Critical Perspect
on Philip Pullm
His Dark Mater....

Critical Perspectives on Philip Pullman's *His Dark Materials*

Essays on the Novels, the Film and the Stage Productions

Edited by STEVEN BARFIELD *and* KATHARINE COX

McFarland & Company, Inc., Publishers

Jefferson, North Carolina, and London

EXTRACTS FROM THE FOLLOWING ARE USED WITH PERMISSION

His Dark Materials: Northern Lights— Philip Pullman. Text Copyright Philip Pullman, 1995. Reproduced with permission of Scholastic Ltd. All Rights Reserved.

His Dark Materials: The Subtle Knife— Philip Pullman. Text Copyright Philip Pullman, 1997. Reproduced with permission of Scholastic Ltd. All Rights Reserved.

His Dark Materials: The Amber Spyglass— Philip Pullman. Text Copyright Philip Pullman, 2000. Reproduced with permission of Scholastic Ltd. All Rights Reserved.

LIBRARY OF CONGRESS CATALOGUING-IN-PUBLICATION DATA

Critical perspectives on Philip Pullman's His dark materials : essays on the novels, the film and the stage productions / edited by Steven Barfield and Katharine Cox.
    p.   cm.
    Includes bibliographical references and index.

    ISBN 978-0-7864-4030-6
    softcover : 50# alkaline paper ∞

    1. Pullman, Philip, 1946– His dark materials.   2. Young adult fiction, English—History and criticism.   3. Fantasy fiction, English—History and criticism.   4. Pullman, Philip, 1946– —Film adaptations.   5. Pullman, Philip, 1946– —Stage history. 6. Allegory. I. Barfield, Steven. II. Cox, Katharine, 1976– .
PR6066.U44Z65   2011
823'.914–dc23   2011026583

BRITISH LIBRARY CATALOGUING DATA ARE AVAILABLE

Front cover images © 2011 Shutterstock

Manufactured in the United States of America

McFarland & Company, Inc., Publishers
  Box 611, Jefferson, North Carolina 28640
  www.mcfarlandpub.com

To my mother and father
for all the fantasy books they bought me as a child
and for all their support over the years.

— *Steven*

To Leo and Leila Maric,
who first introduced me to Pullman — thank you!

— *Katharine*

Table of Contents

Introduction
      KATHARINE COX 1

I. ADVERSARIES AND INFLUENCES

1. Recasting John Milton's *Paradise Lost*: Intertextuality,
   Storytelling and Music
      RACHEL FALCONER 11

2. "When I Grow Up I Want to Be...": Conceptualization of
   the Hero Within the Works of C.S. Lewis, J.R.R. Tolkien
   and Philip Pullman
      PHIL CARDEW 28

3. Constructions of the Child, Authority and Authorship:
   The Reception of C.S Lewis and Philip Pullman
      ELISABETH ELDRIDGE 40

4. "Dark Materials to Create More Worlds": Considering
   His Dark Materials as Science Fiction
      STEVEN BARFIELD 57

II. TRADITIONS AND LEGACIES

5. Revitalizing the Old Machines of a Neo-Victorian London:
   Reading the Cultural Transformations of Steampunk
   and Victoriana
      STEVEN BARFIELD *and* MARTYN COLEBROOK 75

6. Revisiting the Colonial: Victorian Orphans and Postcolonial
   Perspectives
      LAURA PETERS 93

7. Exploring and Challenging the Lapsarian World of Young
   Adult Literature: Femininity, Shame, the Gyptians, and
   Social Class
   NICOLA ALLEN 111

8. "Imagine *Dust* with a Capital Letter": Interpreting the Social
   and Cultural Contexts for Philip Pullman's Transformation
   of Dust
   KATHARINE COX 126

III. RELIGION, SEXUALITY AND GENDER

9. The Man Who Walked with God: Phillip Pullman's Metatron,
   the Biblical Enoch, and the Apocrypha
   JOHN HAYDN BAKER 143

10. The Republic of Heaven: East, West and Eclecticism in
    Pullman's Religious Vision
    J'ANNINE JOBLING 154

11. "Walking into Mortal Sin": Lyra, the Fall, and Sexuality
    TOMMY HALSDORF 172

12. Becoming Human: Desire and the Gendered Subject
    SARAH GAMBLE 187

13. After the Fall: Queer Heterotopias
    SALLY R. MUNT 202

IV. DRAMATIZING *HIS DARK MATERIALS*

14. Staging the Impossible: Severance and Separation in the
    National Theatre's Adaptation
    PATRICK DUGGAN 219

15. Staging and Performing *His Dark Materials*: From the National
    Theatre Productions to Subsequent Productions
    KARIAN SCHUITEMA 239

Bibliography 267

About the Contributors 273

Index 275

Introduction

KATHARINE COX

This volume brings together academics from various literary, philosophical and theatrical fields who read *His Dark Materials* in a range of innovative and original ways. We will offer a survey of some of the key areas of engagement for Philip Pullman, as a writer and as a critic, while locating these themes within Pullman's trilogy.

Pullman: Before and after *His Dark Materials*

Before we discuss his writings in more detail, it's useful to have some background on Pullman as a writer. A useful biography of Pullman is available on his website as well as on the *Literary Encyclopedia*.[1] These short biographical introductions identify his twin urge to inspire and to teach as fundamental to his thinking and writing, and a love of storytelling is a constant throughout. While it may seem strange for a writer so opposed to didacticism, Pullman has firm views on education, especially on the role of the imagination and literature. His response to British educational policy is polemical and "revolutionary" in that his media work is typified by a call to action. This impetus is obvious in his own proselytizing about the power of the creative imagination and his role in protests over the number of tests in Britain (Pullman 2003a), and prescriptive approaches to children's literature in general (Singh 2008). Noting that reading should be a pleasure and not a chore, he has referred to the present dominant thinking in education as "wrong" and "profoundly *vulgar*," full of "false reason" and "incessant, frenzied testing" prompted by "ignorant politicians" (Pullman 2003b). Instead, he points to the role between teacher and child as functioning more like an editor and writer, primarily to allow and encourage the child to enjoy reading, be inspired, and have the space to fail within the learning process.

Pullman clearly recognizes the role of new media in the education and social lives of his child readership. His web pages have been updated (in 2009) to include links to his work and journalism to enable "a more interactive and user-friendly site" (Pullman n.d.c.). This need to teach, entertain and inspire is complemented by the variety of different forms that his work takes in order to reach out to different children and appeal to different age groups. These include plays, screenplays, short stories, fairytales, picture books and novels, as well as the adaptation of his work for television, film and theatre. In addition, he's intrigued by the interaction of picture and language (as an amateur artist, Pullman occupied himself with the production of drawings and engraving for the first two novels in *His Dark Materials*). These engravings recall picture books aimed at young children that play with the interrelationship of word and image. His writing for younger readers includes an entertaining reimaging of *Cinderella* from the perspective of a rat that's transformed into one of the footmen of her coach (*I Was a Rat!* 1999, filmed by the BBC 2001), and a significant number of his writings have been illustrated by a variety of different artists.[2]

For Pullman his interest in teaching is irrevocably intertwined with his approach to writing. His Romanticized view of pedagogy, where writing and reading is child-centered and is predicated upon enjoyment, pleasure, creativity and the imagination, is in polar opposition to what he and other writers consider to be the dry, prescriptive National Curriculum which operates within the English school system. Barely able to disguise his venom for this style of teaching, he points instead to an educational paradigm that is based on the power of stories and storytelling. Concerning the paradox of didacticism within his work, Pullman, accepting the Carnegie Medal in 1996, said:

> All stories teach, whether the storyteller intends them to or not. They teach the world we create. They teach the morality we live by. They teach it much more effectively than moral precepts and instructions [...] We don't need lists of rights and wrongs, tables of dos and don'ts: we need books, time, and silence. "Thou shalt not" is soon forgotten, but "Once upon a time" lasts forever [Pullman 1996].

Pullman's *His Dark Materials* is likely to be enduring for its exploration of complex philosophical and moral ambiguities, inviting, as the essays in this volume demonstrate, re-reading and analysis.

I. Adversaries and Influences

Pullman's work has suffered for both its popularity (how can anything that widely read be any good?) and for its appeal to children. As a publishing phenomenon, like other children's writers before him, including J.K. Rowling,

Pullman has bridged the metaphorical divide between children's and adults' literature and in doing so has made the boundaries between childhood and adulthood less stable. Pullman's writing is often viewed within the canon of children's literature that portrays our fascination with children's progression from innocence to experience, envisaged as the tension between fantasy and reality. The quest, journey or movement between these oppositions is repeatedly evinced in children's literature. Children explore and enjoy but ultimately leave the fantastic realm in such early children's fantasy as Charles Kingsley's *The Water Babies* (1862-3) and Lewis Carroll's *Alice's Adventures in Wonderland* (1865), and this has been a sustained and common feature of children's literature ever since. What is perhaps disquieting in Pullman's work is the opening up of this fantastical and imaginative realm to adults through the sustained device of intertextuality, the consideration of "adult" themes and a motivating and gripping central narrative. Accordingly, Pullman's writing is an uneasy combination of adventure with meta-textual erudition.

Typically fantasy is viewed as escapist and "other," especially when seen in combination with children's literature, and yet Pullman is keen to view fantasy as that which is rooted within representations of the "real" and the everyday as he's "always tried to write about the world that exists" (Pullman qtd. Silverman 2008). When receiving the Whitbread Prize for Fiction for *The Amber Spyglass* in 2002, the author pointedly distanced the book from the fantasy genre, noting that it "has been described as fantasy, but not by me — I like to think of it as stark realism.... The fantasy elements are there to help me say more about being a human being" (Pullman 2002a). Responding to frequently asked questions on his website, Pullman has since moderated his comment that his books are works of "stark realism," preferring to stress the relevance of fantasy when it is linked to the human. This is perhaps a telling reaction to what fantasy is perceived to be and, as this volume explores, perhaps a veiled aside to J.R.R. Tolkien, whose fantastical elves and hobbits are suitably removed from the physical manifestation of human consciousness that Pullman offers us in the shape of his daemons. Though Pullman would distance himself from Tolkien and C.S. Lewis in particular, for their political, religious and didactic worldview, these are the writers that he nevertheless is compared to. In particular, the essays in this volume by Phil Cardew and Elisabeth Eldridge situate Pullman's writing in conversation with these earlier children's authors. Cardew compares Pullman's use of the heroic figure with Lewis' and Tolkien's protagonists, while Eldridge explores the role of authority within Pullman's and Lewis' children's fiction. As these academics note, Pullman's work is heavily allusive, drawing on a variety of myths and canonical literary texts. Pullman spoke of his use of others' ideas and writing in his acknowledgment:

[M]y daemon probably is [... a] Magpie, nothing spectacular to look at but they steal bright things, whether it is a diamond ring or a bit of aluminum foil or whatever it is, an old tin can, if it is bright and shiny they go and pick it up. That is what story tellers do [Pullman 2002b].[3]

Continuing the trend of reading intertextual responses in Pullman's text, Rachel Falconer's essay responds to Pullman's trilogy as a recasting of John Milton's *Paradise Lost*. In doing so, she also explores the hitherto overlooked area of Pullman's musical interests and the musicality of his writing, drawing on the figure of Orpheus, the storyteller. Her argument extends into Pullman's use of fantasy and realism and contends that Pullman's preference is for realism as he finds it morally superior. Another overlooked area of analysis is the influence of science fiction in the trilogy, explored here in Steven Barfield's essay.

II. Traditions and Legacies

When Pullman published the first of his trilogy in 1995 in the United Kingdom, he was already an established writer. Pullman's other work includes the Sally Lockhart quartet (1985–2000), novels that follow the adventures of the plucky (and increasingly modern woman) Sally Lockhart as she battles against a number of villains. Deliberately hackneyed, the quartet revels in the tropes of Victorian melodrama evoking the penny dreadfuls of the period. This writing is in a more straightforward realist mode than his later trilogy, but the Lockhart quartet also dispute received history by showing unpleasant aspects of the British Empire and in centering on a young female detective, confront sexist assumptions about female aptitudes and capabilities.[4]

The quartet has been commissioned by the BBC with Billie Piper playing the central character, broadcast over consecutive Christmases; the first two installments have been televised to date.[5] Influences for these novels include the writings of Mary Elizabeth Braddon, Wilkie Collins and Sir Arthur Conan Doyle, while Pullman's knowledge of Victorian literature and society is underpinned by his undergraduate teaching at Westminster College, Oxford, which included a module on Victorian literature and society. The importance of the Victorian period to Pullman's work is made evident in this collection (particularly in the chapters by Laura Peters, Nicola Allen, Steven Barfield and Martyn Colebrook, and Katharine Cox) but also permeates his other writing and confirms his sentiments that he most admires "the great 19th-century novelists" (Pullman qtd. Silverman 2008).[6] Peters' essay explores Pullman's Victorian reimagining: from the narrative of the hero orphan to the explorations of class and otherness represented by the Gyptians. By re-encountering Victorian concerns, Pullman articulates a world in crisis where technology and religion threaten community and equilibrium. Following on from Peters' focus, Allen's essay links social class with a reading of representations of femininity and shame. Though Pullman's dust has received some academic attention, Katharine Cox resituates its reading by stressing the significance of dust during the nineteenth century, aligned to social and cultural change. Using scientific, religious and ecological examples, Cox argues that attitudes to dust should be re-evaluated as a key aspect of social and cultural practices.

III. Religion, Sexuality and Gender

An amiable and interested writer, Pullman has nevertheless proved deeply controversial. The critic Peter Hitchens observed that Pullman is the "'most dangerous man in England' for his denial of God and Christianity" (Cornwell 2004). As a cultural critic, Pullman has commented on a diverse range of topics, from the possible destruction of an Oxfordshire boatyard to the legality of the Iraqi war that deposed Saddam Hussein, and his strongly held beliefs have often fired controversy. Though Pullman challenges the superiority and dogma of organized religion he doesn't reject faith or spirituality within the trilogy. There have been book-length responses to Pullman's evocation of religion, such as Hugh Rayment-Pickard (2004) and Donna Freitas and Jason King (2007), which have attempted to explore his use of religion. In this volume, John Haydn Baker's work exposes the subtle origins of Pullman's ideas in the Apocrypha, those marginalized texts which challenge the legitimacy of the Gospels. Baker's essay examines the significance of these texts which have previously been forgotten in the fervor over more modern reinterpretations of scripture. Tommy Halsdorf's essay argues that Lyra's Fall is rewritten through the lens of Milton and Blake. In this way Halsdorf places explicit emphasis on the nature of female sexuality. Both essays consider the Bible as text and in doing so place *His Dark Materials* within a continuum of narratives that re-work these stories. In continuing this exploration of Pullman and religion, J'annine Jobling's reading of Pullman sees the author as a post–Christian writer whose engagement with the universe is subtly and perhaps unknowingly informed by Buddhism.

In *The Good Man Jesus and the Scoundrel Christ* (2010), Pullman's most recent work, there is an intensification of interest in religion, with a particular focus on Jesus (after Rowan Williams, the Archbishop of Canterbury, prompted Pullman to tell his story). Pullman divides the character of Jesus into Jesus (the name meaning *salvation OED*) and Christ (meaning *anointed OED*), which implies that Christ is "made." Again, Pullman returns to a vision of a Pantheistic universe through the character Jesus' rejection of organized religion and Christ's embracing of it. In doing so, Pullman is looking to address the difference between Jesus' teachings and the actions of his later followers.

This volume contains a detailed and extensive re-examination of gender politics in *His Dark Materials*. Sarah Gamble's reading of desire and the gendered subject employs Judith Butler's latest work, *Undoing Gender* (2004), and extends the notion of female subjectivity. In particular the work in this section challenges the view of Lyra as a universally positive female role model. In a further innovative reading of the trilogy, Sally R. Munt applies a Foucauldian analysis (principally his writings on heterotopias) and argues that the space within Pullman's multiple-worlds is profoundly sexual and also textual.

IV. Dramatizing *His Dark Materials*

Adapting Pullman's *His Dark Materials* to the stage has proved a commercial and intellectual success despite the author's own doubts, calling the project "impossible" (Pullman n.d.e.). The significance of these theatre adaptations, their scope and success in reimagining Pullman's trilogy, is covered extensively in this collection. Condensing these three rather long novels (especially *The Amber Spyglass*) into a two-part play is a remarkable feat. Importantly, Pullman's early narratives have often begun or gone through the transition of a stage version, and an interest in the theatre is obvious in his work. Pullman has spoken of the influence, power and "sorcery" of the theatre to inspire children (Pullman n.d.e.). Some of his own writing is adapted from school plays and, perhaps because of this creative process, his novels and illustrated books respond well to stage adaptation. Pullman also draws the critic's attention to his knowledge of the theatre by acknowledging the influence of Heinrich von Kleist in *His Dark Materials*.

To date there have been a number of stage performances of *His Dark Materials*, including an adaptation of *Clockwork: An Extraordinary Opera* by the theatre group Unicorn (various 2004), a stage version of *The Firework-Maker's Daughter* (Lyric Hammersmith 2004–2005), and also *The Scarecrow and His Servant* (Southwark Playhouse 2008). This volume analyzes the staging of *His Dark Materials* and presents a theoretical exploration of ideas of severance and separation by Patrick Duggan as well as an analysis of directorial decisions taken by the National Theatre (UK) and Playbox versions by Karian Schuitema.

Less successful perhaps has been the first film version of the opening book. In many ways, it made sense to film *His Dark Materials*: the trilogy had already made Pullman a global phenomenon, had been a critical success, and followed on the back of the highly successful and profitable adaptations of children's books such as J.K. Rowling's *Harry Potter* series (2001–2011), Lemony

Snicket's *A Series of Unfortunate Incidents* (2004) and Lewis's *The Chronicles of Narnia* (2005). Early indications of the remodeling of the books into a film script also seemed to be progressing well with Tom Stoppard working on the screenplay. Stoppard's other film work included Terry Gilliam's *Brazil* (1985), a version of his own acclaimed play *Rosencrantz and Guildenstern Are Dead* (1990), and his Oscar-winning script for *Shakespeare in Love* (1998), but as he confirmed to *The Independent on Sunday*, following the hiring of Chris Weitz to direct, he "assumed his services are no longer required" (Stoppard qtd. Fitzwilliams 2004). Weitz's prior work included the highly lucrative though less esoteric *American Pie* (1999) and *About a Boy* (2002), where he worked on both the screenplay and the script. The decision to replace Stoppard was controversial, especially with Pullman's fans, who feared the "dumbing down" of the novels' themes. The author, however, appeared to be taking a more sanguine approach when he noted, "I imagine this happens in the film world all the time" (Pullman qtd. Fitzwilliams 2004).

Pullman's reticence belies some possible problems he personally identified with Stoppard's vision of his books, such as the focus on the philosophical. While New Line, the film's producers, deemed the script to be "too intellectual" and "not Lyra-centric enough" (Pullman qtd. Rosin, n.d.), Pullman, in discussion over Stoppard's script, identified that the playwright was too engrossed in "the discussions between old men with beards" and that he didn't understand that these needed to be contextualized as the "discussions are only important in how they affect Lyra" (Pullman qtd. Rosin, n.d.). There's some website activity over the quality of the three versions of the script: Stoppard's draft, Weitz's draft and then his final, revised version ("Where Did" 2007). The discussion focuses on the extent to which the intellectual content was compromised at the behest of the production team in order to ensure big, action sequences and to appease a perceived backlash from the American Christian right.

Even before filming had started, the public relations team was already scrambling to impress that Weitz held a first-class English degree from Cambridge and so was capable of the task at hand. It seemed that the director himself wasn't so sure about the enormity of taking on both *His Dark Materials* and the fans of the books (a mistaken question and answer session for the director on the fansite bridgetothestars.net clearly unnerved him as did the fans' reactionary responses) and briefly the film was passed to Anand Tucker (*Shopgirl* 2005). After Tucker's removal, the project was again offered to Weitz, who had remained on as scriptwriter, but the financial aspect and the marketability of the film remained a huge concern. Weitz has spoken about the curtailing of the first book (which excludes the death of Roger, Lyra's betrayal and so forth): "There was tremendous marketing pressure for that [...] Everyone really wanted an upbeat ending" (McGrath 2007).

Everyone, it would appear, apart from the fans of the books. Critically, New Line was "looking for a franchise" (McGrath 2007), a way of filming a changed first book (to appease Christians), with watered-down religious elements, but also building towards the later books in the trilogy. Weitz's prevarication over the script, the compromise of Pullman's key themes and indeed Pullman's own reticence about the adaptation process intensified the media frenzy over the possible adulteration of the books leading to the vitriolic *Times* story "God Is Cut from Film of Dark Materials" (Coates 2004), whose accuracy was directly contested by Pullman himself.[7]

Ultimately, the film of *The Golden Compass* (2007) was not a success: the film grossed $301 million in overseas markets but only $70 million at the American box office (Corliss 2008). *Empire*'s review called the film "a graceless, distracted plod through one of the most interesting and incendiary novels of the past fifteen years" (Richards 2007). What's lacking from the film which is so evident in the books and play versions is the attention to, and the importance of, the story.

Though it remains to be seen whether there is any appetite for a major company to film the rest of the trilogy, it seems inevitable that the books that make up *His Dark Materials* will continue to be read by children and adults alike. Though the trilogy has many contemporary resonances (fundamentalist religious views, organized religion, dark matter and so forth), it has universality through its epic canvas (for example, the central quest, angels, witches and magic) and gravitas through its manipulation of key intertexts (from *Paradise Lost* to comic-book cliffhangers). This collection moves the academic debate on still further and supports the continued study of Pullman's work at undergraduate, postgraduate and academic levels.

A NOTE ABOUT THE TEXT

Philip Pullman's first novel in the trilogy, published by Scholastic Children's Books as *Northern Lights* (1995), was later published by Knopf in the United States as *The Golden Compass* (1996). Pullman has lately commented that he regrets the change of title but that "at the time, I didn't have enough clout to resist" (Pullman n.d.a.). In keeping with Pullman's wishes, this collection will refer to the first book in the trilogy by the British title, *Northern Lights*, however, full bibliographic details are given to both U.K. and U.S. editions. For referencing purposes, the U.K. Scholastic versions of *Northern Lights* (1995), *The Subtle Knife* (1997) and *The Amber Spyglass* (2000) will be known henceforth as *NL*, *SK* and *AS* and the U.S. Knopf version of *His Dark Materials* trilogy (2007) as *HDM*.

NOTES

1. See Pullman (n.d.b.), and Steven Barfield, Katharine Cox and Chris Willis (2005).
2. See, for example, *I Was a Rat!* (UK Peter Bailey; USA Kevin Hawkes, 2000), *Clockwork* (UK Peter Bailey, 1996; USA Leonid Gore, 2000), *Puss in Boots* (Ian Beck, 2000), *The Wonderful Story of Aladdin and the Enchanted Lamp* (Sophie Williams, 1995), *Count Karlstein* (with Patrice Aggs' illustrations, 1991; also published as a novel without illustrations by Knopf, 1998, and in the UK by Doubleday, 2002), *Mossycoat* (Peter Bailey, 1998), *Spring-Heeled Jack* (UK David Mostyn, 1989; USA, 2002) and *The Firework-Maker's Daughter* (UK Nick Harris, 1995;

USA S. Saelig Gallagher, 1999). Significantly, these works often started off as theater or stage pieces for his school children or for theater groups before developing into illustrated books (*Spring-Heeled Jack, Count Karlstein, The Firework-Maker's Daughter, Puss in Boots*) and in the case of *Count Karlstein* this has included the further development into a novel.

3. Ironically, Pullman's sentiments, identifying a magpie as a possible daemon companion, complement his praise of his fellow writer of children's fiction and fantasy chorographer, Alan Garner: "It's as easy to make the mistake that I'm a tight, academic scholar in my work, I'm not. I'm really being a magpie" (Garner 1983 qtd. Hunt 2004). This also reflects the level of intertextual asides in his writing and speaking.

4. For example, at the end of the first novel in the series, *The Ruby in the Smoke* (1985), the protagonist Sally discovers the evils of Britain's lucrative role in the opium trade and throughout the series her evolving independence and ability are central to her success at solving the mysteries which confront her.

5. *Ruby in the Smoke* was shown in 2006 and *Shadow in the North* in 2007 on the BBC in the Britain.

6. As well as the Sally Lockhart quartet Pullman previously wrote a series of stories for the New Cut Gang, a team of guttersnipes and urchins (*Thunderbolt's Waxwork* 1994; *The Gas-Fitters' Ball* 1998) set in *fin-de-siècle* Lambeth (London).

7. See http://www.philip-pullman.com/pages/content/index.asp?PageID=118.

Works Cited

Barfield, Steven, Katharine Cox and Chris Willis. 2005. "Philip Pullman." *Literary Encyclopedia.* http://www.litencyc.com/php/speople.php?rec=true&UID=5064.

Coates, S. 2004. "God is Cut from Film of Dark Materials." *The Times.* December 8. Accessed May 10, 2010. http://www.timesonline.co.uk/tol/news/uk/article400396.ece.

Corliss, R. 2008. "Why Narnia Hits While Golden Compass Flops." *Time Magazine.* May 15. Accessed June 2, 2010. http://www.time.com/time/magazine/article/0,9171,1806790,00.html.

Cornwell, J. 2004. "Some Enchanted Author." *The Times*, October 24. Accessed July 2, 2010. http://www.timesonline.co.uk/tol/life_and_style/article494636.ece.

Fitzwilliam, Malcolm. 2004. "Tom Stoppard Dumped as 'Gross-Out' Director Takes Over 'Dark Materials.'" *The Independent*, November 21. Accessed September 24, 2008. http://www.independent.co.uk/arts-entertainment/films/news/tom-stoppard-dumped-as-gross-out-director-takes-over-dark-materials-534077.html.

Hunt, Peter. 2004. "Alan Garner: Biography." *Alan Garner.* Accessed May 10, 2010. http://www.biographybase.com/biography/Garner_Alan.html.

McGrath, C. 2007. "Unholy Production with a Fairy-Tale Ending." *The New York Times*, December 2. Accessed May 10, 2010. http://www.nytimes.com/2007/12/02/movies/02mcgr.html.

Munt, Sally R. 2007. *Queer Attachments: The Cultural Politics of Shame.* Aldershot: Ashgate.

Pullman, Philip. N.d.a. "Latest Q and A's." *Author's Website.* Accessed May 10, 2008. http://www.philip-pullman.com/about_the_writing.asp.

_____. N.d.b. "About Philip Pullman." *Author's Website.* Accessed September 29, 2008. http://www.philip-pullman.com/about.asp.

_____. N.d.c. "Home page." *Author's Website.* Accessed March 1, 2009. http://www.philip-pullman.com.

_____. N.d.d. "About the Writing." *Author's Website.* Accessed March 1, 2009. http://www.philip-pullman.com/about_the_writing.asp.

_____. N.d.e. "Theatre." *Author's Website.* Accessed March 1, 2009. http://www.philip-pullman.com/pages/content/index.asp?PageID=88).

_____. 1996. "Carnegie Medal Acceptance Speech." *Random House.* Accessed May 12, 2010. http://www.randomhouse.com/features/pullman/author/carnegie.html.

_____. 2002a. "Whitbread Win for Children's Author." *BBC News*, January 23. Accessed May 12, 2010. http://news.bbc.co.uk/1/hi/entertainment/arts/1776393.stm.

_____. 2002b. "Philip Pullman." *CBBC [Children's British Broadcasting Corporation] Newsround*, January 23. Accessed March 10, 2010. http://news.bbc.co.uk/cbbcnews/hi/chat/hotseat/newsid_1777000/1777895.stm.

_____. 2003a. "Complains Grow over School Tests." *BBC News*, February 21. Accessed May 10, 2010. http://news.bbc.co.uk/1/hi/education/2788231.stm.

_____. 2003b. "Isis Lecture." *Author's Website*. April 1. http://www.philip-pullman.com/pages/content/index.asp?PageID=66.

_____. 2010. *The Good Man Jesus and the Scoundrel Christ*. London: Canongate.

Response to Chris Weitz. N.d. Accessed June 2, 2009. http://www.bridgetothestars.net/index.php?d=movie&p=responses.

Richards, O. 2007. "The Golden Compass." *Empire Magazine*, December 5. Accessed June 2, 2010. http://www.empireonline.com/reviews/reviewcomplete.asp?FID=134647.

Rosin, Hannah. N.d. "How Hollywood Saved God." *The Atlantic*. Accessed June 12, 2009. http://www.theatlantic.com/doc/200712/religious-movies/2.

Silverman, Rosa. 2008. "Exclusive Interview with Philip Pullman." *Times Online*. March 22. Accessed November 11, 2010. http://entertainment.timesonline.co.uk/tol/arts_and_entertainment/books/fiction/article3596811.ece.

Singh, A. 2008. "Philip Pullman Leads Author Revolt Against Age Banding for Children's Books." *The Telegraph*, June 5.

"Where Did 'The Golden Compass' Go Astray? And Was Tom Stoppard's Original Script a Masterpiece?" 2007. *New York Magazine*. December 7. Accessed February 2, 2008. http://nymag.com/daily/entertainment/2007/12/golden_compass_scripts.html.

1

Recasting John Milton's *Paradise Lost*: Intertextuality, Storytelling and Music

Rachel Falconer

Introduction: Pullman, children's literature and religion

One of the prevailing views expressed in the media over the past decade or so has been that adult readers have been turning to children's literature because they are looking for comforting or escapist reading, in a word, because they have been "dumbing down."[1] But this view is strangely at odds with the content of many contemporary children's books, which on the contrary, tend to depict characters facing difficult moral dilemmas in extremely dangerous situations. I will argue that far from seeking escapism in children's literature, adults as well as children are preoccupied with questions of coming of age, education and self-fulfillment, one indication of which is the current revival of interest in the classic, nineteenth century *Bildungsroman*. I would suggest that this preoccupation may be one of the factors contributing to the enormous popularity of the trilogy *His Dark Materials* by Philip Pullman, a children's author also read by adults, whose admiration for nineteenth century realism is matched only by his passionate concern over the recent failures of the British education system. Pullman is certainly not alone in thinking that the recent government policies on education are failing. According to John Coleman, director of the Trust for the Study of Adolescence, New Labour's emphasis on standardization, league tables, performance testing and examinations has had an adverse effect on young people across the country. Many pupils are failing to find a meaningful place in the school setting, according to Coleman, and this is "leading to [widespread] pessimism and disaffection regarding the possibilities of adulthood" (Coleman 2002, 59). Despite New Labour's much-vaunted attention to "education, education, education," many professionals feel that the government's reforms (1997–2010) have had a largely negative effect.

Given this immediate social context, the depiction of a dramatic and momentous coming of age of two child protagonists in Philip Pullman's *His Dark Materials* is especially timely. Philip Pullman has been one of the most outspoken critics of the new educational reforms which, he argues, have turned education into a cripplingly dull and joyless experience (see Davies 2005). In his view, education should instruct through delight, and in various senses that I will be exploring here, *His Dark Materials* is a model for how that could be achieved. Not only does Pullman's trilogy provide an alternative model of spiritual education in the Romantic tradition of William Blake, it also engages with one of English literature's best-known works, in which moral education is a central theme: from the adult, literary canon, Milton's *Paradise Lost*.

The title of the trilogy, *His Dark Materials,* derives from Milton's description of the chaos in *Paradise Lost*,[2] and the trilogy as a whole recasts Milton's narration of the Fall of Adam and Eve as a fortunate Fall from inexperience into experience and wisdom. Milton's Christian God is implicitly present in the possessive pronoun His, and even appears as a character in the work, but Pullman re-interprets Genesis as an atheistic story. The dust from which we were made, and which for the religious characters in the story represents original sin, becomes a positive sign of adult consciousness in Pullman's moral scheme. *His Dark Materials* is thus more easily defensible as suitably adult reading matter than other crossover children's fiction (notably, of course, J. K. Rowling's *Harry Potter*). It engages with canonical, adult texts such as *Paradise Lost*, and questions faith and religious institutions which are of obvious concern to adults in the twenty-first century: witness the current spate of books which, on one hand, herald the rebirth of religious fundamentalism, or on the other hand, predict or call for an end to religious thinking altogether.[3] Many of the latter advocate a return to secular humanism, a position which Pullman polemically supports.

Pullman's public diatribes against religious fundamentalism, or "theocratic absolutism" as he terms it, have stirred up far less acrimony than, say, the publication of Salman Rushdie's *Satanic Verses* in 1989.[4] But this may be because the specific target of his ire is a Western religion, rather than Islam. Both authors have used the medium of children's literature to defend secular democracy against its opponents, Rushdie in *Haroun and the Sea of Stories* (1990), a novel written for his son while the author was in hiding following the Ayatollah Khomeini's proclamation of *fatwa* against him. But Pullman is arguably the first British author to ground the debate between absolutism and democracy in terms of the relation between child and adult cultures in Britain. He is scathing of critics who disparage adults' reading of children's literature. In a typically vivid caricature, he describes these gatekeepers as pompously "fierce and stern," patrolling the border against incursions by readers of the wrong age: "They strut up and down with a fine contempt, curling their lips and consulting their clipboards and snapping out orders." But, continues Pullman, "when we step away from the border post, when we go round the back of the guards ... we see ... people are happily walking across this border in both directions. You'd think there wasn't a border there at all. Adults are happily reading children's books; and what's more, children are reading adults' books" (Pullman 2002a, 44). At first glance, Pullman might appear to be supporting the universalist position of one "literature for all" but in actual fact, what he is arguing for is free passage across the borders, and, of course, an end to adult condescension towards children's fiction.

Pullman and the boundaries between childhood and adulthood

Not only does Pullman not advocate a one-size-fits-all view of literature, he makes the differences between children and adults central to the plot and argument of *His Dark Materials*. In Lyra's world, human beings have daemons, external souls that accompany their human hosts everywhere in the shape of animals. Whereas adults in this alternative world have daemons of a fixed shape, children's daemons are constantly metamorphosing into different animals, dependent on the child's changing moods and psychological development. When the child's daemon settles, he or she is said to have crossed over into adulthood. But if this is how coming-of-age should happen, in Lyra's world, the process has been radically disrupted there. In the first volume, it emerges that a theological organization, loosely modeled on the Catholic Church, has been kidnapping children and severing them from their daemons, with the intention of locking them into a permanent state of childhood. Lyra's unmarried parents, the Church militant Mrs. Coulter and the lawless explorer Lord Asriel, are conspicuously inadequate in their parenting skills, being devoted to their various causes and mercilessly willing to exploit children in furthering those causes.

In the second volume, we are introduced to twelve-year-old Will, who cares for his mentally ill mother on his own, since his father has disappeared; Will accidentally kills a man while trying to protect her. When Lyra and Will travel to other worlds, they discover the relation between children and adults to be fraught with danger in other ways. In Cittàgazze, for example, invisible spectres (like Rowling's dementors) reduce adults to zombies, allowing the children of that world to grow feral and wander the streets in lawless packs. These are worlds rather like ours, then, where many children are not innocent or protected, where many adults are not responsible or wise, and above all, where many adolescents find the threshold crossing from youth to maturity has been closed to them, in various different ways.

Lyra's quest in *Northern Lights* is to free the children kidnapped by the Oblation Board, and in a sense, to restore the more natural processes of coming-of-age. Moreover, in *The Amber Spyglass,* the quest of both children is to free the souls of the dead trapped in the underworld, thereby freeing souls terrorized by religious dogma to regard dying as part of the "natural" life-cycle to which, in the humanist view, we all belong. Read in this light, *His Dark Materials* is a highly significant crossover text, not only because it is a children's text that has been enthusiastically endorsed by millions of adult readers, but also because crossing over from one phase of life to a distinctly other phase comes to stand more generally for freedom: freedom both from moral relativism, in which the different stages of life cease to matter, and from religious tyranny. Pullman works toward this goal of moral, intellectual and spiritual freedom by engaging agonistically with a major intertext, John Milton's *Paradise Lost.* As president of the Blake Society, and a self-confessed admirer of the nineteenth-century poet, Pullman's epic trilogy also draws a huge amount of inspiration from the Vulcanic energies of William Blake's verse. But in my view, the dialogues with Milton prove to be the more potent subtext. Perhaps this is because it is an agonist dialogue, and Pullman is a writer whose imagination seems to thrive on controversy.

Being of the Devil's Party: Pullman and Milton

In Pullman's recasting of *Paradise Lost,* Lyra (Pullman's Eve) and Will (his Adam) actually want to escape the Garden of Eden. They desire knowledge, maturity, and an understanding of mortal limit, while it is the representation of the Catholic Church which tries to contain them in a state of permanent innocence. Pullman also represents the Christian God as impotent, and his Regent as a despot; he makes Eve the heroine rather the culprit of Genesis; and he celebrates knowledge and experience as humanity's highest goals. In this way, Pullman reads Milton's *Paradise Lost* against the grain, in the radical Romantic tradition of Blake and Shelley (amongst others). But in other respects, Pullman remains true to the radical politics and even more, the radical poetics, that are themselves expressed in *Paradise Lost.* Just as Milton broke new ground in placing marital relations at the centre of a national epic narrative, rather than war or empire, so Pullman iconoclastically situates two children at the core of his re-narration of Genesis. Of course, many children's books have protagonists who save the world or affect the course of history (in fantasy fiction, superheroes that save the world are almost the genre's *sine qua non*).

But few writers have been so bold as to represent a pair of children as the radical reformers of a major world religion.[5]

Neither Pullman nor Milton seems particularly interested in imagining a state of pure, pre-lapsarian innocence, which is perhaps surprising, given their mutual interest representing the Fall from the Garden of Eden. Pullman characterizes his eleven-year-old heroine, Lyra Belacqua, as a skilful, independent child, with a tendency to break as many rules as she can. In *Paradise Lost,* Milton describes Eden not so much as a place of innocence as a place where evil naturally turns into good and where God's life-affirming energy is directly expressed in every aspect of Creation. In Milton's Eden, Adam can aspire to gain supra-human knowledge (he asks Raphael about angels' digestive systems and whether they can have sex) and Eve can have nightmares and temptations without incurring any spousal or divine wrath. Indeed Milton's God positively encourages intellectual hubris, sexual "conversation," and wild, vegetal overgrowth. This last detail turns out to be quite important, as the reason that Satan finds Eve vulnerably alone is that she has decided she will get more weeding done without Adam around to distract her (*PL* 9.214).

Milton's Adam and Eve are created to possess different but complementary capabilities, and their natural harmony of opposites quickly reasserts itself after the temptation and Fall. Writing in the context of a nation which had (in Milton's view) slavishly regressed back to monarchy, Milton is attempting to re-imagine the relation between the sexes as the basis for a new and just society. Pullman follows suit when he invents complementary qualities for children and adults which differ from the norm, in that there is little emphasis on the traditional innocence of children, and much greater emphasis on their grace, mobility, and mental agility. Adults, in turn, have (or should have) the complementary qualities of self-awareness, experience and wisdom. And in an ideal world, a Republic of Heaven, the two would be bound together by love. As in *Paradise Lost,* heterosexually gendered pairs are also given distinctly complementary characteristics in *His Dark Materials.* Will and Lyra behave very much as a young Miltonic couple in *The Subtle Knife,* Will gaining self-reliance, and the feisty Lyra learning patience and submission. And since nearly all human beings in Pullman's fantasy world have daemons, or souls, of the opposite sex, each individual carries within him or herself a set of heterosexually complementary characteristics, quite apart from the humans they may choose as partners.

If Pullman's aim in *His Dark Materials* was to recreate the grandeur and epic sweep of Milton's *Paradise Lost,* his persona in the media as a controversial moralist is if anything even more Miltonic. In his own times, Milton was known as a pugilistic essayist as well as a poet.[6] By many of his contemporaries, he was considered a dangerous libertarian for his advocacy of the freedom of speech (*Areopagitica* mounts an impassioned case against press censorship), his scandalous defense of divorce (though, it has to be said, the *Divorce* tracts are more sympathetic to male divorcees than female ones) and his unwavering Republicanism (even in the Restoration, he declined to recant his support of the regicide). These views and others, for example on educational reform, Milton published in the form of prose tracts, which were responded to in kind by his opponents. The exchanges were heated, rhetorically elaborate, and often personally abusive. So while Pullman can be seen as offering contemporary young adults a Blakean reading of *Paradise Lost* (Blake famously claimed that Milton was "of the devil's party without knowing it"), he also appears to share Milton's conviction that writers should play a public role in shaping the nation's moral values.[7]

Defending the printing of seditious works, Milton wrote in *Areopagitica*, "I cannot praise a fugitive and cloister'd virtue" (*CP* vol. 2, 548), a line which he actually has Eve restate right before the Fall.[8] Ideas had to be tested out in a public arena, and truth had to emerge "from the dust and heat of battle." In the prose tracts, Milton's strategy is often to carve out his own argument against those of a particular opponent. A post-bellum Milton recalls with obvious relish his heated clashes with the scholar Salmasius, "I met him in single combat and plunged into his reviling throat this pen, the weapon of his own choice" (Milton *A Second Defence of the English People* in *CP* vol. 4.1., 556).

The music of *His Dark Materials*

Pullman's engagement with Milton's language, poetics and moral universe is still pervasive and important. In his introduction to a 2005 Oxford University Press edition of *Paradise Lost*, Pullman writes "no one, not even Shakespeare, surpasses Milton in his command of the sound, the music, the weight and taste and texture of English words" (Pullman 2005b, n.p.). The music or rhythm of words is indeed important to both writers, not least because of the influence they perceive it to have on a listening audience. Milton adopted the legendary Greek singer Orpheus as his poetic persona, because his verses were said to have moved even the queen of the underworld to pity (see Falconer 2006). Blind by the time he finished writing *Paradise Lost*, Milton created a work that above all resonates aurally. Moreover, he shared with his early modern contemporaries the view that hearing was the most susceptible of the five senses to seduction, as well as spiritual enlightenment. For words as aural poison, think of Lady Macbeth, Iago, and Hamlet's play, "The Mousetrap," and for divine inspiration pouring into human ears, think of the opening lines of *Paradise Lost*.[9] It was in fact the very sonority of Milton's verse that T.S. Eliot deplored, as he felt that it had opened a rift in the English tradition between verse that "sounded" and verse that made sense (Eliot 1957). But Pullman is an admirer of Milton's music, and is likewise highly attuned to the aural effects of prose rhythm. Interestingly, in a lecture on adults reading children's literature, he argues that a text's ability to attract a wide audience depends on its possessing a particular musical structure:

> The sort of story we all hope we can write is one that will resonate like a musical note with all kinds of overtones and harmonics, some of which will be heard more clearly by this person's ear, others by that one's; and some of which may not be heard at all by the storyteller. What's more, as the listeners grow older, so some of the overtones will fade while others become more clearly audible [Pullman 2002a, 52].

The crossover text is thus a particular note which will set off other notes than those actually played by the instrumentalist (for example, an A, D, G, or C played on a cello will make the corresponding open string — A, D, G, or C — sound of its own accord). The analogy is an exact one for a text that may impact on another reader besides the one being overtly addressed.

The image of the writer as storyteller, a folkloric figure who charms listeners into a circle round the fire, also recurs frequently in Pullman's remarks on writers and their audiences. Orpheus is, of course, the epitome of the enchanting storyteller as he could draw anyone to listen, whether adults, children, animals, rocks, stones or trees. In their views on the musicality of language, however, Pullman and Milton do differ in one important respect. Milton deliberately set out to charm a "fit audience though few" (*PL* 7.31). Unlike Pullman, he was not, in any sense of the word, a populist. In one of his rare, caustic references to Orpheus, Milton contrasts the legendary poet's catholic appeal with his own desire to address an educated, elite audience:

> Orpheus and Amphion used to attract an audience consisting only of rocks and wild beasts and trees, and if any human beings came, they were at best but rude and rustic folk; but *I* find the most learned men altogether engrossed in listening to my words and hanging on my lips [Milton *The Sixth Prolusion* in *CP* vol 1, 269].

More often, however, Milton represents Orpheus as the poet whose music, like his own, tragically failed to move the cloth-eared masses. "Woods and rocks had ears/ To rapture" but the "savage clamour" of the drunken mob drowned out Orpheus's voice, and eventually he was ripped limb from limb (*PL* 7, 35–36). For Pullman, by contrast, what would be most likely to inhibit the resonance of a fictional work is not the cloth ears of the masses, but a writer's too-obvious articulation of a message:

> if you have a *cause* in mind, a *purpose,* whether it's didactic or moral or social or religious, and you're determined to tell them what it is — and much of what we call children's literature has been disfigured by just such purposes — then those overtones and harmonics are damped down; they just don't ring [Pullman 2002a, 52].

These differences aside, Milton and Pullman share the view that a writer's purpose is to delight and educate, and this sense of purpose is reflected in the language, style and genre of both their works. For Milton, writing when his vision of an English Republic had failed, the poet's task was an enormous one. He had both to "justify the ways of God to men," specifically to explain why God had let the disaster happen, and re-inspire the love of Protestant virtues in a Restoration readership, which seemed inclined to love anything but. The paradox of the Fall of Man is that, once fallen, we lose the capacity to choose the right path again. To prevent the human Fall from becoming demonic, an eternal repetition of the wrong choice, there need to be interventions. On the cosmic scale, there is, of course, the Son of God's sacrifice for Man. But at the local level, a divinely inspired poet could reawaken an audience's desire for grace. As critics like Stanley Fish have shown, Milton was a clever strategist when it came to charming an audience, and then springing a chastening virtue on them, just when they had been lulled into inattention by the verse music (Fish 2003).[10] Milton begins *Paradise Lost* with the charismatic Satan because he knows his post-lapsarian readers will find the Devil more fascinating than the Son of God (as no doubt he did himself). But all the while he is filling his readers' ears with a very un–Restoration sound, not heroic couplets, which were the fashion of the day, but unrhymed verse that rolled on for paragraphs, and required huge breaths to read aloud, and resonated with "ancient liberty," as he explains in his prefatory Note on the Verse of *Paradise Lost*. Gradually he prepares his readers to re-live the fatal moment, when Adam and Eve have to weigh up whether to choose filial service, knowledge (Eve's choice) or love (Adam's).

Modern secular readers like Pullman tend to think they made the right choice. But Milton represents the episode as both a moral Fall, and a fall of language. After they have eaten the forbidden fruit in Book 9, Adam and Eve begin to "converse" (which in the seventeenth century meant both social and sexual intercourse) like Restoration courtiers: Adam "cast lascivious eyes" on Eve, and Eve "as wantonly repaid." Adam's first post-lapsarian address to Eve is full of "dalliance," verbal puns and innuendos, which play on the idea of knowledge and knowingness:

> Eve, now I see thou art exact of taste,
> And elegant, of sapience no small part,
> Since to each meaning savour we apply,
> And palate call judicious [*PL*.9.1017–20].

Here "savour" means both taste (of the fruit) and understanding; Eve has judged well, has prepared an "elegant" meal, by offering him the apple from the tree of knowledge. Thus as Adam and Eve fall, the language also falls from a state of "ancient liberty" into the knowing playfulness and the hypermannerisms of the Restoration. And it never quite recovers, the last three books of *Paradise Lost* de-crescendoeing into a much sparer, more studied and more careful music.

By the same token, the prose rhythm of *His Dark Materials* is a new kind of music in children's literature. Neither straightforwardly realist, nor fizzily magical, and certainly not archly archaic in the tradition of Tolkien's imitators, it more closely approximates the rolling verse paragraphs of Milton's *Paradise*

Lost. Pullman's sentences are longer than one might traditionally expect from a children's author, with phrase after phrase linked loosely by a series of conjunctions (polysyndeton). And like Milton in the Devil-presided Books 1 and 2 of *Paradise Lost,* Pullman makes use of the extended simile and metaphor, the former being a device that features generically in Homeric epic. The following two passages illustrate how Pullman extends the ground between tenor and vehicle (the thing comparing and the thing being compared) to heighten the visual and emotional impact of a scene. The first example (a simile) describes a battle between two bear kings; the second (a metaphor) comes from the end of the trilogy, when Will realizes he has to leave Lyra:

> Like a wave that has been building its strength over a thousand miles of ocean, and which makes little stir in the deep water, but which when it reaches the shallows rears itself up high into the sky, terrifying the shore-dwellers, before crashing down on the land with irresistible power — so Iorek Byrnison rose up against Iofur [*NL* 353; *HDM* 260].

> And at the word *alone,* Will felt a great wave of rage and despair moving outwards from a place deep within him, as if his mind were an ocean that some profound convulsion had disturbed. [...] He felt the wave build higher and steeper to darken the sky, he felt the crest tremble and begin to spill, he felt the great mass crashing down with the whole weight of the ocean behind it against the iron-bound coast of what had to be. And he found himself gasping and shaking and crying aloud with more anger and pain than he had ever felt in his life ... But as the wave expended its force and the waters withdrew, the bleak rocks remained; there was no arguing with fate; neither his despair nor Lyra's had moved them a single inch [*AS* 521–522; *HDM* 910–911].

As these two passages illustrate, Pullman's writing is not only aurally sonorous like Milton's; it is also (unlike Milton) intensely visual. Pullman uses the leisurely arc of his long-breathed sentences to pile up the visual details. For example, when he describes the Aurora Borealis, he lingers sensuously over a delicate tracery of images (see *NL* 183; *HDM* 135–136). This combination of emotive pull and visual detail is one of the most distinctive features of Pullman's style. In his lecture "What! No Soap?," Pullman discusses the importance of "*stance*—not quite the same as *voice,* not quite the same as *point of view* [but] a mixture of where the camera is, so to speak, and where the sympathy lies" (Pullman 2002a, 51). Although he is describing a common feature of narrative, the way Pullman describes the narrator's orientation to his subject seems a particularly apt description of his own technique, with its filmic attention to visual detail together with its heightened emotional tone.

A tension between realism and fantasy

The almost obsessive attention to visual detail — and indeed to the way things taste, smell, feel — are one of the ways in which Pullman signatures his writing as part of a realist tradition of writing. Likewise the emotional intensity of the description signals his distance from the self-consciously ironic writing he seems particularly to loathe. One can immediately detect the parallels between Milton's distaste for Restoration mannerist style and Pullman's dislike of postmodern writing. For him, "the tricksiness and games-playing of modern and post-modern literary fiction" is a sign of post-lapsarian consciousness. It is "a way of coping with [...] with the *self-consciousness* that arises when we lose our innocence about texts and about language — when [...] we suddenly notice what we're doing" (Pullman 2002c, n.p.). In "Miss Goddard's Grave," Pullman elaborates further on the differences between postmodernist and nineteenth century realist fiction. The former "scoffs at the idea of certainty and delights in exposing contradictions and discontinuities and inconsistencies," whereas in reading realist fiction, our "moral understanding is deepened and enriched by the awakening of imaginative sympathy." The education of the reader in this realist "school for morals" is "subtle, fluid [and] all-pervasive" (Pullman 2005c, n.p.). But the contemporary reader's path to the realist school is threatened by monsters on both sides, on the one hand the Scylla of "theocratic absolutism" which dictates that a book (preferably the Good Book) be read rigidly for a singular Truth, and on the other, by the Charybdis of postmodernism which mockingly reduces everything to a vortex of meaninglessness.

Given these strongly held views, it may seem surprising that Pullman wrote *His Dark Materials* in the genre of fantasy rather than realism. Justifying this choice in his essay, "Writing Fantasy Realistically" (2002c), Pullman refers to the psychological depth of characters and the physicality of description in *His Dark Materials* as signs of its realism, but most fantasy writers draw on these realist elements in however varying degrees. But his conviction of the *moral* superiority of realism sets him apart from other fantasy writers. Pullman thus deploys fantasy the way Milton deploys the Devil, knowing that his weak-willed, post-lapsarian audience will be more easily seduced by bears and witches and hot-air balloons than they ought to be. Indeed he appears to have been seduced himself, discovering to his surprise that the fantasy world of *His Dark Materials* "was *home*, in a way that no other world that I've written about has ever been — not even late nineteenth-century London [...] It was *more* than home, actually: I found my imagination leaping towards these things like a flame to a gas leak" (Pullman 2002c, n.p.).

But just as Milton conjured up the classical eloquence of fallen angels in a Protestant poem, so Pullman aims to "find a way of making fantasy serve the purposes of realism." For Pullman, "the Fall happened in literature ... when the first text noticed that it was a text." From then on, the innocence of realism, or one might say the "childhood" of language, was lost. Quoting Kleist's essay on grace and self-consciousness, Pullman writes, "the way *back* to Paradise is barred: [...]We can't go back and regain the same innocence; [...] The only way is forward; the only way is to [...] try to deal as best we can with our own self-consciousness, in life as well as in literature. We discover, in the end, that the remedy for self-consciousness is self-possession" (Pullman 2002c, n.p.). Thus Pullman seems to envisage a Blakean progression of language from a state of innocence (realism, in which language is "transparent," unconscious of itself) to experience (the excess self-consciousness of postmodernity) culminating in wisdom. To pursue the analogy with the phases of life, one might say that in Pullman's scheme, postmodernism constitutes a kind of permanent adolescence, in which we are demonically trapped within the borders of the self. The question is, if this is where we are now and "we can't go back," how do we press forward? How do we acquire the remedy of "self-possession"?

Like Milton, Pullman enacts a "revolution of the psyche" in the Kristevan sense of a radical return to origins (see Kristeva 1984). He takes the reader back to childhood, then into an alternative adolescence, here re-imagined as an educative time-space, a phase of life with a meaningful narrative trajectory: life as quest in pursuit of a heroic goal. At the end of the quest is the promise of adult wisdom, another Fall but in this case a fortunate one. According to the witch clans' prophecy, Lyra has to face a momentous choice without foreseeing it or understanding its consequences. She will have to act in the dark, trusting her intuition. The choice is a complex one, but is roughly analogous to that made by Milton's Eve. Briefly, she will have to betray someone she loves, choose sexual maturity over innocence, and death over an illusion of immortality.

In Pullman's revision of Milton, the moment of choice tests Lyra's willingness to progress from childhood empathy, mobile and flexible thinking, to a more sober adult sense of duty and responsibility. When Lyra discovers that the prophesied betrayal refers to her abandoning her daemon on the shores of the underworld, she is almost physically unable to move on without him:

> And she looked back again at the foul and dismal shore, so bleak and blasted with disease and poison, and thought of her dear Pan waiting there alone, her heart's companion, watching her disappear into the mist, and she fell into a storm of weeping [...] all along the shore in innumerable ponds and shallows, in wretched broken tree stumps, the damaged creatures that lurked there heard her full-hearted cry and drew themselves a little closer to the ground, afraid of such passion [*AS* 296; *HDM* 754–755].

This would be difficult for any human being in Lyra's world, but it is particularly so for Lyra, since her childhood nature is singularly empathetic. In this role, she comes close to the seventeenth century Orpheus, who is likewise famous for being able to move others to pity, as well as being profoundly moved in this way himself. As nameless creatures are moved at the sound of her cry, Lyra becomes the Miltonic Orpheus herself, unable to rescue Eurydice from Hades. Empathy is Lyra's signature key, but Pullman also provides many other examples of species which live in her 'child-like' way, by intuition and imagination. There are supra-rational witches, dragon-fly knights, angels (whom Milton also portrayed as living by intuition rather than reason), and there are the armored bears. Iorek challenges Lyra to fight him with a dueling stick, but she finds he can anticipate and block every parry she makes. Exasperated, she demands, "'How do you *do* that?" "By not being human," he said. "We [bears] can see in a way humans have forgotten. As I am to human fighters, so you are to adults with the symbol-reader'" (*NL* 227; *HDM* 168).

While many of the adults in the trilogy have lost this intuitive sight completely, even the children in Lyra's world seem a little rusty, and need instruction and inspiration to recover their latent skills. Will is a year older than Lyra, and from a world recognizably like ours, so he needs to be taught how to think like a child (that is, intuitively). Thus in Cittàgazze, where he finds the subtle knife, *his* destined instrument, he has to be taught how to use it by the previous bearer, Giacomo Paradisi. Interestingly, in order to master the knife, he has to be able to empty his mind of worries and responsibilities — adult concerns, one might say: "Will tried to do it. But his head was buzzing ... and then he thought of his mother, his poor mother... he put the knife down and cried. It was all too much to bear" (*SK* 191; *HDM* 431). His concerns for his mother are parental, in the sense that until now, he has been her primary carer. Lyra knows how it is done, even if the knife isn't her instrument: "she knew this process [...] so did the poet Keats, all of them knew you couldn't get it by straining towards it. But she held her tongue" (*SK* 192; *HDM* 432). Keats' definition of the imagination as a negative capability is particularly accommodating to an idea of childhood in which inexperience becomes a source of strength.

> "Stop" said the old man gently. "Relax [,,,], This is the subtle knife, not a heavy sword [...] go gently, don't force it." Will tried again. Lyra could see the intensity in his body, saw his jaw working, and then saw the authority descend over it, calming and relaxing and clarifying. The authority was Will's own — or his daemon's, perhaps [...] They watched as Will's body stopped trembling. No less intense, he was focused differently now [...] the knife sat so naturally in his hand [...] Lyra imagined she could see Will's soul flowing back along the blade to his hand, and up the arm to his heart [*SK* 193; *HDM* 432].

The rather oppressive image of authority descending is counter-balanced by the succeeding phrase; it was his own, or his invisible daemon's. But one sees the same process as that undergone by Lyra and Iorek: by some dialogic exchange with another being (Giacomo, the authority), Will enters a natural state, in which his soul flows, his mind and muscles work lightly. In my reading of this passage, he has learned to possess his childhood, therefore to possess himself. Will and Lyra become archetypal figures for an embryonic goodness and wisdom, embryonic because as child characters (unlike Adam and Eve) they are never presented as perfected beings; instead they are an image of human potential.

In *The Amber Spyglass,* the volume which has, not coincidentally, won the highest plaudits as a work of literary fiction (winning the Whitbread Book of the Year Award in 2001), Pullman develops his major theme, that children lose their innate lightness and grace when they become adults but that this inevitable change is positive and morally enriching. We see this change occurring most clearly in Lyra when she will have to re-acquire the skill of reading the alethiometer through long hours of academic study. Another indication of her maturation is when she loses her footing in the underworld, as she and Will and the souls of the dead are making their way around the rim of a vast abyss. She remembers playing on Oxford college rooftops when she was younger, showing off her nimble-footedness to her childhood friend Roger. Casting an Orphic look back at the soul of Roger following her now, she fleetingly recovers a sense of childhood certainty: "she was Roger's Lyra, full of grace and daring; she didn't need to creep along like an insect" (*AS* 378; *HDM* 811). But the next moment, she slips and falls. Luckily, Lyra has powerful allies, and a flying harpy saves her from the endless fall into the abyss.

But the most important change occurs to Lyra as a storyteller, when she abandons fantasy for realism. In the underworld, Lyra at first tries using fictional stories to charm her way past the harpies, whose role here is to guard the entrance to the land of the dead. But they fly at her in rage, and drive her party back. Later, as she tells the dead souls about her life at Jordan College, the harpies crowd round her, listening peaceably. Will asks them,

> "When Lyra spoke to you outside the wall, you flew at her. Why did you do that?"
> "Lies!" the harpies all cried. "Lies and fantasies!"
> "Yet when she spoke just now, you all listened, you kept still. Again, why was that?"
> "Because it was true [...]. Because she spoke the truth. Because it was nourishing.
> Because it was feeding us" [*AS* 332; *HDM* 781].

Will and Lyra strike a pact with the harpies. If they will release the dead souls, then in future years, the dead will return to feed the harpies with true stories about their lives. One might object that Lyra's tales of Jordan College are no truer than her far-fetched fantasies because Jordan College does not exist, but her memories are true to *her* at least. As Pullman glosses this passage in "Writing Fantasy Realistically" (2002c), Lyra "leaves fantasy behind, and becomes a realist. (As the whole story does, you might say)." Thus in Pullman's secular revision of classical myth and Christian theology, acquiring an adult consciousness of mortality requires a shift in the way we frame our lives in narrative. Choice of literary genre becomes no less than an acceptance of adult moral responsibility: we owe it to our deaths to tell the truth. As a corollary to Lyra's conversion to realism, Will discovers that he must use the subtle knife to close up all the windows between different worlds, leaving open only one passage for the souls of the dead to re-enter and dissipate in the material world. Because they come from different worlds, Lyra and Will are essentially fantasies to each other, so in the new realist order, the young lovers are tragically parted.

Like *Paradise Lost*, the moral education of *His Dark Materials* concludes with a pair of lovers making their solitary way from Paradise, with "the world [...] all before them" (Milton *PL*.12.646–49).[11] But the problem remains that for the reader, Lyra and Will are both characters in a fantasy. Is the implication that we should close the book, never read another fantasy, and never re-read this one? In a more general sense, does growing up entail closing all the doors that lead to alternative worlds, except the one by which we exit life? What would be the moral and intellectual implications of closing down consciousness in this way? Pullman's view is that in later life, we cease to change fundamentally; as his image of adult daemons connotes, we become fixed in a certain identity.[12] But this view is at odds with the trajectory of the other moral education depicted in *His Dark Materials*, by which we learn from Lyra's lively ability to empathize with others. Empathy is not the same as identification, but it still requires becoming unfixed from one's own habits of thinking and self-interests. Lyra's moral goodness, as Pullman represents it, stems directly from her intellectual flexibility and openness. And these characteristics also govern her choice of literary form; she is a fantasist because she is easily able to imagine her way into new worlds. In *His Dark Materials* it is easy to see why children have to leave off telling tall stories to become responsible adults. If they continued to give free rein to their fantasies, they would develop into the adult maniacal explorers, scientists and religious absolutists with which *His Dark Materials* abounds.

Conclusion

The trilogy also demonstrates how it might be dangerous and impoverishing to close the door completely to earlier modes of understanding. Many readers have stated their preference for *Northern Lights,* in which this counter theme runs deepest. This suggests a final possible parallel with Milton's *Paradise Lost,* that *His Dark Materials* will be a work frequently read against the grain. That is to say, although Pullman's argument is that adult imaginations are (and should be) limited compared to the quick and graceful flexibility of a child's, nevertheless his trilogy will, on the whole, call this thesis into question as it continues to demonstrate how easily the hearts and minds of adult readers can be set aflame.

Note on the Text

Milton, John. 1998. *Paradise Lost*, 2d ed. Ed. Alastair Fowler. London: Longman. Hereafter cited as *PL*.

Milton, John. 1959–82. *Complete Prose Works of John Milton*, vol. 2. Ed. D. Bush. London: n.p. Hereafter cited as *CP*.

NOTES

1. For example, Jasper Rees (2003) asks, "are we yearning for old-fashioned stories, seeking spiritual solace, or merely dumbing down?" David Aaronovitch wants to know, "What's so smart about being childish?" (2001). Frank Furedi sees adults reading children's literature as a general sign of cultural decline in "The Children Who Won't Grow Up" (2003). Howard Jacobson argues that people are choosing "the lowest common denominator, which is the children's book," on *Lebrecht Live*, BBC Radio 3 (2005). An anonymous writer decries "the juvenalization of everything" in the *Times Literary Supplement* (2005).

2. Into this wild abyss,
The womb of nature and perhaps her grave,
Of neither sea, nor shore, nor air, nor fire,
But all these in their pregnant causes mixed
Confusedly, and which thus must ever fight,
Unless the almighty maker them ordain
His dark materials to create more worlds,
Into this wild abyss the wary fiend
Stood on the brink of Hell and looked a while,
Pondering his voyage [*PL* 2.910–19].

In referring to "his dark materials," Pullman also has in mind the astrophysical concept of dark matter. See *Gribbin and Gribbin* (2005) and Katharine Cox's essay in this volume.

3. Recently published secularist apologias include: Richard Dawkins, *The God Delusion* (2006); Daniel C. Dennett, *Breaking the Spell: Religion as a Natural Phenomenon* (2006); Sam Harris, *The End of Faith: Religion, Terror and the Future of Reason* (2005) and *Letter to a Christian Nation* (2007); Christopher Hitchens, *God is Not Great: How Religion Poisons Everything* (2007); David Mills, *Atheist Universe: The Thinking Person's Answer to Christian Fundamentalism* (2006); and Victor J. Stenger, *God: The Failed Hypothesis. How Science Shows That God Does Not Exist* (2008).

4. On the controversy over *The Satanic Verses*, see Spivak (1993), Appignanesi and Maitland (1989) and Brennan (1989).

5. Philippa Pearce's *Tom's Midnight Garden* (1958) has a pair of Adam and Eve-like children, and Hatty does "fall" from innocence, but their maturation is not given cosmic significance as in Pullman's fable. In Geraldine McCaughrean's *A Little Lower than the Angels* (1987), Gabriel, who is apprenticed to a cruel Master Mason, runs away and joins a group of Mystery Players; he plays Eve to the Adam of another slightly older player boy. Peter Dickinson's *Eva* (1988) presents his eponymous heroine as a new Eve; her consciousness is transplanted into a chimp's body whence the path of human evolution is changed. Other recent representations of child Adam and Eves include: K.L. Going's *The Garden of Eve* (2007) and Elsie V. Aidinoff's *The Garden* (2004). Thanks to Charlie Butler, Monica Edinger, Judith Philo, Leila Rasheed and Alison Waller for these references.

6. On Milton's role as a public polemicist, see Corns (1998); Thum (1993); Kranidas (1983); McCabe (1981) and Lieb (1974).

7. "The reason Milton wrote in fetters when he wrote of Angels & God, and at liberty when of Devils & Hell, is because he was a true Poet, and of the Devil's party without knowing it." William Blake, Plate 6, *The Marriage of Heaven and Hell*. Cf. Pullman (2002).

8. Eve, defending her right to work in Eden alone: "And what is faith, love, virtue unassayed,/ Alone, without exterior help sustained?" (*PL* 9.335–36).

9. Lewis has a similar scene in *The Horse and His Boy* (107) where Aravis is equally irreverent about the adults she is spying on, from behind the couch.

10. Shakespeare, *Hamlet* 3:2. Milton invokes the aid of his "celestial patroness" who "dictates to me nightly slumbering" (*PL* 9.21–23).

11. For a similar point about Rowling's delight in leading her readers astray and later correcting them, see Cooley (2005).

12. The difference being that "solitary" in *The Amber Spyglass* refers to the pair of humans being separation from each other, rather than from God as in *Paradise Lost*.

13. Questioner: "'What would happen if humans changed dramatically in later life? ... would their daemons change also?' Pullman: 'Do people change dramatically in later life? I

think their basic stance towards the world is pretty constant. Opinions can change, but opinions are superficial"' (*Guardian* 2002).

Works Cited

Aaronovitch, David. 2001. "What's So Smart About Being Childish?" *The Independent*, June 6.
Appignanesi, Lisa, and Sara Maitland, eds. 1989. *The Rushdie File*. London: Fourth Estate.
Brennan, Timothy. 1989. *Salman Rushdie and the Third World*. London: Macmillan.
Carey, John, ed. 1997. *Milton: Complete Shorter Poems*. London: Longman.
Coleman, John. 2002. "Into Adulthood." *The Seven Ages of Life*. London: Centre for Reform, 57–80.
Cooley, Ron. 2005. "Harry Potter and the Temporal Prime Directive." In *Scholarly Studies in Harry Potter*. Cynthia Whitney Hallett, ed. Lewiston, NY: Edwin Mellen, 29–42.
Corns, Thomas. 1998. *John Milton: The Prose Works*. New York: Twayne.
Davies, Caroline. 2005. "Author Attacks School League Tables for Killing Off Curiosity and Joy." *Telegraph*, September 3.
Dawkins, Richard. 2006. *The God Delusion*. London: Bantam.
Dennett, Daniel C. 2006. *Breaking the Spell: Religion as a Natural Phenomenon*. London: Penguin.
Eliot, T. S. 1957. "Milton" and "A Note on the Verse of John Milton." In *On Poetry and Poets*. London: Faber.
Falconer, Rachel. 1996. *Orpheus Dis(re)membered: Milton and the Myth of the Poet-Hero*. Sheffield: Sheffield Academic.
Fish, Stanley. 2003. *Surprised by Sin: the Reader in Paradise Lost*, 2d ed. Cambridge, MA: Harvard University Press.
Furedi, Frank. 2003. "The Children Who Won't Grow Up." *Spiked*, July 29. Accessed October 28, 2010. http://www.spiked-online.com/articles/00000006DE8D.htm.
Gribbin, John, and Mary Gribbin. 2005. *The Science of Philip Pullman's His Dark Materials*. London: Hodder.
Harris, Sam. 2005. *The End of Faith: Religion, Terror and the Future of Reason*. London: Simon and Schuster.
_____. 2007. *Letter to a Christian Nation*. London: Simon and Schuster.
Hitchens, Christopher. 2007. *God Is Not Great: How Religion Poisons Everything*. New York: Warner.
Jacobson, Howard. 2005. *Lebrecht Live*, BBC Radio 3, January 27.
Kranidas, Thomas. 1983. "Style and Rectitude in Seventeenth-Century Prose: Hall, Smectymnuus, and Milton." *Huntington Library Quarterly*, 46, 3, 237–69.
Kristeva, Julia. 1984. *Revolution in Poetic Language*. Trans. Margaret Waller. New York: Columbia University Press.
"Letters." 2005. *Times Literary Supplement*, 12–14.
Lewis, C. S. 2000. *The Narnian Chronicles*. New York: Harper Trophy.
Lieb, Michael. 1974. "Milton's *Of Reformation* and the Dynamics of Controversy." In *Achievements of the Left Hand: Essays on the Prose of John Milton*. Michael Lieb and John T. Shawcross, eds. Amherst: University of Massachusetts Press.
McCabe, Richard. 1981. "The Form and Methods of Milton's *Animadversions Upon the Remonstrants Defence Against Smectymnuus*." *English Language Notes*, 18, 4, 266–72.
Mills, David. 2006. *Atheist Universe: the Thinking Person's Answer to Christian Fundamentalism*. Berkeley, CA: Ulysses.
Milton, John. 1959–82. *Areopagitica*. In *Complete Prose Works of John Milton*, vol. 2. Edited by D. Bush. London: n.p.
Pullman, Philip. 1998. "The Darkside of Narnia." *The Guardian*, October 1. Accessed September 24, 2007. http://reports.guardian.co.uk/articles/1998/10/1/p-24747.html.
_____. 2002a. "What! No Soap?" *Notes from the Royal Society of Literature* 20.
_____. 2002b. "I Am of the Devil's Party." *Telegraph*, January 29.
_____. 2002c. "Writing Fantasy Realistically." *Sea of Faith Network*. Accessed October 28, 2010. http://www.sofn.org.uk/conferences/pullman2002.html.
_____. 2005a. "Prize Winning Lecture at the Swedish Royal Library by Philip Pullman at

Swedish House of Parliament — on Receipt of Astrid Lindgren Memorial Award." May 23. Accessed December 1, 2007. http://www.alma.se/templates/KR_Page.aspx?id=3131&epslanguage=EN.

_____. 2005b. Introduction to *Paradise Lost* by John Milton. Oxford: Oxford University Press.

_____. 2005c. "Miss Goddard's Grave." Lecture given at the University of East Anglia. Accessed October 28, 2010. www.philip-pullman.com/assets_cm/files/.../miss_goddards_grave.pdf.

"Question and Answer with Philip Pullman." 2002. *The Guardian*, February 18.

Rees, Jasper. 2003. "We're All Reading Children's Books." *Daily Telegraph*, November 15.

Spivak, Gayatri Chakravorty. 1993. "Reading *The Satanic Verses*." In *Outside the Teaching Machine*. London: Routledge, 219–38.

Stenger, Victor J. 2008. *God: The Failed Hypothesis: How Science Shows That God Does Not Exist*. N.p.: Prometheus.

Thum, Maureen. 1993. "Milton's Diatribal Voice: The Integration and Transformation of a Generic Paradigm in *Animadversions*." *Milton Studies*, 30, 3–25.

2

"When I Grow Up I Want to Be...": Conceptualization of the Hero Within the Works of C.S. Lewis, J.R.R. Tolkien and Philip Pullman

PHIL CARDEW

Introduction

> Who would true valour see
> Let him come hither,
> One here will constant be,
> Come wind come weather.
> There's no discouragement,
> Shall make him once relent,
> His first avow'd intent
> To be a pilgrim [Bunyan 2002, 335–336].

What is C.S. Lewis' *The Lion, the Witch and the Wardrobe* about? Or, to that matter, J.R.R. Tolkien's *The Lord of the Rings* or any part of Philip Pullman's *His Dark Materials* trilogy? To some extent the question is as pointless as it is trite — each book is a narrative and thus to lose ourselves within the narrative is to explore its meaning. However, the extent to which we can delve beneath the "mateere" to the "sentence," to unravel the story from the plot, dictates both the extent to which meaning can be ascribed to the narration of events and the extent to which intertextuality can be said to enrich our understanding.

For it is undoubted that there is an intertextual relationship between the works of Tolkien, Lewis and Pullman. An intertextuality which relies not only on the later works' knowledge of — and in some respects homage to — the earlier (a hermetic great tradition, as it were) but also on each work's relationship to a range of other material, most notably to the Bible but also to a range of medieval and early modern material; a secondary intertextuality which underpins, and reinforces, the primary connections and relationships.

Central to the texts which will form the primary focus of this study, *The Lion, the Witch and the Wardrobe* (1950), *The Return of the King* (1955), and *Northern Lights* (1995), is a representation and conceptualization of the maturing of a hero; maturing not simply in the sense of growing up but also of ripening, as s/he becomes seasoned to the full realization of that which is required to fulfill the role. To some extent, these dual concepts are intertwined as to grow older also entails becoming fully heroic and realizing the needs and aspirations of the narrative and its cast, but in many senses it is through the development of an intellectual (rather than a physical) maturity that a character becomes fully heroic. Frodo Baggins does not mature physically a great deal within the *Lord of the Rings* trilogy, and while the characters of *The Lion, the Witch and the Wardrobe* and *His Dark Materials'* trilogy undergo a maturation process focused on the passage through puberty (with either implicit, or explicit, Freudian analogies) it is their growing intellectual, rather than physical, maturity which has greatest impact upon their heroic *personae*, particularly through the identification and acceptance of human fallacy and unreliability.

At the same time, the connecting feature of these authors' work is a concentration on the fantastic, an exploration of worlds within which the natural laws of science and culture are transcended. For the characters of these novels, heroism takes on a new context within worlds which are populated by darker threats, greater evils, and (thus) more effective heroes than those who operate within our day-to-day existence. In the case of Lewis and Tolkien, such great evils may well be characteristic of the period within which they wrote. As Lutz Röhrich (1991) has discussed, folk tales (and in this respect fantasy novels can be said to embody a modern representation of the folk tale) are often pre-occupied with national stereotypes and concerns. Tom Shippey (2000) has shown that *The Lord of the Rings* as well as presenting an innately medievalized perspective also presents a very English (and particularly pastoral) one. As we will see, later, the desecration of the Shire, in the closing chapters of *The Return of the King*, is a desecration of the pastoral by the industrial. Hobbits take tea and have a fondness for pipes and real ale. They are very much the embodiment of an ideal of English rural life, one that is unspoilt by the harshness of an industrial age. The encroachment of machinery upon a slightly backward society, the imposition of monolithic structures of order and the development of large, unnatural, armies are characteristic of the threatening evils of Tolkien's work, to a far greater extent than Lewis.' Pullman has inherited this perspective too, and presents a distrust of science and experimentation, though perhaps in his eyes, the evils of genetic modification have replaced (or enhanced) the evils of monomania and authoritarian rule.

In essence, a great deal of the work of Lewis, Tolkien and Pullman has to do with growing up. The transition from child to adult, whether that be from schoolboy to prince or from insignificant hobbit to hero of the free world, particularly its relationship to the period of puberty and to the complex emotional forces in operation at this stage of human development, is central to the notion of the hero within the narratives. The fantastic worlds of these authors are worlds in which the trials and tribulations of growing up are either re-emphasized or overcome. The Pevensie children of *The Lion, the Witch and the Wardrobe* mature in Narnia but remain physically unchanged at home.[1] They fight their witches and are supported by their paternalistic heroic father figures, but are separated from their real parents. As this description shows, the allegory of Narnia is as much an allegory of Freud as it is of Christ.[2]

Yet this notion is also one which is, at least, contextualized within a Christian understanding of the possibility of redemption for even the lowest of the low (either in social terms or in terms of sin). Working from such contexts as the Old English poem "The Dream of the Rood" (wherein the transition of the cross from a means of torture and execution to a sign of redemption signifies the possibility of salvation for even the worst sinner), this conceptualization of redemption underpins the very notion of the unlikely hero in a way that (despite its obvious Arthurian similarities) other hero-centered narratives of children (for example J.K. Rowling's *Harry Potter* series, or the works of Susan Cooper) do not.

In the worlds of Tolkien and Lewis, this redemption through the development of the heroic is not complex and is centered on a largely allegorical development of character within the narratives. In Pullman's *His Dark Materials* trilogy, however, concepts of good and evil are neither so clear nor so allegorically charged. The world of the adult intrudes, here, as a world of science and advanced knowledge, and it is a world which is tinged by both a post–Miltonic, and post-holocaust, sensibility.

What is a hero?

Despite the years that have passed since its publication in 1957, Northrop Frye's *Anatomy of Criticism* remains one of the most useful characterizations of the nature of the hero in literature. Frye charts the descent of the status of the hero — from the mythic to the ironic — as a growing relationship between the text and its reader/audience, a relationship in which the power and insight of the reader/audience grows alongside the sophistication of society. When societies are in their infancy then the unexplained needs explanation; when the natural (and supernatural) world is better understood, then we can sympathize with heroes whose capacity to control, or even to understand, the world around them is limited by their ineptitude, or lack of understanding. However, outside the world of folklore, narratives are rarely as single-minded as this approach suggests and it is, indeed, the portrayal of different hero types within a single narrative which provides us with the means to characterize and relate to each individual type. As a reader, especially when operating from what Gérard Genette (1979) would have termed a paraliptic perspective (wherein the reader is operating at the same level of understanding as the characters within the narrative), the plot unfolds alongside the narration and our ability to comprehend what is being narrated is limited by the understanding of the character with whom we interact. When, as is often the case within the texts under discussion, our hero is operating from the perspective of a naïve characterization, then our understanding unfolds with theirs. In these contexts the more knowledgeable, or often more overtly heroic characters act as guides and mentors, but also as interpreters and coaches, to both the less developed characters of the narrative and its reader/audience.

Frye's approach also allows for the concept of the developing hero, the one who begins a narrative as a naïve, or ironic, hero, but who learns from the role models around him (or her), taking the best and worst examples as those to emulate or avoid, and consciously developing towards an ideal. This ideal is embodied in many cases by the most powerful adult characters within the narrative. Often, within a medieval context, such characters embody the notion of the *kolbítr*[3] a character *'óbráðgörr í upprunna'* (unpromising in youth), who changes dramatically as the narrative unfolds. However, as Vladimir Propp (1984) has demonstrated, folk narratives do not seek to explain, or contextualize, such transformations, they simply happen. Lewis and Tolkien, on the other hand, contextualize their essence of perfection in the hero against a Christian context of leadership and self-sacrifice. Pullman's world, however, is less certain about what is good when presenting characters for emulation.

Thus, Lewis and Tolkien are far more easily characterized within Frye's world of western European fiction, which is a world, from its earliest texts, that is dominated by a Christian sensibility and influence on written narrative. It is a truism that most early medieval western European texts are at least tinged with Christian sentiment as it is only the act of Christianization that brings with it the mechanics of writing (and it is only the mechanics of writing which have enabled a modern audience to have access to the text). The narratives of medieval Europe, many of which explicitly or implicitly influence the works of Lewis, Tolkien, and Pullman, operate within a context that cannot escape the Christian world that has recorded them. Thus, an overtly heroic narrative poem, such a *Beowulf,* presents us with a character who is both superhuman (being able to swim underwater for extraordinary periods of time, defeating the monster Grendel with his bare hands) and fallible (falling, finally, to a dragon whose wrath has been unleashed by the actions of his subjects) and who is frequently associated with the Christian deity. While we may suspect (and many have attempted to prove) that the narrative of *Beowulf* existed in a pre–Christian "Bear's Son Folk Tale" form, its iteration to a modern audience presents us with a hero "of God" as well as of his people (see Panzer 1910).

More interestingly, a poem such as "The Dream of the Rood" presents us with the figure of Christ dressed as an Old English hero. In this poem Christ is a *hæleð* (hero, line 39), a *ricne cyning* (mighty king, line 44), a *sigora wealdenden* (wielder of victories, line 67) as well as being *god ælmihtig* (almighty God). The attributes of the hero are the attributes of Christ, as a figure he protects his people and lays down his life for them, in a manner that is unequivocally heroic.

Using another Old English poem for context, "The Battle of Maldon" provides us with a more equivocal, and questioning, relationship between the hero and his Christian context. While the poem depicts some unequivocal representations of heroism (and cowardice), the English "eorl," Byrhtnoth, in allowing an eventually catastrophic concession to his opponents (the overtly pagan Vikings) to cross over a narrow causeway so as to be able to fight the English on a more even footing, declares "for his ofermode" (on account of his pride):

> Nu eow is gerymed, gað ricene to us,
> guman to guþe; god ana wat
> hwa þære wælstowe wealdan mote[4] [lines 93–95].

It may well be suggested that Byrhtnoth's pride in this context is not pride in the perceived prowess of his troops (who are soundly beaten, despite their valiant efforts) but in the power of his Christian God, who alone knows where the victory will lie. This form of pride suggests that Byrhtnoth believes that victory *should* be his because of the fact of his Christianity. However, as John Bunyan would have told him, a Christian soul finds its own path to heaven and it is not predetermined that heaven awaits all Christian souls. This is not to overlabor a point, but the contextualization of heroism, particularly its religious contextualization, colors its representation. Religious and ethical contexts bring a certainty of action to the hero of a narrative which is absent within a more questioning environment.

This, more than anything, accounts for the different feel to the heroes of Pullman from those of Lewis and Tolkien. The latter often represent flawed characters who have the opportunity (in the end) to achieve redemption. The characters of Boromir, in *The Fellowship of the Ring* and of Edmund in *The Lion, the Witch and the Wardrobe*, present two apposite examples, but the nature of good and evil, and of right and wrong, are clear to both the characters of the narratives and their readership. In this respect both Lewis and Tolkien operate within a narrative context which both reflects their Christian faith and also reflects the force of their contemporary society, with evil being as much about totalitarianism as about anti–Christian sentiment. "Power tends to corrupt and absolute power corrupts absolutely," as Lord Acton had it (Acton cited in Duncan *et al.* 2004, 71).

Thus, the naïve heroes of Lewis and Tolkien have a clear framework within both to position their own morality and their perspectives on good governance and heroic behavior. While the lesser mortals of the heroic typology may not aspire to the superhuman or even exceptional deeds of their mythic, romance or high mimetic counterparts (to borrow Frye's terminology), they know what good and evil mean, and can recognize when a ruler oversteps the terms and conditions of their rule and turns from protector to tyrant, from benign lord to despot. This is of central importance, as it is in this way that the adult figures of the narratives reassure both their lesser heroes and their audience that positive role models and reasonable behavior are the path to righteous exaltation. Justice is tempered with mercy, power is not as important as authority and revenge is a dish not served at all.

Tolkien's unlikely heroes

The closing chapters of *The Return of the King*, in the episodes surrounding "the scouring of the Shire" (Book VI, chapter VIII), provide a perfect example of the learned behavior of this form of heroic context. The hobbits, Frodo, Sam, Merry and Pippin, are gradually separated from the more overtly powerful and heroic members of their fellowship (particularly represented by the kingly Aragorn and the wizardly Gandalf—archetypes of Frye's romance and mythic heroes respectively) and are left to return home, to a world which they believe to have been untouched by the distant events of the outside world in which they have been so instrumentally engaged. They arrive, however, to find that, indeed, the security of their home environment has been severely compromised by forces beyond the control of its inhabitants. Emanating from a localized despotism (the desire for wealth displayed by Frodo's wicked cousins the Sackville-Bagginses — and focused within the greedy but ultimately weak figure of Lotho) a greater despotism (in the form of the deposed wizard, Saruman) has taken over. The hobbits, generally presented in a disempowered and child-like context, have been overcome, with Saruman employing men, who are both bigger, and less morally constrained than the hobbits, to tear down homes and countryside, imposing the dark satanic mills of industrialization on a peaceful and pastoral landscape. They are powerless having first given power to one of their own (largely through their inherent lethargy and unwillingness to engage with the potential threats of the outside world) and thus have grown to accept the tyranny which is visited upon them, having no catalyst to provide them with the impetus to rebel.

Into this world step our newly formed heroes. They have been through fire and water and have grown to understand both the devastating power of tyranny and the need for heroism to counter its influence. Their own particular brand of heroism is not, however, in the mould of Aragorn or Gandalf. Although it might be said that Merry and Pippin have acquired a more heroic stature (and height) through drinking the "ent draft" given them by Treebeard, Frodo and Sam are physically unchanged. The added stature that the party have acquired is the stature of maturity, the self-confidence of knowing what a true villain looks like and knowing that villainy, even the essence of evil itself (in the figure of Sauron) can be overcome.

Thus, it is in the guise of generals and not warriors that Frodo and Sam confront the challenges facing the shire. They organize a resistance, they stand up to bullies who are otherwise powerless, and they face the malignance of the usurped sorcerer, Saruman. At the same time, they demonstrate that their maturity has taught them as much about good government as it has about heroism. They prevent the wholesale slaughter of the thugs who have overtaken the Shire, and Frodo is even prepared to show mercy to Grima Wormtongue and to Saruman himself. In this, Frodo reflects the attitude of his chief mentor, Gandalf, who has, previously, counseled against the slaying of Gollum on the grounds that he might still have a part to play in the story of the Ring (as proves, ultimately, to be true). However, this is no mere slavish emulation, it is a wisdom born of experience. While Beowulf teaches us that he may demonstrate *fortitudo* but finally fails to exhibit *sapientia*, Frodo shows us the gentle application of both of the kingly virtues.

Most importantly, the four heroic hobbits have been consciously set on their path by their most authoritative and fatherly role-model, Gandalf, who leaves them on their return to the Shire, with the explicit sentiment that they are now capable of dealing with what they find there. There is no element of luck in this assumption, but one of trust. They are children no longer having passed the test of transition into adulthood and are now free to make their own judgments. While, in earlier passages, the tests have been those which invite failure as well as defeat (as are the tests, largely, for the Pevensie children) the scouring of the Shire invites a display of prowess and accomplishment and a realization that these characters have achieved what was not expected of them at the outset of the narrative.

Lewis' straightforward model of heroism

Unlike the subtleties of Tolkien's later text, Lewis's characters in *The Lion, The Witch and The Wardrobe* are both more straightforward and more obvious. As with many allegorical roles, their task is to be read on many levels and to make overt the link between the narrative on the page and the narrative of faith. In many ways, it is the characters of Lewis' (still overtly Catholic) science fiction — particularly *Out of the Silent Planet* (1938) and *That Hideous Strength* (1945) which displays a more complex presentation of heroic realization.

Despite the fairly heavy handed imagery of the Oyarsa, angelic figures who are far removed from Pullman's, the narratives approach the concept of the pre-lapsarian and post-lapsarian worlds of Mars and Earth with more subtlety, overt allegory giving way to suggestion and ethical dilemma.

The children of Narnia have a more straightforward and more naïve set of choices before them. Characters may "seem fair and feel foul" (as Sam Gamgee initially says of Aragorn, in *The Fellowship of the Ring*), but their true natures are really very near the surface. Along with Tolkien, and most probably as a result of the time at which they were writing, it is the characters who could go one way or the other that are most vexing to their straightforwardly good counterparts. Just as some hobbits had sided with Saruman and embraced the descent into the fall brought on by Saruman, some of nature is seen to embrace the evil presented in Lewis' work as: "some of the trees are on her [the White Witch's] side" (Lewis 1950, 1).

Models of heroism in *His Dark Materials*

The children of the *His Dark Materials* trilogy are not so fortunate in their adult or heroic role models as those of Lewis, or as the hobbits of *The Lord of the Rings* (1954). Pullman's world is not a straightforward one of good and evil, and this is manifested in the social and ethical context that the series presents. Society is both a theocracy and a corrupt semi-despotic tyranny. Scholarship and education are to be admired, even aspired to, but are ultimately weak and divorced from the harsh realities of the real world. The Jordan scholars are apparently impotent against the power of Mrs. Coulter and yet by passing the alethiometer to Lyra they provide her with the means to expand her intellectual capacities and in turn defeat the tyrannical organizations who control her world. Parental figures may, or may not, be true parents and may, or may not, cherish or threaten in equal measure. Central to the message of the narratives is that the adult world is a world of mistrust, politics, self-interest and fear.

In this respect, Pullman holds out little hope of a perfect world in which all these problems will disappear. There is no Nirvana, no Heaven (aside from the fleeting experience of a knowledgeable Eden in *The Amber Spyglass*), only other. Escape to other worlds only presents as many challenges, fears and threats as whichever is currently viewed as reality. Everything is, finally, transient. We are merely dust and will return to dust (in both a symbolic and actual sense) and so the outlook is pretty bleak for anyone growing up with any fancy ideas otherwise. Indeed, in a web interview, Pullman explicitly states that his world is overtly non-fantastic:

> The story I was trying to write was about real people, not beings that don't exist like elves or hobbits. Lyra and Will and the other characters are meant to be human

beings like us, and the story is about a universal human experience, namely growing up. The 'fantasy' parts of the story were there as a picture of aspects of human nature, not as something alien and strange [Pullman n.d.].

From this perspective, it is as much class, as religion, that imbues and underpins the essence of heroism within Pullman's work. In *Northern Lights*, the truly heroic characters, characters who display selflessness and bravery in order to protect the immature central characters, are either lower class (occasional college servants and the Gyptians, who despite their internal hierarchy and pecking order are marginal and outside the world of polite society) or socially classless (Lee Scoresby who is at best a flawed hero, others might include the armored bear, Iofur Raknison, and the witches). All these characters operate within a world view that is in opposition to the social class that is so important to Lyra's autocratic and aristocratic world, as it is a world view that does not consider learning or religion, but which values common sense and bravery above all else.

Indeed, the Gyptians, especially in the context of the motherly Ma Costa, the fatherly Faader Coram and the kingly John Faa, present the most straight-forwardly positive representations of adulthood within the novel.[5] These representations are particularly pertinent given Lyra's ambivalence, lack of certainty and separation from her real parents. In this respect, she shares much with Frodo Baggins (who is an orphan) and the Pevensie children (who are evacuated, and thus separated from their parents), in that she has to rely on a range of adult figures as role models. Both Frodo and the Pevensies, however, have stable concepts of an ideal to draw upon. Lyra's world is less certain and more problematic.

It is also arguable that Pullman's naïve heroes never fully achieve their transition to adulthood and satisfactory heroic status. While the journeys of the hobbits, and the Pevensies, are internal as well as actual — the characters achieving moral strength, maturity of outlook and certainty of purpose — the paths traveled by Pullman's characters are far more the paths of growing complexity and ultimate cynicism. To some extent, this is embodied by the use of tools within the novels, whether the alethiometer or the subtle knife, which supplant the need for the child characters to grow up, replacing the mature realization of adulthood with a growing proficiency with gadgets: a type of Excalibur for the Game Boy Generation.

The ultimate danger of Pullman's world, however, rests with stasis: the inability to change, to adapt, to reflect the forces around you and to respond to them. Just as a theocracy looks towards stability and, finally, sacrifice (oblation being an offering to God), adulthood brings with it a different kind of stasis the permanent shape of the daemon, a freezing into a particular role, or character and a loss of the innocent delight of experimentation. This delight, the delight in another being that is demonstrated by Lyra, in particular, summons to mind the innocent and unquestioning love of the very young, which is unequivocal and absolute. It shows us a world before the Fall, a world where questions are not asked and promises are not broken. With age comes experience, with experience comes betrayal (or, at the very least, disappointment) and maturity brings a solidification of attitude and inherent prejudice.

This is not an inspiring image, and, it could be suggested, is not meant to bring hope to its audience. While we have characters to admire in the works of Tolkien, and to understand and emulate in the works of Lewis, Pullman gives us heroes fit for the world he presents us, where there is no salvation, and little hope. We might say these are very ordinary heroes fit for a modern, complex and postmodern world in which the very idea of traditional heroism has become so problematic. This may be one reason why Pullman often refers to the books as "stark realism," which is to say that Will and Lyra are heroes but not in a traditional sense as we identify and empathize with their limitations as much as their successes.

Conclusion

If Lewis and Tolkien's worlds are influenced by their contemporary society, with a distrust of despotism and a need to demonstrate that the heroism of the little people can ultimately win through, Pullman's is equally rooted in a society which is as concerned with the continual forces of democratization and a distrust of traditional elites and meritocracies. Lewis and Tolkien inhabit a world of choice, where one character's choice at one time can determine the fate of the whole of society, but Pullman gives us a world of choices as opportunities, each one possible, each one valid, each one presenting a different prospect for success or failure. To emulate Will and Lyra is to emulate how ordinary adolescents might act under extraordinary circumstances and find a reluctant heroism within themselves which is not as far from the model seen in Lewis and Tolkien as might at first be supposed.

Notes

1. Although, as Rachel Falconer contends in this volume, the children are returned to their physical youth they retain their adult intellectual capacities.

2. Useful discussions of the extent to which symbolism within fairy tale and the fantastic can be viewed as symptomatic of Freudian theory can be found in Brewer (1988) and Bettelheim (1991).

3. Meaning literally "coal biter"— traditionally a character who sits very close to the fire in early youth.

4. Translation: "Now room is granted to you, come swiftly to us, warriors to war. God alone knows who at the end shall possess this battle's field."

5. See Nicola Allen's essay in this volume for further discussion of the Gyptians and social class in trilogy.

WORKS CITED

Aarne, Antti. 1961. *The Types of the Folktale: A Classification and Bibliography*, 2d ed. Trans. and enlarged by Stith Thompson. Helsinki: Suomalainen Tiedeakatemia.

Andersen, Flemming G., Esther Nyholm, Marianne Powell and Flemming Talbo Stubkjær, eds. 1980. *Medieval Iconography and Narrative: A Symposium*. Odense, Denmark: Odense University Press.

Andersson, Theodore M. 1970. "The Displacement of the Heroic Ideal in the Family Sagas." *Speculum* 45, 575–93.

Aristotle. 1932. *Aristotle's Theory of Poetry and Fine Art, with ... the Poetics*. Trans. and ed. S.H. Butcher. London: MacMillan.

Auerbach, Erich. 1953. *Mimesis: The Representation of Reality in Western Literature*. Princeton: Princeton University Press.

Barthes, Roland. 1981. "The Discourse of History." Trans. Stephen Born. In *Comparative Criticism*. E.S. Shaffer, ed. Cambridge: Cambridge University Press, 3–20.

"The Battle of Maldon." 2004. In *Old and Middle English c. 890-c. 1400: An Anthology*, Elaine M. Treharne, ed. Oxford: Blackwell, 141–155.

Bauschatz, Paul C. 1982. *The Well and the Tree: World and Time in Early Germanic Culture*. Amherst: University of Massachusetts Press.

Bekker-Nielsen, Hans, Peter Foote, Andreas Haarder and Preben Meulengracht Sørensen, eds. 1979. *Medieval Narrative: A Symposium*. Odense, Denmark: Odense University Press.

Benson, Larry D. 1970. "The Originality of *Beowulf*." In *The Interpretation of Narrative: Theory and Practice*. M.W. Bloomfield, ed. Cambridge, MA: Harvard University Press, 1–32.

Bettelheim, Bruno. 1991. *The Uses of Enchantment: The Meaning and Importance of Fairy Tales*. Harmondsworth, Middlesex: Penguin.

Brewer, Derek. 1988. *Symbolic Stories: Traditional Narratives of the Family Drama in English Literature*. London and New York: Longman.

Bunyan, J. (2002) *The Works of John Bunyan*. Project Gutenberg. Accessed February 17, 2011. *http://www.gutenberg.org/dirs/etext04/jbun310.txt*.

Chadwick, Nora K. 1959. "The Monsters and Beowulf." In *The Anglo-Saxons: Studies in Some Aspects of Their History and Culture Presented to Bruce Dickins*. Peter Clemoes, ed. London: Bowes and Bowes, 171–203.

Chambers, R.W. 1929. "Beowulf's Fight with Grendel and its Scandinavian Parallels." *English Studies* 11, 81–100.

_____. 1963. *Beowulf: An Introduction to the Study of the Poem with a Discussion of the Stories of Offa and Finn*, 3d ed. With a supplement by C.L. Wrenn. Cambridge: Cambridge University Press.

Davidson, H.R. Ellis. 1976. "Hostile Magic in the Icelandic Sagas." *The Witch Figure*. Venetia Newall, ed. London and Boston: n.p., 20–41.

_____. 1978. "Shape-Changing in the Old Norse Sagas." In *Animals in Folklore*. J.R. Porter and W.M.S. Russell, eds. Ipswich and Cambridge: n.p., 126–142.

Dégh, Linda, and Andrew Vázsonyi. 1976. "Legend and Belief." In *Folklore Genres*. Dan Ben-Amos, ed. Austin: University of Texas Press, 94–123.

"The Dream of the Rood." 2004. In *Old and Middle English c. 890-c. 1400: An Anthology*, Elaine M. Treharne, ed. Oxford: Blackwell, 108–115.

Duncan, Walter Raymond, Barbara Jancar-Webster and Bob Switky. 2004. *World Politics in the 21st Century*. London: Pearson and Longman.

Dundes, Alan. 1966. "Metafolklore and Oral Literary Criticism." *The Monist* 50, 505–16.

Finnegan, Ruth. 1977. *Oral Poetry: Its Nature, Significance and Social Context*. Cambridge: Cambridge University Press.

Foote, Peter. 1984. "Observations on 'Syncretism' in Early Icelandic Christianity." In *Aurvandilstá*, 84–100. Odense, Denmark: Odense University Press.

Frye, Northrop. 1957. *Anatomy of Criticism*. Harmondsworth: Penguin.

Garmonsway, G.N., and Jacqueline Simpson. 1980. *Beowulf and its Analogues*. London: Dent.

Genette, Gérard. 1970. *Narrative Discourse: An Essay in Method*. Trans. Jane Lewin. Ithaca: Cornell University Press.

Gramsci, Antonio. "Language, Linguistics and Folklore." *Selections from Cultural Writings.* Eds. D. Forgacs and G. Nowell-Smith. Trans. W. Boelhower. London: n.p., 164–195.

Hammond, Paul, ed. 2002. "Bunyan, John." *Restoration Literature: An Anthology.* Oxford: Oxford University Press, 335–336.

Hand, Wayland D. 1974. *From Folk Legend to Folk Custom: The Shift from Narrative to Dramatic Contexts.* Helsinki: n.p.

Heinrichs, Anne. 1976. "'Intertexture' and its Functions in Early Written Sagas: A Stylistic Observation of *Heiðarvíga saga, Reykdæla saga* and the Legendary *Oláfssaga.*" *Scandinavian Studies* 48, 127–145.

Jerome, Jeffrey, ed. 1996. *Reading Monsters/Reading Cultures.* Minneapolis: University of Minnesota Press.

Kalinke, Marianne E. 1981. *King Arthur, North-by-Northwest: The "matière de Bretagne" in Old Norse-Icelandic Romances.* Copenhagen: Reitzel.

Ker, W.P. 1897. *Epic and Romance.* London: Macmillan.

Kermode, Frank. 1979. *The Genesis of Secrecy: On the Interpretation of Narrative.* Cambridge, MA: Harvard University Press.

Klaeber, Fr., ed. 1950. *Beowulf and the Fight at Finnsburg,* 3d ed. Cambridge, MA: Harvard University Press.

Lawrence, W.W. 1928. *Beowulf and Epic Tradition.* Cambridge, MA: Harvard University Press.

Lewis, C. S. 1950. *The Lion, The Witch and The Wardrobe.* Accessed October 28, 2010. *http://www.mylibrarybook.com/books/674/C.S-Lewis/The-Lion-the-Witch-and-the-Wardrobe-1.html.*

Liberman, Anatoly. 1977. "The Concept of 'Literary Theme.'" *Enclitic* 1, 49–56.

Lindow, John. 1976. *Comitatus, Individual and Honor.* Berkeley: University of California Press.

Lodge, David. 1990. "Mimesis and Diegesis in Modern Fiction." In *After Bakhtin: Essays on Fiction and Criticism,* 25–44. London and New York: n.p.

Maranda, Pierre, ed. 1971. *Structural Models in Folklore and Transformational Essays.* The Hague: Mouton.

Mitchison, Rosalind, ed. 1908. *The Roots of Nationalism: Studies in Northern Europe.* Edinburgh: Canongate.

Ó Giolláin, Diarmuid. 1990. "Folklore, History and the State." *Arv: Scandinavian Yearbook of Folklore* 46, 169–174.

Ong, Walter J. 1982. *Orality and Literacy: The Technologizing of the Word.* London and New York: Methuen.

Panzer, Friedrich. 1910. *Studien zur Germanischen Sagengeschichte I Beowulf.* Munich: C.H. Beck.

Patterson, Lee. 1987. *Negotiating the Past: The Historical Understanding of Medieval Literature.* Madison: University of Wisconsin Press.

Pizarro, Joaquín Martínez. 1989. *A Rhetoric of the Scene: Dramatic Narrative in the Early Middle Ages.* Toronto: University of Toronto Press.

Pratt, M.L. 1977. *Towards a Speech Act Theory of Literary Discourse.* Bloomington: Indiana University Press.

Propp, Vladimir. 1984. *Theory and History of Folklore.* Ed. Anatoly Liberman, trans. Ariadna Y. Martin and Richard P. Martin. Minneapolis: University of Minnesota Press.

Pullman, Philip. n.d. "Frequently Asked Questions." Accessed May 4, 2007. *http://www.philip-pullman.com/about_the_writing.asp.*

Röhrich, Lutz. 1991. *Folktales and Reality.* Trans. Peter Tokofsky. Bloomington: Indiana University Press.

Scholes, Robert, and Robert Kellogg. 1966. *The Nature of Narrative.* New York: Oxford University Press.

Shippey, Tom. 2000. *J.R.R. Tolkien: Author of the Century.* London: HarperCollins.

Smalley, Beryl. 1974. *Historians in the Middle Ages.* London: Thames and Hudson

White, Hayden V. 1975. "Historicism, History and the Figurative Imagination." *History and Theory* 14, 48–67.

3

Constructions of the Child, Authority and Authorship: The Reception of C.S Lewis and Philip Pullman

Elisabeth Eldridge

Introduction

Since the first book in Philip Pullman's *His Dark Materials* trilogy was published in 1997, Pullman has become one of the most interviewed and written-about authors in Britain. His viewpoint on religion, education, reading, children and the process of writing has been the subject of numerous media articles, garnering as much interest and comment as his novels. Time and again these articles can be read as turning upon the ideas of the author and critic C.S. Lewis, a personality that is re-constructed anew in each media piece. Pullman's opinions are repeatedly set against attitudes claimed to be those of Lewis. It could be argued that this continual focus on the idea of the authors of *His Dark Materials* and the *Narnia* books is a result of the allegorical nature of these texts. That is, when allegory is defined as the medium through which fantasy exerts a didactic function, as Colin Manlove (1975) has suggested, the text can be said to constitute an idea of an author forming and guiding that didacticism, fuelling the text with intention.

As Michel Foucault argues in "What Is an Author" (2000), an author can only exist as a product of a text but does so within a broad, systematic and historically changing discourse of authorship. So this is not to return to an idea of a writer who can be understood entirely through his work because his intentions are in complete control of the text *contra* Roland Barthes' thesis regarding "The Death of the Author," nor to resurrect an author or who puts himself into his work, but to suggest that these texts themselves strongly construct the concept of just such a figure. Not all texts do this, so it is a special case for C.S. Lewis and Pullman I will argue in part because they are so publicly used to embody certain arguments about the relations of religion and atheism to the discourse of children's literature. This function as a kind of shorthand for attitudes and contrasting positions and so the ideas of "Lewis" and "Pullman" are constructed in the public arena and in many critical writings, as polemic authors whose novels, interviews, media articles and so on, proselytize the personal religion, or anti-religion of these men.

This essay will explore this public constitution of these notions of author and text. The articles discussed can be read as being informed by anxieties concerning the role of both authors as writers of children's literature and their responsibility to, and effect upon, child readers. In order to track the constructions of intentional authors as aspects of the Foucauldian idea of an author function that relates to specific discourses; and to deconstruct the notion of an actual authorial self central to the texts through my reading, I will use quotation marks when using the authors' names. This is not to deny that there are authors named Lewis and Pullman, but to consistently emphasize that when the texts I examine here use these names, they are constructing an idea of an author that has only something to do with a real person. It is these constructions of authors, narrated within texts, that I discuss and critique here.

"Philip Pullman's" construction of "C.S. Lewis"

The British children's book website ACHUKA published an interview with Pullman in which he is asked to reflect on his childhood experience of *The Chronicles of Narnia*.

> *Did you read the Narnia books when you were a boy, and if so were you as uneasy about them then as you are now?*
> No, I didn't read the whole of Narnia as a boy: I read *The Voyage of the Dawn Treader*, and felt slightly queasy, as if I were being pressured to agree to something I wasn't sure of. Now I can see what that was, and why I felt odd. Reading the whole sequence for the first time as an adult, I was angered and nauseated by the sneakiness of that powerful seductive narrative voice, that favourite-uncle stance, assuming my assent to his sneering attitude to anything remotely progressive in social terms, or to people with brown faces, or to children who don't seem like his own favourites [ANCHUKA, n.p.].

Though a short passage, it is valuable to engage in some close linguistic and semiotic analysis, and in the first instance to consider the possibility of coherence. The question begins with the you of the present tense, now, and asks whether the you of the past was in some sense the same. The notion of coherence functions here in two ways: whether the you of the past is the same you, the same subject and identity, as the you of now; and whether both you's can be described as "uneasy" about "the Narnia books."

The answer engages with the productions of the self and of childhood established in the question by constructing an adult "Pullman" looking back at the memory of the reading boy. Despite the repeated production of an I, implying coherence and consistency (that is, that the I of boy is the same I as now), the narrated I is split between the I attached to the boy described in the past tense and the I attached to the now of the present tense. The construction of I in this text can be read as undermining the implication that memory and remembering are straightforward and stable notions that reveal fact or truth by disrupting the coherence constructed between boy and adult and introduced initially by the terms of the narrated question.

This is further troubled by the slippage back into a past tense after the assertion of a present tense now: "I *was* angered" (emphasis added). While it might be argued that the re-establishment of the past tense can be read as associating the two distinct I's, the past-tense is fractured by the divided self produced by the two I's and by the insertion of a present tense now. The slippage back into a past tense functions to further destabilize the narration's production of reading as an adult compared with doing so as a child. The narration implies that, as an adult, the reading experience is different, that the adult reader "Pullman" can now recognize something in the text ("now I can see what it was") that explains the intuitive unease ("I felt") narrated as the boy's experience. The implication is that the adult reader has a more experienced and perceptive reading than the child. Aside from the undermining of the coherence between boy and adult, the disjunction between tenses following the claim to a now can be read as a further split in the already divided I. The reading experience of the adult cannot be accepted as truth, despite the I's claim to a clarified understanding; the reading as an adult is also a memory and, as such, more complicated and less stable than is implied by an assumption of coherence between the two adult I's. Like the recollection of the boy's feeling of queasiness, the anger and nausea are remembered feelings and, as such, are memories constituted after the event.

The boy narrated here feels that something is amiss as he reads, yet cannot pinpoint the reason for this feeling. It is feelings, how the "boy [...] felt," that construct this image. It is *as if* the boy is "being pressured to agree to *something* [he] *wasn't sure of*" (emphasis added). There are no exact or direct claims and yet the "boy [...] felt odd." The "slightly queasy" feeling seems to be associated by the narration with the ambiguity and elusiveness of the experience. "Pullman" is constructed as being "angered and nauseated" by his reading. The narration of "sneakiness," "powerful seductive," "assuming my assent," suggests that "Lewis" text is somehow deceptive or beguiling. The narration's construction of boy and adult implies that the boy reader is vulnerable to this seduction because he could not "see what it was," and yet feels "pressured." The adult

"Pullman" "can now recognize" that the "narrative voice" is "seductive" and sneaky; the books are narrated in the language of pretence and performance ("voice," "stance," "assuming," "attitude," "seem"). The book is produced as though it was trying to lure the reader, and will assume the reader's assent.

The quotation from the ACHUKA interview is immediately followed by "Pullman" claiming: "[n]o-one has expressed this better than John Goldthwaite, in his marvelous *A Natural History of Make-Believe.*" This volume first published in 1996 has a long section on Lewis and Narnia, in which "Lewis" is at once adult and child, teacher and pupil, underpinned by the idea that "Lewis" can be read and identified through the narration of his books and through the documentation of his biographers and critics. Other texts are produced as insight into "Lewis" as author, and so in turn into his book, so that "Lewis" is constructed as at once within the text, and yet also as being a real person. Goldthwaite produces numerous images of "Lewis," often setting one idea against another so that "Lewis" is compared with a bullying, cowardly schoolmaster and then with a little boy "making a grab for the whistle and clipboard" (Goldthwaite 1996, 227) and "post[ing] his own keep-out signs on the clubhouse door" (1996, 227). "Lewis" is, therefore, constructed as an uncomfortable and wholly malignant combination of both child and adult.

It is interesting to compare another text in which Stuart Wavell interviews Pullman, which in its turn constructs "Pullman" as saying of "Lewis": "He had an odd view of children. Either he had never been a child himself or he had never stopped being a child," evident in "Lewis'" "popular Narnia stories" (Pullman in Wavell 2001, 3). "Lewis'" "odd view of children" is thus attributed as either the absence *or* the incessancy of being a child. "Pullman" is narrated as identifying this "odd view" from "Lewis'" "fixat[ion] on innocent children in Narnia," which led him to "kill them rather than let them go through adolescence" (Pullman in Wavell 2001, 3). The implication seems to be that either "Lewis" had no personal experience of adolescence and so prevents the children from experiencing what he did not or could not, or that "Lewis'" childhood somehow perpetuated through his own adolescence. Alternatively, "Lewis'" childhood had been effectively non-existent, leading him to idealize and idolize a notion of childhood. "Lewis" is, then, himself constituted as a sort of Peter Pan figure, or the inverse of that. This construction is based upon what is produced here as "Pullman's" reading of "Lewis'" book, so that "Lewis" is again constituted through his work.

Gender and "C. S. Lewis"

In returning to Goldthwaite's critique of Lewis, there is employed a distinction between the reception of the texts idealized boys and girls:

> The seduction here for girls, I suspect, is their implicit induction into a private club previously reserved for boys only. As they read along, they may not care what an elitist clique for Top Boys and Girls it is, or how exclusion from it will be for everyone else the quite literal loss of heaven in the end. Harvey Darton had noted the Victorians' "modest feeling of prerogative audience." In Lewis' keeping, this feeling has turned immodest and smug, allowing him to post his own keep-out signs on the clubhouse door [Goldthwaite 1996, 227].

"Lewis" is constructed as engaged in a "seduction" of his girl readers, as courting them by offering a "bouquet" of girl characters who acquit themselves well (Goldthwaite 1996, 227). This imagery and suggestion can be read as functioning throughout Goldthwaite's text. "The first adventure had begun in the spirit of a school holiday, but this was a deception," the narration claims (Goldthwaite 1996, 226). Then he remarks that: "Lewis is sly"; "the lessons are being insinuated; the method is one of innuendo"; "Lewis will sometimes even cosy the reader into a conspiracy"; "it is a betrayal"; it is an "implicit induction"; "this feeling has turned immodest and smug" (Goldthwaite 1996, 226–227). "Lewis" is in effect produced through the language of the narration as a figure of deception, seduction and insult (Goldthwaite 1996, 227). The claim is made by Goldthwaite that

> the relationship between Lewis and his characters is here exposed: he is the false friend of their need, ever ready to throw a wink over their shoulders to the reader [Goldthwaite 1996, 227].

Here, "Lewis" and his characters are produced as being in a relationship founded on deception and betrayal. This relationship can be exposed through a reading of the book, and is set alongside the invocation of "Lewis" through "the man's public testimony": text and biography are once again brought together to expose "Lewis." "Lewis" is a "false friend" who hypocritically behaves one way towards the characters but another towards the reader. Moreover, the girls criticized in the public testimony are treated with the same lack of conviction as those in the pages of the books; they are assumed to be in some sense the same girls. The generalizing function of "we" suggests all readers will all notice the same things in the text and so find the real or correct "Lewis" who conceals himself from his characters.

The language of "sneakiness" and "seduction" used here can be read alongside that employed in the ACHUKA text. The discussion can be read as producing a seduction based on a construction of sexual difference: girls are subject to the seduction that is "being offered them in Narnia," but "boys [...] sense" something in the text that leads them to reject it. Further, the implication seems to be that girls like what is being offered, and that, furthermore, "it is natural that they should be attracted." By reading and liking the stories, the narration argues, the girls are joining Aslan's "Smart Set frolicking down the avenue" (Lewis 1951, n.p.) as described in the text as the "vilest passage ever to poison a children's book" (Goldthwaite 1996, 228). The suggestion seems to be that girl readers are complicit in their seduction that is to say they have incorporated patriarchal and sexist ideology and, "they may not care what an elitist clique for Top Boys and Girls it is, or how exclusion from it will be for everyone else the quite literal loss of heaven in the end" (Goldthwaite 1996, 227). Whether this view of Lewis is correct or incorrect is not really my concern in this essay, rather what interest me is the peculiarity of this construction of Lewis as an example of an adult author writing for children and the ideological forces that underlie this view.

There are of course different and contrasting views possible and it is worth contrasting the views above, against say Polly Toynbee's (2005) caustic and extremely funny attack on C. S. Lewis after the release of the film of the *The Chronicles of Narnia: The Lion, The Witch and the Wardrobe* (2005). She feels that luckily today's secular children are not so easily beguiled and caught by Lewis' allegory (his "bully-pulpit," as she calls it), but rather it is adults who have most to fear going to see the film:

> Does any of this matter? Not really. Most children will never notice. But adults who wince at the worst elements of Christian belief may need a sickbag handy for the most religiose scenes. [...] Everyone needs ghosts, spirits, marvels and poetic imaginings, but we can do well without an Aslan [Toynbee 2005, n.p.].

The point here is that it is not the child who has most to fear from "Lewis" and Christina propaganda in the shape of allegory, because their parents are the barriers and in any case most children will thankfully not notice the allegory. What is wrong instead with Lewis' work for Toynbee is that it insults the intelligence of adults who recognize Christianity (or "Lewis'" brand of it at least) as deeply unpalatable, destructive as well as wrong-headed:

> Of all the elements of Christianity, the most repugnant is the notion of the Christ who took our sins upon himself and sacrificed his body in agony to save our souls. Did we ask him to? Poor child Edmund, to blame for everything, must bear the full weight of a guilt only Christians know how to inflict, with a twisted knife to the heart [Toynbee 2005].

What is interesting is that while Toynbee is as critical (if not more so) of Lewis as Pullman and Goldthwaite, she does not hold to their notion of needing to protect a child reader from seductive adults (a kind of Christian stranger danger): rather she simply wants to meet Lewis's belief system head on, adult to adult.

Constructions of the child

Jacqueline Rose's seminal text on children's literature and its criticism, *The Case of Peter Pan or the Impossibility of Children's Fiction* (1984), describes J. M. Barrie's "The Little White Bird" as being a story about "the difficulty of the relation between adult and child, and a question about the sexuality of each. What is the sexuality of the narrator? What is the origin of the child? What is *going on* between them?" (Rose 1984, 5) The same questions I would argue can very usefully be asked of the texts discussed here. In both the ACHUKA and the Goldthwaite texts, the narration is positioned as adult in comparison with a notion of the child readers constructed within the text. The adult Pullman and the narration of the Goldthwaite text (which is also positioned as adult) are narrated as being able to both recognize and resist the seduction of the narrative voice in the Lewis text, which nonetheless is produced as affecting the innocent child, whether in terms of the constructed remembered boy or in terms of girls today. The difference between adult and child is therefore firmly demarcated.

Rose's text argues that limited or partial readings of Freud have resulted in an elision of "the question of childhood — its threat to the idea that we have neatly picked up and resolved everything that came before on the way to where we are now" (Rose 1984, 14). It is this now that is in the foreground in the ACHUKA text: "as an adult," the narrated I referring to the construction of "Pullman" "can see" that the "narrative voice" was "seductive." The adult narration constructed in the texts discussed produces a notion of child, whether girls, boys or a memory of the self "as a boy," that is distinct and separated from the I of the text; that is, despite the coherence implied in the ACHUKA text (that the I then is the same I as now), childhood is something that has finished and is set apart from adulthood. The ACHUKA and Goldthwaite texts narrate an I who, having left childhood behind, can recognize the "powerful seduction" being asserted over the child. The narration of the Goldthwaite text constitutes itself as neither girl nor child, and thus as able to objectively examine the process of seduction it identifies. The continual conjecture and supposition by the narration can, in this sense, be read as a repeated emphasis on the difference between the girls and the I; the I can only "suspect" and "suppose" because, as an adult, childhood and the realm of, perhaps, the female or feminine, are assumed to be entirely separate and beyond what I can even "pretend to understand."

Rose argues that there is a tendency, played out in many texts, to understand childhood as a progressive narrative, to "see in the child merely a miniature version of what our sexuality eventually comes to be" (Rose 1984, 4). The seduction of the child in the ACHUKA and Goldthwaite texts is, I would argue, constructed by the narration as a threat to the adult I produced there. The idea seems to be that if the child can be textually and sexually seduced, then so can the adult: if the boy is "being pressured to agree to something," then so is the adult, unless the I can construct a demarcation between constructions of then and now that will represent a development in the self, enabling it to recognize and resist the seduction. Securing the child allows it to be preserved as a sealed-off site where sexual difference, and indeed, sexuality itself (understood as polymorphous, perverse and unstable) are denied. If childhood has not been resolved and left behind, then the threats against Goldthwaite's girls and boys, and "Pullman's" production of a childhood self, may remain a threat. Moreover, this anxiety seems to inform "Pullman's" production of "Lewis" as being imprecisely adult or child. In that reading of "Lewis," boundaries between adult and child are unrecognizable, so that it is unclear from where the perceived danger comes.

Like the children's literature and its criticism explored by Rose, the texts I am discussing are concerned with the textual seduction of the child, of the fixing of the notion of child as the focus for the adult's investment, and in particular its interest in holding "the whole problem of what sexuality is, or can be [...] at bay" (Rose 1984, 4) by sealing off the child as either asexual, or as in a sexual stage that the adult has grown up from and left behind. In *Child-Loving: The Erotic Child and Victorian Culture* (1992), James R. Kincaid similarly argues that "the 'child' has been constructed as a centre of adult desire and investment [...] an irresistibly erotic Other" (Kincaid 1992, 360). The Goldthwaite and ACHUKA texts can be read as fixing the child according to the constructions they produce: the child is constituted as known and understood within the text. It could be argued that the Goldthwaite and ACHUKA texts are concerned, not with "Lewis'" inappropriate "loving" of the child, but rather his mistreatment of them: damning them to Hell, killing them, bullying them, spying on them, and so on. However, as argued above, these constructions of textual abuse are produced in the ACHUKA and Goldthwaite texts as turning upon a sexualization of child and of "Lewis," that, it is important to note, is constituted within these two critical texts and attributed to "Lewis." This process is an ambivalent act, as Kincaid identifies when he argues that, "[b]y insisting loudly on the innocence, purity, and asexuality of the child, we have created a subversive echo: experience, corruption, eroticism," thereby allowing us to construct a pedophile "other," which is required "to assure us that our own profiles are proportionate" (Kincaid, 1992, 3–5). The Goldthwaite and ACHUKA texts can be read, then, as a construction of "Lewis" in the role, not straightforwardly of pedophile, but as representing that same otherness, that corruption and inappropriateness towards the child that Kincaid reads pedophile as suggesting within culture and literature. By thus positioning "Lewis," these critical texts can be interpreted as positioning themselves, not as perpetuating the eroticism and desirability of the child that Kinkaid suggests, but rather as guardians of the child.

The critical texts which construct these relationships position themselves, however, as a voyeur to the textual seduction of the child reader it reads the other guilty of, and as such are inextricably bound up in the very violation they denounce in the other position whether they like it or not. Consider all the faults that Pullman using Goldthwaite lay at "Lewis'" door; do not Lewis" defenders simply reverse the terms of these faults and place a structurally similar and contiguous mirror image of this blame in Pullman's camp? The construction of the child reader and thus the child implied within these texts is validated by such relationships and perhaps most importantly it is because such texts and debates as these exist that a certain value of innocence amidst threats continues to be such a well word cliché about what it means to be a child in society. In identifying the risk made to the child reader, the narrations discussed here seal themselves off as separate from the child and, as such, as safe from the perceived threat, which is to say they separate the adult from the child as distinct categories of humanity and engage in producing the adult reader as the opposite of the child reader. The announcement of a textual seduction of the child reader assures the safety of the adult narration itself: it is a seduction that happens only to the weak reader, the vulnerable audience. Ultimately childhood cannot transcend adulthood for either "Lewis" or "Pullman" whatever power that can be granted to it, because adulthood is something that is embedded in the constructions "Lewis" and "Pullman."

Moreover, the texts present their own readings of the books they critique as a truth that has been concealed by a deception that also lies within their texts; this again marks them as adults as they can penetrate to depths beyond that of where the child reader cannot go. The textual trickery they perceive is a production of their own reading but is pinned very firmly upon the construction of an intentional author whether that is "Lewis" or "Pullman."

Philip Pullman's relationship with "Lewis"

Various media interviews with Pullman allow him to critique the characterization of Susan in the *Chronicles of Narnia*, and condemn "Lewis" for what is portrayed as his cruel and misogynistic treatment of her, as though she were in some way an actual teenage girl rather than a character in a book (*cf.* Roberts n.d.; Wavell 2001). The repeated setting of Susan alongside Pullman's Lyra seems to invite comparisons between them. In both the novels and media texts, both are at least partly defined by their womanhood. In *His Dark Materials*, Lyra is heralded as the new Eve (see for example *AS* 71, 74–75; *HDM* 597, 600), while Susan, along with Lucy and other human female characters, is known as a "daughter of Eve" (see for example Lewis 1980a, 64, 75, 177). This suggests Lyra and Susan's association as girls/women with betrayal, apostasy, disobedience and the Fall; significantly, it also suggests that Lyra may to some extent be regarded as Pullman's revised and revisited version of the character of Susan. Lyra is destined to bring about a second Fall that will be the first step towards the Republic of Heaven, while Susan's "Eve-ness" contributes to her own Fall from grace, apparently rooted in her pursuit of the trappings of femininity: "nylons and lipstick and invitations" (Lewis 1980b, 128). Susan's desire to become grown-up (by forgetting Narnia and being interested in boys) can be read usefully alongside Lyra's almost accidental discovery of love and sexual desire through her relationship with Will.

Their individual experiences of what are constructed as adult emotions result in both characters being isolated in some sense. Lyra realizes that she and Will must eventually find someone else to love, but she also understands that their separation will be felt forever (*AS* 537–538; *HDM* 921–922). Susan is declared to be "no longer a friend of Narnia" and is excluded from heaven (Lewis 1980b, 128). It could be argued that Lyra's grief is a personal sacrifice for the greater good, having played the central role in the cosmic drama that has unfolded, while Susan seems to have unwittingly condemned herself after just one among many falls by the wayside.

Lyra's own decisions can be seen to shape her future, yet, the Church and the witches recognize her as one destined through prophecy to Fall, and as Stephen Thomson argues, she is also compelled by the destiny inherent in her own genetic lineage as Asriel's daughter. Thomson refers to Serafina Pekkala's "notion of the necessary illusion of free will: we are all subject to fate but must act as if we are not" (2004, 153). The age-old opposition of free will versus pre-destination, played out in the actions and fate of Lyra and Susan seems to relate to the question of reading these books as they demand to be read: allegorical writing constructs a didactic function even though it is possible to read against the text. However, by reading against the didactic demands of the allegory, a reader must acknowledge those demands and respond to them.

Constructing "Pullman": religion and the author

His Dark Materials have attracted a substantial amount of criticism, and from religious publications in particular, for the novels' depiction of images and characters associated with Christianity; so much so, that numerous interview and review texts open by quoting these comments and using them as a springboard to reveal what is constituted as the real author or the correct way to interpret the books (Billen 2003, 14–15; Roberts n.d., n.p.; Wavell 2001, 3; "Pullman Don't" 2001).[1] The extreme responses to Pullman's writing, and his authorial stance, construct an ambivalent "Pullman." For example, Alan Jacobs' essay "The Republic of Heaven" constructs an ambivalent version of "Pullman" as an author that accuses Lewis of dishonesty, but in fact "dishonesty is perhaps the signal moral trait of Pullman's trilogy (2004, 149). He continues: "Pullman the storyteller has also been cheated — by Pullman the village atheist. Powerful alternative versions of the Biblical narrative can only be told by people who are themselves passionately theological" (Jacobs 2004, 148). This sweeping claim divides "Pullman" into two positions, storyteller and atheist, one of which is responsible of swindling the other, so that "Pullman's" deception is so pervasive that it even convinces himself. Jacobs argues "Pullman" has a "more insidious method" of employing the "multiple-worlds device," which allows an alternative Calvin to be denounced as a child-killer (Jacobs 2004, 149). For Jacobs, this is "a nice trick," underpinned by "Pullman's" personal hatred of Christians, and one which Jacobs assumes will work just as "Pullman" surely intends: "who knows how many readers go away from this book believing that John Calvin massacred innocents?" (Jacobs 2004, 150). Jacobs's argument constitutes the text of the novels as a revelation of the truth of "Pullman's" personal beliefs, which are concealed by "Pullman" through a deception that in is turn presented as a "dark truth" (Jacobs 2004, 150).

Jacobs' argument assumes that his knowledge of the truth means that he is not taken in by "Pullman," while less educated or perceptive readers are at risk from the "trick." Jacobs knows that Calvin did not order the murder of children, but implies many others might not. Similarly, texts critical of *His Dark Materials* can often be read as framing their censure in terms of what is good or damaging for child readers, supported by the assumption that adult readers can discern this, while children cannot. The back cover blurb for John Houghton's *A Closer Look at His Dark Materials*, for example, maintains that

> the trilogy is surrounded by controversy because of its blatant and outspoken anti–Christian message, advocating as it does a profoundly cynical view of God and the church. Many are concerned at the impact this may have on children [Houghton 2004, n.p.].

Children are supposed to be more particularly at risk, or it is assumed that any impact on them will be greater than upon adults. "Poisoned pen?" by Mark Greene, published first in *Christianity and Renewal* magazine, specifically questions whether *His Dark Materials* are good for Christian readers, and for Christian child readers in particular. Greene's critique of the novels recalls the language of violence implicit in the interview text constructions of "Lewis" discussed earlier, and its concerns for the Christian child recall the language of seduction that functions in many of the texts discussed here. Curiously enough (and perhaps he is oblivious of this) Greene's argument is in essence an inversion of what Pullman and many others have long argued about "Lewis'" work, that his Narnia books functions in effect as religious propaganda in favor of Christianity to innocent child readers and thus is guilty of seducing them into a position they would not otherwise take; while Greene's unnamed daughter in turn inverts the traditional defense of the Narnia books from such charges, which is that child readers are quite capable of ignoring the propaganda of Lewis' allegory and just reading the books for the story alone.

> I first encountered these stories through the enthusiasm of my then 12-year-old god-daughter who admired the brilliance of Pullman's adventure but was able to dismiss

his anti–Christian propaganda with the nonchalance of a donkey flicking away a fly. "Pullman's God," she said, "is nothing like the God I worship." Indeed, he is not. But you only need to go back to the Garden of Eden to see how dangerous it can be when a subtle wordsmith whispers in someone's ear that God is not really good, that he does not have your best interests at heart, that he does not mean what he says [Greene 2002, 73].

The 12-year-old god-daughter is constructed by the text as making a distinction between two productions of God: "Pullman's God" and "the God I worship." The god-daughter's statement seems to acknowledge the constructedness of the notion of God but the text collapses this comprehension even as it corroborates it ("Indeed he is not"): the God whispered about by the "subtle wordsmith" seems to be produced as the same God worshipped by the god-daughter after all. God here is a product of the I that worships and is thereby constructed as her God. The text destabilizes this construction with the supplement "but." The implication is that this construction of God is volatile because it is subjective and subject to influence from another position or argument. The authoritative I of the text is re-established through the construction of a "you" and reference to a "someone": in arguing for a potential destabilizing of the position held by the god-daughter, the I enacts this possibility by challenging it within the text.

Elsewhere in the text, the I warns that: "Pullman may succeed in turning many a child away from the true God he calls 'the enemy'" (Greene 2002, 73). This God is "Pullman's" in the sense that "Pullman" constructs and names him as "the enemy," yet the I is identifying him as simultaneously "the true God." Again, the I seems to be both asserting two distinct productions of God and undermining that assertion. However, it could further be argued that while the text posits a true God in opposition to "Pullman's" God, which is constructed through his "call[ing ... it] the enemy," that very calling in relation to what the narration cites as true positions that true God as existing. The text constructs different productions and meanings of God, which it both conflates and tries to seal off from the other. It also claims that: "After all, a God who will deliberately sacrifice himself out of love is a long, long way from the malevolent and impotent cripple of Pullman's imagination" (Greene 2002, 73). Again, Pullman's God is described as personal production that greatly differs from notions of a God produced by the I that is Greene.

In this text, the Garden of Eden is the arena for the dangerous whispering of a "subtle wordsmith" to someone associated by the I with its 12-year-old girl. The suggestion of what might happen, what is still at risk, foregrounds her nonchalance so that her dismissal of the propaganda is not through differentiation but indifference; the propaganda is not dangerous but merely an irritation, like the buzz of a fly. The constructed child is not perceptive, but unaware and enthusiastic and, as such, at risk. Like the narrative voice constructed in the Goldthwaite and ACHUKA texts (sly, insinuating, deceptive) the threat here is subtle, understated: it *whispers*. The narration produces a you who, like the adult "Pullman" constructed in the ACHUKA text, can see what the nonchalant child of this text cannot; the danger of the voice whispering to the child is seen by the I and the you it produces here.

In this passage, the Garden of Eden is not indicated as a textual reference, but as a temporal location: it is not story but rather a time (and one would presume the writer Greene believes the events of the Fall happened). It is somewhere to which you need to go back: it can be reached, but only by a recession or a return. Is need functioning as a reference to what you must do to get to the Garden of Eden or is it a directive associated with the argument here? That is, that you *need* to see, to recognize, the danger of this situation? The Garden of Eden seems to be associated with "the God I worship" and so is distinct from Pullman's God. The "subtle wordsmith" here, however, seems to refer to both "Pullman" (both "Pullman" and the "subtle wordsmith" are constructed within the text as producing an idea of God that differs from that of their audience) and to an idea of a tempter-figure, a Satan, who is implicitly associated with a Garden of Eden produced as connected to "the God I worship." The God whispered about by the "subtle wordsmith" becomes, in this sense, the same God as that worshipped by the god-daughter's I.

The text constructs a child who "feel[s] [...] abandoned — by divorce and overwork, for example — [...] who must make their own way in the world," and yet is vulnerable to the heady mix offered by the novels and to the whispering of the "subtle wordsmith" (Greene 2002, 72–73). "Pullman" is constituted as having "drawn his readers (and me) into" his tale where "along the way we learn more about God who is not a loving God" (Greene 2002, 70), but with the implication, as in the ACHUKA text, that the adult in the text is capable of recognizing this drawing in, of realizing he is being manipulated, while the nonchalant child readers might not have this perception. The text distinguishes between his readers and me, as though this me is not one of his readers, despite having read the texts. Both the readers and me are drawn into his tale; being drawn in is produced as different from reading: it seems that one can be drawn in without being a reader. It is specifically he, "Pullman," who draws in the readers and the me, further strengthening the association of "Pullman" with the "subtle wordsmith" later in the text.

In the terms of Rose's argument, "Pullman" is constructed here as being engaged in the child's seduction by "draw[ing] in the child" (Rose 1984, 2). Moreover, the narration's claim that "along the way we learn" certain ideas about God suggests that, having been drawn in along with, but distinct from, the readers, the me nevertheless becomes part of the we here: readers and me are conflated and learn as one group. However, the critique of "Pullman" and the books would seem to imply that the I of the text has not learned what it suggests "Pullman" is teaching. Again, and as in Jacobs' text, the first person of the narration is distinguishing itself from others in the sense that it is able to see how dangerous the stories can be.

The text constructs "Pullman" and the novels as at once subtle and yet direct. The readers are drawn into the story and its propaganda, vulnerable to the whispered suggestions of a "subtle wordsmith," and yet "Pullman's" assault on the Bible is "direct [...] no concealing of the identity of God," "his cause [is] clear," there is not "much subtlety of characterization" and "Pullman has laid down his gauntlet in public" (Greene 2002, 73, 70, 71, 73). The "Pullman" constituted in this text is at once devious and blatant. The argument that "Pullman may succeed in turning many a child away from the true God" and the repeated use of the word "propaganda" to describe the novels claims that this is "Pullman's" aim and intention for the books. The text opens with the statement that, "His ['Pullman's'] cause, as he himself has made clear, is to destroy Christianity, and to liberate the world from any faith in a personal God" (Greene 2002, 70).

In comparison with Lewis' writing though it is the explicitness of the text that grates as it is an "assault in the most direct way — no allegory for [Pullman], no concealing the identity of God behind invented names like Lewis' Aslan" (Greene 2002, 70). Here, the narration seems to critique "Pullman" for *not* being devious. The absence of allegory is described as "the most direct" form of "assault." The text constructs "what Pullman does to the Bible" and to God as entirely obvious: God is directly God. "Lewis" is produced as using "invented names" to intentionally conceal "the identity of God," while "Pullman," it is implied, allows there to be no ambiguity over the target of his assault: God is attacked as God.

The text does not seem to resolve how such a direct approach can seduce the child reader so subtly, except through its construction of dangerously nonchalant and naïve child readers and sharply perceptive adult readers. However, the I constitutes "adults who have never known the love of the living God" (Greene 2002, 73) in a way similar to its production of children. Both "children and adults" alike who do not know God's love are narrated as the easiest targets for "Pullman's propaganda" (Greene 2002, 73). Further, "the explicitness of his attack may well provide Christians of all ages with many an opportunity to present the truth" (Greene 2002, 73). Here, adults who "have never known" God are demoted to a position of vulnerability that exceeds that of the Christian child, nonchalant as she may be. The explicitness of "Pullman's" "attack" is here presented as providing opportunities to "present the truth," while "Pullman's propaganda [...] may simply confirm [the] prejudices" of "children and adults" who do not know God.

Children are produced here as vulnerable to "Pullman's" own agenda, which is at once concealed and yet exposed in his work. To read *His Dark Materials* is, then, to be drawn into the text and to allow "a subtle wordsmith" to whisper suggestions that might corrupt the faith of even a devout child or destroy any possibility of belief in the adult atheist or agnostic. The books are equated with a construction of "Pullman" himself, so that they constitute a direct reflection of "Pullman's" apparently anti–Christian intentions. The very substance and essence of the books, then, produces a stable meaning which cannot be alternately interpreted. This is undermined by the possibility of reading Greene's text as representing in part such an alternate meaning. Although the I concurs with many of "Pullman's" supposedly dangerous constructions of God, the Church, and so on, it also reads against these productions of what it reads as Christianity. The I is able to resist being "turn[ed] away" from his faith (as, indeed, is the young god-daughter) and can understand it as what it calls an "edifice of untruth," implying that the texts' meanings are not universal. The narration's production of its own ability to perceive "Pullman's" novels in this way is attributed, it seems, to a constitution of itself as being an *adult* who *has* "known the love of the living God": that is, through producing itself as adult, rather than child, and Christian as opposed to non–Christian. Again, this construction is destabilized by the construction of the child, his god-daughter, who, despite being a child, *is* able to resist the text's apparently intended meaning. Nonetheless, the narration persists in distinguishing between constructions of wise, Christian adult, and impressionable Christian or non–Christian child and non–Christian adult.

Conclusion

Using Rose's work on children's literature and its criticism to inform a reading of the texts discussed here, both "Lewis" and "Pullman" can be understood as productions bound up in anxieties about the child reader, its relationship with an author figure, and the implications of that for criticism and notions of an adult reader. The novels these texts discuss produce a strong sense of an authorial *persona* who has an intense and definite meaning to press upon the child and it is this which allows critics to return to what is one of the oldest ways of explaining the value of children's fantastic literature which is that of didacticism to teach specific values to innocent and inexperienced children. Although "Lewis" and "Pullman" are constituted differently in each text, it is possible to read a recurring use of the language of deception and persuasion to describe a relationship between author and child reader, a relationship initiated by the author in order to convey a particular and hazardous message to a child reader. These relationship between Lewis/Pullman and their possible child reader are almost uncanny mirror images of one another (from the religious/non religious point of view), while the child reader is consistently produced as vulnerable and ignorant of the designs made upon him/her. Such readings do not just depend upon replaying the opposition of innocence to experience as that between child reader and adult critic (ironically the former is a major opposition in both Christianity and *His Dark Materials*); rather I would argue they help to formulate such dualisms.

The authorial figures that are the constructions "Lewis" and "Pullman" seem like uncanny twins of one another we can suggest for two reasons. First, this is because in structural terms they are rather similar as figures and depend upon very similar notions of child and adult, seduction and knowledge, as well as relationship between these terms. Second, because "Lewis" and "Pullman" constitute an essentially *agonistic* relationship: without the construction called "Lewis" then Pullman's texts would have little to operate against and "Lewis" becomes an effectively adversarial precursor for "Pullman." But, equally so without "Pullman" then "Lewis" in the terms in which he is defended by his admirers would lack an adversary worthy of the anxieties behind his own texts; "Pullman" for Lewis' admirers is the very opposition that needed to be invented because it did exist at the time the Narnia books were written. This then is not so much "an anxiety of influence," as Harold Bloom (1997) once called it, but instead an anxiety of opposition. The anxiety is that underneath it all and as this article suggests there may be more in common between "Lewis" and "Pullman" than what at first meets the eye.

NOTES

1. The negative response to Pullman's treatment of Christianity and his influence as a result are widely reported. Rather than repeat them, I think it is valuable to stress that this reaction has been mixed with notable support coming from Dr. Rowan Williams (Archbishop of Canterbury) and from several books which claim to be written for and from a Christian viewpoint, which adopt a stance sympathetic to the trilogy and to Pullman. See for example Rowan Williams (2004), the BBC (2004) and Tony Watkins (2006).

WORKS CITED

ACHUKA. n.d. "ACHUKA Interview: Philip Pullman." Accessed December 30, 2002. *http://www.achuka.co.uk/ppint.htm*

Barthes, Roland. 1978. "The Death of the Author." *Image-Music Text*. Stephen Heath, ed. New York: Hill and Wang, 142–148.

BBC. 2004. "Archbishop Wants Pullman in class." March 10. Accessed October 29, 2010. *http://news.bbc.co.uk/1/hi/education/3497702.stm.*

Billen, Andrew. 2003. "The Andrew Billen Interview: A Senile God? Who Would Adam and Eve It?" *The Times*, January 21, 14–15.

Bloom, Harold. 1997. *The Anxiety of Influence: A Theory of Poetry*. Oxford: Oxford University Press.

Bruner, Kurt, and Jim Ware. 2007. *Shedding Light on His Dark Materials: Exploring Hidden Spiritual Themes in Philip Pullman's Popular Series*. Carol Stream, IL: Salt River.

Chrisafis, Angelique. 2002. "Pullman Lays Down Moral Challenge for Writers." *Guardian*, August 12. Accessed December 30, 2002. *http://education.guardian.co.uk/Print/0,3858, 4479940,00.html.*

Foucault, Michel. 2000. "What Is an Author?" In *Modern Criticism and Theory: A Reader*, 2d ed. David Lodge with Nigel Wood, eds., 174–187. Harlow: Pearson Education.

Goldthwaite, John. 1996. *The Natural History of Make-Believe: A Guide to the Principal Works of Britain, Europe and America*. Oxford: Oxford University Press.

Greene, Mark. 2002. "Poisoned Pen?" *Christianity and Renewal*. London: Monarch CCP.

Houghton, John. 2004. *A Closer Look at His Dark Materials*. Eastbourne: Kingsway.

Jacobs, Alan. 2004. "The Republic of Heaven." *Shaming the Devil: Essays in Truthtelling*. N.p.: Wm. B. Eerdmans.

Kincaid, James R. 1992. *Child-Loving: The Erotic Child and Victorian Culture*. New York and London: Routledge.

Lesnik-Oberstein, Karín. 1994. *Children's Literature: Criticism and the Fictional Child*. Oxford: Oxford University Press.

Lewis, C. S. 1980a. *The Lion, the Witch and the Wardrobe*. London: Lions.

_____. 1980b. *The Last Battle*. London: Lions.

Manlove, Colin. 1975. *Modern Fantasy: Five Studies*. Cambridge: Cambridge University Press.

"Pullman Don't Preach." 2001. *Oxford Student*. January 11.

Roberts, Susan. n.d. "Interview with Philip Pullman." Accessed December 30, 2002. *www.fish.co.uk/culture/features/pullman_interview.html*.

Rose, Jacqueline. 1984. *The Case of Peter Pan*. London and Basingstoke.

Thomson, Stephen. 2004. "The Child, the Family, the Relationship. Familiar Stories: Family, Storytelling, and Ideology in Philip Pullman's *His Dark Materials*." *Children's Literature: New Approaches*. Basingstoke and New York: Palgrave Macmillan, 144–167.

Tonynbee, Polly. 2005. "Narnia Represents Everything That Is Most Hateful About Religion." *The Guardian*, December 5. Accessed June 15, 2008. *http://www.guardian.co.uk/books/2005/dec/05/cslewis.booksforchildrenandteenagers*.

Watkins, Tony. 2006. *Dark Matter: Shedding Light on Philip Pullman's Trilogy His Dark Materials*. Downers Grove, IL: Intervarsity.

Wavell, Stuart. 2001. "The Lost Children; Interview; Philip Pullman." *The Sunday Times*, November 11, 3.

Williams, Rowan. 2004. "A Near-Miraculous Triumph." *The Guardian*, March 10. Accessed July 15, 2005. *http://arts.guardian.co.uk/features/story/0,1165873,00.html*.

4

"Dark Materials to Create More Worlds": Considering *His Dark Materials* as Science Fiction

STEVEN BARFIELD

Pullman and science fiction as genre

Focusing on the *His Dark Materials* trilogy, this chapter will offer a reading which is contextualized by exploring different aspects of science fiction. The epigraph to *Northern Lights* is from John Milton's *Paradise Lost* (Book II, ll. 915–916; Milton 2008, 70), and these are the lines that provide the trilogy as a whole with its memorable title:

Unless the almighty maker them ordain
His dark materials to create more worlds

Milton's lines catch that startling moment in his epic poem when Lucifer, the fallen and rebel angel, contemplates the abyss across worlds that he must traverse in his journey to earth to challenge God. From this vantage point, he views the contending elements of primordial chaos of the abyss which he believes that only the creator can make into new worlds. This sublime moment, as Lucifer pauses and reflects on the sheer size of the cosmos and the fantastic and hazardous journey stretching before him, could perhaps also be construed as a classic science fiction scenario; a space-traveling alien sets out for earth across the near infinite cosmos. Despite the fact that for most critics, as Michael Collings (1997, 7–24) suggests, the religious world view that *Paradise Lost* originates from would preclude it as a progenitor of either science fiction or fantasy, this is not true for a modern, hybridized and radical re-conceptualization of Milton's epic poem such as Pullman's trilogy, which we will suggest in this chapter is significantly informed in sometimes surprising ways by conventions of science fiction. However, whatever the disputes regarding the generic location of Milton's work, the business of making or at least imagining new worlds into being from chaotic, dark materials is also an accurate appraisal of the business of science fiction writers and thus at least in the realm of imagination, challenges what might be thought of as the power reserved for a higher being alone.

Using an unusually broad range of science fiction genres and hybridizing their elements allows Pullman to comment on our present world in a variety of rich, complex and nuanced ways. There are significant elements and conventions from the genre of science fiction in Pullman's novels. These include the accounts of spatial exploration and discovery;[1] the creation of non-humanoid aliens with their own highly particularized and internally consistent society and ecology (such as the *mulefa*), or real world animals with re-imagined quasi-human characteristics;[2] the representations of scientists as heroes and as anti-heroes,[3] and the representation of scientific practices such as experimentation and the use of scientific theories.[4] In particular, Pullman makes use of more recent genres of science fiction with their retro-futurist, Victorian derived technology such as Victoriana and steampunk;[5] the creation of utopias (the world of the *mulefa*) and dystopias (Lyra's world, the Land of the Dead), for the purpose of deliberate estrangement from our actual world, thus making the reader think critically about his/her own culture and society. The aim of this chapter then will be to explore a necessarily limited selection of these science fiction elements in greater depth and to consider how they function in *His Dark Materials* where their associated conventions are often deployed in the themes, settings and strategies of Pullman's text.

Pullman and science fiction

Definitions of the science fiction genre that appear to strongly distinguish it from fantasy or romance are numerous. Adam Roberts, in *Science Fiction: the New Critical Idiom*, refers to the "grounding of SF in the material, rather than the supernatural" (2005, 5), effectively emphasizing the science in the fiction and seeking to differentiate a science fiction reader's expectations from the conventions of more typical fantasy texts where magic may the norm. Earlier, Kingsley Amis argued:

> Science fiction is that class of prose narrative treating of a situation that could not arise in the world we know, but which is hypothesized on the basis of some innovation in science or technology, or pseudo-science or pseudo-technology, whether human or extra-terrestrial in origin [1960, 14].[6]

As Roberts, Amis and many other similar definitions suggest, such differentiation functions principally in terms of issues of the inner scientific probability of the non-realistic elements of the text which it is often assumed must typically conform to known laws of science or else be informed and rational speculations about future scientific developments. For example, consider Isaac Asimov's celebrated Three Laws of Robotics:

1. A robot may not harm a human being, or, through inaction, allow a human being to come to harm.

2. A robot must obey the orders given to it by human beings, except where such orders would conflict with the First Law.

3. A robot must protect its own existence, as long as such protection does not conflict with the First or Second Law [Asimov 1990, 423–5].

These laws were created to help Asimov make sense of how robots might behave in the future real world for the needs of his science fiction stories, but significantly they have also been considered as issues worth debate by scientists working in Artificial Intelligence (AI), as if they might offer something to real world scientific researchers.[7] In this respect, what matters is the way the three laws establish ideas of consistency and probability within actual scientific thinking, rather than just in terms of a secondary fictional world. However, as is suggested later in this essay, while this type of technical definition is germane and useful to identifying the genre of science fiction, there are many examples of texts that render such clear definitions problematic.

While it is unclear from Pullman's published comments whether or not he is a great reader of science fiction, nonetheless it is informative that he contributes the short, but incisive foreword to Russell T. Davies and Benjamin Cook's *Doctor Who: The Writer's Tale* (2008) and that he also produced a dramatic adaptation of Mary Shelley's *Frankenstein* (1990), intended for school children. The *Doctor Who* series is a staple of British popular science fiction and *Frankenstein* is usually considered by critics one of the earliest examples of the genre of science fiction, despite or perhaps because of its relationship to the Gothic (see Fred Botting 2008, 111–127). *Frankenstein* is another text much influenced by Milton's *Paradise Lost* and uses an epigraph from the poem: "Did I request thee, Maker, from my clay / To mould Me man? Did I solicit thee / From darkness to promote me?" (Book X, ll. 743–744; Milton 2008, 306) suggesting that man and woman too can be guilty of behaving badly towards what they create. In addition, *Frankenstein,* at least in its original 1818 edition, as Marilyn Butler (2008) has argued, can be thought of a radical text that explores alternatives to conservative, establishment values through its positive depiction of science. Significantly, Pullman's stage version of the novel for young adults emphasizes the perspective and humanity of the creature, rather than legitimating any straightforward notion of the dangers of science in challenging God's prerogative and authority.

Pullman is by no means the first to create mixed or hybrid texts which deploy conventions from different kinds of science fiction, or indeed mixing generic conventions from science fantasy and indeed older models of fantasy or romance; nor is he the first to employ such hybrid texts towards the goals of social and political commentary. There is in fact an existing tradition of such cross-genre texts which undermine hard and fast distinctions between science fiction and fantasy beginning perhaps with *Frankenstein* (in that Victor Frankenstein combines science with sorcery in creating the creature). For example, Christopher Stasheff's *The Warlock in Spite of Himself* (1969) features Rod Gallowglass, the space-traveling agent of SCENT and his robot Fess on a mission to the planet Gramarye. Gallowglass does not believe in magic nor that he is himself a warlock, as Gramarye's populace insist (although his name, Gallowglass, is suggestive), because he recognizes only an established scientific paradigm. Nonetheless after his final victory over various magical forces he admits to being a warlock in order to marry one of the planet's inhabitants. Stasheff's suggestion would seem to be that a scientifically advanced space-traveler is more or less indistinguishable from a warlock in real terms, and consequently magic is indistinguishable from any sufficiently advanced technology; thus rather cannily reversing for fun the terms of the relationship between science and magic made famous by Arthur C. Clarke's famous "Third Law of Prediction": "Any sufficiently advanced technology is indistinguishable from magic" (Clarke 2000, 2). Pullman's own early novel *Galatea* (1979) can claim to be a cross-genre text of this hybrid type, as Pullman has remarked:

> "I don't know how you'd classify it; but then classifying anything is terribly hard. I don't know what's fantasy and what isn't fantasy. I suppose sort of magical realist [...] it's a year or two too early for the magic realist thing, otherwise it'd have ridden that wave, but it didn't" [Brown 2000, n.p.].

From the viewpoint of science fiction it is significant that several critics have attempted to explain the speculative physical science of *His Dark Materials*, while actual scientists seems to have found Pullman's world of interest;[8] no doubt this is because scientific theories of various kinds play a significant part in the books themselves. In addition, the existence of the multi-verse and parallel worlds within the trilogy is a long time staple of science fiction and has some grounding in developments in quantum mechanics in the shape of the many-worlds hypothesis.[9] However, *His Dark Materials* also presents worlds where science and magic seem to co-exist and, because of the peculiar consciousness of Dust which lies behind the thematic framework of the books, it is particularly hard to decide what might separates magic from science. But what if dark matter were indeed conscious (the "if," it were, of science fiction) then would it be able to explain the kinds of events we see in Pullman's multiverse, as dark matter is something that lays within the realm of science? It is difficult to answer this typical science fiction style question because information is largely lacking.[10]

Pullman's trilogy shows many kinds of technological elements, much like traditional science fiction and sometimes with a neo–Victorian retro-futurist flavor akin to the conventions of the science fiction genre of Steampunk in the presentation of Lyra's world. Her earth contains late Victorian technology in the present; for instance, zeppelins, hot air balloons and bolt action rifles. Rather more futuristically, there is the example of the Gallivespian's lode-stones resonator which allow communication across worlds in the multi-verse because of the possibility offered by the (real) scientific hypothesis of "quantum entanglement" (AS 184–185; HDM 677). However, the trilogy also shows worlds in which various kinds of magical events and beings are common. This combination of elements intertwines something we associate with science fiction conventions (technology based on scientific possibility) with something we strongly correlate with the marvelous qualities of the fantastic (magical and inexplicable occurrences). Both Lyra's symbol laden alethiometer and Will's subtle knife are technological artifacts that seem to mix science and magic in their constitution and what they actually do and so make problematic the boundaries of science fiction and fantasy. The alethiometer, which was created in Prague in the seventeenth century as an astrological instrument, tells those who can read it the truth in response to any question they ask; while the subtle knife created some three hundred years ago by the masters of the Guild of the Torre degli Angeli, in the city of Cittàgazze, has the ability to slice through anything, as well as the capability to cut windows between separate worlds within the multi-verse (NL 173; HDM 128 and SK 189–196; HDM 430–435). Probably such artifacts are powered in some way by the Dust, as both require the same state of child-like grace in which to be used, as does Mary's computer system when reading the shadows in The Subtle Knife or indeed her I-Ching. In the end then, the reader is unsure whether to turn to science or magic to explain the inner consistency of the world they find in His Dark Material because of the hybridity of science and magic, science fiction and fantasy being deployed.

Alternative histories

The employment of science fiction strategies towards socio-political commentary is also relatively common in the history of science fiction, and texts have made commentaries on significant political events or debates about social policies, just as His Dark Materials does regarding religion. For example, H. G. Wells' The Wars of The Worlds (1898) draws explicit comparisons and parallels between the imagined Martian conquest of earth and British colonialism, suggesting that philosophies of Social Darwinism that contend that human evolution is driven by a struggle for survival between different races and groups might easily be turned against those in the British Empire who regarded themselves as inherently superior[11] to other races:

> And before we judge them [the Martians] too harshly, we must remember what ruthless and utter destruction our own species has wrought, not only upon animals, such as the vanished Bison and the Dodo, but upon its own inferior races. The Tasmanians, in spite of their human likeness, were entirely swept out of existence in a war of extermination waged by European immigrants, in the space of fifty years [Wells 2005, 9].

It is by no means clear, if Wells means anything more here than to create a *frisson* for those self-centered humans (the British) who imagine themselves without good reason the masters of the universe, by means of his text's structural and metaphoric displacement of Imperialism from the British onto the Martians, thereby reworking the then popular genre of German invasion narratives into something much more overwhelming. There is much disagreement among critics if Wells is actually and consciously critiquing the principles that underlay Victorian and Edwardian Imperialism, so much as producing a warning against his compatriot's complacency in the face of competition with the burgeoning German Empire.[12] While it would be overstating the case to say that there is an easily locatable tradition of science fiction texts focused on debates which had social and political implications (such as how far science undermined religion and *vice versa*), it is certainly true that an Edwardian and Victorian tendency in science fiction towards exploring utopias and dystopias leads to a relationship between science fiction and implied social and political values of science. As Edward James (2003, 219–230) suggests, this is an inherent tendency in science fiction due to the genre's intimate connection with utopias and dystopias[13] and James is following the influential argument of Darko Suvin (1973, 121–145) that science fiction and utopias have much in common because utopia is consequently the main driver for science-fiction.

A similar imaginative correlation between socio-political events in our world and another made via a speculative fictional strategy is also found in Pullman's *His Dark Materials*. Here his imagination of an alternative, but parallel earth, in which the Reformation and thus the Enlightenment did not happen (as they did in our history), has produced the dystopia of Lyra Belacqua's world in which a misogynist, classist theocracy governs that world in the shape of the Magisterium. Unlike the case of Wells there is, however, little for critics to dispute about any possible ambiguity or ambivalence in Pullman's use of science fiction for political intervention.

Pullman's strategy here has much in common with the conventions of another science fiction genre, that of the alternate history genre of science fiction. Alternate history typically asks: "What if a historic event had turned out differently and what consequences would this then have?" (Duncan 2003, 209). For example, consider some recent examples of alternate history: Harry Turtledove's *How Few Remain* (1997) is a novel that asks what might have happened if the Southern Confederacy had won the Civil War and been reluctantly recognized by the Northern Union. The same author's *Agent of Byzantium* series of stories, features a Byzantium and Eastern Roman Empire that never fell, because the Prophet Mohammed instead of founding Islam converted to Christianity and became a Saint; while Robert Harris' *Fatherland* (1992) imagines a world in which Nazi Germany won World War II and in which America had remained neutral and uninvolved

In fact as was first noted in passing by Michael Billington (2004), there is a probable source for Lyra's world in Kingsley Amis' much earlier alternate history from 1976, *The Alteration* (2004). In Amis' parallel world the Reformation never took place, as Martin Luther became Pope and Henry VIII never ascended to the throne and as a result the English Isles (Eire is just West England) is a theocracy and monarchy where the Convocation of the Catholic Church wields absolute power through a secret police. Catholic controlled Europe is engaged in a Holy Cold War with the Ottoman Empire, the Republic of New England is a breakaway Protestant state and various forms of technology (such as electricity) are banned, while science is suppressed. The alteration of the title refers to the plight of ten year Hubert Anvil, a chorister who the Church has decided must be castrated in order that his perfect child's voice might be saved for the sake of Christian art from the onset of puberty and sexuality. There are many close parallels between this alternate world and Lyra's both in terms of theocratic rule, historical causation and the theme of suppressing children and adult's sexuality to show how it is embedded in the alternate history genre. However, Pullman very considerably extends the scenario through fantasy and cosmology and crucially, while Hubert Anvil does not escape his fate, Lyra and Will bring down the Church and save the multiverse.

His Dark Materials therefore shows us by means of a alternate history dystopia how our world too might have become if Christianity had remained the dominant and univocal political force within the West, the Reformation had never happened and thus the Enlightenment had failed to take place and as a consequence secular liberalism and accompanying ideas about human rights, the need for a secular civil society and the rule of law had never become established. In Lyra's world, Calvin becomes Pope and unifies Catholicism and Protestantism (*NL* 31; *HDM* 23). Thus this alternate history is part of Pullman's intended critique of Christianity as organized religion and social practice by means of creating the dystopia of an alternative earth are carefully linked to our world's own history. Catherine Gallagher (2002, 11–31) sees alternate history as aiming to deconstruct and question present historical actuality in order to interrogate how we understand the process of historical causation and its relationship to our representation of the past, through creating a present retrospective moment. These events have also altered the geopolitics of Lyra's earth (as is common in alternate histories) and there is a changed political map of the world; surprisingly the United States of America does not exist as Lee Scoresby is a New Dane from the country of Texas (*NL* 178; *HDM* 132).

However, unlike the other examples of alternate history fiction discussed above, which often refer to political tendencies and entities that cannot realistically be revived (the American Confederacy, the Byzantine Empire, German National Socialism); Pullman intends his alternate history to relate primarily to what he perceives as a clear and present danger to our liberal and secular tradition. This danger is located in the contemporary growth of extremist religious tendencies in western society, such as Protestant Christian fundamentalism, and the re-establishment of more aggressive Catholic values, with the consequent intolerance towards others that such identities typically display. The witch, Ruta Skadi learns after traveling to meet Lord Asriel accompanied by angels that the aim of the agents of the Authority (God) in various worlds is to destroy all "the joys and truthfulness of life" thus reversing the conventional arguments of theism that God holds the key to joy and truth (*SK* 283; *HDM* 496).

Perhaps the place where the purity of the joy and truthfulness of life is felt most obviously is in the world of the *mulefa*. One of the most interesting features of science fiction has always been the ability to construct entirely new and believable worlds and this is a feature of *His Dark Materials*. Asimov's celebrated story *Nightfall* (1941) is a classic example of a science fiction story which investigates the possibilities of a world that is radically different from our own in terms of elements of its physical nature, and how the internal consistency of the elements of its civilization (which look rather like our own society), would be affected by extraordinary events made possible by these physical aspects. Much as with Asimov, Pullman's world of the *mulefa* attempts a thoroughgoing creation of a radically different, but internally consistent world within the multi-verse of *His Dark Materials*. In this case it is also the site of utopia: the *mulefa* live in apparent ecological harmony with their world unlike humans; the Church is completely unknown there; it will be the new garden of Eden in which the second Fall (that of Lyra) will occur at the end of *The Amber Spyglass*; and it becomes the dimension where the dead will leave their gloomy underworld to re-enter the Universe (*AS* 455–456; *HDM* 864–865). Like much science fiction, Pullman's trilogy mirrors current anxieties about global warming and looming ecological catastrophe. The trilogy shows melting ice-caps causing flooding and rising river levels in Nova Zembla and the Northern territories of the witches, while the armored bears have to flee their polar home due to the melting of the ice and the consequent loss of their food sources (*NL* 225; *HDM* 166 and *AS* 39–42, 116–117; *HDM* 574–576, 630–631). The disturbed magnetic poles and other environmental problems are warnings which suggest global warming, even if they are played out in Lyra's world not ours and are contrasted with the ecological positivity of the existence of the *mulefa*, which is also threatened by similar problems from elsewhere in the multi-verse that may destroy their utopia (*AS* 246–248; *HDM* 720).

The *mulefa*, as Mary Malone discovers, are non-humanoid aliens and their world is dominated by an evolutionary path which produced an invertebrate diamond shaped species (*AS* 460–461; *HDM* 868–869). In addition each "zalif" (an individual *mulefa*) has an extraordinarily dexterous and prehensile, elephantine-like trunk (*AS* 129–131; *HDM* 638–640). While highly intelligent they do not use metals, but as tool-using animals, use disc-shaped seed pods from their planets gigantic seed-pod trees to turn themselves into astonishingly wheeled creatures. It is the simultaneous combination of interaction between the basalt rock formation of long roads on this prairie planet, the seed-pod trees themselves with their oiled seed pods which contains sraf (dark matter, Dust) and the *mulefa* themselves which allows this existence: without the trees the *mulefa* would lose their intelligent consciousness due to lack of "sraf," while without the *mulefa* the trees would not have their hard seed pods broken up (*AS* 132–135; *HDM* 641–642). What is most impressive here is the level of detail which Pullman provides and the internal consistency he achieves in letting us see this unique world and ecology through Mary's eyes and much like Asimov's protagonist the world is made concretely real through the inter-relationship of new causal connections altered by an individual element. For just one example of this, consider the fact that their lack of hands means the *mulefa* must always work together to undertake tasks such as tying knots for fishing nets, which helps explains their intensely communal existence without perceivable organized government (*AS* 134–135; *HDM* 642–643) In addition the *mulefa* are taught in their own positive version of the Fall in Eden how to first use wheels by a snake, which explains their veneration of snakes (*AS* 236–237; *HDM* 713–714). In this sense the utopianism of the *mulefa* world counterbalances not just the dystopia of Lyra's theocratic world ruled by the Magisterium, but also the underworld of the dead which Will and Lyra must travel to in order to liberate the ghosts.

Exploring and challenging Christian science fiction from within

His Dark Materials combines science fiction motifs with a theological underpinning; however, within the context of science fiction this strategy is better known as defining the existing genre of Christian science fiction; in itself an example of hybrid science fiction. An early example is Victor Rousseau's loosely allegorical *The Messiah of the Cylinder* (1917) in which the hero, kept artificially asleep for many years, becomes the messiah who will liberate a future world dominated by socialism, atheism and mechanistic science. More significant for Pullman's own practice though, is the example of C. S. Lewis' three science fiction novels (called by critics, the Space Trilogy or Cosmic Trilogy) and set in our solar system: *Out of the Silent Planet* (1938), *Perelandra* (1943) and *That Hideous Strength* (1945). These novels attempt to combine Christian cosmology with science fiction, as has been discussed by critics such as Sanford Schwartz (2009) and Walter Hooper (1987).

First, the novels originate in part from Lewis' attempt to argue that science fiction and Christianity are not necessarily incompatible and that scientific explorations of space will not render Christianity less credible and thus undermine Faith.[14] Second, the trilogy suggests that human beings are still flawed due to the Fall of man and that any encounter with other worlds will generally be harmful to inhabitants of such a world, thus criticizing as immoral the view that Lewis took to be represented in Olaf Stapledon's *Last and First Men: A Story of the Near and Far Future* (1930) where Lewis thought Stapledon was suggesting that future colonization of other planets may inevitably might include genocide of inferior alien races for the needs of settlement, paralleling European colonization in the new world. Third, Lewis' novels also attempt to rebut the arguments of Wells' own science fiction, such as *The Shape of Things to Come* (1933) in which Wells portrays a future rationalist and socialist world, in which all religion will be banned as harmful to the human beings of this imagined Utopia.

In Lewis' the Space Trilogy the explorers leave earth (the Silent Planet, because it is divided from the rest of the universe after the events of this cosmological version of the Christian Fall) and encounter various alien races, but the most significant of these are the eternal, celestial Eldila. The Eldila, guardians of individual planets in our solar system are science fiction depictions of angels, appearing as energy based, pan-dimensional beings. They explain to the humans that the universe is as it is because Maleldil, the highest Eldila (paralleling God), once ruled the entire solar system, before the Bent One (an *Oyarsa* and thus one of the highest of the Eldila specific of earth and paralleling Lucifer), rebelled against Maleldil and the other Eldila. The Bent One, was imprisoned on the Earth, which he subsequently recreated as a domain of evil (the story parallels Genesis) Maleldil then chose to become a human (paralleling the story of Christ), in order to sacrifice himself by death to redeem Earth. In effect, Lewis has remade Christian cosmology into science fiction by means of broad allegory.

Another writer who combines Christian cosmology with science fiction is Madeleine L'Engle in *A Wrinkle in Time* (1962) and others in the loose series of books featuring the Murry and O'Keefe families. L'Engle has rather more liberal and humanist Christian views than Lewis[15] and while not allegorical, her science fiction cosmology is not that dissimilar from Lewis' structurally speaking, insofar as it focuses on re-imagining angels, and hybrids Christian doctrine about the universe with science fiction themes. In *A Wrinkle in Time*, the Black Thing takes the place of Satan and he/it is slowly taking over the universe. The Black Thing kidnaps the children's father; who in turn are helped by three angelic star-beings (rather more human and less like Old Testament angels than Lewis' Eldila). As L'Engle's main critic Carole F. Chase (1998) has argued, selfless love it would appear can indeed conquer all in our universe and the texts are much more child-centered than anything Lewis created (angels help but significantly the children take center stage).

Such combinations of science-fiction and theology as those of Lewis or L'Engle have traditionally been positive about Christianity. As Rolland Hein's (2002) useful survey of this genre suggests, such a didactic function by means of allegory (Lewis) or symbolization (L'Engle) has been made because of the dangerous secularism which Christians often consider to be implicit in the genre of science fiction. A key element of such texts as those by Lewis and L'Engle is the depiction of angels as being who are infinitely more powerful, distant and different from the humans than they meet and while they are re-imagined within a science fiction context, they still maintain the traditional characteristics and position of angels towards humanity. It is noticeable that Pullman is avowedly critical of Christianity, while still deploying a similar cos-mology,[16] *because* he is contesting the traditional Christian understanding of the universe. While Lewis and L'Engle work through allegory and symbolization of Christian cosmology respectively, disguising angels as star-beings and super-aliens and so forth because they see Christianity as more or less literal truth, Pullman, in contrast, works directly with Christian cosmology because he sees it as a dangerous myth which must be contested on its own level.

Unlike Lewis and L'Engle, in Pullman's world, God is represented by the senile figure of the Authority in his crystal casket (*AS* 431–432; *HDM* 848) and actual power is wielded by his angelic and tyrannical Regent Metatron. But we learn that the Authority did not create the universe, he was merely the first angel to appear out of Dust and he then masqueraded as if he had created the universe and consequently set up a Kingdom of Heaven with himself in charge over everything else in the Universe, as Mrs. Coulter discovers to her absolute astonishment from King Ogunwe (*AS* 221–222; *HDM* 702–703). How far this represents Pullman's use of the marginalized traditions of Gnos-ticism within English literature, particularly the Ophite heresy[17] may be a moot point: what is certain is that this reworking of the myth of God represents Pullman's deliberate and also very determined subversion of the kind of attitude towards God we see in Christian science fiction.[18]

While Pullman powerfully re-utilizes the idea of multi-dimensional beings called angels (although this time, unlike in Lewis and L'Engle they are actually named as angels in *His Dark Materials*), he both works to humanize them in a way Lewis and L'Engle do not. In addition, he includes non–Christian and pagan elements in his text, though now seen in a positive light, as the witches led by Serafina Pekkala and Ruta Skadi and a shaman. The shaman is John Parry, Will's father who originated from our earth and he will play a key role in the successful rebellion against God/the Authority. The witches who are seen as the enemies of the Church of Lyra's world and indeed traditional Christianity, will become some of the principal guardians to Will and Lyra throughout the trilogy and staunch adversaries of the Church.

Pullman imbues the angels of Christian science fiction with human-like characteristics and personalities, as well as wishes and desires, to enter into various kinds of relationships (sometimes of equality) with humans.[19] These are all key ways *His Dark Materials* undermines and subverts the place and nature of the angels in the cosmology of Christian theological science fiction through humanization. In addition, to emphasize angelic materiality the 'fastidious' Balthamos tastes some of Will Parry's Kendal Mint Cake in *The Amber Spyglass* (*AS* 27; *HDM* 565), parodying how Raphael shares a meal with Adam and Eve in Book V (lines 320–460) of *Paradise Lost*.

While Pullman's fallen angels are both proudly rebellious they are at the same time seen as capable of mixed feelings and making mistakes, which thus makes them as sympathetic to the reader. This humanization of the angels' characters is particularly evident in terms of the depiction of the loving and passionate relationship between the two key rebel angels who appear in the novels from the end of *The Subtle Knife*: Balthamos and Baruch. Raphael's remarks on angelic love in *Paradise Lost* (Book VIII, ll. 618–29) suggest the physicality of angels; however. Pullman's two male angels, Baruch and Balthamos would appear truly, madly and deeply in love with one another and Balthamos refers to Baruch as his "beloved" (*AS* 496; *HDM* 892). As minor angels they are not much more powerful than humans (in comparison for instance to Metatron or Xaphania) and can be easily injured by other angels and in the case of Balthamos, can suffer from anxiety, grief, self-doubt, guilt and despair. Baruch's dying word is his lover's name: "Balthamos" (*AS* 65–66; *HDM* 592–593). Though the grief-stricken Balthamos promises to help Will because of his lover and companion's sacrifice, he deserts Will from what appears to be cowardice when they are struggling with the Swiss Guard, after Will has rescued Lyra from Coulter, and for a time the grieving angel will be consumed by guilt and despair over his desertion, again representing a humanization of angelic nature (see for example *AS* 165–166, *HDM* 664–665).

Apart from Baruch, Balthamos, Metatron and Xaphania, we more often see anonymous angels flying through the sky in the books, such as those angels the witches led by Serafina Pekkala and Ruta Skadi and who Ruta Skadi then accompanies to Lord Asriel's fortress (*SK* 143–150; *HDM* 399–403). The angels the witches see are described as "more like architecture than organism, like huge structures composed of intelligence and feeling" on which a light shines from somewhere than cannot be seen, rather than physical entities which it is suggested is how they appear to mortals (*SK* 143–150; *HDM* 399–403). This more traditional description filled with awe is not the normal way that angels are presented in *His Dark Materials*. Metatron is also humanized as part of this transformative process of the original apocryphal Biblical myths of angels who had sexual relationships with women, who then bore them children and it is the angel's desire for a physical human lover in the shape of his sexual desire for Coulter, which leads to his literal downfall in *The Amber Spyglass*. He is memorably wrestled into the abyss between worlds (caused by the multi-verse jumping bomb intended to kill Lyra), by Asriel, Coulter and their respective daemons (*AS* 424–430; *HDM* 843–847).

If Pullman draws from the motifs of Christian science fiction, then he does so to challenge and subvert them; for example, by reversing the genre's transformation of angels into science fiction cosmological aliens, he forcefully reads them back into their original theological sources (often via Milton) and then works carefully to humanize his angelic rebels and reactionaries, while simultaneously placing pagan elements within his imaginative world to offset Christian lore. Matthew Uselton has helpfully suggested the relevance to Pullman's use of religious material of Casey Fredericks' (1982) structuralist discussion of the transformative use of myth.[20] Myth for Fredericks is not over-determined by the original context, but its systematic grammar can serve to allow new combinations of meaning and possibility through that of the older mythology: "In modern SF mythology, humanity is a self-creator. The future remains in our hands, to fail or succeed in the great adventure of the future" (Fredericks 1982, 176). For Pullman making explicit the link between Christina theological cosmology and science fiction representations of the same allows him to use the past to interrogate the possibility of the future within the present by changing structural relations within the biblical myth and its subsequent literary variations.

At the same time, Pullman's careful and original use of other science fiction genres and strategies such as world creation, alternate worlds, utopias/dystopias, and indirect commentary on the socio-politics of the present allows him additional purchase on the territory of science fiction because his work is so well integrated at the philosophical level in terms of aims. This is combined with a deliberate exploration of the hybrid space between science fiction and fantasy that allows him to unravel many of the traditional conventions by which science fiction and Christian cosmology have been linked together for deliberately religious purposes by Christian writers. Pullman put this last point of view trenchantly and amusingly in interview in 2002: "Blake said Milton was a true poet and of the Devil's party without knowing it. I am of the Devil's party and know it" (Pullman 2002).

Conclusion

Pullman's practice reminds us that science fictions are determined by political, social and cultural aims. In addition, at least part of *His Dark Materials* is set in our realistically depicted actual world, which is the world Will Parry originates from, and bringing this world into contact with the other imagined worlds is crucial to the way the trilogy advances not just the development of its principal characters, but as we have already argued, for the trilogy's use of characteristic science fiction tropes of utopia and dystopia. Suvin (1979, 63–84) has suggested in an influential thesis that science-fiction as a form requires there to be a dominating "novum" created for a text, that is to say the imagining by the writer of something historically new, extraordinary and radically different from the author and reader's actual and lived environment, which then allows the interplay of cognitive estrangement from our world and cognitive logic in the working through of validity of the new world created (Suvin 1979).[21] Such defamiliarization of our world by the novum is often shown most powerfully in utopias and dystopias and acts to encourages us to think again about elements we take for granted about our own world and to reflect and change them (Shklovsky 1965, 3–25).

Feminist and other writing concerned with gender in science fiction has found that the scientific paradigm used in a text may alone be insufficient to allow effective critique of masculine and patriarchal ideology, or else may restrict the gender of the possible readership. We may notice regarding this issue how Pullman consistently works to balance male with female characters throughout the trilogy showing his interest in gender politics: Lyra and Will; Asriel and Malone; the witches and a shaman; Xaphania and Metatron; male and female Gallivespians.

More than one feminist writer from Ursula K. Le Guin to Joanna Russ has adopted textual strategies familiar from fantasy in what is ostensibly science fiction as has been surveyed by Veronica Hollinger (2003, 125–136) and by Lucie Armitt (1990). This is also true of Pullman, though this is perhaps unsurprising in a work where gender and religion are of so much importance.[22]

Pullman's engagement with the science fiction genre through both convention and context is an extremely rich, complex and productive one that repays careful critical analysis. Pullman's worlds are both multiple and inter-related, with a bold architectural design at the heart of the trilogy including opposing novums in the shape of utopias and dystopias as part of the multiverse. Pullman's aim is both estrangement from our world as we have seen to make us think again about how it is constituted, but more powerfully still, it is to produce estrangement from and critical reflection upon the histories, traditions, mythologies and ideologies of organized Christianity itself. Pullman's final aim then is to explore the possibility of "a republic of heaven" (*AS* 548;

HDM 929), which does not answer to God and which puts humanity firmly at the center of the universe with the possibility to shape their own democratic utopian aspirations. But the people of the multi-verse as Will and Lyra discover to their cost, can never truly come together except in imagination; instead utopia for Pullman is always radically incomplete. It is something distant and worth striving for, but where we are is always the most important place and where we must begin to build towards the distant gleam of utopia.

NOTES

1. For example, the characters' expedition to the melting Arctic ice cap and the ability to travel between different worlds and explore them within the context of a multi-verse of parallel worlds.

2. Such as the *Panserbjørn,* who are iron-working, intelligent and conscious polar bears.

3. See for example the contrasting scientists represented by the characters of the physicist and former nun, Dr. Mary Malone, and the eccentric and powerful Lord Asriel.

4. The trilogy positions the importance of dark matter and the value of various scientific theorizations about the structure of universe to the imaginative cosmology. It also explores quasi-scientific theories such as Terence McKenna's novelty theory; whereby, novelty theory considers the universe a living system (broadly similar to a pantheistic world view), in which the novelty and complexity of living entities increase exponentially as time progresses due to a universal law towards extropy (the opposite of entropy). Interestingly enough, McKenna made determined use of the I-Ching to develop the numerological patterns that underlay his thesis, while Dr. Malone in *His Dark Materials* recognizes how the I-Ching can serve to contact the conscious and living Dust (dark matter/angels; see *SK* 99; *HDM* 369) as well tell her how to proceed on the journey she makes in the third volume of the trilogy, to the world of the *mulefa* (*AS* 84; *HDM* 607). See Terence McKenna and Dennis McKenna, (1994) *The Invisible Landscape: Mind, Hallucinogens, and the I Ching* and, Ralph Abraham, Terence McKenna and Rupert Sheldrake (1992) *Trialogues at the Edge of the West: Chaos, Creativity and the Resacralization of the World.*

5. The use of these forms creates an alternative present where social consequences are due to changes in past events of the historical timeline, thus following the conventions of the science fiction genre of alternate history.

6. For good discussions of the problem of defining science fiction see Roberts (2005, 1–35) and Roger Luckhurst (2005, 1–29).

7. For example, Asimov himself provided the foreword to Shimon Y. Nof's *Handbook of Industrial Robotics* (1999) and the three laws have been discussed with regard to their practical value for future robotic design by Lee McCauley (2007).

8. *C.f.* John Gribbin and Mary Gribbin (2008); Robert A. Metzger (2006), and Arthur B. Markman (2006).

9. *C.f.* Merali (2007); Miller (1987); De Witt and Graham (1973), and Peter Nicholls and John Clute (1996).

10. For example, do science *or* magic determine genre conventions when it comes to the following: the powers of apparently supernatural beings such as Pullman's angels or witches; polar bear society with language, armor made from fallen meteorites and self-consciousness; the capabilities of the Lilliputian-like Gallivespians with their short lives of nine years and their poisonous heel spurs; or indeed, how the mysterious six-legged intention craft of *The Amber Spyglass* works or is powered (*AS* 210–233; *HDM* 695–710).

11. On Social Darwinism, see Mike Hawkins (1997).

12. *C.f.* Patrick Parrinder (1996); Alexander Irvine (2004), and John Hawley (2004).

13. *C.f.* Phillip Wenger (2008, 79–95).

14. Lewis also makes this argument in his earlier essay "Religion and Rocketry" (2002, 83–93).

15. Her work is less concerned with the significance of the Fall for instance and much more an avocation of Christian ideals of love or *agape* and how it can contest evil.

16. For instance, he inverts the accepted Christian binary opposition between traditionally good and obedient angels who remain faithful to God, and their rebellious and evil counterparts.

17. This is the speculation that the serpent in the Garden of Eden may actually have been Christ disguised; this is a tradition in English literature that has been discussed by Anthony Nuttall (1998).

18. Pullman in his William Blake Society lecture of 2005, "I Must Create a System… " discusses Gnosticism and indeed mentions Nuttall's monograph. For a useful introductory discussion of the complex history of Gnosticism see also K. L. King, (2005) *What Is Gnosticism?* and for the inventive and lucid (if finally unconvincing) argument that Pullman seeks to reform the understanding of the Christian God rather than to argue for atheism, see Donna Freitas and Jason E. King (2007) *Killing the Imposter God: Philip Pullman's Spiritual Imagination in His Dark Materials.*

19. Such as Balthamos' companionship and service to Will Parry, Metatron's palpable lust for Coulter, or Xaphania's work as Lord Asriel's commander or assistance in closing the portals between worlds (*AS* 524–525; *HDM* 912–913).

20. See Matthew Uselton (n.d.) and Casey Fredericks (1982).

21. For discussions of the impact of the "novum": see Adam, Roberts (2005, 7–10); Istvan Csicsery-Ronay Jr., (2008, 47–50) The *Seven Beauties of Science Fiction*; and while Patrick Parrinder collection of 2001 is entirely devoted to Darko's work.

22. For example, in *His Dark Materials* Dr. Mary Malone, despite her scientific training, must rely upon intuition to interpret what the dark matter is saying to her (*SK* 98–100; *HDM* 362–364; *SK* 248–265; *HDM* 471–483) and it is her emotional rapport with Lyra rather than any scientific, rational process of analysis, which allows Malone to make decisions that will allow her to play her part in the unfolding cosmic narrative.

Works Cited

"Parallel Worlds." 1995. In *The Encyclopedia of Science Fiction.* Peter Nicholls and John Clute, eds. New York: St. Martin's, 907–909.

Parrinder, Patrick. 1996. *Shadows of the Future: H. G. Wells, Science Fiction, and Prophecy.* Syracuse: Syracuse University Press.

Pullman, Philip. n.d. "Philip Pullman Interview Transcript." Scholastic Books. Accessed March 1 2009. http://web.archive.org/web/20000816094721/http://teacher.scholastic.com/authors andbooks/authors/pullman/tscript.htm.

_____. 1979. *Galatea.* New York: E.P. Dutton.

_____. 1990. *Frankenstein: The Play.* Oxford: Oxford University Press.

_____. 2000. "Revisiting Suvin's Poetics of Science Fiction. In *Learning from Other Worlds: Estrangement, Cognition, and the Politics of Science Fiction and Utopia.* Patrick Parrinder, ed. Liverpool: Liverpool University Press, 36–51.

_____. 2002. "I Am of the Devil's Party." Interview by Helena de Bertodano. *Daily Telegraph,* January. Accessed March 1, 2009. http://www.telegraph.co.uk/culture/donotmigrate/3572490-/I-am-of-the-Devils-party.html.

_____. 2009. "'I Must Create a System…': William Blake Society Lecture 2005." Accessed March 1, 2009. http://www.philip-pullman.com/pages/content/index.asp?PageID=110.

Roberts, Adam. 2005. *Science Fiction: The New Critical Idiom,* 2d ed. New York and London: Routledge.

Rousseau, Victor. 2008. *The Messiah of the Cylinder.* N.p.: Wildside.

Schwartz, Sanford. 2009. *C. S. Lewis on the Final Frontier: Science and the Supernatural in the Space Trilogy.* Oxford: Oxford University Press.

Shklovsky, Victor. "Art as Technique." In *Russian Formalist Criticism: Four Essays,* Lee T. Lemon and M.J. Reis, eds. Lincoln: University of Nebraska Press, 3–25.

Stapledon, Olaf. 1999. *Last and First Men: A Story of the Near and Far Future.* N.p.: Gollancz.

Stasheff, Christopher. 2004. *The Warlock in Spite of Himself.* N.p.: Ace.

Suvin, Darko. 1973. "Defining the Literary Genre of Utopia: Some Historical Semantics, Some Genology, a Proposal and a Plea." *Studies in the Literary Imagination* 6. 2, 121–145.

_____. 1979. *Metamorphoses of Science Fiction: On the Poetics and History of a Literary Genre.* New Haven: Yale University Press.

Turtledove, Harry. 1994. *Agent of Byzantium.* N.p.: Pocket.
_____. 1998. *How Few Remain.* New York: Hodder and Stoughton.
Uselton, Matthew. n.d. "A Structural Study on the Emergence of Evil in Philip Pullman's *His Dark Materials.*" Accessed March 1, 2009. http://www.darkmaterials.com/spyinter02.htm.
Wells, H.G. 1993. *The Shape of Things to Come.* N.p.: Phoenix.
_____. 2005. *The War of the Worlds.* Harmondsworth: Penguin Classics.
Wenger, Phillip E. 2008. "Utopia." In *A Companion to Science Fiction.* David Seed, ed., 79–95. Oxford: Blackwell.

II. TRADITIONS AND LEGACIES

5

Revitalizing the Old Machines of a Neo-Victorian London: Reading the Cultural Transformations of Steampunk and Victoriana

STEVEN BARFIELD AND MARTYN COLEBROOK

Introduction: Defining steampunk and Victoriana

There are two relatively recent and overlapping genres within science fiction,[1] steampunk and Victoriana, both of which grew out of the earlier science fiction genre of cyberpunk, which we will argue in this chapter are utilized by Philip Pullman in *His Dark Materials*. They are used in ways that are innovative in terms of the genre and in augmenting Pullman's central aims within the trilogy, but Pullman also make us aware of new possibilities within these two areas. This discussion therefore provides further opportunity for the critical exploration of how thoughtfully Pullman uses science fiction tropes and conventions within the complex architecture of *His Dark Materials*.[2]

Steampunk and Victoriana have definitions that are loose, somewhat overlapping, and which have been and still are keenly debated and contested. An attempted representative anthology such as that of Ann and Jeff VanderMeer's *Steampunk* (2008) present a considerable range and variety of texts, although the selection may perhaps be considered problematic because so much of the development of the genre has occurred in the form of novel-length texts. Rick Klaw's essay in the same volume (2008) serves to catalogue the range and varieties of material, and interestingly includes Pullman's trilogy as one of his favorite examples of the genre.

There is still a lack of academic and critical materials on the genre, although there have been important articles in *Steampunk Magazine*, produced by radical aficionados of the genre with anarchist or socialist leanings. Jess Nevins (2008) in an introductory essay and Cory Goss (2007) in *Steampunk Magazine*, both suggest that in certain ways the forebears of the genre are the mid-nineteenth to early-twentieth century examples of science fiction of the period. These forebears are what Nevins (2008) terms the Edisonades[3]; while Goss (2006) identifies the genre's precursors as found in the differing but related tendencies of the scientific Romance writers of the Victorian and Edwardian period, such as H.G. Wells and Jules Verne.

While this precursor history has a certain appeal, as many steampunk texts would appear to see themselves as self-consciously continuing the project of the Victorian and Edwardian fiction of Wells and Verne, or the Edisonade magazine stories about Victorian inventor/explorer figures, steampunk's roots as a self-conscious genre arguably lie nearer to the present. Victorian and Edwardian science fiction was not using the technology in a retro-futurist way, but rather the point is this technology and attitude has been recreated as a stylistic and thematic precursor by contemporary science fiction writers reacting against and thus modifying the vertiginous, dazzling and postmodern computer-human interfaces and imagined near futures for human society that are familiar from cyberpunk. Steampunk therefore restores imaginatively a nineteenth or early twentieth century idea of the machine which is more organic and individualized that our digital and high-technology world permits and so allows a more direct relationship to the material world for humans than with present technology: "Steampunk machines are real, breathing, coughing, struggling and rumbling parts of the world. [...] The technology of steampunk is natural; it moves, lives, ages, and even dies" (Catastrophone Orchestra and Arts Collective 2006, 4).

This type of attitude towards this retro-futurist technology is shown effectively at the end of *The Subtle Knife*, where the four zeppelins of the Muscovite Imperial army that are chasing Lee Scoresby and John Parry/Stan Grumman/Jopari (who have landed their own balloon in the forest to hide from the pursuing zeppelins), are dispatched by various physical means.[4]

Steampunk was codified primarily an offshoot from the genre of cyberpunk, which was so dominant in the 1980s and 1990s.[5] In contrast to cyberpunk, steampunk and Victoriana have mostly if not exclusively focused on the past of the long nineteenth century (thus including the Romantic and Edwardian periods and stretching from *circa*. 1780 to about 1930) as opposed to cyberpunk's emphasis on the future and technological speculations therein. It is worthwhile stating though, that one of the principal differences of setting between *His Dark Materials* and most steampunk and Victoriana texts is the Lyra's alternate Earth is not in fact set in the past, but rather in a present parallel Earth. In part this allows Pullman to be exempted from the charge of a simple escapism through cultural nostalgia, both technological and social of which examples of both steampunk and Victoriana are sometimes accused of by theorists of the genre.[6]

Both steampunk and Victoriana re-imagine the world of the nineteenth century, especially the British Empire and create pastiche, retro-futurist neo-Victorian worlds in terms of their settings as a result of this specific re-imagining. However, in steampunk the texts usually have a central theme of technology derived from that of the nineteenth or early twentieth century (the steam of steampunk), although it may be a fictional technology or real technology that was in fact invented later, or combinations thereof, such as for instance steam-powered computers or robots or atomic power. In addition, texts in this genre according to critics such as Goss (2006) and Nevins (2008) often display a radical edge in exploring issues of social class, race and gender through the text (the punk of steampunk). Goss (2006) suggests the relationship to the Victorian past should be melancholic and critical of the politics of the period (following H.G. Wells as exemplar), rather than simply nostalgic and politically uncritical (following Jules Verne as exemplar), that is to say it should favor a critical dystopia located in that past over an expansive utopia.

In contrast, in Victoriana, neither the emphasis on early technology nor the more radical political critique of the earlier historical period is typical, but the science fiction setting itself will still be explicitly one that is derived from the Victorian or Edwardian period. According to John Clute and Roz Kaveney (1999), the "Gaslight romance" is a version of Victoriana that emphasizes the mode of fantasy most often in a troubled and melancholic frame, focusing on mythologically resonant, but historical characters such as Sherlock Holmes or Dracula from the *fin de siècle*.[7] Although Pullman does not re-use characters from the science fantasy or gothic novels of the period, he does reuse many of the typical ways of portraying an industrialized, dark and gritty London which are familiar from such texts, such as in the way the rumors of the child stealing Gobblers are spread among the population.

The last point of locating the difference between steampunk and Victoriana is liable to cause some confusion in terms of the study of more mainstream contemporary fiction. In particular, Pullman's work it should be stated does not set out to be science fiction or even science fantasy and is thus not ostensibly within the genre, but as we argue in this account rather uses the genre as part of its complex and rich textual architecture. As several critics have argued, much contemporary neo–Victorian literature and culture is defined by its intention to be critical of the Victorian period and often this seems to be to a greater extent than is found in the steampunk genre.[8] This is in part because steampunk has the twin problems that while set in the past it links to science fiction, which was in its nineteenth century incarnations more often about technology-centered escapism rather than social critique and, insofar as steampunk's generally realist style (often based around scientific consistency) does not allow it to disrupt its relationship to the past, it tends to colonize it.

If the steampunk genre shows social change often driven by technological factors, with technological deviation, absences or inventions occurring earlier than they did in the real world (technological determinism); then in Pullman's case it appears rather that it is social and political change that determines technology and the events of an alternative history that has lead to the technology of a different present. In this case the fact that the Reformation and Enlightenment did not happen in Lyra's alternative world is the defining factor of its history, rather than any deviation in the history of technology alone.

In Lyra's theocratic world for example, while physics as we know it still exists (and indeed is carried out at Jordan College), it is called experimental theology and not experimental physics because in Lyra's world the entire paradigm is still controlled by the Church and everything is seen as being about the study of God, rather than as in our world the study of a natural universe. It is probable that while much modern technology does exist in Lyra's world and much else could, some of it has never developed because the Church does not wish it to be and the bourgeoisie, much less the working-class, never developed any effective challenge to the establishment. In an aristocratic world where democracy seems absent, there is presumably no need for modern conveniences necessitated by consumer capitalism as the latter seems largely held in check by conservative social arrangements reminiscent of the pre–1832 Great Reform Act period that have managed to survive into the present.

Hence such objects as ring-pull cans, can-openers, refrigerators, bank ATM machines, and the cinema are all absent from Lyra's world because of social and economic retardation, rather than technological divergence. Ordinary working people seem to be treated if anything worse than their mid-nineteenth century forebears[9] and there is to our contemporary views an extreme set of social hierarchies in place. For instance, in *The Subtle Knife*, Lord Asriel's faithful manservant Thorold tells Serafina Pekkala that despite having served Asriel for almost forty years: "He wouldn't confide in me anymore than his shaving-mug" (*SK* 46; *HDM* 332). Additionally, Lyra when she first meets Will in Cittàgazze, shows that she can't cook and then refuses to wash the dishes after Will has cooked an omelet, as that is a job in her world that only servants do (*SK* 27; *HDM* 319).

Pullman's steampunk technology

In *The Amber Spyglass* Mrs. Coulter, her daemon and Lord Roke the Gallivespian try unsuccessfully to destroy Father MacPhail and Dr. Cooper's multi-verse hopping bomb. Powered mainly by the *intercision* (separation) of a human from its daemon which process releases we are told almost unimaginable energy, this extraordinary device will also require the entire energy output from the huge *anbaric* (electricity) power generating station of Saint-Jean-les-Eaux in Lyra's world's Switzerland just to trigger it.[10] In addition, this impressive smart bomb has been programmed genetically by means of a few strands of Lyra's hair stolen from Mrs. Coulter's locket while she is sleeping, by a nervous Brother Louis, so that it will find the child in whatever universe she inhabits. We are presented with Mrs. Coulter's view of the bomb's futuristic technology: "Mrs. Coulter could see it clearly in the wash of the flood lights, an ungainly mass of machinery and wiring slightly tilted on the rocky ground [...] she could see no principle behind the coils, the jars, the banks of insulators, the lattice of tubing" (*AS* 363; *HDM* 801).

The view we obtain of this singularly advanced piece of technology is one from the annals of a Victorian or Edwardian science laboratory, complete with coils, jars, insulators and tubing. All suggest the intricate technology of the past rather than the streamlined technology we associate with the future. Though this is a retro-futurist technology,[11] we are also told the bomb uses the "many-worlds" hypothesis of quantum mechanics as Dr. Cooper informs Father MacPhail (*AS* 350; *HDM* 793). As technology it seems curiously at odds with itself, when we compare what we see of the device through this representation with the fact that the immense blast of the bomb, which Will luckily manages to divert underground into a different universe, is so great that Lyra and the others still feel its force in the underworld of the dead even though it misses (*AS* 371–374; *HDM* 807–810).

The portrayal of the bomb emphasizes its physical elements: the machine has an elaborate set of components and requires Lyra's actual hair to be present within it. This account of the bomb also includes elements of nineteenth-century gothic, as one end of the machine is connected by cables to two mesh cages separated by the guillotine which will allow the severance of the human victim from their daemon (*AS* 363; *HDM* 800–801). Fatally, Father MacPhail triggers the guillotine which separates him from his unfortunate daemon and thus unleashes the bomb's full power, in a theatrical, suitably amateur and improvised fashion by bringing the "two wires together with a spark" (*AS* 368; *HDM* 805). Were it not for the fact that we have become so used to seeing technology in Lyra's earth which reminds us of the past, from the Victorian and Edwardian periods in particular, we might find this description surprising: how can such an old-fashioned looking weapon yet be so devastating and sophisticated? The report of the bomb seems less *Star Trek* than "Steam Trek."

The sublimity achieved through this thrilling scene is that of Edmund Burke's sense in his treatise *A Philosophical Enquiry into the Origin of Our Ideas of the Sublime and Beautiful* (1756). Here the sublime is something which brings forth both fear and consequently pleasure in the human subject. The scene's calculated affect upon the reader lie both in Pullman's use of a traditionally sublime setting (the mountaintop generating station in Switzerland, the obscurity caused by driving wind and rain during the night which impedes Mrs. Coulter's vision), and by the complexity, size and power of the bomb, presented more as if it were a kind of huge and complex infernal machine than state of the art futurist technology.

To accompany this enormous technology, a zeppelin,[12] that the party had originally traveled in to Saint-Jean-les-Eaux, towers overhead throughout: "the great ribbed belly of the zeppelin bulked over the bomb, straining at its cables in the wind, its silver sides running with moisture" (AS 366; HDM 803). If the bomb almost looks like something put together using do it yourself technology ("there was the lock of hair: held between rubber bands in a metal clasp" [AS 367; HDM 804]) we might ask how this incredible feat of genetic tracking is possible, when Lyra's world apparently lacks computers? Lyra suggests this in The Subtle Knife when she is so surprised to discover what she calls Mary Malone's engine, that is to say the project's computer integrated with the shadow particle detector and she tells the police from Special Branch that her father lacks such an "engine with the words on the screen" (SK 158; HDM 409).[13]

Lyra's Earth, however, is not ours and to a considerable extent, it is a dystopia which we would suggest is imagined by Pullman using the tropes and language of steampunk and Victoriana and the retro-futurist technology which so often signals the two genres, as much as by the conventions of fantasy that also exist in the book (witches, angels, daemons and so forth). The apparently retro-technology shown in the description of the unnamed bomb suggests an appeal to a fear and admiration of the physicality of the machines and devices of the long nineteenth century, akin to that which Margaret P. Ratt (2006) locates in the manifesto-like editorial of Steampunk Magazine: "We love machines we can see, feel and fear. We are amazed by artifacts but unimpressed by 'high technology.'" When Asriel presents information to the Jordan College scholars he does so using what at first seems much like a Victorian style magic lantern show as the device needs to be pumped by hand and the device is significantly called a projecting lantern, but it in fact shows photograms, which seem essentially similar to our concept of photographic slides rather than magic lantern slides which were hand drawn and colored (NL 20–24; HDM 16–18).

The bomb as we have suggested is as physically tangible and visible as any fan of steampunk could ask for, despite its seeming high technology. As Rebecca Onion (2008) has argued very cogently, the mechanical contraptions of steampunk such as zeppelins and steam-powered robots and computers represent a distinctly anti-modernist desire to embrace "the affective value of the material world of the nineteenth century" (2008, 150–151), in contrast to what is seen as the abstract technology of today. As Onion (2008) suggests, the more organic-looking contraptions of steampunk possess sublimity determined around the twin markers of intricacy of design and sheer magnitude, which was so important to views of nineteenth-century industrialism. Father MacPhail and Dr. Cooper's bomb is both intricate and immense as is emphasized in Pullman's language in the scene; but is also simultaneously humanized insofar as Mrs. Coulter, her daemon and Lord Roke can hope to stop it from reaching its target Lyra, by purely physical means alone in terms of either removing Lyra's hair, or else by preventing Father MacPhail from successfully separating from his daemon.

This dystopic aspect of the technology in *His Dark Materials* can be contrasted usefully with one of the most celebrated steampunk novels, Bruce Sterling and William Gibson's *The Difference Engine* (1990) which unlike many is also an example of alternate history. In this case due to Charles Babbage's success in creating a steam-powered mechanical computer (the difference engine of the title, which was planned by the real Babbage but never constructed), the British Empire became in the nineteenth century far more powerful and dominant on the world stage than in historical reality. While this leads in *The Difference Engine* to social changes such as the dominance of a new pro-Industrial pro-bourgeois political party, it represents finally a techno-determinist view that society is primarily the product of technology, rather than that technology depends upon social innovations to become available and taken up by society. While the alternate history of *The Difference Engine* does have an effect on the world's geo-political organization, not unlike the case of Lyra's world, it certainly does not retard the growing bourgeois and forces of capitalism as is the case in her parallel Earth.

For Sterling and Gibson it is the economic and military success of the revitalized British Empire as occasioned by Babbage's computers that affects and prevents the rise to global dominance of the Unites States of America as well as other European powers. However, for Pullman in what is admittedly only a sketchy history in the trilogy, the United States of America never comes to exist in Lyra's world (instead we have New Denmark, which includes a separate country called Texas). We are informed Calvin shifted the seat of the Papacy to Geneva, and the Papacy itself was then dissolved after Calvin's death in favor of the competing theocratic forces that make up the Magisterium, unifying as it does Catholicism and Protestantism. We assume that there is consequently no unique Protestant ideology to create the ideological drive necessary for American exceptionalism to thrive and flourish and to create its own identity. In this respect the divergence from our historical timeline in Lyra's Earth occurs far earlier that the Victorian period and within the sixteenth century.

Another example of this use of steampunk tropes is the machine Lord Asriel uses at the end of *Northern Lights* to build the bridge between worlds of the multi-verse. It's powered just like the bomb by the *intercision* of a child, Lyra's friend Roger, and triggered by the power of the Aurora Borealis. This is a scene whose depiction plays on the strong sublimity of the staggering natural setting, but combines with the retro-futurist technology of an amateur's Victorian science laboratory and the image of a nineteenth century scientific adventurer, clad in heavy furs and driving a dog sledge:

> Fifty yards away in the starlight Lord Asriel was twisting together two wires that led to his upturned sledge, on which stood a row of batteries and jars and pieces of apparatus, already frosted with crystals of cold. [... as] Lord Asriel connected his wires, the Aurora blazed all of a sudden into brilliant life. Like the long finger of blinding power that plays between two terminals, except that this was a thousand miles high and ten thousand miles long: dipping, soaring, undulating, glowing, a cataract of glory [*NL* 391–392; *HDM* 237–238].

Asriel is himself portrayed as an example (as we see above) of the Victorian adventurer-explorer-scientist on whom steampunk texts so often focus; a single-minded amateur whose startling ambition is nothing less than to kill the Authority and destroy the Church across all worlds. Like the characters we often find in nineteenth century science fiction, he is presented as possessed of self-belief and an indomitable will, to the point of obsession. Lyra thinks he is mad at one point and his snow leopard daemon, Stelmaria, symbolizes his "proud," fiercely solitary, "beautiful" and "deadly" nature (*NL* 377; *HDM* 277). We should also remember that Asriel will be shown to be a child-killer in the first book, when he separates the unfortunate Roger from his daemon. However, he is also a long time friend to the Gyptians, several of whose children he once saved from drowning in the floods of '53 (*NL* 136–137; *HDM* 101), which suggests he is more of an ambivalent and complex anti-hero than is common in typical scientific romances or Edisonades of the Victorian era.

Lord Asriel has an appropriate setting for his experiments and preparations against the Authority: his fortress is described as an amazing technological marvel and a hive of industry, while its description recalls the tropes of traditional sublime images of fantasy and mythology. As Ruta Skadi tells the other witches: "Sisters it is the greatest castle you can imagine — ramparts of basalt, rearing to the skies, with wide roads coming from every direction, and on them cargoes of gunpowder, of food of armor-plate" (*SK* 282; *HDM* 495). Later, Mrs. Coulter sees the armory of the fortress, where in an atmosphere thick with sumptuous fumes she sees gigantic hammers "flattening baulks of iron the size of tree trunks" to make weapons and the "brilliant, seething flood" of a river of molten metal that is entering moulds (*AS* 224–225; *HDM* 705).

Re-interpreting steampunk and Victoriana:
Pullman's use of magic

Pullman's usage of steampunk and Victoriana is perhaps best thought of as a unique and sophisticated re-interpretation of these genres within the design of the trilogy as a whole and it is significant that he uses the genre conventions almost exclusively in the account of Lyra's alternative Earth in the present, and not for these other worlds. Lyra's world is not in fact set in the actual past (as is common in both steampunk text and neo–Victorian historical fiction), but rather in the present. It is worth remembering that the four principal other Earths of Pullman's multi-verse in *His Dark Materials* (our contemporary Earth, the world of the *mulefa*, the underworld of the dead and the city of Cittàgazze) are not presented in terms of any noticeable Victorian or steampunk tropes or conventions.

In Lyra's alternate Earth there are no aircraft, we see instead Victorian and Edwardian-style zeppelins and gas-powered balloons (in the case of Lee Scoresby) as the predominant means of transport, and while these employ heavy machine guns these seem of late nineteenth century or world war one vintage rather than their modern equivalents. The soldiers that appear, like their Victorian forerunners, lack modern automatic assault rifles and depend instead on their bolt action guns.[14] Such tropes certainly suggest the steampunk genre, as we have seen in the case of the bomb, but Lyra's world directly parallels our late twentieth century society in certain ways despite such archaic uses of technology. We learn, for example, that Lyra's world surprisingly has the capacity for distinctly twentieth-century innovations: such as atomic weapons (called "atom-craft" in Lyra's world). Experimental physics in our world does exist in a fashion in Lyra's worlds and is called "experimental theology" in her theocratic society but seems to be much the same in terms of its subject matter; so for instance, our world's dark matter, which Mary Malone and her team are investigating, has become Dust and is reinterpreted by the all powerful Church as the evidence of original sin (*NL* 370–378; *HDM* 272–278).

Sometimes the situation is further complicated by what seems to be magical and fantastic elements that are mixed in with the retro-futurist technology. In this regard Pullman's creation of Lyra's world is similar to other authors who have combined steampunk elements with fantasy ones,[15] but, in this case, Pullman also draws on religious, mythological and literary traditions (for instance in terms of the angels or Gallivespians) in a practice that is different because it is more explicitly intertextual, spans a variety of worlds and has such a strong dystopic vision at its core in comparison to other steampunk fantasy writers.

As we have already suggested as Lyra's world seems to lack any computers, it is hard to see how such technologies as the bomb designed by Dr. Cooper are possible and even more so how it can lock onto Lyra via her hair follicle's genetic material, especially in another world of the multi-verse such as the world of the dead? But here there is perhaps more than a hint of traditional witchcraft and magic (in which an object connected to a person traditionally yields some power over that person) mixed in with the science in the process of this device.[16] Technology in Lyra's world is a curious hybrid between that of the retro-futurist technology of the steampunk and Victoriana genres based on the long nineteenth century with technology now available in our contemporary world, but differently named and constructed. Pullman complicates this further with artifacts which add a considerable element of the magical to these, already hybrid, Victoriana constructs. For example, consider the clockwork and mechanized spirit (thus a kind of magical cyborg) in the shape of a beetle that attacks Lyra on the Gyptians' ship in *Northern Lights*, but which is powered by a spell-bound spirit rather than any conventional source of power. "There's a clockwork running in there, and pinned to the spring of it, there's a bad spirit with a spell through its hearts" (*NL* 156; *HDM* 115).

Along with the ubiquitous steam power, clockwork is another significant trope sometimes found in steampunk.[17] In the context of steampunk and its display of archaic technological devices the significance of the alethiometer as a tool for answering truthfully seemingly impossible questions and predicting future events, combined with Lyra's capacity to interpret these while she is a child, also represents a striking transformation of the conventions of the steampunk genre (*NL* 74; *HDM* 55). Not only is the device disruptive of the borders between scientific technology and magic (since we do not know exactly how it works to answer the questions put to it, although Lyra recognizes it is due to communication with Dust), the means of operation of the device suggest occult rather than scientific practices: such as reading the Tarot pack which also uses a multiplicity of signs whose rearrangements alter the possible meanings of an individual reading. The instrument's complex iconography of myth and legend shows its Renaissance origins, which is confirmed by the witch consul, Dr. Lanselius, as having been made in seventeenth-century Prague and he also claims that it was an object originally designed for astrological purposes to discern the influences of the planets (*NL* 173; *HDM* 128). While certainly archaic technology, the alethiometer is clearly not derived from that of the Victorian period and instead takes us back to the early modern period before science and technology as we know it separated distinctly from investigations of the magical. It is linked as an object to Will's subtle knife which he becomes the bearer of in the second volume of *His Dark Materials* which was created some three hundred years before the events of the trilogy and thus once again has pre–Victorian origins in the seventeenth century, though this time in an alternate Earth which resembles a continuation of the Italian Renaissance.

The knife was made by the masters of the Guild of the Torre degli Angeli and obtained by Will after single combat in the Tower of Angels in the city of Cittàgazze; the knife has the ability to cut through anything, as well as the ability to cut windows between worlds within the multi-verse. A highly ambivalent tool at best, it is to be the weapon that offers salvation to the cause of those who rebel against the Authority by being the means by which the Authority will be freed from the 'crystal cell' in which he is imprisoned and allowed to dissipate gratefully into the world (*AS* 432; *HDM* 848). It is also the tool which will allow an exit to be cut from the world of the dead which Lyra and Will visit in *The Amber Spyglass* therefore freeing those imprisoned there (*AS* 381–382 ; *HDM* 813–814).[18] However, we also discover the knife is the means by which the Spectres of indifference came to enter the world in which Cittàgazze is located and to terrorize and destroy the adult population (*SK* 196; *HDM* 435). Coupled with this later revelation, Lyra also recognizes that the blade has the same constitution and color as the blade of the guillotine used to separate daemons from their children in the first book of the trilogy (*SK* 190; *HDM* 431). This ambivalence is evident when Lyra consults the alethiometer at Iorek's request, prior to his repairing the broken knife for her and Will, and it tells her how the knife can do either harm or good, held in a delicate balance by the intentions of the bearer (*AS* 192; *HDM* 682).

The idea that a blade which is formed of matter and thus is at the molecular level could be able to cut through such things is both an indication of a retro-futurist orientation similar to that of Lyra's world towards physical objects and a hint of the possibility of some kind of magical force as opposed to science. While the work that produced the subtle knife began as a scientific enquiry into the bonds of the smallest particles, it appears as having consistently magical qualities because of its ability to cut pathways between the various worlds of the multi-verse and to be possessed of intentions of its own, as first Giacomo Paradisi suggests (*SK* 189; *HDM* 430) and then Iorek Byrnison confirms (*AS* 190; *HDM* 681).

Sometimes the relationship between the conventions of science and magic seems to shift into reverse, as for instance in the description of the mysterious Intention Craft which Lord Asriel's forces invent and which seems a physical counterpart to Dr. Cooper's bomb intended to kill Lyra. This is a mechanical object and one whose method of operation and propulsion is obscure and mystifying which might suggest magic: "there was no sound of an engine, no hint of how it was held against gravity. It simply hung in the air" (*AS* 227; *HDM* 707). However, its description is as much an example of steampunk tropes as the bomb. It appears to Mrs. Coulter when she first sees it as having a cockpit like a "complex drilling apparatus [...] or, the cabin of a massive crane" and furthermore: "[i]t stood on six legs, each jointed and sprung at a different angle to the body, so that it seemed both energetic and ungainly; and the body itself was a mass of pipework, cylinders, pistons, coiled cables, switchgear and valves and gauges" (*AS* 227; *HDM* 706). Later on when it is tested against an airborne raiding part of Metatron's army it destroys the entire party with smooth efficiency: "a series of nearly silent flashes lit the mountainside, accompanied by short hisses like the escape of steam" (*AS* 229; *HDM* 707–708).

The classic site of steampunk: London

London is a central location and setting for steampunk, Victoriana and mainstream neo–Victorian historical texts and the imaginative world of *His Dark Materials*. There are a number of reasons for this and in terms of steampunk in particular they are worth exploring. First and foremost it is because nineteenth century London was so important as a site of modernity, both in terms of its ever-spiraling size as a globalized city at the heart of the world's largest Empire, and because it underscored the connection between the rise of the bourgeoisie and the capitalist mode of production, technological innovations and the social problems caused by these same aspects. As Lawrence Phillips has shown (2007), there are a varied range of literary representations of the city which became quickly mythologized as both exhilarating utopia and dismal dystopia. In this sense, part of the discourse of the representation of London that developed in the poetry of the Romantic period was that of the sublime based not upon nature but in terms of the city itself, as sign of excessiveness that could awe the individual (see Spaar, 2009). Science fiction too as a medium was drawn to represent London as the city that seemed to represent sprawling, speeding, excessive, chaotic modernity and thus the possibility of the future, as Darko Suvin has explored (1983). Consequently, we can see why as Andrew Milner (2004) argues, cities and the fabric of the urban have so often served as the means by which the logic of utopias and dystopias have been worked out in the genre of science fiction: in one sense steampunk writers are returning to the prototype world city, London.

For steampunk then it becomes clear why Victorian or early Edwardian London are so important as a talismanic space they wish to re-present and revisit, as the metropolis serves as the specific ground zero of modernity. Yet, at the same time, nineteenth-century London also offers a place where Romantic individualism was still more important and possible. Additionally, machines still had all the physicality of steam, gears and a mechanical life. This can be contrasted with the futuristic digital metropolis of cyberpunk usually found in the form of newer cities such as Los Angeles, a reshaped Tokyo or more recently Shanghai. Peter Nicholls also points to an ambivalence that the largely American writers of steampunk feel towards the moment of Victorian London:

> Victorian London has come to stand for one of those turning points in history where things can go one way or the other, a turning point peculiarly relevant to SF itself. It was a city of industry, science and technology where the modern world was being

born, and a claustrophobic city of nightmare where the cost of this growth was registered in filth and squalor [1995, 1161].

In particular London offers the possibility of alternating between dystopia and utopia, which Nicholls sees as a door largely opened by one of the greatest London writers and shapers of the city's imaginative life in a combined mode of fantastic/ realistic literary representations: Charles Dickens. As Jeremy Tambling (2008) has argued, the task of writing London is crucial to understanding Dickens' creative *oeuvre* and its significance. Although Nicholls (who is cited with approval at length by Goss 2007), may go too far in arguing for Dickens as the progenitor of steampunk, he does have a point about the value of Dickens' dystopic vision of the city and we would add this is equally true for the mainstream literary writers involved in critical, neo–Victorian historical novels, as it is for the grittier examples of steampunk.

Pullman's depictions of Lyra's alternate Earth's London borrows many of the tropes from more dystopic steampunk views of Victorian London, but in terms of his work as a whole, such dark and Dickensian representations of the metropolis can be found earlier in the realist Sally Lockhart series. Sally's experience of Victoriana is matched by the description of Lyra's world's Limehouse, from where Tony Marakios with his drunken mother and mixed immigrant heritage will be kidnapped in *Northern Lights*. The reader reaches Limehouse after a long sweeping description of the river journey down the Thames from Oxford to London. We are reminded how Lyra's world is different from ours as the description progresses: the river just as the Thames was in Victorian times is still thronged with boat traffic unlike the river of today's London, in this case corn-tankers and brick-barges. The Elizabethan magician Dr. Dee's mansion still stands at Mortlake rather than having been burnt down and destroyed, Falkeshall (an older name for today's Vauxhall) still has its eighteenth-century pleasure gardens and they were not built upon by early nineteenth century property developers, and White Hall Palace has not burned down and been replaced by Whitehall, and is still the seat of the King and his Council of State.

However Limehouse is still Limehouse, much the same now as it was in the Victorian period in our world: "the river, wide and filthy now, swings in a great curve to the south [... Tony] wanders through the market, between the old-clothes stalls, and the fortune-paper stalls, the fruit-mongers and the friend -fish sellers" (*NL* 41; *HDM* 30). The docks and their river traffic has managed to not only survive but to prosper, unlike in our own contemporary London. There seems to have been no equivalent of the Clean Air Act of 1956 in Lyra's London and this helps to give it a sense of its Victorian forerunner. Lord Byron had memorably described Don Juan's arrival in the metropolis, sailing up the Thames in the early nineteenth century and seeing London as a "mighty mass of brick and smoke" (1999). Byron's portrayal thereby emphasizes the qualities of the city as at once sublime and rampantly industrialization. This industrial sublime of the machine age is at once alarming and worthy of awe because of what human manufacturing and trade can achieve. Lyra sees her world's London with her outsider's view as something much the same and Pullman may indeed be alluding to Byron's famous portrayal as he remarks: "murky London air laden with fumes and soot and clangourous with noise" (*NL* 100; *HDM* 74).

Lyra's London we are told, still has tramcars and canals that form a significant mode of transport as they did in the Victorian period and there are "great gaunt factories behind wire fences," as well as, "endless streets of little identical brick houses, with gardens only big enough for a dustbin" (*NL* 102; *HDM* 76). This makes London sound more like one of the northern industrial cities such as Manchester and suggests that industrialization in Lyra's London is still in many ways following a nineteenth century model, the city has not been remade into a more modern twentieth century city to meet the needs of an increasing bourgeoisie, much less the desires of a more affluent working-class. London in *His Dark Materials* is in fact repeatedly described as an old-fashioned and labyrinthine city, where street lighting seems less common than in the contemporary world despite the availability of *anbaric* (electric) power, leading Lyra to perceive the city as composed of: "dark alleys [that] all around were alive with movement and secret life and she knew none of it" (*NL* 99; *HDM* 74). This description perhaps recalls a London even earlier than the Victorian period and the 1762 decision to ban trade signs in London for reasons of safety to passers-by and to introduce street numbering as a more coherent alternative, an action that was reinforced by the subsequent Paving Acts in 1766 and 1768.[19] Movement within Lyra's London, as she is seeking to avoid detection by Mrs. Coulter, is constrained by the need to avoid discovery, but concealment is made much easier by the layout and size of streets compared to our real contemporary London: "She walked quickly away from the river, because the Embankment[20] was wide and well-lit. There was a tangle of narrow streets between there and the Royal Arctic Institute, which was the only place Lyra was sure of being able to find, and into that dark maze she hurried now" (*NL* 99; *HDM* 74).

In contrast, Mrs. Coulter's flat is on London's Embankment itself echoing the great palaces of the English aristocracy that existed along the Whitehall stretch of the Thames during the early modern period, but which had largely disappeared by the late Victorian period. Presumably, Mrs. Coulter's home is within the older aristocratic environs of Westminster and closer to the seat of the King's government in White Hall place (there is significantly no mention of the Houses of Parliament in *His Dark Materials*). The dividing line between the seat of royal power at Westminster and the City of London does not seem to have become blurred as began to happen in the nineteenth century in our own world, but has instead remained much as it was in the earlier era.

Conclusion

The representation of Lyra's London and indeed the entirety of her steampunk-influenced world is not a result of technological determinism, but rather it takes the form of a dystopic novum.[21] As Adam Roberts suggests, for a reader the: "systematic working out of the consequences of a difference and differences, of a novum or nova, becomes the strength of the mode" (2005, 7). Tom Moylan has suggested that dystopias can provide ample force for novums that work politically to provide estrangement through a "utopian pessimism" and in providing examples where: "social conditions are explained in terms of the material processes of history" (2000, 63). In the case of Pullman's creation of Lyra's world, this would be an accurate appraisal, since for all the attractiveness of the steampunk-aligned world that we see, it is a world which points continually to severe social and political retardation which we as readers are meant to acknowledge and learn from. *His Dark Materials* also counterpoints its pessimistic dystopia against the successful possibility of change and activity and the transformation of its steampunk influenced dystopia into a human-centered utopia of the future: the Republic of Heaven where the sentient beings of the multi-verse will strives to represent a new way of living and at that point in the trilogy's architecture, it would seem that steampunk and the neo–Victorian has been left behind.

NOTES

1. See Steven Barfield's chapter in the present volume for a discussion of Pullman and science fiction.

2. Pullman writes Victoriana having already used the Victorian period to locate the Sally Lockhart series; he's also penned a comic series of two historical neo–Victorian novels, *Thunderbolt's Waxwork* (1994) and *The Gasfitter's Ball* (1995). Their descriptions and lifestyle inform the depiction of Lyra's rough but rowdy gang of young children in the Oxford scenes in *Northern Lights* (36–37; *HDM* 26–27).

3. This is where technology is put into use within the dime store magazines of the day often featuring gentlemen scientist-inventor-tinkerers, exemplified by Garrett Serviss' *Edison's Conquest of Mars* (1898).

4. One zeppelin is destroyed by a lightning bolt from the storm that the shaman John Parry conjures up (*SK* 298; *HDM* 506); a second airship is ruined when its pilot succumbs to a Spectre of indifference that the shaman convinces to float up and attack him in his cabin and which leads to the machine crashing into a rock scarp (*SK* 305; *HDM* 511); a third crashes after John Parry's daemon, the osprey Sayan Kötör, brings all the birds of the forest into action to obscure the pilot's vision and damage the zeppelin's gas envelope, which in turn led to a fatal crash into another rocky scarp (*SK* 307–308; *HDM* 512); the fourth is grounded by a single rifle shot from Scoresby at the beginning of his stand against the Muscovite troops which damages the engine mount and is then devastated by a further shot fired by the dying Scoresby at the stranded, hydrogen-filled behemoth (*SK* 318; *HDM* 520).

5. In cyberpunk, dystopic and high-technology near futures based around the growth of computing technology and cyberspace saw the genre linked successfully to more general theorisations of postmodernism and it became quickly regarded by more mainstream literary theorists as a powerful and critically reflective account of the way the future might look. See for example discussions by the following: Richard Kadrey and Larry McCaffery (1991); George

Slusser and Tom Shippey (1992); Dani Cavallaro (2000); Graham J. Murphy and Sherryl Vint (2010).

6. See Goss (2006), Nevins (2008), and Pagliasotti (2009a).

7. This is a world described in detail in Nevins' exhaustive *The Encyclopedia of Fantastic Victoriana* (2005).

8. See, for example, Christian Gutleben (2001), and Cora Kaplan (2009).

9. Significantly, Lyra's world is much less populated than ours; for instance, she is shocked by how populous our world's Oxford is and how international the inhabitants are.

10. The device seems modeled in its action on the way that a thermonuclear bomb using fusion requires a nuclear bomb using fission as a detonator (*AS* 351; *HDM* 793).

11. This is technology based on speculations about the future as though it was portrayed in the past, and seems more fitting to the laboratory of a nineteenth-century fictional scientist, like Victor von Frankenstein or Dr. Jekyll.

12. This is, according to Rebecca Onion (2008, 160), one of the dominant tropes of steampunk as genre. This occurs also in one of the earlier and now recognized progenitors of the steampunk genre in Michael Moorcock's novel *The Warlord of the Air* (1971; see Nevins (2008, 3)). With its zeppelins and Edwardian pastiche it also offers a critique of Victorian imperialism and imperial values. Moorcock's novel, while critical of Empire, is not driven by the contemporary critical force explicit in Pullman's vision of the social and human consequences of what a theocratic dystopian world driven by all pervasive religious fundamentalism might be like; as religious fundamentalism, unlike the historical British Empire, seems to be engaged in a strong contemporary global revival.

13. "Engine" perhaps refers to Charles Babbage's plans for a steam powered difference engine which would have been an early computer if it had been built. The use of the term may also allude to Bruce Sterling and William Gibson's *The Difference Engine* (1990), which is often regarded as one of the earliest steampunk novels.

14. See, for example, the battle of Alamo Gulch between Scoresby and the Muscovite Imperial Guard at the climatic conclusion of *The Subtle Knife*.

15. See, for example, China Miéville's *Perdido Street Station* (2003) or Stephen Hunt's alternate world Victorian-based fantasy books for young adults, such as *The Court of the Air* (2007).

16. For this use of magic see, for example, the spell performed by the witches to try to heal Will's wounded hand at the end of *The Subtle Knife* (*SK* 266–269; *HDM* 484–486).

17. See, for instance, the short story "Mother of the Dispossessed: A Winter's Seasonal Tale Designed to Educate and Illustrate" in *Steampunk Magazine* ("Mother of," 2006, 11–19), Jay Lake's novel, *Mainspring* (2007), his short story "The God Clown is Near" (2008, 97–106) and S.M. Peter's *The Whitechapel Gods* (2008).

18. Pullman's phrase alludes perhaps to William Blake's poem "the crystal cabinet" and its fantastic and uncanny depiction of a parallel world inside the cabinet which is apposite to the multi-verse of the trilogy as a whole (see Wu 2005, 244–245).

19. See Emily Cockayne (2007, 180–185) and Roy Porter (2000, 122–128).

20. In *His Dark Materials* (American version) the Embankment is spelt with a lower case letter which suggests a generic physical feature rather than a specific location. The Embankment in London is an area of land reclamation (achieved in the nineteenth century) which runs alongside the Thames river but which includes a number of prestigious buildings and landmarks.

21. Can be defined as historically new, extraordinary and radically different from the author and reader's actual and lived environment (Suvin 1979). For an extended discussion of novum see Steven Barfield's essay on science fiction in this present volume.

WORKS CITED

Achebe, Chinua. 2006. *Things Fall Apart*. Harmondsworth: Penguin Classics.

Barfield, Steven, and Lisa Russ Spaar. 2009. "'Eternal London Haunts Us Still': Thirteen Contemporary Poets Reflect on London as Muse." *Literary London: Interdisciplinary Studies in the Representation of London*. 7.2. Accessed February 1, 2010. *http://www.literarylondon.org-/london-journal/russ.html*.

Barnes, Julian. 2006. *Arthur and George*. London and New York: Vintage.

Blake, William. 2005. "The Crystal Cabinet." In *Romanticism: An Anthology*, 3d ed. Ed. Duncan Wu. Oxford: Blackwell, 244.

Botting, Fred. 2008. "'Monsters of the Imagination': Gothic, Science, Fiction." In *A Companion to Science Fiction*. Ed. David Seed. Oxford: Blackwell, 111–127.

Bowler, Alexia L., and Jessica Cox. 2010. "Introduction to Adapting the Nineteenth Century: Revisiting, Revising and Rewriting the Past." In *Neo-Victorian Studies*. 2:2 (Winter): 1–17. Accessed January, 10 2010. *http://www.neovictorianstudies.com/*.

Burke, Edmund. 2008. *A Philosophical Enquiry into the Origin of Our Ideas of the Sublime and Beautiful*. London: Routledge.

Byron, Lord George. 1999. *Don Juan*. Boston: Adamant Media.

Carey, Peter. 1998. *Jack Maggs*. London: Faber and Faber.

Catastrophone Orchestra and Arts Collective (NYC). 2006. "What, Then, Is Steampunk? Colonizing the Past So We Can Dream the Future." *Steampunk Magazine* 1 (Fall): 4–5.

Cavallaro, Dani. 2000. *Cyberpunk and Cyberculture: Science Fiction and the Work of William Gibson*. London: Athlone.

Clute, John, and Roz Kaveney. 1999. "Gaslight Romance." In *The Encyclopedia of Fantasy*, rev. ed. Ed. John Clute and John Grant. New York: St. Martin's Griffin, 390–391.

Cockayne, Emily. 2007. *Hubbub: Filth, Noise, and Stench in England, 1600–1770*. New Haven: Yale University Press.

Dickens, Charles. 2004. *Great Expectations*. Harmondsworth: Penguin.

Forster, E.M. 2005. *A Passage to India*. Harmondsworth: Penguin.

Goss, Cory. 2006. "Varieties of Steampunk Experience." *Steampunk Magazine* 1 (Fall): 60–63.

_____. 2007. "A History of Misapplied *Technology*: Exploring the History of the Steampunk Genre." *Steampunk Magazine* 2 (Summer): 54–61.

Gutleben, Christian. 2001. *Nostalgic Postmodernism: The Victorian Tradition and the Contemporary British Novel*. Amsterdam: Rodopi.

Hunt, Stephen. 2007. *The Court of the Air*. London: Harper Voyager.

Hutcheon, Linda. 1988. *A Poetics of Postmodernism: History, Theory, Fiction*. London: Routledge.

Kadrey, Richard, and Larry McCaffer. n.d. "Cyber Punk 101: A Schematic Guide to Storming the Reality Studio." In *Storming the Reality Studio: A Casebook of Cyberpunk and Postmodern Science Fiction*. Ed. Larry McCaffery and Richard Kadrey. Durham: Duke University Press.

Kaplan, Cora. 2007. *Victoriana: Histories, Fictions Criticisms*. Edinburgh: Edinburgh University Press.

Klaw, Rick. 2008. "The Steam Driven Time Machine: A Pop Culture Survey." In *Steampunk*. Eds. Ann VanderMeer and Jeff VanderMeer. San Francisco, CA: Tachyon, 348–359.

Lake, Jay. 2007. *Mainspring*. New York: Tor.

_____. 2008. "The God Clown Is Near." In *Steampunk*. Eds. Ann VanderMeer and Jeff VanderMeer. San Francisco, CA: Tachyon, 97–106.

McCaffery Larry, and Richard Kadrey, eds. 1991. *Storming the Reality Studio: A Casebook of Cyberpunk and Postmodern Science Fiction*. Durham: Duke University Press.

Miéville, China. 2003. *Perdido Street Station*. New York: Del Rey.

Milner, Andrew. 2004. "Darker Cities: Urban Dystopia and Science Fiction Cinema." *International Journal of Cultural Studies*, 7. 3, 259–279.

Moorcock, Michael. 1974. *The Warlord of the Air*. London: Quartet.

"Mother of the Dispossessed: A Winter's Seasonal Tale Designed to Educate and Illustrate." 2006. In *SteamPunk* 1: 11–19.

Moylan, Tom. 2000. "Look into the Dark: Dystopia and the Novum." In *Learning from Other Worlds: Estrangement, Cognition, and the Politics of Science Fiction and Utopia*. Ed. Patrick Parrinder. Liverpool: Liverpool University Press, 51–72.

Murphy, Graham J., and Sherryl Vint, eds. 2010. *Beyond Cyberpunk: New Critical Perspectives*. London: Routledge.

Nevins, Jess. 2005. *The Encyclopedia of Fantastic Victoriana*. Austin: MonkeyBrain.

_____. 2008. "The Nineteenth Century Roots of Steampunk." In *Steampunk*. Ed. Ann VanderMeer and Jeff VanderMeer. San Francisco: CA: Tachyon, 3–13.

Nicholls, Peter. 1995. "Steampunk." In *The Encyclopedia of Science Fiction*. Ed. Peter Nicholls and John Clute, 1161. New York: St. Martin's.

Onion, Rebecca. 2008. "Reclaiming the Machine: An Introductory Look at Steampunk in Everyday Practice." *Neo Victorian Studies* 1:1 (Autumn): 138–163, accessed January 21, 2010. *http://www.neovictorianstudies.com/*.

Pagliassotti. Dru. 2009a. "Does Steampunk Have Politics?" *The Mark of Ashen Wings.* Accessed March 1, 2009. *http://drupagliassotti.com/2009/02/11/does-steampunk-have-politics/*.

_____. 2009b. "Does Steampunk Have an Ideology?" *The Mark of Ashen Wings.* Accessed March 1, 2009. *http://ashenwings.com/marks/2009/02/13/does-steampunk-have-an-ideology/*.

Peters, S.M. 2008. *The Whitechapel Gods.* New York: Rok.

Phillips, Lawrence, ed. 2007 *A Mighty Mass of Brick and Smoke: Victorian and Edwardian Representations of London.* Amsterdam: Rodopi.

Porter, Roy. 2000. *London: A Social History.* Harmondsworth: Penguin.

Pullman, Philip. 1996. *Thunderbolt's Waxwork.* Harmondsworth: Puffin.

_____. 1998. *The Gasfitter's Ball.* Harmondsworth: Puffin.

_____. 2006. *The Ruby in the Smoke.* London: Scholastic.

Ratt, Margaret P. 2006. "Putting the Punk Back Into SteamPunk." *SteamPunk* 1 (Fall): 2.

Roberts, Adam. 2005. *Science Fiction: The New Critical Idiom,* 2d ed. London: Routledge.

Scott, Paul. 2007a. *Raj Quartet I: The Jewel in the Crown, the Day of the Scorpion.* London: Everyman.

_____. 2007b. *Raj Quartet 2: The Towers of Silence, a Division of the Spoils.* London: Everyman.

Selvon, Sam. 2006. *The Lonely Londoners.* Harmondsworth: Penguin Classics.

Slusser, George, and Tom Shippey. 1992. *Fiction 2000: Cyberpunk and the Future of Narrativ.* Athens: University of Georgia Press.

Sterling, Bruce, and William Gibson. 1996. *The Difference Engine.* London: Gollancz.

Suvin, Darko. 1979. *Metamorphoses of Science Fiction: On the Poetics and History of a Literary Genre.* New Haven: Yale University Press.

Suvin, Darko. 1983. *Victorian Science Fiction in the UK: The Discourses of Power and Knowledge.* Boston, MA: G. K. Hall.

Tambling, Jeremy. 2008. *Going Astray: Dickens and London.* London: Longman.

VanderMeer, Ann, and Jeff VanderMeer, eds. 2008. *Steampunk.* San Francisco: Tachyon.

Waters, Sarah. 2002. *Fingersmith.* London: Virago.

6

Revisiting the Colonial: Victorian Orphans and Postcolonial Perspectives

LAURA PETERS

Introduction

In his concluding remarks to *His Dark Materials* Philip Pullman acknowledges three literary debts, *On the Marionette Theatre* by Heinrich von Kleist, John Milton's *Paradise Lost*, and the works of William Blake. Not surprisingly, exploring the relationship between the novels of *His Dark Materials* trilogy, Milton and Blake has garnered significant critical attention. In identifying such a literary influence, Pullman distances himself from the tradition of Oxford-based writers such as the Inklings, a group which included J.R.R. Tolkien and C.S. Lewis, objecting to attitudes implicit in their work:

> Well I passionately disagree with [Tolkien's comments]. The physical world is our home, this is where we live, we're not creatures from somewhere else or in exile. This is our home and we have to make our homes here and understand that we are physical too, we are material creatures, we are born and we will die [Pullman 2002a].

Although critical of the Inklings, Pullman's own acknowledgment to *The Amber Sypglass*, "I have stolen ideas from every book I have ever read," highlights the complex web of intertextuality in and surrounding *His Dark Materials* within English Literary tradition beyond the more obvious examples.

As can be seen elsewhere in this collection, Pullman's narrative is continuously in dialogue with both John Milton's *Paradise Lost* and William Blake's revision of it. But Pullman is in dialogue with other literature beyond these examples throughout the trilogy. Through his engagement with past literary tradition

Pullman searches out "fresh streams of story" (Pullman 2002b) to offer a solution based on an "interrelated module of art, identity and ethics" (Shohet 2005). Pullman's indebtedness to Victorian narratives and contexts is apparent throughout *His Dark Materials*. Despite Pullman's admission of widespread indebtedness, little work has been done to explore the specifically Victorian influences on Pullman's thinking beyond considerations with regard to Lewis Caroll and *Alice and Wonderland*. I will argue that Pullman revisits the nineteenth century to narrate the legacy of the problems with which we are confronted today.

One of the central problems Pullman addresses is the result of imperial expansion, and its relationship to system of orientalism as outlined by the literary critic Edward Said in his work *Orientalism*. Orientalism, Said argues (Said 1978, 7), is never far from an "idea" of Europe in which the idea of such a European identity is viewed as superior to non–European identities. Pullman directly addresses the notions of racial and cultural difference underlying such assumptions in his work in order to expose not only the hegemony of orientalism but also the hegemony of the largely European church whose legacy is to denigrate life on earth. To turn to the Victorians for Pullman is a way of critically considering the relationship between our world and theirs and in particular the legacy of Empire and stereotyping of non–Western others. Neither straightforward historical fiction set in the past nor "historiographic metafiction"as outlined by Linda Hutcheon (where such novels are typically both self-reflexive and also document historical events and real people); Lyra's neo–Victorian world that is an alternative to our own allows certain key ideas of the period to be investigated in terms of the legacy they may have for the present.

Accordingly, I will be exploring a context that might at first seem unexpected: the dynamic relationship between Pullman's epic trilogy and children's literature written about orphans and the more general significance of the figure of the orphan in the post–Romantic Victorian period more generally. While neither Lyra and Will are orphans in the usual sense (though Lyra becomes so over the course of the trilogy) they do conform to some of the stereotypes of the Victorian orphan; in particular, Lyra's journey from supposed orphan to the discover of her parents and a reappraisal of her situation. It is true that many children's books as well as fairy stories and folk tales feature orphaned protagonists; from Lucy Maud Montgomery's Anne in *Anne of Green Gables* to Dorothy in L. Frank Baum's *The Wizard of Oz* to J.K. Rowling's Harry Potter. As Melanie Kimball (1999) has suggested, this is in part because such a plot event at the beginning of these narratives allows adventures to occur without the hindrance of parents and for the reader to see the child growing up and becoming independent and self-reliant in their attitude to the world around them.

Both Lyra and Will are in nuanced ways something like the classic orphan figures of such texts. Lyra thinks she is an orphan when *Northern Lights* begins (as does the reader) and that her uncle Lord Asriel has placed her in the care of Jordan College until she becomes an adult. Much later in the trilogy we discover that in fact Lord Asriel and Mrs. Coulter are indeed her parents, but in effect she has been brought up as if she is an orphan with all the resourcefulness and independence that we might expect. While Ma Costa nursed her when young, she was given too quickly to the bemused scholars of Jordan College who did what they could but failed to provide the nurturing and comforting protection of a parent. She herself suggests as much: "I just grew up on my own, really; I don't remember anyone ever holding me or cuddling me, it was just me and Pan as far back as I can go" (*AS* 194, *HDM* 684). Will has lost his father, the explorer John Parry who has been lost on a mysterious expedition to the North Pole. While he has been brought up by his mother and is therefore technically a child of a single parent rather than an orphan, his mother's mental illness has led to him to becoming her primary carer, rather than her looking after him and thus in a sense he has suffered a kind of orphaning because of this deprivation. Will remarks that: "his mother, after all, had not protected him; he had had to protect her" (*AS* 149, *HDM* 653).

Revising the tropes of Victorian orphanhood

Pullman's trilogy revisits the triple decker format of publishing made popular in the nineteenth century, expanding it from three discreet volumes to an extension of the narrative over three volumes. One of the best known of the triple decker publications was that written with contributions from Currer, Ellis and Acton Bell (the Brontë sisters), namely *Jane Eyre*, *Wuthering Heights*, and *The Tenant of Wildfell Hall*. Two of these narratives within this triple decker, published in 1848 the year of widespread European revolutions and unrest, tell of orphan figures who rebel against the established authority of the family, class and religion. By breaking rules and social taboos, these texts (and especially the orphan figures within them) keep rebellion against tradition alive. It is the trope of orphanhood central to Victorian culture that interests Pullman. But, what did the orphan figure represent in Victorian culture? In a society organised around familial identification which established name, genealogy, social place and a fixed, rooted home, the orphan was a liminal figure outside of this space. There were endless efforts to recuperate the orphan figure in order to reinforce the familial structure. The central paradox was that the orphan was often the *product* of social structures such as the workhouse with its enforced separation of parents and children. As a figure outside the family structure, the orphan embodies ambivalence. Though problematic, the orphan simultaneously offers endless possibilities for reinvention and social mobility. Alongside this, in its rootless state, the orphan became a powerful metaphor for racial and cultural difference found both within Victorian society, in the form of the Traveling and Jewish communities, and in empire. The most popular mode of narrating the orphan, the adventure of romance, lends itself to the narrative that Pullman has to tell.

While one could argue that the Victorian interest in the orphan figure arose out of its valorization of the family as social structure and imperial metaphor, Pullman's work highlights the same fragmentary social structures and problematic families producing orphans. This figure was an attractive target for proselytizing Victorian Evangelical efforts, taking the form of cheap popular tracts and various impetuses for conversion and social reform. Pullman's engagement with the orphan figure is not a coincidence; Pullman contests the moralizing, reforming and patronizing impulse of the Evangelicals in his larger argument with the controlling nature of organised religious establishments and their life-denying teachings.

These Victorian evangelical publications traced their own genealogy to Hannah More's tracts and the tracts of the Cheap Repository which first started publishing, significantly, in March 1795 during the turbulent decade of revolution which characterized much of the Romantic literature. One could argue that these publications sought to nullify the revolutionary tendencies of the working-class. These tracts were written to influence popular culture in order to prevent perceived moral degeneration and to reinvigorate the ties of "hierarchy and dependence between rich and poor" by stressing the importance of order and hierarchy within the family (Pederson 1995, 94). Pullman resists this controlling impetus, reversing the structure in *His Dark Materials*: Lyra Belacqua's family is the site of destruction and disorder; it is Lyra who tries to liberate children and reunite families throughout the narrative. Rather than the upper classes patronizing and reforming the poor, it is the skills Lyra learns while running wild in Oxford with the children of the poor and the Gyptians that prove vital in the battle for the salvation of the world. Similarly, Will Parry's longing for his father, "as a lost child yearns for home" highlights his lack of home (*SK* 321; *HDM* 523). Yet the narrative is ambivalent: contrary to Victorian Evangelical assumptions, home for working-class Will was a place where he gave and received nurture. Forced to abandon this nurturing home, Will becomes "wild outside [...] and wild within" (*SK* 331; *HDM* 529). Will's powerful memories of his mother making him feel safe sitting "on his bed in the dark, singing nursery rhymes, telling him stories" in her "dear voice" (*AS* 194; *HDM* 684) is in stark contrast to aristocratic Lyra who has never known a mother's love. In the cave it is made clear that the accomplished Mrs. Coulter does not even know the words to the simplest lullabies, yet her attempts to care for Lyra mediate her cruel image and poor parenting.

Rather than reaffirming the family unit, Pullman's narrative requires both Lyra and Will to embrace their (metaphorical) orphanhood in order to accomplish their quest; the family has to be sacrificed. Coulter suffers the pain of separation from Lyra like an intercision, "tearing" at her heart (*AS* 169; *HDM* 667) as Lyra rejects her mother. Ultimately, Lyra's bad parents Asriel and Coulter sacrifice themselves to save her, "to give Lyra time to find her daemon, and then time to live and grow up" (*AS* 426; *HDM* 844). Likewise, in order to succeed, Will orphans himself by forgetting about his mother: "If you want to succeed in this task, you must no longer think about your mother. You must put her aside. If your mind is divided, the knife will break" (*AS* 204; *HDM* 690–691). Both Lyra and Will can only achieve their quest outside the family.

The nature of the orphan is multi-faceted in Victorian literature. The legacy of Romanticism throughout Victorian culture informs the suggestive power of this figure; the orphan held a special place within the Romantic conception of childhood which invested it with a holy power. As one immersed in Romanticism, Pullman would not have missed the possibilities embodied by the orphan figure resonating throughout the Victorian period. In William Wordsworth's Ode, "Intimations of Immortality from Recollections of Early Childhood," the orphan arrives "trailing clouds of glory" (in Wu 2005, 539, l. 64) and in possession of considerable creative and redemptive power. "Mighty Prophet! Seer blest!" (in Wu 2005, 540, l. 114). Pullman draws on this literary inheritance: he represents this visionary ability figuratively, Lyra's unique ability to read the alethiometer intuitively and Will's possession of the knife. As children, Lyra and Will are immune to family-destroying spectres who create "spectre-orphans" (*SK* 142; *HDM* 398). They are unique in their fates: Lyra as both Eve and the "final weapon" (*SK* 287; *HDM* 499); and Will as savior, who has "a task that is greater than [... he] can imagine" (*SK* 334; *HDM* 531).

Returning to Wordsworth, this spiritual nature, manifested most strongly in the child who was fresh from the Creator, progressively diminished throughout adolescence until it disappeared in adulthood: "The Youth, who daily farther from the east / Must travel, still is Nature's Priest, [...]. At length the Man perceives it die away, / And fade into the light of common day" (Wu, 2005, 539, ll.71–6). For Pullman this pattern is the natural progression into adolescence with its accompanying development of sexuality underlying his conceptualisation of Dust; it is a natural and inevitable movement but one which Pullman feels the Church represses as evidence of fallen nature.

Pullman is attracted to the freedom from the "prison-house" (Wu 2005, 539, l. 67) that, according to Wordsworth, the child, particularly the orphan possesses. This sense of individual freedom, as a defining characteristic of the Romantic child and of the artist, became increasingly important during the course of Victorian literature as the orphan figure, the outcast, as seen in Wordsworth's autobiographical epic poem, *The Prelude: The Growth of a Poet's Mind,* at times embodied the redemptive power and personal freedom of the child/Poet. Book I of *The Prelude* shows a striking image of the Rousseauesque child protagonist, the young Wordswoth, running freely in nature, amid the hills of the lake district; easily as wild and barbaric as Lyra is when we first encounter her in *Northern Lights*. He hangs from the crags to rob birds nests and further on in Book I, he even steals a skiff for a joy ride, only to be chased by his guilty conscience in the shape of the looming sublimity of a mountain (Wordsworth 1996, 54, Book I, ll. 320–350; and Wordsworth 1996, 58, Book I, ll. 394–427). Like Lyra the protagonist of *The Prelude*, Wordsworth as young child, is a great storyteller and while he lives a solitary life in nature as opposed to Lyra's more sociable life with her friend Roger; neither seem much unencumbered by adult concerns such as going to school. As Wordsworth reminds us later he will become a literal orphan which still at school: "Ere I to school returned / That dreary time, ere I had been ten days / A dweller in my father's house, he died, / And I and my two brother (orphans then)" (Wordsworth 1996, 484, Book XI, ll. 363–366). Wordsworth later makes the linkage between young poet and presumably pagan priests of the tribe, it is his reverence for nature that is at stake here as that is the temple in which he worships and where he will serve: "Poetic numbers came / Spontaneously, and cloth'd in priestly robe / My spirit, thus singled out, as it might seem, / For holy services" (Wordsworth 1996, 38, Book I, ll. 60–3) The Poet's task then is to transcribe for others the vision that he has the ability to perceive. Both Lyra and Will are similarly chosen for their tasks: Lyra's role has been the subject of witches' prophecy and she has an intuitive ability to read the alethiometer, while the knife chooses Will to be its bearer, marking him accordingly. Like Wordsworth, Pullman's focus is partly on the self: the spirituality of the self; and the self in nature extending to contemporary concerns about the environment. For the Victorians, the orphan emerges as the metaphor for the detached self whose "solitude energises him as a visionary artist" and whose "orphanhood becomes his glory" (Auerbach 1975, 395, 404).

Pullman uses this figure and its Romantic inheritance to develop a new heroic. Complimentary to each other, Will and Lyra work with the armored bear King Iorek Brynison to forge the knife. They both undertake the ultimate in self-sacrifice in denying their daemons (though Will's is not yet visual), in their journey to the land of the dead; in return they share the authority over the whole mass of the dead and over the narrative (see *AS* and *HDM:* "The Harpies" chapter). Lyra gathers in children for nurture, and they both fulfill the role of redeemer leading the dead to the promised land, although in this case the promised land is a return to the elements of which the universe is made up. This is an inversion of the child emigration schemes in *Northern Lights* which Coulter plays a key role as head of the General Oblation Board (with the evangelical and purifying connotations of the organization's name); gathering up what the Victorians termed street arabs, waifs and strays, Lyra now leads the children, but this time to happiness, renewal, and harmony rather than intercision and the life-denying doctrines of the Church: "This child has come offering us a way out and I'm going to follow her" (*AS* 336; *HDM* 783). Will and Lyra's orphanhood is the required self-sacrifice that the children make.

However, like the popular Victorian orphan narrative, Lizzie Bowen's *Cared For; Or the Orphan Wanderers* (1881), which narrates the journey of the two central orphan figures, Philip and Susie Arnold, from the Australian periphery to an English centre which does welcome returning migrants, Lyra and Will have become true orphans with no home to return to; they cannot be reintegrated.

> "Mmm," said Will. "D'you think *we'll* ever go home?"
> "Dunno. I don't suppose I've got a home anyway. They probably couldn't have me back at Jordan College, and I can't live with the bears or the witches. Maybe I could live with the gyptians" [*AS* 482; *HDM* 883].
> Will: "when I go back I'll be made to go into some kind of institution."
> "No! Like an orphanage?" [*AS* 486; *HDM* 886].

Ironically, in a narrative that emphasizes the importance to live in one's place, Will and Lyra discover on their return to their respective worlds that they do not have a home: Lyra's days running free in Jordan College are over; Will's mother is ill and needs to be taken into care.

Pullman is also aware of the life-denying doctrines of the Church, at play within the Victorian trope of the orphan. The Calvinistic doctrine which viewed children as born evil, in need of firm instruction in order to develop into moral adulthood, contested the Romantic legacy celebrating childhood and the status of orphanhood. Both these trends inform Pullman's narrative: pervasive throughout is a celebration of the naturalness of children and the wild, unfettered time running through the canals and streets of Oxford; the General Oblation Board with its excoriation of adolescence as the moment of sexuality seeks the most repressive instruction, intercision, in order to tame the wild spirit, to "suppress and control every natural impulse" (*SK* 52; *HDM* 336). The narrative puts forth the argument that to rebel against the Church (the Authority) was right and just given the "cruelties and horrors all committed in the name of the Authority, all designed to destroy the joys and the truthfulness of life" (*SK* 283; *HDM* 496) to perpetuate the belief that the world was made of "foulness, betrayal, and lassitude" (*SK* 329; *HDM* 528).

Home and abroad: Locating the Victorian orphan

In addition to debates over the nature of childhood, the family and larger debates surrounding Evolution and Creationism, there was a wider social context in which to view children, particularly orphans in Victorian times. From the fledgling scheme of the Board of Guardians of Marylebone in 1850, ruled illegal by an inquiry in 1851, orphan children were emigrated out to empire in increasing numbers, initially by Boards of Guardians responsible for their care and eventually through an increasing number of schemes. In 1870, two philanthropic women, Miss Rye and Miss Macpherson started a scheme to address the burgeoning numbers of homeless and ragged children, specifically targetting "street arabs," the children of costermongers and street traders, "waifs and strays" and "gutter children." Macpherson and Rye were also sanctioned to emigrate pauper children by the Poor Law Board.[1] By 1879 an Act of Parliament was passed empowering the Boards of Guardians "to subscribe to any Association or Society for aiding boys and girls in service." Emigration was seen as a solution to a burgeoning urban social problem in Victorian times, the orphan population comprised some sixty per cent of the population of the reformatories. Estimates of how many orphan children were to be found amongst the burgeoning number of street children of urban areas are imprecise, but most agree there were thousands. The destiny of a large number of orphan children, including a number of workhouse orphans, to become criminals is a testament to the neglect suffered by many of these children.

In *The Workhouse Orphan*, the pamphlet written in response to the 1860 Committee of Inquiry on Education the author, in reviewing the current state of the New Poor Law provision, argues that the institutions for the care of the poor, particularly the orphan children of the poor, are still failing in their duty. Orphan children living on the street were most likely to be criminalized both by need and by association. Once on the street the author argues "they were all lost characters; old in vice, though still young in years" (Workhouse Orphan 1861, 10). The subsequent criminalization of the orphaned children of the poor generated a sense of social failure within Victorian culture. However, the emigration schemes were dodged with controversy from the beginning. It was unclear whether all the children emigrated were in fact orphans; if they were not, it was unclear whether the required parental consent was obtained. The overriding image of the two ladies, Macpherson and Rye, and later Mrs. Louisa Birt, Miss Macpherson's younger sister, rounding up children on the streets and shipping them abroad informs the image of Coulter rounding up children off the streets and shipping them to Bolvangar. Ironically, her own daughter, Lyra is represented as a savage, what Maude Hines terms "a street urchin in the tradition of Dickens and Alger" (Hines 2005, 36–8) resisting her mother's belated attempts to civilize her.

In the Victorian discourse of the street arab and the criminal, the orphan figure came to embody a threatening difference. With the expansion of empire, this difference took on racial and colonial overtones. In using the orphan to represent difference, Victorian society replicates colonial and orientalist discourses in the construction of notions of civilisation and savagery identifiable within the orphan adventure narratives. Peter Buchan's *The Orphan Sailor: A Tragic Tale of Love, of Pity, and of Woe* (1834), whose main character William is of the impoverished migrant street population, perpetuates gendered discourses of civilisation, patriotism and imperialism, deeply masculinist in their emphasis. Pullman challenges this gendered emphasis by placing Lyra in a format which often relied on a masculine heroic. In *The Orphan Sailor* the victimized and enslaved orphan has ample opportunity to display inherent qualities such as bravery, daring and resourcefulness.[2] In the tale, the orphan William is taken prisoner by Algerian pirates and is sold as a slave in Algiers. After a series of tragedies, William ultimately remains "friendless and forlorn." In *His Dark Materials*, instead of battling barbarous pirates, Lyra battles fierce Tartars, the General Oblation Board, witches, armoured bears, and her parents. Although the foreign enemy is as fierce and savage as found in the Victorian narratives, *ut infra* the real savagery lies within Lyra's own family and culture. At this moment it is possible to situate Pullman's project within an orientalist tradition, yet Pullman works to subvert this tradition from within reversing the conceptual binary of opposition between civilisation and barbary. Pullman's setting is not the heat of Victorian imperial expansion into Africa, Asia and the South Pacific, but rather the extreme cold of the North. The threat of being sold as a slave permeates the children's stories, as well as the threat of being eaten by Tartars. Unlike the solitary, forlorn William, Lyra always has Pan: together they enter the new worlds.

The opening of the second volume, *The Suble Knife*, introduces Will by evoking the popular Boy's Own narratives[3] of the nineteenth century:

John Parry has been a handsome man, a brave and clever officer of the Royal Marines, who had left the army to become an explorer and lead expeditions to remote parts of the world. Will thrilled to hear about this. No father could be more exciting than an explorer. From then on, in all his games he had an invisible companion: he and his father were together hacking through the jungle, shading their eyes to gaze out across stormy seas from the deck of their schooner, holding up a torch to decipher mysterious inscriptions in a bat-infested cave.... They were the best of friends, they saved each other's life countless times, they laughed and talked together over campfires long into the night. [...] All his games were going to come true. His father was alive, lost somewhere in the wild, and he was going to rescue him and take up his mantle.... It was worth living a difficult life, if you had a great aim like that [*SK* 10; *HDM* 307–308].

Not only is Will's introduction reminiscent of *Boy's Own* stories, but his search for his soldier/explorer father echoes the real-life search parties sent out to find the missing naval hero and explorer Sir John Franklin during the 1850s which were covered extensively in the print media at the time. Both Frankin and Parry disappeared while trying to uncover the mysteries of the North. The disappearance of John Parry was also covered in the newspapers and the subject of endless search parties, but for a different reason, the mystery he was trying to uncover would pose fundamental challenges to life as one knew it.

Other Victorian orphan narratives represent an idealised return to a pastoral existence as a response to the problems caused by expanding urbanization.

Charles Wall's *The Orphan's Isle* (1838) is an example of such a pastoral retreat depicting a timeless and unchanging society. In *The Orphan's Isle* the ship-wrecked middle-class orphans (as opposed to being sold into slavery or labour-ing onboard ship), live with the indigenous people on the orphan's isle. In this pastoral landscape, the orphans are instructed by the natives and ultimately are re-assimilated back into society. Such a retreat becomes essential to ensure the proper education that has been lost in the pressing urban conditions. This use of pastoral retreat combined with the construction of difference to be dis-cussed next, is a way of understanding Lyra's excursion with the Gyptians.

Orphans: Ethnicity, race and nationhood

One of the strategies used to construct difference within these Victorian popular orphan narratives is the association of the orphan figure with traveling peoples (gypsies) who, by their lifestyle, disrupt certain notions of rootedness, family, home, Christianity and nationhood. In this strand of writing, the orphan is linked, however tenuously, to traveling peoples, in an exploration of a mar-ginalized difference within Victorian society articulating difference through racial, ethnic and sectarian terms such as that found in Mootoo's (pseudonym*)* *The Orphan: A Romance* (1850). *The Orphan: A Romance* is about the life of Squire Hawthorn's son who is sold to Gypsies by the Squire's evil brother in order that Caleb may claim the family inheritance. The tale narrates the child's life with these gypsies. When the old Gypsy Reginald finally confesses to what has taken place, the orphan is restored to his rightful family estate and inher-itance. There are several things to note. The narrative in its consideration of the life of the orphan with the Gypsies works to establish the traveling peoples and their culture as "other": the Gypsies are constructed as savage heathens and demo-nized as a corrupting threat to the "civilized" members of society as represented by their willingness to work with corrupt elements within the mainstream society to destroy the family unit by subverting the line of familial succession.

The Gypsies have no hesitation in purchasing or even stealing children away from their families; yet paradoxically having worked to destroy one family, the gypsies form another by raising the child as their own. The Gypsies are represented as barbarous and corrupt but they work in conjunction with truly corrupt and barbarous elements within the society — in the figure of the uncle willing to sell his nephew in order to steal his inheritance. The root of the threat is twofold. The existence of the Gypsies within (albeit on the margins of) Victorian England and the racialised difference they embody poses uncom-fortable problems for the construction of Victorian society as a family. Home-lessness and a traveling lifestyle disrupt a family narrative and established social structures. But even more difficult for this construction is the existence within the heart of this society of elements, like the uncle, who seek to disrupt the family narrative, do not respect the bonds of family, and display traits antithetical to the civilised values which the society used to distinguish itself from other barbarous cultures. The allegorical project of this romance is most clearly identifiable in the figure of the orphan child who retains the essential qualities of purity and morality claimed by the society as its own civilised nature even while being raised by Gypsies. The retention of such traits allows this child to assume his rightful inheritance espousing the values of rootedness, family, and Christianity — all component values of the English subject.

Thus in Victorian popular culture Gypsies, by virtue of their traveling lifestyles, posed problems for notions of home, place and eventually civilization the key criteria of which depended on specific notions of rootedness. Furthermore, gypsies embodied a direct threat to the notion of the family as they were, rather stereotypically, associated with child-stealing and hence the destruction of the family. Gypsies also embody the racial difference found within Victorian society which needed to be excluded according to the logic of racism; they existed in a marginalised fashion. While these three modes of narration testifies to anxieties about belonging and foreignness as related to home, class, and national identity, Pullman's narration of Will and Lyra does not display the same anxious probing of these concepts. Rather Pullman inverts the orientalist premises underlying these Victorian discourses.

Lyra's time with the Gyptians (Gypsies or Roma) is more of a pastoral retreat. The nobility found within the so-called barbarous savages instructs Lyra. Lyra receives nurture from Ma Costa, she learns of her past and family from John Faa, she learns about her power to read the alethiometer from Farder Coram. In Pullman's narrative, it is the spectres not the Gyptians who destroy families and create orphans; the spectres are orphans themselves, orphans of the abyss. In a telling moment, the spectres are under the command of Coulter, the Church's representative. One could conclude that it is the Church destroying the very family that it claims to espouse.

In *Northern Lights* Lyra's time with the Gyptians challenges this popular representation of gypsies. First, Lyra is saved from the grasp of actual child-stealers, Turk traders, who capture Lyra as she is fleeing from the grasp of the other child-stealers, Coulter and the Gobblers. In *His Dark Materials* racial difference is embodied primarily from those outside of the culture, Turks, yet the threat to the family is posed equally between various elements. There are foreigners, Tartars depicted as cannibals who eat children, the society itself (in the form of Coulter, the General Oblation Board and the Church) and the family, Coulter is Lyra's mother while Asriel, who kills Roger, is her father. In Victorian times the threat to the family was partly posed by the state and its representatives under the guise of the child emigration schemes. Along the lines of Macpherson and Rye in the 1870s, Coulter and the Gobblers operate their own child emigration schemes with the consent of the state, "the landloper police and the clergy. Every power on land is helping 'em" (*NL* 116; *HDM* 86); they "reach out by night and pluck little children out the hearts of their families"(*NL* 135; *HDM* 100). Although here emigrating the children is not the primary objective of the Board as they have a more simister motive. Gyptian children are stolen as well; the Gypsies are not the child-stealers but the child-losers in this narrative whose families have been "hit worse" (*NL* 110; *HDM* 82) by the Gobblers. The villians are not part of any specific racial grouping, when Lyra sees the face of the man purchasing her at Bolvangar she describes him as "not a Samoyed or a Tartar. He could have been a Jordan Scholar" (*NL* 238; *HDM* 175).

As in Victorian narratives, the Gyptians live in a marginalised fashion, but in *Northern Lights* Pullman takes the reader into the heart of the Gyptian community gathering at the Fens and on the excursion to the North; it is a representation which gives voice to the community and its structures in a way that Victorian narratives do not. It shows the humanity of the culture and its own civilization denied to the gypsies in Victorian culture. Yet Pullman weaves enough of the Victorian assumptions together for recognition to challenge these very assumptions through his detailed and sympathetic representation of the community. Legacies of old social order are still apparent, the gyptian community still exists uneasily: it has no recourse to law or the courts and its membership is both exclusive and excluded. Their central homeland is indeterminate in its composition, it is part-land, part-water situated on the margins of inhabitable land, and in its definition, it mingles "indistinguishably" with seas and other lands. The wild nature of the Fens provides safety for the gyptian muster. The fact that the Fens has never been settled at all identifies it as other and unknowable, the difference within once more. The police can only operate on the margins of the Fens. Lyra is denied membership in the Gyptian community on account of her being "a fire-person" in contrast to the Gyptians who are "water people" (*NL* 113; *HDM* 84).

Elaborating the contradictions within Victorian popular culture, in *Northern Lights* it is this gyptian community which best embodies the family values. Prior to Lyra's orphanhood, Ma Costa nurtured her, hiding her from Mr. Coulter's murderous rage. It is the Gyptian community that took an interest in Lyra's life. Ma Costa is denied guardianship of the child by both the courts who do not value the Gyptian community and by the implicit message of the trilogy that one sticks to one's own kind. Even the earth-preserving love of Will and Lyra cannot overcome the narrative's injunction to live in one's own world. Lyra's strong evocative memories of home are "to see Ma Costa's broad arms, to smell the friendly smells of fish and cooking that enfolded you in her presence" (*NL* 346; *HDM* 255). The Gyptian community organises a rescue expedition to free all the children which requires all the valor, knowledge and resources possessed by the community. After first rescuing Lyra from the Turk traders and indirectly from Coulter, Lyra is welcomed on to the Costa's boat with real affection. She learns the truth of her parentage, and subsequent abandonment, from the Gyptians. She was metaphorically orphaned, a foundling removed from the grasp of the Church and placed into the hands of the Scholars. Here Pullman draws on the tradition of narrating the foundling in Victorian culture; the best known example given Pullman's place within an Oxford tradition of writers, is the ancient Oxford legend, *The Orphan; The Foundling; Abiah* (1643), reprinted in 1842 by Leapidge Smith under the title *Abiah, Or, The Record of a Foundling* in order to raise money for a foundling child discovered in Newgate Market in May 1842.

Pullman uses these traditions in order to highlight the failure of the Church in its duty to children, best exemplified by the General Oblation Board and the experiments at Bolvangar. The emphasis on the rewards to be found in heaven, "A happy home in heaven above, / Safe in the arms of Jesus' love; / Nor sad the little Foundling's story, / Who thus attains a home of glory" (Smith 1842, 9, ll. 15–18), is exactly the life-denying impulse by religion which Pullman attacks. Pullman is firm in his assertion that life has to be lived now, on earth. Pullman's evocation of Lyra's foundling status challenges the impetus of the Oxford legend, Abiah, the underlying assumption of which is the embrace of the orphaned and foundling children by God and the Church. In Victorian culture the ideal of the family was the spiritual one, with God the patriarch and all Christians part of the same family. In Pullman's narrative, the Church poses the largest threat to the family and to children.

Pullman evokes the Victorian orientalist assumptions regarding race and difference in order to deconstruct them. The real evil and savagery lies within those identified as Europeans rather than in the racialised others: "dangerous as the Tartars were, far more dangerous were the adults of Bolvangar" (*NL* 293; *HDM* 215). Added to this, Coulter imports bad practices from the south in a way which demonstrates that evil is widespread; intercision, circumcision and castration all conflate together as horrors perpetuated by religion throughout the world. "She's travelled in Africa, for instance. The Africans have a way of making a slave call a zombi. It has no will of its own; it will work day and night without ever running away or complaining. It looks like a corpse." Equally chilling is the "horrible phantoms they have in the Northern Forests" (*NL* 375; *HDM* 276). Ruta Skadi, from the North, is "mysterious" and "uncanny" (*SK* 51; *HDM* 335). At times, the North is demonised in the narrative but there is slippage around the sense of otherness. Will and Lyra are foreign wherever they go, as orphans they find no home, no family, no belonging anywhere. Ultimately, they unknowingly adopt the custom/ritual of others, such as voluntarily separating from their daemons in order save the world; the solutions to the global crisis are to be found in a number of cultures.

Intriguingly, while some African troops are zombies, King Ongunwe and his troops offer the best hope for Will and Lyra's survival. Magnificent warriers, King Ongunwe and his troops offer an example of civilization at its highest when he assures Mrs. Coulter that he and the Heavenly Republic's many troops from so many varied worlds are not colonialists they "haven't come to conquer, but to build" (*AS* 222; *HDM* 703). It is pertinent that Lord Asriel respects the African King Ongunwe enough to give him one of the key command roles in his campaign. This isn't then a narrative of reverse colonization and degeneration, a prevalent fear in late–Victorian writing, rather it is about building something new. The narrative offers both a confidence in one's own identity and an acceptance of difference:

> And now we've been travelling [...]. I've learned that there are some people who don't seem to have daemons, like Will doesn't, and I was scared till I found out they were just ordinary like me really. So maybe that's why someone from your world might be just a bit sort of nervous, when they see us, if you think we're different [*AS* 272; *HDM* 737].

Finally, it is in the company of the Gyptians that Lyra is able to develop not only her ability to read the alethiometer but also to tell stories.

The legacy of the storyteller

Lyra's characterisation of storyteller, visionary, poet, priest of tribe draws on the legacy of the Romantic conception of childhood in Victorian culture which informs Pullman's work, the best example of which is the witches' prophecy which Dr. Lanselius relates to Farder Coram:

> The witches have talked about this child for centuries past [...] they hear immortal whispers from time to time [...] they have spoken of a child such as this, who has a great destiny but that can only be fulfilled elsewhere — not in this world, but far beyond. Without this child, we shall all die. So the witches say. But she must fulfil this destiny in ignorance of what she is doing, because only in her ignorance can we be saved [*NL* 175–176; *HDM* 130].

The linkage Pullman develops is not only the inherent innocence of the child and the radical potential of this to change the established order, but the connection outlined previously between salvation and creativity, particularly storytelling. Pullman continually highlights the link between storytelling and deception, as "Lyra and liar were one and the same thing" (*AS* 308; *HDM* 763). The power of storytelling is "intoxicating" to Lyra who holds Iofur, "the great bear [...] helpless" (*NL* 343; *HDM* 253) earning her new name "Lyra Silvertongue" (*NL* 348; *HDM* 257). Lyra's power lies in her storytelling: it starts off as lies but through experience and knowledge deepens to a storytelling gift, an ability which is redemptive. Tialys castigates Lyra as a "thoughtless insolent child" (*AS* 178; *HDM* 672)[4] to whom "fantasy comes so easy," so that her "whole nature is riddled with dishonesty" (*AS* 280; *HDM* 743). Ultimately, it is only by telling true stories that salvation can occur. It is of no coincidence that when Lyra loses the ability to lie convincingly she also starts to lose the ability to read the alethiometer: the two are interrelated. Pullman links the power of the imagination (storytelling) a way of seeing (*AS* 535; *HDM* 920) with a visionary ability, reading the alethiometer. What Lyra was able to do by "grace" she can regain by a lifetime of work (*AS* 520; *HDM* 909). The extension of the ability to see through conscious application offers an understanding which is deeper than that which comes freely; there is an important role for rationality in matters of imagination and seeing. Lyra starts to tell powerful, true stories. In doing so, Lyra realizes the importance of good stories, the nourish the soul and help see the best in people rather than the worst.

> "You all listened, [...] why was that?"
> "Because it was true, [...]. Because she spoke the truth. Because it was nourishing. Because it was feeding us. [...] Everyone of these ghosts has a story; every single one that comes down in the future will have true things to tell you about the world.[...] If they live in the world, they *should* see and touch and hear and love and learn things" [*AS* 332–333; 334; *HDM* 781–782].

Lyra's story earns redemption for the dead; the harpies agree to lead them to a part of the land of the dead where Will can cut an exit. In the logic of the narrative, these stories, celebrating the best in people and life on earth, are the key to saving people from the Church's unrelenting narrative that seeks to denigrate life on earth and to see the worst in human nature.

However, Pullman tempers the Romantic cult of childhood. Throughout the trilogy, childhood is narrated as a suggestive moment but the logic of the narrative is always that it must end. Like the Romantic project, Pullman's narrative does encourage the retention of a childhood sensibility in adulthood because it allows adults to perceive that a world can be reimagined and then changed, rather than just to blindly accept the social staus quo. The trial of achieving separation from their respective daemons is part of the maturation process Lyra and Will undergo. When they reunite with their daemons it is in a different way: the daemons then allow the expression of sexual desire. The experiments at Bolvangar are a warning for those who fetishize the innocence of children: in their desire to prevent children from assuming adult consciousness and adult sexuality, Coulter and the Bolvangar project ironically destroy the very curiosity fundamental to the creativity of children.

Conclusion: Pullman's Victorian reimaginings

One can only speculate why Pullman revisits Victorian popular literary culture to address present-day concerns. It is perhaps that within Victorian society he found a time of extreme conditions: industrialisation and the expansion of the urban environment with the subsequent population explosion, poverty and homelessness produced a social crisis; while the expansion of empire produced other challenges, introducing the concept of the global.[5] The Victorian's sense of a world in crisis has as its present-day counterpart the global environmental crisis and interrelated world poverty and famine. Thus Victorian society offers an urban environmental crisis which has expanded from the local to the global today. The desolated landscape of much of Pullman's narrative characterised by floods, landslides, melting Arctic ice, and fraught with danger, testifies to climate change and global warming. The balance of the eco-systems has been lost as the *mulefa* have discovered; the opening into other worlds causes disasters such as global warming. "All the Arctic peoples had been thrown into panic, and so had the animals, not only by the fog and the magnetic variations but by unseasonal crackings of ice and stirrings in the soil" (*SK* 45; *HDM* 331).

Elsewhere in Cittàgazze, a Mediterranean city of great science and learning the greed of scientific endeavour and the Guild's consequent ability to steal from many worlds, released the spectres; the heaven on earth of the city was turned into hell, full of spectres created by the guild members desire for elsewhere. The existing abyss between the worlds is made larger by the man-made bomb unleashed to kill Lyra, threatening to drain consciousness out of the whole universe; the spectres unleashed through man's folly are the uncanny children, orphans, of this very abyss. In Will's instruction to Lyra one finds the basis of Pullman's argument about the environment: "We've got to treat this place *right*" (*SK* 28 author's emphasis; *HDM* 319 no emphasis).

A denigration of the world we live in and the desire for elsewhere is the crux of the difference Pullman has with the teachings of the Church, with all churches. Pullman emphasises the unity of all churches in their desire to "control, destroy, obliterate every good feeling" (*SK* 52; *HDM* 336). In *His Dark Materials*, the General Oblation Board are united by their fear of consciousness, the experience into which innocence transforms. The desire of the Authority to destroy joy and truthfulness highlights the suspect nature of the Authority; Pullman does not seek to consolidate the hegemony and power of the Church and Europe implicit within orientalism, rather Pullman unravels it in the final revelation of the ancient but child-like state of the Authority. The center, lacking in will, cannot hold. Rather it vanishes completely with "a sigh of the most profound and exhausted relief" as the aged Authority simply melts away when freed from his casket by Will and Lyra (*AS* 432; *HDM* 848). The legacy of the Church is destructive, best exemplified in the assassin, Father Gomez, who enlists the help of the most foul and destructive of beings we probably see in the trilogy, the Tualapi. Once Father Gomez is able to show the Tualapi the concept of death and its connection to him, he is confident he has the basis for "a fruitful understanding" based on "fear" (*AS* 389; *HDM*

819). The distorted nature of the Church is made manifest in the view that consciousness, as embodied by the *mulefa*'s use of the seedpods, is satanic and Lyra is the figure of evil. Pullman argues that to rebel is right and just when one considers what the Church's agents did in its name. In essence, Pullman's disagreement, as a storyteller, is with the Church's narrative and the ideology that it puts into this narrative.

The epigragh, from William Blake to Chapter 31 entitled "Authority's End," "for empire is no more" celebrates, perhaps prematurely, the loss of the controlling systems — empire, capitalism, the Church. In order to achieve a post-empire, post-colonial moment Pullman returns to the importance of storytelling in literature and in life. The post-colonial writer has an even greater responsibility. As a guardian of the culture and the values it embodies, the task of the writer is to recover pre-colonial customs and values in order to help forge new ones in opposition to the values imposed by the old colonial masters. Pullman's injunction is to live vital lives; one can only live in the world in which one is born, there is no deferral. The sacrifice required is not for the afterlife but for here and now. Ultimately Will and Lyra need the harpies, the Church-designated tormentors of the dead, to succeed as the central value of the narrative is the value of collaboration and not confrontation. This is embodied in the paradise-on-earth community, the *mulefa* who live a communal lifestyle, working together, in sympathy with the environment rather than imposing on it. The final image of this paradise is one which accepts difference, the people of three worlds break bread together in a new communion which celebrates the here and now. The final voice heard is that of Lyra, the master storyteller. She gets the last word.

NOTES

1. This was not the only scheme emigrating orphans and street arabs to empire. Dr T. Bowman Stephenson, the founder of the National Children's Home and Orphanage, started a scheme in 1873.

2. The historical specificity is that of the Mediterranean under the control of Algerian piracy and the Barbary coast. By orientalizing the Algerians as a barbarous foreign threat to the English, the tale works to justify the English imperial impulse as a civilizing impulse.

3. Pullman acknowledges his awareness and delight in these *Boy's Own* stories in "All This Belongs to Me" (Pullman n.d., n.p.).

4. Tialys repeats this viewpoint when he calls her "a thoughtless, irresponsible, lying child" (*AS* 280; *HDM* 743).

5. In this sense, *His Dark Materials* seems to progress considerably in terms of form and complexity from Pullman's earlier and historical Sally Lockhart novels, which are set directly in the Victorian period, although it should be noted they do address the colonial problems of the period such as the opium trade in *The Ruby In The Smoke* (1985), while also featuring a heroine as the protagonist.

WORKS CITED

Auerbach, Nina. 1975. "Incarnations of the Orphan." *English Literary History* 42: 395–419.

Bowen, C.E. 1881. *Cared For; or the Orphan Wanderers.* London: Partridge.

Buchan, Peter. 1834. *The Orphan Sailor: A Tragic Tale of Love, of Pity, and of Woe.* Edinburgh: Thomas Stevenson.

Hines, Maude. 2005. "Second Nature: Daemons and Ideology in *The Golden Compass.*" In *His Dark Materials Illuminated: Critical Essays on Philip Pullman's Trilogy.* Millicent Lenz with Carole Scott, eds. Detroit: Wayne State University Press, 37–47.

Hutcheon, Linda. 1988. *A Poetics of Postmodernism: History, Theory, Fiction.* London: Routledge.

Kimball, Melanie. 1999. "From Folktales to Fiction: Orphan Characters in Children's Literature." *Library Trends* 47, 3: 558–578.

Mootoo [pseud.]. 1850. *The Orphan; A Romance.* London: Arthur Hall, Virtue, & Co.

Pederson, Susan. 1986. "Hannah More Meets Simple Simon: Tracts, Chapbooks, and Popular Culture in Late Eighteenth-Century England." *Journal of British Studies* 25 (January 1986): 84–113.

_____. 1995. *Family, Dependence, and the Origins of the Welfare State: Britain and France 1914– 1945.* Cambridge: Cambridge University Press.

Peters, Laura. 2000. *Orphan Texts: Victorian Orphans, Culture and Empire.* Manchester and New York: Manchester University Press.

Pullman, Philip. 1985. *The Ruby in the Smoke.* Oxford: Oxford University Press.

_____. 2002a. "Faith and Fantasy." *Radio National Encounter Interview,* March 24, 2002. Accessed October 29, 2010. *http://www.abc.net.au/rn/relig/enc/stories/s510312.htm.*

_____. 2002b. "The 2002 May Hill Arbuthnot Lecture, 'So She Went into the Garden.'" *Journal of Youth Services in Libraries* (JOYS), 15.4, 35–41.

Said, Edward. 1978. *Orientalism.* Harmondsworth: Penguin.

Shohet, Lauren. 2005. "Reading Dark Materials." In *His Dark Materials Illuminated: Critical Essays on Philip Pullman's Trilogy.* Millicent Lenz with Carole Scott, eds. Detroit: Wayne State University Press, 22–36.

Smith, Leapidge. 1842. *Abiah: Or, The Record of a Foundling.* L. Smith, ed. London: n.p.

Wall, Charles. 1838. *The Orphan's Isle; A Tale for Youth, Founded on Facts.* London: W.S. Orr & Co.

Wordsworth, William. 1996. *The Prelude: A Parallel Text,* rev. ed. Jonathan Wordsworth, ed. Harmondsworth: Penguin.

_____. 2005. "Intimations of Immortality from Recollections of Early Childhood." In *Romanticism: An Anthology,* 3d ed. Duncan Wu, ed. Oxford: Blackwell, 538–542.

The Workhouse Orphan. 1861. London: Hatchard.

7

Exploring and Challenging the Lapsarian World of Young Adult Literature: Femininity, Shame, the Gyptians, and Social Class

Nicola Allen

Introduction: Class and selected contemporary children's fiction

This chapter aims to discuss the previously under-represented issue of the link between social class and the concept of lapsarian shame in Philip Pullman's *His Dark Materials*. Lapsarian shame is the Christian idea that human beings, but women in particular, discovered shame about their bodies (such as what it means to be naked), after Adam and Eve's ate from the forbidden tree of knowledge and were consequently expelled from Eden in the Fall. While there may have been gender before the Fall, it is the postlapsarian world in which femininity becomes an important construction. While much has been written concerning the importance of themes such as gender and religion in Pullman's trilogy,[1] Pullman's depiction of social class remains an issue that is not examined at length in critical discussions of the trilogy.

This chapter will situate *His Dark Materials* within the wider context of children's fiction that depicts the movement of a central character between different social classes, and will include a comparison between Pullman's text and the wider body of children's fiction; including, but not limited to, a discussion of the similarities and differences in the treatment of social class that exist between Pullman's trilogy and that found in the works of J. K Rowling (the *Harry Potter* series) and Kevin Crossley-Holland (*Gatty's Tale*). These texts are worthy of interrogation alongside Pullman's since they represent a similar engagement with the theme of social mobility and how such social mobility is engaged in the construction of normative femininity. As Bob Dixon (1977) reminds us in *Catching Them Young 1: Sex, Race and Class in Children's Fiction*, one of the key formative functions of children's literature has always been the didactic one of teaching children how to grown into adults in such a way that they will follow the accepted norms, conventions and prejudices that constitute the ideology of the society they live in. In this case texts often strive through complex narrative negotiations to help form in the child reader appropriate adult attitudes for that individual subject's own social class, race and gender and to those other subjects whom they as they grow up must come to recognize do not share their own particular status. This interiorization of society's power by the subject requires that the individual child subject as it grows up comes to own and indeed actively participate in its own limitation and formation within social constraints. If all such differential subject positions within society are to a large extent performed as differing social identities as Judith Butler (1990) would have it, then the child subject must learn how to carry out a successful performance within the masquerade of social interaction.

These texts are of interest here because the search for, and acquisition of, knowledge forms a vital part of all three novels' treatment of their female characters, thus, to a certain extent allowing each of the heroines to act as ameliorated Eve figures. It is interesting to note that Hermione, who is always top of her class, often saves the lives of the other characters because of her immense knowledge and skill for logical reasoning, is often referred to on fan sites and general (non-academic) reference sites for the text as an overachiever,[2] as though there are unwritten limits to the amount of knowledge that she should attempt to accrue. Potter, who is equally extraordinary, is rarely described in such negative terms. In comparison, Gatty begins *Gatty's Tale* as an illiterate and unschooled peasant farmer's daughter, who is selected to partake as a servant in a pilgrimage to Jerusalem and on the way learns to read and write, and who ultimately realizes that she must now take the lead in gaining acceptance from the people of Caldicot, now that her learning and experience marks her out: "I'm the same but not the same because I seen so much and learned so much" (Crossley-Holland 2006, 372).[3]

Hermione's, Lyra's and Gatty's quests for knowledge sees all three writers attempting to redeem the role of knowledge in the development of their female protagonists/characters which itself marks them out as contemporary texts informed by a notion of female equality with men. But whereas the female protagonists of the *Potter* series and *Gatty's Tale* take a holistic approach and embrace their final feminization,[4] Pullman's trilogy ends equivocally with Lyra refusing to fully take on a feminized body image, and still deciding what to do with the rest of her life. Thus while Hermione's and Gatty's stories can be said to encompass both the successful search for knowledge, each also incorporates the realization that this must be tempered with other qualities, that includes a desire for others both male and female to acknowledge their emergent sense of their own femininity. In Rowling's *The Goblet of Fire*, Hermione can be found reminding Ron that she is female, and wants to be acknowledged as such: "Just because it's taken you three years to notice, Ron, doesn't mean no one else has spotted I'm a girl!" (2007, 25).

Within Pullman's text there is a more complex relationship between the female protagonist and her attitude towards femininity, and this is focused on body image. Mrs. Coulter initially follows the patterns we can find in the *Potter* series and *Gatty's Tale* as an exemplar of femininity as a kind of knowledge, and is thought to be a positive influence by Lyra because she is linked to the search for knowledge. Upon first meeting her, it is this that Lyra finds so attractive, we learn that Lyra "gazed at Mrs. Coulter with awe, and listened rapt and silent to her tales of igloo building, of seal hunting, of negotiating with the Lapland witches" (*NL* 69; *HDM* 51). However, whereas Rowling and Crossley-Holland attempt an overt amelioration of the search for knowledge in female protagonists, Pullman's trilogy exhibits a more complex relationship between the protagonist and the bearers of knowledge. Although Lyra is intrigued by the knowledge that Mrs. Coulter can teach her, Lyra ultimately feels stifled by the demands of Marisa Coulter's adjacent version of femininity, and so rejects this version of the feminine and runs away instead to join the Gyptians. Thus, Pullman's text implies that in order to function as the Eve figure (the Betrayer), Lyra has to both originate from, and ultimately to some extent return to, that bourgeois world, but that she must also experience enough of the Gyptian's freer, less inhibited body image in order to reject the version of femininity that Marisa Coulter first outlines for her in *Northern Lights*.

Constructions of shame and femininity

In order to facilitate an analysis of this process within Pullman's trilogy, and particularly to provide an examination of how *His Dark Materials* relates to the feminine body image expressed in other children's fiction, the chapter will detail the depiction of female characters that might be said to interact with the figure of Eve in some way — particularly the link between social class and the desire (or restraining of the desire) for knowledge (including but not limited to an emergent sexual knowledge) in female protagonists of young adult/teenage fiction. This chapter will examine, in particular, the implied link that Pullman draws between the biblical Fall and issues of social class, and will principally explore the dichotomy between Mrs. Coulter's London set and Pullman's depiction of the "shameless" Gyptians.

The theorists Simone de Beauvoir and Michel Foucault provide an appropriate analytical framework for an analysis of the treatment of the female subject in these texts since, as political theorist Sonia Kruks (1999, n.p.) outlines in her essay, "Panopticism and Shame: Reading Foucault through Beauvoir":

> [the] creative appropriations of Foucault's genealogical methods have enabled feminist scholars to explore the ways in which representations of "woman" have shifted over time. His insights into the inseparability of power and knowledge, and his explorations of the disciplinary practices that produce "subjectified" subjects, have also made his methods a valuable resource for a wide range of feminist analyses of women's subordination.

Thus, this chapter will utilize Kruk's assertion of the value of reading Foucault through de Beauvoir in order to reveal the link between the perpetuation of subjective feminine identities and the way in which shame and particularly concepts of body shame could be used in order to perpetuate restrictive social structures. This will be utilized in this chapter in order to demonstrate that Pullman's text implies a link between feminine body shame and the social structures of Mrs. Coulter's recognizably bourgeois London community which Lyra is invited to learn. Pullman achieves this alignment of body shame with the bourgeois, in part by depicting the traditional femininity of the London female characters. Pullman makes it clear that with *His Dark Materials* Mrs. Coulter's postlapsarian femininity is both based upon a sense of quasi–Christian shame concerning the female form and is correlated to the Magisterium (which believes as a woman she is unequal to men);[5] and therefore is also related broadly to notions of conservatism, reserve and ideological and moral hypocrisy. This is contrasted within the novel with Pullman's fictionalized other space, in the form of the liberated world of the Gyptians, which is reminiscent in certain of its aspects of historically fictional representations of the British working class.

The Gyptians, a fictional ethnic group whose lifestyle and name are analogous with the original English name for the Roma, Gypsies, Egyptians or Gyptians,[6] are depicted very much within a tradition of fictionalized (sentimental) and positive representations of the working class in much literature and culture. They have a tightly knit community, a travelling lifestyle, identifiable use of a rich and non-standard colloquial language and a romanticized sense of verve, humor and localized, participative democracy[7] all of which help to situate them within this sentimental tradition of how the Roma and the working-class are often represented in a positive fashion. Abby Bardi (2006) in comparing Victorian and modernist representations of the Roma in British literature has drawn attention to how when the Gypsy is represented in a more positive way by twentieth-century writers such as D.H. Lawrence and Virginia Woolf.[8] They function as images of social and sexual liberation because they are at the margins of society and associated with non-normative social practices towards sexuality, work and marriage. As discussed in Deborah Epstein Nord's

Gypsies and the British Imagination, 1807–1930 (2006), while the Romantic representations of the Roma were often more positive than in much popular culture of the time, they simultaneously created the Gypsy as a stereotype of wild and primitivist society, who lived at the margins and therefore offered an innocence and spontaneity which bourgeois civilization had lost. In keeping with the more positive Romantic and modernist tradition, the Gyptians in *His Dark Materials* prove to be a spiritually and emotionally fulfilling force for Lyra, providing her with a liberating space in which to critically assess her situation, and in which to shed the demands of conformity to the feminine ideal and live a baser existence that is freer from the concept of shame.

This is not an entirely new literary trope by any means in either children's or adult literature and children's literature in particular often shows an ambivalence towards the figure of the Gypsy ranging between negative and positive stereotypes (see Binns, 1982). As Jessica Duchen (2008, n.p.) reminds us, "It's fascinating that century after century, Gypsies are both the most romanticised people on earth and the most vilified: this is almost as much the case now as it was two centuries ago." Therefore, not only does the trilogy uphold de Beauvoir's starting point outlined in *The Second Sex*—"One is not born, but rather becomes, a woman" (1989, 265)—it also prioritizes the importance of social class and the positive (albeit stereotyped) representation of the Gyptians in this process. Such that if, as de Beauvoir claims, not every female is a woman: "[W]e are exhorted to be women, remain women, become women. It would appear, then, that every female human being is not necessarily a woman; to be so considered she must share in that mysterious and threatened reality known as femininity" (de Beauvoir, 1989, ix).

In Pullman's text, the femininity that de Beauvoir outlines predominates in the middle class world of Mrs. Coulter, but is almost completely absent from the world of the Gyptians, and from the isolated world of Jordan College. Lyra does not initially refer to the female scholars at Jordan as women but rather as "poor things, they could never be taken more seriously than animals dressed up" (*NL* 67; *HDM* 50), and Lyra's enchantment with Mrs. Coulter on first meeting her is intrinsically bound up in her fascination with the performance of a traditional femininity that represents a hitherto unexplored territory for Lyra. When Mrs. Coulter talks to the captive children they note that "she was so gracious and sweet and kind that they felt they hardly deserved their good luck, and whatever she asked they'd give it gladly so as to stay in her presence a little longer" (*NL* 44; *HDM* 33). De Beauvoir herself suggests the existence of a link between social class and gendered identity but does not extend this beyond a suggestion that the types of marginalization suffered by women and the proletariat might be linked if ultimately different in manifestation:

> Most assuredly the theory of the eternal feminine still has its adherents who will whisper in your ear: "Even in Russia women still are women" [...]. The parallel drawn by

Bebel between women and the proletariat is valid in that neither ever formed a minority or a separate collective unit of mankind. And instead of a single historical event it is in both cases a historical development that explains their status as a class and accounts for the membership of *particular individuals* in that class. But proletarians have not always existed, whereas there have always been women. They are women in virtue of their anatomy and physiology [de Beauvoir 1989, ix].

De Beauvoir's conviction that the "eternal feminine" is a fallacy sees her taking a position that Pullman explores textually. De Beauvoir raises the issue of femininity and communism, suggesting that under a different system where the bourgeois cultures of the middle classes have been all but eliminated, although some may argue that "women still are women" for de Beauvoir this is a simplistic view that denies the effect that social structures have on the processes of the construction of femininity.

Femininity and social class

Pullman maintains and develops an interaction with this emphasis on the relationship between notions of feminine humility and social class. In *His Dark Materials* upon reaching sexual maturity a person's daemon (a physical manifestation of the soul) takes on its final form, and loses the ability to shape shift into animals that represent the feelings of their human partner. Significantly there seems to be one exception to this rule in the form of Lyra's Gyptian mother-figure, Ma Costa's daemon however, maintains the ability to shape shift.[9] This works as a metaphor for Ma Costa's lack of awareness of the corruption of original sin that should have fixed her and her daemon's identity, and prevented the expression of her changing emotions through her daemon's form. This is linked to her lifestyle, which is less concerned with shame, and more concerned with the practicalities of day-to-day existence: "[o]n the Gyptian boat, there was real work to do, and Ma Costa made sure she did it" (*NL* 111; *HDM* 83).

Social class is almost constantly referenced in Lyra's Oxford and Mrs. Coulter's London, Lyra is told that she can't travel by public transport because it would be unseemly for someone of her social standing: "Mrs. Coulter had said that is was not really intended for people of their class" (*NL* 102; *HDM* 76). Although the link between class and female body shame is hinted at in Oxford, it is once Lyra is removed into the world of Mrs. Coulter's upper-class London set that the link between body shame and social class is made increasingly more explicit, Lyra's body becomes both less visible and more static and confined:

Helping Mrs. Coulter had all been very well, but Pantalaimon was right: she wasn't really doing any work there; she was just a pretty pet. On the Gyptian boat, there was real work to do, and Ma Costa made sure she did it. She cleaned and swept, she peeled potatoes and made tea, she greased the propeller, she washed dishes, she opened the lock gates, she tied the boat up at mooring-posts, and within a couple of days she was as much at home in this new life as if she'd been born a Gyptian [*NL* 111; *HDM* 83].

Pullman's insistence on the overwhelming presence of traditionally female jobs in this list of Lyra's boat duties allows the novel to make a statement about the link between lapsarian body shame and social class rather than making a broader statement about gender roles. Both the Gyptians and Mrs. Coulter's "ladies who lunch" occupy traditional female roles, and so Lyra's world is seemingly a definite pre-feminist space. However, the key difference lies not in attitudes towards female equality but in the specifics of body image and particularly lapsarian body shame; the more working class Gyptian female is confined to traditionally female tasks, but their body image is seemingly freer from the concept of shame that so typifies Mrs. Coulter's middle class, Christian world.

Once, made aware of it, for Lyra aspects of this shame or humility persist until the trilogy's conclusion and are present in the depiction of Lyra's final reunion with the Gyptian King, John Faa, Lyra is at first shy until Faa initiates physical contact:

Such an age had passed since Lyra had last seen these dear men! They'd last spoken together in the snows of the Arctic, on their way to rescue the children from the Gobblers. She was almost shy, and she offered her hand to shake, uncertainly; but John Faa caught her up in a tight embrace and kissed her cheeks, and Farder Coram did the same, gazing at her before folding her tight to his chest [*AS* 530; *HDM* 916].

This residual shyness is analogous with Foucault's belief that the repressive power of the state, by which he meant the overriding ideology, was becoming insidious, and no longer used force to perpetuate or verify its own existence, but rather could do so by more surreptitious means.

Pullman depicts a manifestation of the power of shame that is able to penetrate the most intimate aspects of life. In a similar fashion to Foucault's model of the Panoptic State as something that was all-pervasive but did not manifest itself through force,[10] rather through the power of its discursive practices, "which circulates its ideology throughout the body politic" (Barry 1995, 176).[11] Foucault argues that the discursive practices within any system of belief that surround sexuality, and more specifically what is permissible and what is deemed to be vice, can be viewed as a means of controlling the very bodies that exist under that system. Such discursive practices produce knowledge and in the case through shame they discipline the bourgeois woman's body into a model of femininity as she passes from childhood into adulthood. This is why Lyra is so "shy" in the extract cited above when she meets John Faa and Farder Coram at the end of *the Amber Spyglass,* after she has become a young woman who is now also aware of her aristocratic origins. Accordingly, any deliberate representation of something which has been deemed deviancy will be considered, because of the very presence of the censoring, as something which is avant-garde and risqué by any movement which wishes to disrupt that state. As a result, by evoking such contentious representations of sexuality Pullman immediately posits his art on one side of the process of discourse, on the side of protest, without overtly even mentioning a political agenda; simply because of the fact that the discursive practices of the power of the state have entered even the most intimate aspect of the daily life of those living under its reach. This makes any writing concerning anything that has been deemed unworthy of artistic attention, immediately an act of political interest.

Children's literature as an alternative space: *Gatty's Tale*

In his interview with Angela Lambert, Pullman implies that children's fiction provides a space for drawing up alternative world views that simply isn't possible in adult fiction, Pullman tells Lambert: "Children's fiction is to do with hopes and aspirations, the still-existing sense that there is something to be striven for, whereas adult fiction is so often about the destruction of aspirations and adult non-fiction is full of ghastly autobiographies (Lambert 2002, n.p.).

The work of children's writer Kevin Crossley-Holland also incorporates this "sense that there is something to be striven for." Crossley-Holland's *Gatty's Tale* is set in the medieval world of 1203, in a no man's land between Wales and England, and its heroine 12-year-old Gatty is selected (because of her lack of family and her beautiful voice) to join a group of Christian pilgrims on their journey to Jerusalem. As Christopher Ringrose (2007) suggests, it is part of a genre of children's literature where the past is investigated by contemporary writers through literary pastiche in order to consider the present, I would argue this is also true for Pullman's descriptions of the neo–Victorian world in which Lyra comes from. For Gatty the feminine is a realm that has hitherto been denied her because of her lack of social status. Like Lyra, the character of Gatty begins the novel with a sense of bodily innocence that has arisen from her orphaned and penurious status. She sleeps with her cow in the barn, and is described in animalistic terms as the novel opens; significantly, we do not know what Gatty's gender is until halfway down the first page:

> "Light of light! Oh, flight! Oh, flight!" trilled the early birds.
> In one corner of the cow-stall, the heap of dirty sacking shifted. Something buried beneath it made a sound that began as a gentle murmur and ended as a grouse.
> Then the cook crowed and that loosed the tongues of his disciples. Half the neighers and brayers and bleaters and grunters in the manor of Caldicot welcomed the day's dawning, chill and misty as it was.
> As soon as Hopeless joined in and mooed, the heap of sacking shrugged and then tossed. In one fluid movement, Gatty stood up, crossed herself, reached for her russet woollen tunic lying on a bale of hay and pulled it on over her undershirt and baggy drawers [*GT* 1].

This movement from unidentified moving thing to a gendered being mirrors the text's overall movement towards Gatty's feminization as the narrative progresses. As she embarks upon a Christian pilgrimage to Jerusalem as the servant of a female aristocrat, Gatty is expected to acquire a more traditionally Christian, feminine manner.

Upon first entering the great hall at Caldicot, the henchman guarding the door responds to Gatty's disdain at being searched before she is permitted entry with an interesting conflation of gendered reference (the guard knows that he is talking to a girl as he refers to Gatty by name, upon seeing her, but uses the phrase "No one enters this hall without *he's* searched"); this is followed by a description of Gatty's first view of Lady Gwyneth in all her finery, that serves to emphasize Gatty's lack of identifiable feminine qualities:

> "Orders is orders," the first man replies. "No one enters this hall without he's searched."
> Gatty stepped into the hall, and she caught her breath.
> She saw Lady Gwyneth at once, standing at the far end of the hall, very tall and slender and fair, with a girl on her right and a big man on her left, but in that same first long moment she saw the kind tapestries hanging on the walls and the soft honey-light of dozens and dozens of candles, she smelt scents sweeter and thicker than Fallow field in June [*GT* 17].

Like Pullman's Mrs. Coulter, Crossley-Holland's Lady Gwyneth's femininity seems to both originate from and infect her surroundings; thus firmly locating the feminine within a particular (high) social class. The femininity that Gatty witnesses in the hall both entrances and starkly contrasts with the heroine of the tale:

> Had Gatty been able to look at herself through Lady Gwyneth's eyes, what would she have seen?
> A grubby parcel of sackcloth and, sticking out the top, a freckled and dirt-streaked face; large river eyes, set quite wide apart; and a storm of curls, now in the candle-light more silver than gold [*GT* 18].

Like Pullman's early descriptions of Lyra, Crossley-Holland depicts Gatty in terms that are stereotypical of ancient depictions of the unfeminized female as urchin and ragamuffin and thus link her to the elemental and the earthy. Like Lyra, Gatty's physical journey is accompanied by a metaphorical journey into the constructed feminine adult world of the contemporary era, during which, the heroine embraces some aspects of that femininity but discards others, rejecting the body shame that accompanies most typical versions of aspirant femininity at the time and which in certain ways continue into the present.[12] In the final scenes of *Gatty's Tale*, Gatty can be found preparing for her big entrance into a church service held in her honor at Caldicot, after her return from the pilgrimage to Jerusalem.

The final moments of the novel's action begin with Gatty getting dressed and applying a medieval version of lipstick, thereby conforming to a lady-like ideal, despite her worries that this could be construed as an attempt at social climbing:

> Gatty drew her beautiful yellowy-green silk dress from her saddle-bag, and carefully spread it out on the flagstones.
> No she thought. I can't! I can't wear it. Who does she think she is? That's what they'll say. Everyone will.
> Gatty stared down at the dress.
> Maybe Joan's right. I'm not the same. Not the same as I was.
> I am, though. I'm the same but not the same because I seen so much and learned so much. But being different isn't wrong, is it? That old man in the pound, he said difference can be a threat but it can be a wonder [*GT* 372].

After asserting Gatty's right to occupy this feminine space, the final section of the novel sees Gatty choosing to shed the accoutrements of certain aspects of that femininity. Indeed, Gatty consciously reverses the gender roles of the traditional marriage ceremony as she places her ring on Arthur's finger: "she took Arthur's strong, warm right hand and slipped the ring on to his fourth finger" (*GT* 383).

Versions of femininity in *His Dark Materials*

Within *His Dark Materials,* Pullman implies such a link between a lapsarian body image; one marked by a concept of shame, and social class, suggesting that female body shame is felt more keenly and perpetuated within the middle classes, while the working classes remain freer from the shame of a post-pubescent body, and are freer to partake in a less classical and therefore less restrictive body image. Pierre Bourdieu's (1993) important theory of cultural capital is relevant here, insofar as the accumulation of the knowledge, of how to produce a femininity determined by bourgeois notions that respond to shame, is itself a kind of social capital that can in reciprocal fashion mark the female subject out as of a higher status in terms of social class. It is no less a form of cultural capital which may then be traded and utilized to the subject's advantage as having the right accent or the having been educated in the right kind of school. In one sense this is the lesson Mrs. Coulter is trying to teach her natural daughter Lyra to become a lady rather than a working class woman. A dichotomy is set up therefore at the start of the trilogy between the snobbish attitude of Jordan's scholars and Lyra's inner barbarism (making her an outsider to the social body of her world) which is imbued with a sense of physical freedom: "Lyra was a barbarian. What she liked best was clambering over the college roofs with Roger, the kitchen boy who was her particular friend, to spit plum stones on the heads of passing scholars" (*NL* 35–36; *HDM* 26).

This can be set against the supercilious attitude that is rooted in the college environment; we learn that Lyra likes to boast of her college's eminence to the various urchins and ragamuffins she played with by the canal or the claybeds; and she regarded visiting scholars and eminent professors from elsewhere with pitying scorn, because they didn't belong to Jordan and so must know less, poor things, than the humblest of Jordan's under-scholars [*NL* 35; *HDM* 26].

This battle between competing ideologies is continued throughout the trilogy as Lyra's urge for the body freedom that she sees in the world of Gyptians and in Will Parry's post-feminist Oxford, battles with the internalized values of Lyra's rather more antiquated world, which represents a particularly pre-feminist space.[13] Pullman distances himself from accusations of sexism by ensuring that the fact that this is Lyra's perspective which is emphasized and this is one which must incorporate the sexist and misogynistic attitudes of the world she originates from. Once Lyra's journey is complete her views on the female scholars change: "this Dame Hannah was much cleverer, and more interesting, and kindlier by far than the dim and frumpy person she remembered" (*AS* 541; *HDM* 924).

In this Lyra exhibits similar characteristics to the character of Hermione Grainger in J.K Rowling's *Harry Potter* series, who has a similar internalized snobbery that battles with the adventurer within; but unlike Hermione, Lyra remains irritated at the end of the trilogy by the fact that she will now have to re-learn how to use the alethiometer from books; having lost her instinctive ability to read the device. Hermione is in contrast intrigued by female scholars: "That's what Hermione does. When in doubt, go to the library" (*CS* 7), and can often be relied upon to inform the other adventurers of scholastic matters: "Aren't you ever going to read Hogwarts, A History?" / "What's the point?" said Ron. "You know it by heart, we can just ask you" (*GF* 28). However, Hogwarts while very different from contemporary Britain is still dominated by its norms. Like Lyra, however, Hermione's mixed blood (she is human born) means that she is granted access to different worlds which could be regarded as being analogous to the different social classes of our world.

The bath scene in *Northern Lights* that takes place at Mrs. Coulter's flat symbolizes the new feminine space that Lyra is expected to occupy in order to fulfill the rules of female propriety (*NL* 78; *HDM* 58). Mrs. Coulter's forcing of modesty onto Pan and Lyra during the highly theatrical bath scene highlights that there is nothing innate about the shame that Lyra's body is supposed to induce in her male daemon, but rather that this is to be learnt and created through an intentional process of the removal of intimacy between Pan and Lyra to produce what are significantly referred to as "feminine mysteries" (mysterious because the performance is so naturalized that it cannot be explained as a learned role). It also may explain one reason why daemons normally appear to be the other gender from their human companions in the trilogy, insofar as apart from helping to embed heterosexual normativity (same sex humans and daemon combinations are very unusual), it also shows how the patriarchal gaze becomes internalized within the female subject's own perception of herself. This has echoes of de Beauvoir's insistence of the vital role that the perception of the male gaze plays in constructing female modesty, as Kruks notes:

> Beauvoir's account of how one "becomes a woman" requires developing an awareness of one's "permanent visibility," learning continually to view oneself through the eyes of the generalized (male) inspecting gaze and, in so doing, taking up as one's own project those "constraints of power" that femininity entails. But becoming a woman is, for Beauvoir, still an intentional process, even though it is enacted within the constraints of power [Kruks 1999, n.p.].

De Beauvoir also draws the reader's attention to the biblical and specifically Judeo-Christian religious origins of this version of femininity, which relies on instilling the need and the desire to hide the female body because of its perceived inferiority to the masculine; Beauvoir reminds us that "St. Thomas for his part pronounced woman to be an 'imperfect man,' an 'incidental' being. This is symbolized in Genesis where Eve is depicted as made from what Bossuet called 'a supernumerary bone' of Adam" (1989, xxii). As Kruks' analysis demonstrates, there are similarities between Foucault and Beauvoir's concepts of the link between becoming body consciousness and succumbing to a western, post-enlightenment, quasi Christian ideological structure:

> Foucault reverses traditional forms of mind-body dualism by privileging the body as the site of the formation of the self, yet he is still caught up in this dualism. If the interiorization of power takes place through "the body," then it can of course bypass that — allegedly — distinct entity called "consciousness." But if, with Beauvoir (who here draws on Merleau-Ponty) we insist that the body is *not* distinct from consciousness but rather is the *site* of their interconstituency, and the site of a sentient and intentional relation to the world, then the modalities through which we interiorize and/or resist the panoptic gaze can be explored more adequately [Kruks 1999, n.p.].

Pullman's text also shares this belief in the wider ideological implications of becoming body conscious. The adults in Lyra's Oxford attempt to instill her with a sense that because of her social class she has to be treated differently to the other children who populate the college, Lyra embarks upon a dialogic process of interiorizing and resisting this notion. The Master of Jordan College informs Lyra: "You're not a servant's child [...] we couldn't put you out to be fostered by a town family. They might have cared for you in some ways, but your needs are different" (*NL* 70; *HDM* 52) this is followed in the next chapter in the trilogy by another reminder that there are some key differences between the women of the various social classes set up in Pullman's trilogy; and this is again specifically related to their bodies, of Mrs. Coulter's friends Lyra notes that they are "women so unlike female scholars or Gyptian boat-mothers or college servants as almost to be a new sex altogether, one with dangerous powers and qualities such as elegance, charm and grace" (*NL* 82; *HDM* 61).

The description of the most typically feminine women of the novel as "a new sex altogether" in Pullman's text echoes Beauvoir's description of the feminine as occupying a different class to the masculine:

> In truth, to go for a walk with one's eyes open is enough to demonstrate that human-ity is divided into two classes of individuals whose clothes, faces, bodies, smiles, gaits, interests, and occupations are manifestly different. Perhaps these differences are superficial, perhaps they are destined to disappear. What is certain is that they do most obviously exist [de Beauvoir 1989, xx].

Femininity in Foucault's terms (1981) is a kind of discourse, a regulated and systematically ordered representational system which works through dif-ferences and exclusions to allow what is and isn't femininity to be understood as such and therefore to become reproducible. Pullman's use of the word "grace" in his description of the most traditionally feminine character in the trilogy sets up an interesting dichotomy between Lyra and Mrs. Coulter, and suggests that if Lyra works as a redeemed Eve figure then Mrs. Coulter at this point in the novel is set up as a contrasting Mary figure. The mention of grace reminds the reader of the Christian and specifically Catholic prayer "Hail Mary / Full of Grace" but in Pullman's world while knowledge is redeemed and ameliorated, grace is perjorated, allowing a complete reversal of Christian female sexuality as would have been understood for example in representations of idealized women that stem from the courtly literature of the middle ages. The witches of Lapland form perhaps the most obvious example of this form of reversal of traditional bourgeois femininity, they occupy an overtly female space, and despite the cold refuse to cover their bodies, Serafina Pekkala explains to Lyra:

> "We feel cold, but we don't mind it, because we will not come to harm. And if we wrapped up against the cold, we wouldn't feel other things, like the bright tingle of the stars, or the music of the Aurora, or best of all the silky feeling of moonlight on our skin. It's worth being cold for that" [NL 313; HDM 231].

Pullman's witches occupy, in many respects, a long-established version of the feminine, which locates the female within the broader category of nature, and links woman to the lunar cycle. The witches reveal their love of moonlight, and describe an elemental existence; although it must be noted that Pullman distances himself from the accusation of sexism and overemphasizing their innate naturalness by ensuring that the reader is told that witches do make good warriors and skilled archers and that they exist in non-patriarchal, women only communities. In addition there is something about their existence which is almost existential (in Kierkegaard's sense of the term [1973]) in the way they choose face the cold of their wilderness existence. It is not that they don't feel the cold we are told, but rather that they prefer to suffer the cold in order to have a more unmediated relationship with being sensuously alive and aware of the moment and living in the world, as opposed to being mired in civilized habits that would deaden their existence. In this respect at least the witches offer an unusual complement to the Gyptians as both outcast groups exist at the very margins of the conventions of bourgeois society and its disciplined construction of the body as a site of shame, albeit it in different ways. Perhaps unsurprisingly the trilogy shows much mutual respect between the Gyptians and the witches, best epitomized in the story of Farder Coram's genuine love for the witch Queen Serafina Pekkala whose life he once saved.

The traditional, elemental aspect of the witches however, and indeed the notion that they can be easily grouped together as a body of women who all share the same characteristics is noteworthy, since it works to locate Pullman's argument firmly within a discussion of the detrimental effect of feminine modesty on the female subject, rather than engaging determinedly with the broader issues of difference within feminism.

Conclusion

In an interview for *Prospect Magazine* with Angela Lambert, Pullman reveals that the materialist, more democratic and less shame centered world of the Gyptians who are not so concerned with innocence and the prevention of sin might offer a didactic message, Pullman tells Lambert:

> "Every story does teach, whether you intend it to or not. [...] We have to grow up and leave childhood; our task is to become wise and to leave our innocence behind. That means engaging with our bodies and a reverence for this life here on this earth; making moral choices that involve compromise, because we're usually involved with competing goods, not a good and a bad" [2002, n.p.].

Thus Pullman prioritizes a more complex, less binary world view that would regard the absence or abandonment of body shame as a necessary part of the process to becoming more engaged with our bodies and which will at the same time challenge inequitable and undemocratic social hierarchies based on gender as well as those of social class which serve to prevent human beings from facing up to living this life here on earth.

NOTES

1. Most notably Claire Squires' discussion of such issues in *Philip Pullman, Master Storyteller: A Guide to the Worlds of His Dark Materials* (2006), and Mary Harris Russell's detailed analysis of Lyra's function as an Eve figure, "'Eve, Again! Mother Eve!': Pullman's Eve Variations' in Millicent Lenz and Carole Scott's collection (2005).

2. For examples of the term "overachiever" being applied to Hermione see the following sources: http://www.helium.com/items/329996-class-hogwarts-school-witchcraft; http://en.wikipedia.org/wiki/Hermione_Granger; http://www.imdb.com/character/ch0000986/bio; http://www.modthesims2.com/showthread.php?t=263625.

3. Henceforth, *Gatty's Tale* is cited in references as *GT*.

4. Gatty "marries" herself to lifelong sweetheart Arthur and we learn that Hermione and Ron marry and have children.

5. The Magisterium is Pullman's term for the Established Church of Lyra's world, which forbids females to enter its ranks and forces the nuns that serve the Pope to be silent.

6. Based on a folkloric narrative that they originated from Egypt.

7. Consider the discussions on what to do about the missing children at the Roping in *Northern Lights/The Golden Compass* (see Chapter "John Faa").

8. As opposed to being used to represent a melodramatic male villain who threatens British female purity, which is more common in the nineteenth century representations.

9. When Ma Costa is worried about Billy her daemon takes the form of a hawk. After Tony rescues Lyra in London it becomes a grey dog.

10. Foucault used Jeremy Bentham's prison design, the "panatope," which consisted of tiered ranks of cells which could be surveyed by a single warder who was to be positioned at the centre of the circle, to explain his idea of the all-seeing state. See Foucault (1977).

11. The term "discursive practices" is perhaps somewhat problematic, and requires greater definition, Glenn Ward's interpretation becomes useful here; he argues that: "Discourses can be seen as controlled systems for the production of knowledge. Though regulated they are not completely closed systems and have to allow for change and dissent" (Ward 1997, 129).

12. See Ernst Robert Curtius (1953) for discussions of the representations and attributes of lady-like women in medieval literature.

13. See for example Lyra's disdain of the female scholars (*NL* 67; *HDM* 50).

WORKS CITED

Bardi, Abby. 2006. "The Gypsy as Trope in Victorian and Modern British Literature." *Romani Studies* 16.1, 31–42.

Barry, Peter. 1995. *Beginning Theory*. Manchester: Manchester University Press.

Binns, Dennis. 1984. *Children's Literature and the Role of the Gypsy*. Manchester: Manchester Travellers School.

Bourdieu, Pierre. 1993. *The Field of Cultural Production*. Cambridge: Polity.

Butler, Judith. 1990. *Gender Trouble*. New York and London: Routledge.

Crossley-Holland, Kevin. 2006. *Gatty's Tale*. London: Orion.

Curtius, Ernst Robert. 1953. *European Literature and the Latin Middle Ages*. London: Pantheon.

De Beauvoir, Simone. 1989. *Le Deuxième Sexe* [1949].

Dixon, Bob. 1977. *Catching Them Young 1: Sex, Race and Class in Children's Fiction*. London: Pluto.

Duchen, Jessica. 2008. "Jessica Duchen's Top 10 Literary Gypsies." The *Guardian*, August 12. Accessed August 12, 2008. *http://www.guardian.co.uk/books/2008/aug/12/1*.

Foucault, Michel. 1977. *Discipline and Punish: The Birth of the Prison*. Trans. A. M. Sheridan-Smith. Harmondsworth: Penguin.

_____. 1981. "The Order of Discourse." In *Untying the Text: A Poststructuralist Reader*. Trans. and ed. R. Young. London: Routledge.

Kierkegaard, Soren. 1973. *Fear and Trembling and the Sickness Unto Death*. Trans. Walter Lowrie. Princeton, NJ: Princeton University Press.

Kruks, Sonia. 1999. "Panopticism and Shame: Reading Foucault Through Beauvoir." *Labyrinth* 1.1. Accessed May 5, 2008. *http://h2hobel.phl.univie.ac.at/~iaf/Labyrinth/Kruks.html*

Lambert, Angela. 2002. "A Golden Age for the Kids? Is Children's Fiction More Interesting Than That Being Written for Adults? Angela Lambert Talks to Philip Pullman." *Prospect Magazine*, March: 72. Accessed May 1, 2008. http://www.prospect-magazine.co.uk/article_details.php?id=4989.

Lenz, Millicent, and Carole Scott. 2005. *His Dark Materials Illuminated: Critical Essays on Phillip Pullman's Trilogy*. Detroit: Wayne State University Press.

Nord, Deborah Epstein. 2006. *Gypsies and the British Imagination: 1807–1930*. New York: Columbia University Press.

Rowling, J.K. 2007. *Harry Potter Boxed Set*. London: Bloomsbury.

Ringrose, Christopher. 2007. "A Journey Backwards: History Through Style in Children's Fiction." *Children's Literature in Education*, 38.3. 12, 207–218.

Squires, Claire. 2003. *Philip Pullman's His Dark Materials Trilogy: A Reader's Guide*. London: Continuum.

_____. 2006. *Philip Pullman, Master Storyteller: A Guide to the Worlds of His Dark Materials*. London: Continuum.

Ward, Glenn. 1997. *Postmodernisms*. London: Hodder and Stoughton.

8

"Imagine *Dust* with a Capital Letter": Interpreting the Social and Cultural Contexts for Philip Pullman's Transformation of Dust

KATHARINE COX

Introduction

Dust is significant and pervasive in Philip Pullman's *His Dark Materials*. This Dust is elevated above ordinary dust through the use of a capital letter, is intrinsically linked to the characters' central quest and is an ever-present motif that connects the multi-worlds of Pullman's vision. Of particular note is the initial ambiguity of the Dust and its development within the trilogy, as it is variously interpreted as original sin, evil, good, consciousness, light, dark matter and wisdom by those who encounter it. As a result, the interpretation of Dust is fundamental to the narrative and forms the detective pulse at the heart of the books, as the protagonists and reader try to unravel the meaning of Dust. The repeated misunderstandings about Dust within the trilogy, and the competing attempts by the characters to control, destroy or understand it, would appear to make a singular reading of Dust difficult. Pullman has repeatedly spoken of writing a *Book of Dust*[1] to offer further insight into this ambiguous substance, and this task promises to extend the trilogy further[2] but also confirms Dust as an ongoing concern.

One of the problems in understanding Pullman's Dust is the difficulty of analyzing a metaphor that is plural, elusive and is, as Anne-Marie Bird notes, "a confusing babble of narratives" (2005, 195). Dust is used to progress some complex theological, philosophical and ecological concepts and concerns. It evades the interpretations ascribed to it by the characters within the text, growing in importance, until it threatens to overwhelm the characters and reader alike. It would be tempting to ascribe a postmodern tendency to the substance, as Bird does (2005), were it not for the end of the trilogy where the substance is re-envisaged as non-radical and unifying, ultimately enabling closure. The reason that Dust is difficult to define and understand is that it is revealed to be *everything*. In this revelation, Pullman uses this complex metaphor to communicate a consistent vision, that of a united and multi-dependent universe. This is achieved through a manipulation of our historic and contemporary attitudes towards dust, inverting God's cursed material into a means of redemption, by transposing dark matter into Dust, and by making this integral to organic and in-organic matter and ultimately the universe. This essay will explore Pullman's use of science, religion and nature to resituate a Monotheistic paradigm, represented by the concept of dust in the Bible,[3] with the apparently non-theistic science of dark matter in order to promote ideas of a Pantheistic universe.[4] Dust becomes a possible worldview that knits together these disparate and competing conceptual strands. In this way, the small and apparently inconsequential is revealed as the most significant thing in the universe.

As evidenced above, Pullman's use of Dust is an intriguing and wide-ranging topic for investigation. Existing research has drawn on the religious application of Dust as a metaphor for consciousness (see Bird 2005; Shohet 2005), as well as a term for dark matter (see Gribbin and Gribbin 2008). Bird's earlier work on Dust, in a significant insight into Pullman's Romantic influences, identifies the interpretation of the substance as based on Blake's concept of "contraries" (Bird 2001). These prior investigations emphasize the possibilities of Dust as a research concern. Critically though, these writers do not delve into the social implications and cultural history of dust to consider what *it* is that Pullman transforms. To understand Pullman's theology it is first necessary to analyze the transformation of dust into Dust in *His Dark Materials* through an exploration of dust's associations. Pullman's invention of Dust is a manipulation of prior literary sources, cultural and social meanings and also galvanizes theological and scientific concepts into a comprehensive whole.

What is dust?

Though we live with dust, this commonplace reminder of "matter out of place" whether generated from industrial activity, effluence or decay, is so mundane as to be overlooked. Pullman's attention to dust places an emphasis on the small and apparently inconsequential, but it also reflects nineteenth and twentieth-century concerns about the connections between dust and its relationship to health and illness. In order to contextualize our historical and present cultural responses to dust it is first necessary to consider what we mean by dust. Definitions of dust suggest that it is small pieces of dry solid matter, light enough to be airborne when disturbed (see *OED*). More scientific observers of dust argue the substance may be classified either by its size, the diameter of which, as David Lide (1994) notes, is between 0.001–10,000 μm; by its constituent parts, which the nineteenth-century scientist John Tyndall argues were composed mainly of organic material (cited Flint 2000, 43); or by its location.[5] These compositional and social concerns are at the forefront of Pullman's usage as protagonists vie to elucidate what Dust is, to attribute its social meaning, and take the necessary action.

Despite its size, dust has been growing in importance and significance, particularly since the late nineteenth century. Although it has many negative associations, dust is richly allusive and has been variously deployed as a metaphor both to describe the very low, evident in such idioms as "to bite the dust" or "eat my dust," and conversely to things of worth, quality or magic, such as gold dust or fairy dust.[6] In keeping with these oppositions, Pullman's Dust is also described ambivalently, from the negative interpretations ascribed by the Church to Mary's discussions of love.

For the Roman poet Lucretius dust represented the minute, that which was at the margin of our sight and also our understanding (see *De Rerum Natura*); comparably its first mention in the books by Asriel emphasizes a lack of knowledge about the Dust but a desire to know more (*NL* 24; *HDM* 18). The reference by Lucretius is an interesting one as this writer is often perceived as an antecedent of Romantic atheism as one who offered a "materialist alternative to God" (Preistman 1999, 7). In his poem *De Rerum Natura*, he mediates on death as a leveler of men and dissipater of power and uses dust as a metaphor to illustrate this process.

Though dust was once defined as the smallest perceptible substance, Robert Hooke's seventeenth-century publication of *Micrographia* (1664–5) opened up a world of the minute, demonstrating that there were monsters lurking amongst the dust (*c.f.* Hooke's depiction of mites). For Hooke his investigations of the miniature were often hampered by the dust; he writes that his observations of mercury ran smoothly providing the table "surfaces be not *dusty*" (Hooke's emphasis 1664–5, Observation VI). Had he access to an electron microscope, rather than one he was forced to chase his animate subjects with (Observation L), Hooke might have been rather more interested in these complex dusty topographies. The development and advancement of microscopes illuminated what had previously been obscure; the marginal and the previously invisible came into view and the viewers didn't always like what they saw.[7]

Dust as a foe in the contemporary imagination can be largely traced back to nineteenth-century practices of cleanliness and hygiene. Joseph Amato, in his analysis of dust, opines that substance has become "transformed from an enduring condition to an enemy of sanitary civilization" (2000, 12). The author and critic John Ruskin clearly indicates that it is a woman's duty to defend the home against dust in his quixotic *The Ethics of the Dust: Ten Lectures to Little Housewives on the Elements of Crystallization* (1866), while some four years previously, Doctor Charles Murchison had made the link between wet dust (dirt)[8] and disease in his *Continued Fevers of Great Britain* (1862).[9] This cultural shift, obviously in combination with Biblical associations, encourages the Church to read D/dust as a negative entity and one which should be cleaned up (this happens both historically and also in Pullman's novels).

It is worth exploring the connection between dust and threat as a precursor to Pullman's use of Dust, as these insights are relevant to the experience of the city which informed Romantic thinking (especially London). Writing late in the Victorian era, Alfred Russell Wallace observed that the irritation of dust as a feature of daily life was not in question but that dust is also "a serious source of disease" (qtd. Flint 2000, 40). These investigations into dirt and disease complemented the notion of diseases being caused by miasmas (polluted or bad air). The effects of dust intensified during the industrial revolution as additional airborne pollutants were released and encountered. Dust as a byproduct of the process of industrialization is experienced by Lyra in the drastically reduced air quality during her flight through London, which is the experience of an industrial landscape (*NL* 100; *HDM* 74). Though Pullman's Dust is intrinsically linked to all forms of dust (unavoidably so when he chose the name), in particular, Pullman's usage is indebted to and involves a re-imagining of nineteenth-century narratives about dust. These negative associations intensified over the twentieth century and are part of the semantic inheritance that Pullman navigates. The trilogy partly traces this historical process, from dust's position of acceptance within our lives to one of containment, to fear and finally the desire to eradicate it. This is evident in the Church's anxiety to destroy Dust which is based upon D/dust's perceived ability to infest and contaminate which in turn parallels attitudes toward dust from the end of the nineteenth century onwards, through its connections to disease.

Dust and the Church

Pullman has notoriously written against and spoken out about the "dangers" of organized religion; these religious institutions, he argues, seek to narrow interpretation. In the Church's response to Dust in his trilogy, Pullman is able to explore the problems of a narrow vision of sin and experience. Ironically though, Pullman himself repeats this narrowing of interpretation by imposing a singular meaning on Dust. Over the course of the books, various characters strive to understand or master the Dust. As the physical embodiment of original sin, Dust is treated as evil by Coulter and the Church, while Asriel wishes to harness its scientific possibilities and power. Pullman's Dust is ubiquitous and conscious and as such reflects directly the meaning of Pantheism (from the Greek παυ meaning "all" and θε-óς meaning "God"). Pullman's dust flood deliberately inverts the biblical narrative of the Flood (Gen 6:17) where human sin resulted in mass extermination and a cleansing of the earth. His flood is an ecological catastrophe where nature is seen as "crying out and hurling [... itself ...] into the struggle to keep the Shadow-particles in this universe, which they so enriched" (AS 476; HDM 880). Against this collective display of nature, love, the nobleness of the two children, various angels, witches, friends and *mulefa*, Pullman sets the negative and controlling religious ideologies that seek to destroy Dust as they perceive it to be evil. Pullman works this dialectic to its fictional conclusion, achieving a triumph of love through experience and knowledge, and in doing so rewrites the Fall.

The association between Dust and evil is an exaggeration of cultural responses to dust, which perceive dust as a frightening concept and entity, and is an extension of the biblical references to dust. In the Bible, dust is the epitome of a life without redemption, one that is arid and infertile; see for example Job's protest: "wilt thou bring me into dust again?" (Job 10:9). Though perhaps best remembered as God's curse to Adam, dust is repeatedly used as a device to imply spiritual death without God.[10] Without redemption the body is destined to return to the dust of the earth. This reminder that dust is a metaphor for our mortality is explored by both William Shakespeare (*Hamlet*) and T.S. Eliot (*The Waste Land*) amongst others.[11] However Pullman's emphatic combination of body and soul (child/adult and daemon) ensures that this connection between body and spirit cannot be broken. Rather than confirming that "the dust return to the earth as it was: and the spirit shall return unto God who gave it" (Eccles 12:7), Pullman portrays a semantic reclamation that views Dust as embodiment of matter and spirit.[12]

The Church's desire to eradicate or nullify through intercision the effect of the Dust can be seen as an extension of the cultural anxieties surrounding dust.[13] Biblical usages connect it firmly with death (without redemption) while contemporary investigations into its composition reveal that it includes skin material, pollution, and waste. This scientific research suggests that dust ultimately, and ironically given Pullman's adoption of the idea, evidences the process of the loss of human consciousness as it signifies the transformation of sentient beings through a return to inert matter. Drawing on this association between dust and death, these usages connect the substance with decay and decomposition to which living tissue is returned.

By consolidating the Church's response to Dust as one of eradication without consideration, Pullman casts the young protagonists firmly against the status quo or sanitary civilization as represented by the Church: "if *they* all think Dust is bad, it must be good" (NL 397; HDM 292). For the Church, the negativity associated with dust combines with biblical associations, so that Dust is firmly equated with experience. The Church identifies Dust as a threat as it appears to them as a physical manifestation of sin. In addition, Astriel's experiments seem to suggest that at adolescence a child/young adult attracts increased levels of Dust, which confirms for the Church a definitive connection between experience and sin. Dust's attraction to adolescence is represented by a physical threat in Cittàgazze as the specters feed off this consciousness, rendering adults vacant and stripped of their humanity. The Church's experiments seek to prevent this increased connection with the Dust, by severing the daemon from its child and so preventing the daemon settling on a single form, they hope to reverse the process of sin.

This moment of transition is evinced by the inability of the daemon to change, a moment that is dreaded by Lyra as she connects it with inflexibility and loss; and yet when Pan does settle on a form it is through choice, instigated by sexual experience which is pleasurable and which connects Lyra and Will. Pullman places positive emphasis on this transition from child to young adult and so writes a variation of *felix culpa* (the fortunate fault/Fall), whereby this sin is recast as love, experience and knowledge and so should be welcomed. In defying the Church's imposed readings of Dust, Lyra and Will ultimately conclude that the Dust represents knowledge and wisdom, recognizing it as a consciousness that has become externalized (see Dodd 2004). The young couple's understanding that links knowledge and dust recalls God's curse to the serpent that tempted Eve: "dust shalt thou eat all the days of thy life" (Gen 3:14). Here the curse is inverted as for Pullman and his characters Dust is revealed as a nourishing and loving consciousness; so to eat of this Dust is good and fulfilling.

Knowledge, love and understanding are highly valued by the writer and by the Romantic tradition in general. In an elaboration of William Wordsworth's early Pantheistic sentiment, Pullman's ghosts return with joy to the universe becoming "mist or smoke [...] becoming part of the earth and the dew and the night breeze" (*AS* 455; *HDM* 864). Here the lowly or the commonplace is viewed as significant, which is an extension of Pullman's decision to valorise the humble dust mote. The Kingdom of Heaven is overthrown and with it their biblical understanding of dust to be replaced by the positive community of characters from the trilogy, with the diminutive Lyra (the child) at their core, who are tasked with developing a republic of heaven based on Dust.

Dust and dark matter

Though these cultural and textual elements of dust are the most obvious, Pullman deliberately consolidates the fictional theoretical model of dark matter into his investigations into Dust. This discussion of dark matter is highly topical and in this next section of the essay I intend to explore some of these contemporary connotations, including an example from recent physics.

On 10 September 2008, in a series of underground bunkers that stretch beneath the borders of France and Switzerland, the Large Haldron Collidor initiated its first cycle in an experiment designed to discover both the Higgs boson or "God particle"[14] and its relationship to dark matter (Fallon 2008).[15] It was anticipated that the experiment, designed to collide two high speed beams of particles head on within the Collidor, would artificially create or prove the presence of dark matter for the first time. In an environment at the vanguard of particle physics, on the threshold of both science and imagination, these scientists optimistically sought to recreate the conditions as close as possible to the start of the beginning of the universe (illustrated by the scientific theory of the Big Bang)[16] (Ananthaswamy 2007). However, just nine days later, on 19 September 2008 the experiment was compromised (CERN 2008), ensuring for the time being at least that our understanding of dark matter would see no significant breakthrough.

The continuing absence of a scientific answer to the conundrum of dark matter and its place in the universe allows Pullman greater flexibility in his incorporation of dark matter into the larger concept of Dust in *His Dark Materials*. Pullman's fictional response to the question of dark matter is prominent amongst literary works; for example, Annalee Newitz (2008) lists it as one of the top ten fictional responses to the possibility of dark matter. It is important to note that dark matter is a theoretical model which has not been proven (or even shown to exist), and so should be considered a fiction itself (although one that has gravitas as it is postulated by leading scientists). It complements Pullman's fictional purposes that he is drawing on this paradigm as there has not yet been an answer to the missing mass of the universe as posed by Newtonian physics (the reason for a model of dark matter) and while an answer would not vitiate his concept, he has previously expressed concern that it might (Pullman n.d.).

Following Pullman's lead in such articles as "The Science of Fiction" (2004) and his interview with Celia Dodd (Dodd 2004), this essay will demonstrate that although Pullman uses physics to build the conceit of Dust, its depiction is not limited to scientific antecedents. Although Pullman is self deprecating about his knowledge of science, "I might deceive the moderately intelligent reader" (Pullman 2004), his interest in dark matter and its inspiration for the Dust in his trilogy are well documented. Since the publication of *His Dark Materials*, he has lectured in Britain at the Oxfordshire-based Rutherford Appleton Laboratory (2005b), has discussed science with Lord Robert Winston at the Cheltenham Science festival (2005b)[17] and *His Dark Materials* has even spawned a popular science guide (Gribbin and Gribbin 2003). Yet despite this apparent scholarly interest in science he has confirmed that "I don't do science" (Pullman 2004); instead as a writer of fiction Pullman utilizes science, specifically the investigation of dark matter as Dust, as a background to the action of *His Dark Materials*.

When considering a title for his trilogy, Pullman was drawn to the links between science and creativity inherent in the phrase from John Milton's *Paradise Lost* (Book II), where Milton refers to God's "dark materials" as a creative principle.[18] Though Milton's usage was to associate this creative principle with God, Pullman extends this further and as author recasts this notion in a more egalitarian light. The conceptualization of Dust manipulates this "apt symbol of creative formlessness" (Douglas 1984, 161), and by giving it form or multiform, teases out its rich associations. The idea of Dust as a creative force repositions God's angry words to Adam in Genesis ("for dust thou *art,* and unto dust shalt thou return" Gen 3:19) and combines this notion with the mysterious dark matter alluded to by contemporary scientists. In doing so, Pullman offers a comprehensive vision of a creative consciousness that is both of the universe but which also *forms* the universe (rather than Milton's God, Pullman offers a universe that *is* God and a God that is *part* of the universe).

This combination of creativity and dust is appropriately described in Wordsworth's response to archaeological discoveries of poetry at Herculaneum in his poem "September, 1819":

> a genuine birth
> Of poesy; a bursting forth
> Of genius from the dust [lines 55–57].

For contemporary readers Pullman as literary archeologist salvages fragments of Romantic thought and theology and combines this with his adventure narrative, and so forms a similar bursting forth from the dust. The trilogy is infused with this blend of creativity or consciousness, the implication being that we (humanity and aliens alike) as originators of Dust are envisioned in a dependent ecological cycle that elevates our consciousness (wisdom, knowledge and love) as the firmament of the universe. This places an emphasis on the importance of the individual and the community as active creators of their spiritual environment and undermines the binary opposition of divine power offered by the passive presence of the Authority and the dictatorial force of the Regent, Metatron. In doing so, Pullman moves from Monotheistic principles (God as originator of the universe) to Pantheistic (universe *as* God). Dust is a direct challenge to the process of worship propagated by the Church as mediators of the faith in Lyra's world and instead empowers the individual in a democratic "republic of heaven" (*AS* 548; *HDM* 929).

Dust, location and gender

From the particles of the Aurora,[19] the dark materials of Milton's vision, to Mary Malone's investigations, the Dust, and that which is at the periphery of our vision, is a major concern across the numerous worlds of Lyra's and Will's explorations. The Dust is protean and allows the viewer glimpses of other possibilities or worlds; for example, the figure of a child engulfed in the Dust (*NL* 22; *HDM* 17) enables Asriel to finance his expedition into the mysterious phenomenon, while the Dust-rich Aurora is a point of disjuncture that stands as a gateway between worlds.

The Aurora illuminates the great city of Cittàgazze, whose "towers, domes, walls ... buildings and streets, [are] suspended in the air!" (*NL* 24; *HDM* 18). Just as the light of the Aurora in Lyra's world indicates the dislocation between her world and Cittàgazze, so too clouds of dust are typically natural indicators of turbulence and chaos. Dust as an indicator of the chaotic is sustained in Pullman's writing through his identification of the Dust-stream that removes Dust from the worlds. The flow of the Dust-stream is deemed to be unnatural and unordered. This "terrible flood of Dust" (*AS* 496; *HDM* 892) heralds the disaster that is the loss of consciousness, as without the Dust there will be no sentient, loving life; instead conscious life would be degraded into a "brutish automatism" (*AS* 476; *HDM* 879).

When we first meet Lyra she is in the progress of a spatially transgressive act, as she infiltrates and later eavesdrops within the inner sanctum of the Jordan scholars' Retiring Room. It is from her cramped hiding place there that she first hears of the Dust: "Something in the way he said it made Lyra imagine *Dust* with a capital letter, as if this wasn't ordinary dust" (*NL* 22; *HDM* 16). Though Pullman, through Lyra, attempts to draw a division between the commonplace dust and the Dust of the novel's investigations, as this essay demonstrates, the social and cultural responses to dust are significant for Pullman's usage as he is unable to maneuver his readers fully from their cultural competences. The significance of Dust is maintained at the end of the first volume with Lyra vowing to journey and learn about Dust until she understands its meaning (*NL* 398; *HDM* 293). The grandeur of Lord Asriel's speech about the mysterious Dust and the strange cold expanse of the Northern territories, where the act of trepanning brings individuals closer to the Dust, prefigures Lyra's quest North and confirms the connection between Dust and knowledge throughout the trilogy.

Initially, dust and dirt can be read as indicators of Lyra's adventures along the boat yards in Oxford which confirm a city that is the site of industrial change. This is an environment that Pullman feels strongly about, observing that the "boatyard and its work is part of a complex human ecology that sustains all kinds of life" (2005a). This reference suggests a counter-cultural response to dust and dirt which is at odds with the popular desire to eradicate or contain it. It reminds us that Pullman perceives dust as an intrinsic part of an ecological system and that his use of the substance as Dust is a transformative one based in part on the negativity ascribed to dust but also its ambivalence. Ordinary dust is important to Pullman's Dust as he uses the ecological features of the substance to stress fertility and the possibility for growth (this is in direct conflict with the biblical associations of dust).

Lyra's escapades through Oxford usually result in her being marked by the filth of the city or the mud of the river bank. In Oxford, unlike the amoral London of Pullman's vision, the progress of industrialization and the knowledge represented by its colleges are allowed to grow together in harmony. Being marked by dirt or dust from the boatyards or being affected by industrial pollutants reveals an activity. Typically, dirty or dusty activities are linked with work and as such "Dust is linked to social class" (Fine and Hallett 2003, 6). Lyra is chastised for her movement and her activities as they are unbecoming of her rank and her gender. As her father Asriel notes in his appraisal of his daughter, she is "Dirty" (*NL* 38; *HDM* 28). He takes this dirt as a sign that she spends a lot of time outdoors as the dirt speaks of other things, and other places. He perceives "matter out of place" (James qtd. Douglas 1984, 164) and his supposition is backed up by his empirical observations "I saw you on the roof only yesterday" (*NL* 39; *HDM* 28). Asriel's detective ability recalls Sherlock Holmes' first (yet flawed) case when he remarks "I could read all that in the dust" (Doyle 1994, 24). His examination of her hands and fingernails, a reading rather like the predictions of a fortune-teller, indicates that his daughter's fate is aligned to the Dust.

In a repetition of Asriel's inspection of her and just before her first meeting with Mrs. Coulter, her mother (*NL* 66; *HDM* 47–48), Lyra is roughly washed to remove these indicators of the outside. As Douglas shows in her seminal work *Purity and Danger: An Analysis of the Concepts of Pollution and Taboo* (1966) dirt or dust within the house is a transgressive sign of the chaotic and the desire to banish such symbols is a "positive effect to [organize] the environment" (1984, 2). Unlike Lyra's intellectual father who merely comments on her behavior, the Housekeeper, Mrs. Lonsdale takes remedial action to combat this transgressive signifier:

> "Wash," she said ferociously.
> "You get all that dirt off."
> "Why?" Lyra said at last [...]. "What've I got to do this for? You don't care about Roger" [*NL* 65; *HDM* 48].

As Lyra indicates, the treatment towards her differs from her friend Roger and is a direct result of her social status and gender. Although Lyra rails against various attempts to socialize her as a young woman during the trilogy, there is an ambiguity about her final acceptance of a place at Dame Hannah's college, which if she decides to accept feels like contrition (*AS* 545; *HDM* 928). This is after her consummation of her relationship with Will and so suggests that this normative heterosexual behavior guides her into a more traditional model of gender. As Sarah Gamble argues in this collection, Lyra is ultimately returned tamed to the college environment and so suggests that her natural habitat is within the privileged walls of society. This appropriate location, which she initially refers to as "her world" (*NL* 63; *HDM* 46), severs her completely from her young companion, Roger, who is from a different class.

The need to cleanse Lyra indicates a social desire to purify her of her worldliness and experience,[20] and to inculcate her into the ways of feminine society. Adult reactions to Lyra's appearance remind us that dust is a complex marker of taboo, informing the transgression from innocence to experience. As Sally R. Munt and Gamble emphasize in this collection, Coulter's washing of Lyra is a deeply symbolic act. In Coulter's London flat the sheer brightness of the place with its "wide windows [which] faced south" (*NL* 76; *HDM* 56), indicates an absence of dust and an attention to cleanliness. In such an environment, dust as "[f]orm and form-giver, light and light-bearer" (McGuiness 2004) would be out of place and so demonstrates that Coulter's philosophical attitudes towards Dust, evident in her work for the Church, and her domestic politics are convergent.

Coulter's first act upon welcoming her daughter to this overly feminine apartment is to instruct her to wash, and so symbolically cleanse her of the outside and also her previous life in Jordan. This process is repeated the very same day upon their return to the flat with a luxurious and extravagant bath, which she immediately contrasts with the behavior of Mrs. Lonsdale with her rough flannel. It is appropriate given Coulter's alliance with the Church that she should so instruct her daughter in these cleansing rituals and "feminine mysteries" (*NL* 78; *HDM* 57) that conform to John Wesley's proverb that "Cleanliness is indeed next to Godliness" (1791). Lyra's ultimate rejection of her mother, and her attention to washing and cleaning, implicitly conveys her rejection of her belief system (although it appears Coulter is primarily concerned with power rather than religion). In choosing dirt and the Dust, Lyra rebuffs the Church.

Lyra's first experience of Coulter's bathroom stresses the strangeness of this environment and the newness of the elaborate ritual of washing. Its otherness to Jordan is emphasized and the gendering of the two places are contrasted with the "magnificent" beauty of the all-male Jordan's college set against the trinkets of Coulter's "pretty" environment (*NL* 76; *HDM* 56). These linguistic hints imply that she is more closely associated with the outside and with the world of experience than Coulter's mannered femininity. Initially overwhelmed by this new place and beautified by Coulter's feminizing treatments, the young girl fails to recognize her own reflection in the mirror and quickly finds herself bored by the performance of gender that a life with Coulter entails. The enveloping language of this episode (*NL* 76–79; *HDM* 56–59) with its repeated use of terms "pretty," "little," "soapy," gentle," "brushed" and "soft" suggests an excessiveness and contrived nature of the situation and location until Lyra is finally "too enchanted to question anything" (*NL* 79; *HDM* 59). Unlike a fairy tale character who might have been lulled to sleep at this point and hence encounter misfortune, Lyra's Pantalaimon[21] directs her wakefulness towards the alethiometer, and so towards her destiny to defeat the Church.

Pullman's ecological vision

As critic Claire Squires notes, the ecological focus of Pullman's trilogy has been under assessed (Squires 2006) and this is often at the expense of discussing Pullman's theological position. So it is surprising then given the prominence of Dust, which combines Pullman's theological perspective with an ecological one, that this has not generated more ecologically-focused attention. Pullman places a great deal of emphasis upon the relationship between conscious life and its environment and this is heightened by his reclamation of D/dust, ultimately, as a positive, all encompassing motif. Dust is transformed from a dry, arid and negative substance into a fertile and life-affirming concept. In doing so, Pullman is partially mimicking the natural role of dust in our environment. By drawing attention to the life of dust, Pullman supports the idea of a cycle of life which he terms an ecological "feedback system" (*AS* 476; *HDM* 879). Ultimately, Lyra and Will succeed as they stem the flow of the Dust while the closing of the doors into other worlds and so lock this physical manifestation of consciousness into the local ecology.

This notion of a feedback system is amusingly portrayed by David Staume (2009), who offers a revealing fairytale concerning a king who wished for no more dust. In Staume's short story, the world dies as a result of the loss of dust which, though a nuisance to the king, is intrinsic to sustaining life as well as providing beautiful sunsets (Staume 2009). Staume connects the dust with beauty and its intrinsic role in sustaining life. Readers of Staume's story are encouraged to focus on this minuscule material and reassess it as an enduring, positive and necessary part of our environment.

An emphasis on ecological harmony in the trilogy is deliberate: Pullman has written polemically about the changing planet (2005a) and followed this up with the idea of climate change as a religious issue in a collection of essays about faith and the environment (*c.f.* Pullman in Simms and Smith 2008). In the trilogy there is a repeated threat to the environment through cultural attitudes (the Church) and technological advancement (intercision and Astriel's machines). Pullman's ecological zenith is presented in the final book through the characters of the *mulefa* with their balanced relationship to their environment, in what Lauren Shohet terms their "ideally adapted ecological synergies" (2005, 31). Dust plays a crucial role here as it is integrated into the basic biological technology of the *mulefa* where it nurtures and suffuses the oil and seed pods that they use as "wheels." In addition, they respond to the Dust in natural terms, referring to it as "*like the light on water*" (*AS* 234; *HDM* 712; Pullman's emphasis). Their Dust, which they term *sraf*, awoke their consciousness some thirty-three thousand years ago (*AS* 236–237; *HDM* 712–713) and unlike their human counterparts they do not require technology to view the Dust. The role of sentient life is paramount to this ecological vision and calls for all life-forms to live in harmony with their environment.

The focus on this primitive world after the sophistication of the technology of the previous worlds forms a regression to a paradise in preparation for the Fall. Though the *mulefa* use technology it is integrated into their physiognomy and adapted from the world around them. A supreme example of symbiosis, the *mulefa* use seed cases as wheels which once split allow for germination; these "broken wheels" are as valued as the initial seed pods as they're viewed holistically by the *mulefa*. These sentient beings are thus the guardians of this world in an interrelated hierarchy as "[e]ach species depended on the other" (*AS* 135; *HDM* 643).

A possible contradiction can be anticipated here as Pullman both praises and elevates individuals and community actions (for example, the notion of Lyra as hero is juxtaposed with the *mulefa* and other cooperative systems) and yet renders all as equal through his version of Pantheism. Despite individual endeavor, Pullman's enduring image is of assimilation within the environment, forming part of the universe, and this can be seen in his release of the dead in *The Amber Spyglass*, where: "[Roger] laughed in surprise as he found himself turning into the night, the starlight, the air ... and then he was gone, leaving behind such a vivid little burst of happiness" (*AS* 382; *HDM* 814).

Though Roger is gone he not lost as the emphasis on his emotions here demonstrates. This description of the dissipation of the dead appears to be a joyful rewrite of Wordsworth's final Lucy poem, "A Slumber Did My Spirit Seal," where when released by death Lucy becomes one with nature:

> A slumber did my spirit seal;
> I had no human fears: [...]
> No motion has she now, no force;
> She neither hears nor sees;
> Rolled round in earth's diurnal course,
> With rocks, and stone, and trees [lines 1–2; 5–8].

This emphatic revision of Wordsworth is interesting as it causes Pullman to associate himself with this ecological Romantic poet, and there are further connections to Wordsworth present in his writing. Principally, Pullman adopts a Romantic ecological vision which is similar to that conveyed by Wordsworth, especially in his early period. Jonathan Bate has written extensively on the notion of the Romantic ecology (see 1991 and 2000) and cites Wordsworth as the primary figure in the Romantics' relationship with nature, as a writer who experienced an "unalienated relationship with nature" (Bate 1991, 29). This "unalienated relationship" is one that Pullman espies in the children's relationship to their surroundings and allows, through them, the reader to experience. Just as the Romantics encouraged the reader to see and feel again as a child, Pullman accesses this world-view for his adult readership which helps explain his cross-over success.

Pullman is clearly indebted to the Romantics, as Bird (2001) and Falconer in this present volume have demonstrated, and persuasively continues this Romantic tradition, as William Gray (2008) has argued. There is a clear engagement with the Romantics, especially in *The Amber Spyglass* where Pullman opens each chapter with a quotation (of the 37 chapters that use such epigraphs, 13 can be thought of as being written by the Romantics). Pullman's focus on the ecological places him within a Romantic tradition of writers of place that primarily includes John Clare and Wordsworth, but which can be extended into the contemporary and seen in the work of Ted Hughes and Seamus Heaney. There is a sense of a healing connection (both for the individuals and their environment) to be had by the ecological experience. These characters are seen to fully dwell in the natural world of which they are a crucial part.

Pullman's extends the limits of most ecological writings by going a step further; for Pullman the universe is sentient and meaningfully alive and, in turn, Dust is revealed as the physical manifestation of Pantheism (God/love/consciousness is all-pervasive). It is a vision of ecology and spirituality that Wordsworth articulated in his poem "Composed a Few Miles Above Tintern Abbey, on Revisiting the Banks of the Wye During a Tour. July 13, 1798," where

> I have felt
> A presence that disturbs me with the joy
> [...] and in the mind of man;
> A motion and a spirit, that impels
> All thinking things, all objects of all thought,
> And rolls through all things [lines 93–94; 99–102].

Although Pullman's Pantheistic use of Dust appears closely associated with Wordsworth's ecological writings, Pullman does not quote Wordsworth in his chapter headings; rather the content and underlying Pantheistic themes connect the two.

Conclusion

Pullman's multifarious use of Dust draws directly upon its social and cultural contexts, and the effect of this in his writing is to foreground this marginal and ambiguous material. Pullman's Dust is both old and new: the sum total of textual, social and scientific attitudes towards the material as well as his own reading of the Dust. The presence of Dust and its apotheosis within the *mulefa* environment is pro-marginal, ant-bourgeois and anti–Monotheistic. Pullman subverts the dusty Old Testament curse directed at Adam and Eve (and their descendents) after they have eaten from the Tree of Knowledge and instead, in elevating Dust and the importance of consciousness and knowledge, causes Dust to be a symbol of redemption through collective engagement with one another and our planet. In doing so, emphasis is placed firmly upon the ecological relevance of dust and our individual and collective responsibility to our planet.

NOTES

1. Pullman's regular columns in 2006 allude to the writing of this book and in his interview with Andrew Ffrench for the *Oxford Mail* he suggests that it "could be published in 2009" (Ffrench 2007). At the time of this volume going to press it is still not available and it is unclear whether his work on this book has stopped.

2. Building upon the short adventures contained in *Lyra's Oxford* (2003) and *Once Upon a Time in the North* (2008).

3. For example, God's words to Adam — "For dust thou *art,* and unto dust shalt thou return" (Gen 3: 19) — effectively denies him (and his offspring) eternal life, and so redemption is not possible until after Christ's sacrifice.

4. Dust as a Pantheistic idea has been mentioned in passing by Bird (2005) and Squires (2006). Bird's research in particular links the Dust to Blake's notion of contraries (2001); however, this requires further elaboration as Blake's religious view though highly unusual can still be considered Monotheistic. Pullman's Pantheistic tendencies align him far more closely (as I'll demonstrate) with William Wordsworth's radical early writings and the Pantheistic leanings of P.B. Shelley and John Keats.

5. For a discussion of dust as a social indicator see, for example, Thompson (1979).

6. See for example the unusual Harmon Mounds in Dickens' *Our Mutual Friend* who makes a living from his mounds of dust. These so-called dust heaps created by the new industrial age represent both the unwanted jetsam of urban living but conversely offer the opportunity for financial gain. For further examples of idioms involving dust see Amato (2000, 18).

7. These observations of dust led to steps to eradicate it and nullify its presence; the use of chemical sprays, the invention of the vacuum cleaner, laminate flooring and so forth all point to this social need to re-order and regulate the space in which we live.

8. The differences between dust and dirt are blurred. Critically, dust is usually defined as dry (*OED* 2) so that dirt might be thought to be dust particles which have become wet or contaminated which allows them to stick to other surfaces more readily. Alternatively critic Amato (2000) suggests that dirt is contaminated dust that has been combined with excreta and so is treated with more suspicion and fear. Given the similarities between dust and dirt it's not surprising that the connotations and meaning attributed to each have become blurred.

9. For an example of the connections between dust and disease in literature see Elizabeth Tilley's reading of Bram Stoker's story "The Burial of the Rats" (2004). I'm grateful to Dr. Catherine Wynne who made me aware of this little-known Stoker story.

10. Conversely, dust can also be considered positively in the Bible as although God curses Adam to the dust it was also the material from which he was made. As H.P. Maler poetically notes, the creation of dust prefigures the birth of Adam, as on the third day God created the land and, in so doing, the dust was born (Maler 1877, 14).

11. There are numerous literary texts that combine dust and death, indicating that dust as a commonplace substance is to be feared as it reminds the reader or onlooker of their own mortality. Hamlet is made to contemplate his father and ultimately his own "dusty death" while Eliot's pithy "I'll show you fear in a handful of dust" encapsulates the ambivalent relationship that we have with dust.

12. See Bird (2001) for a more detailed discussion of body and spirit in *His Dark Materials*.

13. Mary Douglas' *Purity and its Dangers* (1964) is a seminal work on dirt and taboo.

14. The "God Particle" is the common term used to describe the Higgs Boson particle after Leon Lederman's accessible science book, *The God Particle: If the Universe is the Answer, What is the Question* (1994). It is hoped that this theoretical particle, if it exists or can be found, will help provide missing knowledge about the start of the universe.

15. The concept that the universe was missing matter was first postulated by Fritz Zwicky (1933). Dark matter is a scientific term which came into usage to explain the undetected matter which scientific calculations suggest should be present in the universe (usually based around the effects of gravity). These calculations identify a discrepancy between the mass of the known universe and the calculations of anticipated mass (afforded by effects of gravity). Pretzl's work (in Greiner 2004) suggests that of the 27 percent of the universe made up by matter, only a small proportion of this is known, the rest is dark matter. Another way of referring to dark matter is through its other name, cosmic dust, which has stronger associations with the dust we encounter. These scientific allusions to dust promote the importance of the apparently inconsequential and associate the mundane with the scientific and indeed the marvelous.

16. Big Bang theory is a popular scientific model used to explain the development of the universe to its current state; specifically this model refers to the rapid transformation of dense matter resulting in an expanding universe. For more information see Hawking (1995).

17. Lord Winston is Professor of Science and Society and Emeritus Professor of Fertility Studies at Imperial College London. For more information see his website: http://www.robertwinston.org.uk/.

18. See Rachel Falconer in this collection for her discussion of this phrase and for Pullman's use of Milton generally.

19. The Aurora is another name for the Northern Lights which are illuminated charged particles and which can be agitated by atmospheric dust.

20. This use of dust and dirt as an indicator of the outside recalls Thomas de Quincey's *Confessions of an English Opium Eater* where the dust is a marker of the pedestrian. And like de Quincey who loses his working-class companion Ann, Lyra is quickly separated from her kitchen friend Roger.

21. Pullman's all-encompassing philosophy is suggested in the name of Lyra's daemon, Pantalaimon. Perhaps named after Saint Panteleimon, the word suggests: all-forgiving. It's interesting to note the naming of the daemons as there appears to be no imposition of these names, rather they reflect the essential nature of the character.

WORKS CITED

Amato, Joesph. A. 2000. *A History of the Small and the Invisible: Dust.* Berkeley: University of California Press.

Ananthaswamy, Anil. 2008. "Higgs Boson: Glimpses of the God Particle." *NewScientist.com.* March 2. Accessed: October 2, 2008. *http://www.newscientist.com/channel/fundamentals-/large-hadron-collider/mg19325934.600-higgs-boson-glimpses-of-the-god-particle.html.*

Bird, Ann-Marie. 2001. "'Without Contraries Is No Progression'": Dust as an All-Inclusive, Multifunctional Metaphor in Philip Pullman's *His Dark Materials.*" *Children's Education in Literature* 32, 2, 111–123.

_____. 2005. "Circumventing the Grand Narrative: Dust as Alternative Theological Vision in Pullman's *His Dark Materials.*" in *His Dark Materials Illuminated: Critical Essays on Philip Pullman's Trilogy,* edited by Millicent Lenz and Carole Scott. Detroit: Wayne State University Press, 188–198.

CERN. 2008. "Incident in LHC Sector 3–4 — Press Release." September 20. Accessed October 2, 2008. *http://press.web.cern.ch/press/PressReleases/Releases2008/PR09.08E.html.*

Coupe, Laurence, ed. 2000. *The Green Studies Reader: From Romanticism to Eco-criticism.* Manchester: Routledge.

Dodd, Celia. 2004. "Debate: Human Nature: Universally Acknowledged." *The Times.* May 8. Accessed June 1, 2005. *http://www.timesonline.co.uk/tol/life_and_style/health/features/article417383.ece.*

Douglas, Mary. 1984. *Purity and Its Dangers.* Manchester and London: Routledge.

Doyle, Arthur Conan. 1994. "A Study in Scarlet." *The Adventures of Sherlock Holmes*. London: Wordsworth Classics.

Evans, Aneurin. 1994. *The Dust Universe*. Chichester: John Wiley and Sons.

Fallon, Amy. 2008. "Leak Delays CERN Tests Until Spring." *The Guardian*, September 24. Accessed January 9, 2009. *http://www.guardian.co.uk/science/2008/sep/24/cern.nuclear*.

Ffrench, Andrew. 2007. "Pullman Adds to Trilogy." *Oxford Mail*, December 16, 2007. Accessed October 27, 2010. *http://www.oxfordmail.co.uk/news/1908126.pullman_adds_to_trilogy/*.

Fine, Gary Alan, and Tim Hallett. 2003. "DUST: A Study in Sociological Miniaturism." *The Sociological Quarterly* 44, 1, 1–15.

Flint, Kate. 2000. *Victorians and the Visual Imagination*. Cambridge: Cambridge University Press.

Hawking, Stephen. 1995. *A Brief History of Time: From the Big Bang to Black Holes*. London, New York: Bantam.

Holmes, Hannah. 2001. *The Secret Life of Dust: From the Cosmos to the Kitchen Counter, the Big Consequences of Little Things*. New York: John Wiley and Sons.

Lederman, Leon. 1994. *The God Particle: If the Universe Is the Answer, What Is the Question*. New York: Delta.

Lenz, Millicent, and Carole Scott, eds. 2005. *His Dark Materials Illuminated: Critical Essays on Philip Pullman's Trilogy*. Detroit: Wayne State University Press.

Lide, David R. 1994. "Characteristics of Particles and Particle Dispersoids." *Handbook of Chemistry and Physics,*75th ed. Boca Raton, FL: CRC.

Lucretius. 2008. "*De Rerum Natura* [On the Nature of Things]." Trans. William Ellery Leonard. *Project Gutenberg*. Accessed February 12, 2009. *http://www.gutenberg.org/files/785/785-h/785-h.htm*.

McGuiness, Patrick. 2004. "'[Dust].'" *London Review of Books*. June 3. Accessed February 12, 2009. *http://www.lrb.co.uk/v26/n11/mcgu01_.html*.

Newitz, Annalee. 2008. "What Will Happen When the LHC Turns On?" *io9*, September 10. Accessed January 9, 2008. *http://io9.com/5047040/what-will-happen-when-the-lhc-turns-on-10-scifi-stories-have-the-answer*.

Pretzl, K. 2004. "Dark Matter, Massive Neutrinos and Susy Particles." In *Structure and Dynamics of Elementary Matter. Vol. 166 of Nato Science Series*. Walter Greiner, et al. n.p.: Springer.

Pullman, Philip. 2004. "The Science of Fiction." *The Guardian*, August 26. Accessed June 1, 2005. *http://www.guardian.co.uk/science/2004/aug/26/lastword.sciencefictionfantasyandhorror*.

_____. 2005a. "Boatyard Statement." *Philip Pullman's Website*. March 8. Accessed June 1, 2005. *http://www.philip-pullman.com/pages/content/index.asp?PageID=112*.

_____. 2005b. "Folio Society Edition of *His Dark Materials*." *Philip Pullman's Website*. September. Accessed February 12, 2009. *http://www.philip-pullman.com/pages/content/index.asp?PageID=119*.

Rosen, G. 1999. *The Victorian City: Images and Realities*, vol. 2. Eds. H.J. Dyos and Michael Wolff. London: Taylor and Francis, 625–668.

Ruskin, John. 1865. *The Ethics of Dust: Ten Lectures to Little Housewives on the Elements of Crystallization*. London: Blackfriars.

Shohet, Lauren. 2005. "Reading Dark Materials." In *His Dark Materials Illuminated: Critical Essays on Philip Pullman's Trilogy*, eds. Millicent Lenz and Carole Scott, 22–36. Detroit: Wayne State University Press.

Squires, Claire. 2006. *Philip Pullman, Master Storyteller: A Guide to the Worlds of His Dark Materials*. New York, London: Continuum.

Tilley, Elizabeth. 2001. "Stoker, Paris and the Crisis of Identity." *Literature and History* 10, 2 (Autumn): 26–41.

Zwicky, Fritz. 1933. "Die Rotverschiebung von extragalaktischen Nebeln."*Helvetica Physica Acta* 6, 110–127.

9

The Man Who Walked with God: Philip Pullman's Metatron, the Biblical Enoch, and the Apocrypha

JOHN HAYDN BAKER

Introduction

The angel Metatron, Regent to the Authority, is, Mrs. Coulter aside, the principal villain of Philip Pullman's *His Dark Materials* trilogy, even though he only actually seen in its final volume. He first appears at the start of *The Amber Spyglass*, sweeping down from the sky at Will and his angelic companions, his gaze filling Will with terror at his "vast, brutal and merciless intellect" (*AS* 32; *HDM* 568–569). We later learn more of Metatron from the dying angel Baruch, who reveals the Regent's megalomaniacal plan to permanently usurp the senile Authority's power and "intervene much more directly in human affairs," establishing a totalitarian control over all conscious life (*AS* 63; *HDM* 591). Like Martin Bormann in Adolf Hitler's Germany, he is the real power behind the Authority's (empty) throne. Baruch goes on to reveal that Metatron was not always an angel; like Baruch, he was once a man — his own brother, in fact: "I was his brother ... that was how we found our way to him in the Clouded Mountain. Metatron was once Enoch, the son of Jared, the son of Mahalalel.... Enoch had many wives. He was a lover of the flesh" (*AS* 65; *HDM* 592–593). Later in the novel Lord Asriel tells King Ogunwe that "they speak of him in the apocryphal scriptures: he was a man once, a man called Enoch, the son of Jared — six generations away from Adam" (*AS* 393; *HDM* 822).

It is, ultimately, Metatron's residual fallen humanity that leads to his destruction. Mrs. Coulter confronts him in the Clouded Mountain, and trembles before "a being made of light" of terrifying power: "he was exactly like a man in early middle age, tall, powerful, and commanding. Was he clothed? Did he have wings? She couldn't tell, because of the force of his eyes. She could look at nothing else" (*AS* 417–418; *HDM* 838). Metatron gazes pitilessly into Mrs. Coulter's soul, and sees nothing but "corruption and envy and lust for power"; his own wickedness blinds him to her love for Lyra, and the "cess-pit of moral filth" he sees within her reflects his own callous brutality (*AS* 419; *HDM* 839). His inability to perceive the goodness in Mrs. Coulter is compounded by his physical desire for her: in Pullman's marvelous phrase, "his next words pierced her flesh like darts of scented ice" (*AS* 419; *HDM* 839). He declares that he "had wives in plenty" in his human form:

> "When I was a man I was known as Enoch, the son of Jared, the son of Mahalelel, the son of Kenan, the son of Enosh, the son of Seth, the son of Adam. I lived on earth for sixty-five years, and then the Authority took me to his kingdom."
> "And you had many wives."
> "I loved their flesh. And I understood it when the sons of heaven fell in love with the daughters of earth, and I pleaded their cause with the Authority. But his heart was fixed against them, and he made me prophesy their doom" [*AS* 419–420; *HDM* 839–840].

Metatron's twin human failings — his lust for power and for female flesh — lead him to follow Mrs. Coulter to the edge of the abyss. We are told that "the Regent was a being whose profound intellect had had thousands of years to deepen and strengthen itself, and whose knowledge extended over a million universes. Nevertheless, at that moment he was blinded by his twin obsessions: to destroy Lyra and possess her mother" (*AS* 425; *HDM* 844). He is lured into a trap, and, following a desperate struggle, Lord Asriel and Mrs. Coulter succeed in dragging Metatron into the abyss. Like Satan, he plunges into the void — unlike Satan's fall, however, his will have no end. The death of God and the destruction of the being that so longed to reign in his stead leaves conscious life throughout the manifold universes free to decide its own destiny.

Although he appears only in *The Amber Spyglass*, Metatron is a major figure in Pullman's trilogy. In his cruelty and lust for absolute power, he symbolizes Pullman's cynical view of organized religion. However, despite his name, which seems more suited to an evil robot in a bad science fiction novel, he is not simply a figment of Pullman's powerful imagination. As the quotations above suggest, his origins lie thousands of years ago in ancient myth, and an examination of his relationship to his sources — biblical and otherwise — will prove illuminating to students and scholars of *His Dark Materials*.

Enoch as a biblical figure

The figure of Enoch, the man who would become Metatron, is one of the most mysterious and haunting presences in the Old Testament. He is, first of all, not to be confused with Cain's son, after whom Cain named a city in the land of Nod after his murder of Abel (Genesis 4:17). Our Enoch is a somewhat later figure, some seven generations after Adam. Genesis deals with him in a few short but deeply mysterious verses:

> And Jared lived an hundred sixty and two years, and he begat Enoch: And Jared lived after he begat Enoch eight hundred years, and begat sons and daughters: And all the days of Jared were nine hundred sixty and two years: and he died. And Enoch lived sixty and five years, and begat Methuselah: And Enoch walked with God after he begat Methuselah three hundred years, and begat sons and daughters: And all the days of Enoch were three hundred sixty and five years: and Enoch walked with God: and he was not; for God took him [Genesis 5: 18–24].

Enoch's earthly span of three hundred and sixty five years is nothing special by Patriarchal standards; his son, the venerable Methuselah, would live nine hundred and sixty nine years, and Enoch's own father Jared managed only seven years less (Genesis 5: 20, 27). In fact, nine hundred years seems to have been a pretty average span in those days. One would be inclined to write Enoch off as cut off in his prime, were it not for the tantalizing declaration that he "walked with God: and he was not: for God took him" (Genesis 5: 23–24). This does not necessarily mean he died, unlike all his ancestors. It seems to indicate that God somehow took him to heaven, presumably as a reward for his piety, without him dying. Unsurprisingly, this bizarre idea — a living man "walking with God," in heaven, yet still living — has fascinated and compelled readers of Genesis, including Pullman, ever since. Enoch is never mentioned again in the Old Testament, but this compelling reference has lingered in the Jewish, and later Christian, imagination.

That this is the case is confirmed by the fact that Enoch is referred to twice in the New Testament, the collection of specifically Christian documents found in the latter part of the Christian Bible. He is mentioned by the author of the Epistle to the Hebrews, traditionally ascribed to the Apostle Paul, but probably not by him; as part of an argument about the importance of faith, we are told that "By faith Enoch was translated that he should not see death; and was not found, because God had translated him: for before his translation he had this testimony, that he pleased God" (Hebrews 11:5). The writer of this letter, who probably wrote some time in the second half of the first century CE (Common Era), was almost certainly addressing an audience of Jewish converts to Christianity, and would have assumed a familiarity on their part with the Enoch of Genesis. The anonymous author plainly believed Enoch to be an exceptionally pious man, whose faith had earned a spectacular reward, and who could serve, like Abel (mentioned in the preceding verse) as a model for contemporary believers (Hebrews 11: 4).

At about the same time the author of the combative Epistle of Jude, who some scholars believe may have been a younger brother of Jesus, made a brief reference to Enoch that has long puzzled commentators: "And Enoch also, the seventh from Adam, prophesied of these, saying, Behold, the Lord cometh with ten thousands of his saints, To execute judgment upon all, and to convince all that are ungodly among them of all their ungodly deeds which they have ungodly committed, and of all their hard speeches which ungodly sinners have spoken against him" (Jude 1: 14–15). Jude's letter is full of dire threats against those he sees as "ungodly men" who have "crept in unawares," and here he co-opts the pious Enoch, who "walked with God" and is therefore worth heeding (Jude 1:4). As we shall see, this reference seems to indicate some familiarity on Jude's part with the apocryphal Book of Enoch, which stresses Enoch's prophetic role. There are no further biblical references to Enoch, except the author of Luke's citation of him as a distant ancestor of Joseph, Jesus' putative father (Luke 3: 37).

Is this biblical figure Pullman's Metatron? To a degree, but not entirely. His account of his ancestry to Mrs. Coulter is identical to that of the Enoch of Genesis — as Lord Asriel informs King Ogunwe, he is indeed "six generations away from Adam" (AS 393; HDM 822). In his own words, "the Authority took me to his kingdom"— he was "translated" without dying, just like the biblical Enoch (AS 419; HDM 839). There is a minor alteration, in that Pullman's Enoch was whisked away to heaven at sixty-five, three hundred years before his biblical equivalent — presumably Pullman alters this for the sake of verisimilitude (AS 419; HDM 839). His transformation into a powerful angel is not biblical, however — Genesis gives no hint as to Enoch's state following his translation, and neither do the Epistle of Hebrews or the Epistle of Jude. Pullman's inspiration here, as we shall see, seems to be entirely apocryphal. Metatron's excessive lust for female flesh, too, is nowhere to be found in the biblical Enoch. All we can assume about him is his extreme piety. We are told he fathered Methuselah at the age of sixty-five, and "sons and daughters" thereafter, but Genesis says nothing of his wife (or wives), or his attitude towards them (Genesis 5: 22). He was a patriarch, so much is certain, but whether he was an unusually lusty one is unclear.

Metatron's lustful nature is his most striking feature, along with his megalomania. Even his dying brother Baruch finds it necessary to point out that, in his human form, he "had many wives" and was "a lover of the flesh"; thus, Pullman artfully prepares us for his subsequent downfall (AS 65; HDM 592–593). Interestingly, Pullman may be hinting at a degree of homophobia on Metatron's part in this scene; the love between Baruch and Balthamos is plainly homoerotic, if such a term can be used in relation to angels, and Baruch hints that this offended the thoroughly heterosexual Enoch: "my brother Enoch cast me out, because I.... Oh, my dear Balthamos" (AS 65; HDM 592–593). If this is the case, it adds to the force of Pullman's condemnation of the sort of authoritarian religion Metatron represents, particularly for the contemporary Western reader.

Nevertheless, the biblical Enoch is not depicted as a "lover of the flesh," at least not in this disfiguring way. Even the apocryphal Enoch is not so described. Why, then, does Pullman make lust one of Metatron's deadly sins? The answer may lie in another mysterious, and much debated, biblical passage, to which Metatron himself refers. Later in Genesis we are told that

> when men began to multiply on the face of the earth, and daughters were born unto them, That the sons of God saw the daughters of men that they were fair; and they took them wives of all which they chose. And the Lord said, My spirit shall not always strive with man, for that he also is flesh: yet his days shall be an hundred and twenty years. There were giants in the earth in those days; and also after that, when the sons of God came in unto the daughters of men, and they bare children to them, the same became mighty men which were of old, men of renown [Genesis 6: 1–4].

Who are these mysterious "sons of God" who, like Metatron, were "lovers of the flesh," and whose union with human women produced "mighty men"? Most commentators have argued that they were fallen angels, whose unnatural desires bred a race of fearful crossbred monsters (the giants, or Nephilim), and whose misbehavior so disgusted God that he decided to destroy all mankind except Noah (Genesis 6: 7–8). The story indicates that at least some angels (presumably the fallen variety) feel physical desire, and are capable of both sexual intercourse and procreation with human women. Pullman doesn't make it clear if Metatron is capable of the latter, but he certainly feels the former — on his way to the fight with Lord Asriel, he seems to "gulp at the scent of [Mrs. Coulter's] flesh" in a very physical manner (*AS* 425; *HDM* 843). He is perfectly capable of battering Asriel within an inch of his life, for all his insubstantiality. Pullman seems to have transposed the sexuality of the fallen "sons of God" onto Metatron, despite the fact that he is anything but fallen. It is a reminder of his humanity, and thus of his fallibility.

Metatron himself makes a brief reference to this biblical passage. During his conversation with Mrs. Coulter, he tells her that he "understood it when the sons of heaven fell in love with the daughters of earth, and I pleaded their cause with the Authority. But his heart was fixed against them, and he made me prophesy their doom" (*AS* 419–20; *HDM* 840). Nowhere in the Bible do we find this strange link — and sympathy — between Enoch and the sons of God, but a clue to its origin lies in Lord Asriel's brief remark to King Ogunwe that "they speak of [Enoch] in the apocryphal scriptures" (*AS* 393; *HDM* 822). Before a consideration of these strange texts, however, we must briefly consider perhaps Enoch's most shadowy role — as an Occult figure.

Dr. John Dee, the celebrated magus and advisor to Queen Elizabeth I, attempted to communicate with angels using their own language, a language which he believed to have been that used by God and Adam in the period immediately following the creation. He believed that Enoch was the last human speaker of this language, and therefore this language has come to be known as

Enochian. Occultists, most famously, Aleister Crowley and the Order of the Golden Dawn, have developed a whole system of Enochian magic, based on this revealed language. The complexities of Enochian magic are rather beyond the scope of this chapter, but it should be pointed out that there is very little evidence that it has anything to do with either the Biblical Enoch or his apocryphal counterparts. John Dee, or his equivalent in Lyra's parallel world, is mentioned briefly in *Northern Lights* as a "great magician," but, that aside, Pullman seems to have little interest in Enoch as an Occult figure (*NL* 40; *HDM* 30). The origins of his Metatron lie, instead, in the Old Testament apocrypha, and it is to these mysterious texts that we must now turn.

The apocryphal Enoch

The Greek word "apocrypha" means "those who have been hidden away." When Lord Asriel refers to the apocryphal scriptures, he means the bewildering variety of texts of uncertain authenticity that never made it into the Bible's official canon. For all the protests of fundamentalists, the Bible is not a single unified text, but a collection of texts.[1] This collection was essentially fixed by the end of the fourth century CE. Most Christian churches today use Bibles containing a broadly similar canon of texts, though there are several important differences between them — the King James Bible, for example, contains an inter–Testamental section called Books called Apocrypha, containing fourteen books, such as Tobit and Ecclesiastics, while other English Bibles lack this. The term "the Apocrypha" is most commonly used to refer to this particular collection of texts.

Unless Lord Asriel's world's Bible is rather different from the King James version,[2] Enoch does not appear in this collection of apocrypha. However, there are many other apocryphal texts, both Jewish and Christian, and some of them feature Enoch. Lord Asriel seems to be referring to these texts, the most famous of which is known as *The Book of Enoch* (also known as *1 Enoch*). Metatron himself makes reference to this particular text as I shall explain (*AS* 419–20; *HDM* 839–840).

The Book of Enoch was considered lost for centuries until the Scottish explorer James Bruce brought two contemporary manuscript copies back to England from Abyssinia (now Ethiopia) in 1773. It was first translated into English in 1821 by Richard Laurence. Like many apocryphal texts, it is a complex, mystical and heterogynous work, probably assembled from a collection of originally independent texts written over at least three centuries. When considering the origins of Pullman's Metatron, the most relevant part of the text, and the best known, is The Book of the Watchers, in which Enoch expands upon the curious story of the lustful angels and the daughters of men from

Genesis. The Watchers are angels sent by God to watch over humanity. Swiftly, however, they found themselves drawn to the "handsome and beautiful daughters" of their human wards: "and the angels, the children of heaven, saw them and desired them; and they said to one another: 'come, let us choose us wives from among the daughters of men and beget us children'" (Charlesworth 1983, vol. 1, 15). The Watchers, who number two hundred, swear an oath to defy God's wrath and proceed to father a race of terrifying giants upon their human wives; the giants prove ungovernable, and wage war both upon mankind and each other (Charlesworth 1983, vol. 1, 16). The Watchers compound the chaos by teaching the hitherto innocent human race how to make weapons and — unforgivably — cosmetics: "and there were many wicked ones and they committed adultery and erred, and all their conduct became corrupt" (Charlesworth 1983, vol. 1, 16). Informed of this shocking behavior by his loyal angels, God condemns the errant Watchers to imprisonment until Judgment Day (and, of course, eternal torment thereafter), while the human race is to be entirely obliterated except for Noah and his family (Charlesworth 1983, vol. 1, 17–19).

Enoch, it would appear, had been taken into heaven before this period: "before these things (happened) Enoch was hidden, and no one of the children of the people knew by what he was hidden and where he was. And his dwelling place as well as his activities were with the Watchers and the holy ones" (Charlesworth 1983, vol. 1, 19). Enoch is ordered to bring the unhappy news to the Watchers, and does so (presumably he has been granted the ability to travel between realms): "fear and trembling" seizes them and they beg him to "write for them a memorial prayer," and deliver it to "the Lord of heaven" (Charlesworth 1983, vol. 1, 19). Enoch does not tell us how he received this request, but he agrees to intercede on their behalf; after writing their petition, he falls asleep and is given God's ferocious reply in an awe-inspiring dream, which he proceeds to recount to the weeping Watchers (Charlesworth 1983, vol. 1, 19–29). Particularly terrifying is Enoch's description of the place in which the Watchers will be imprisoned: "[I] saw a terrible thing: a great fire that was burning and flaming; the place had a cleavage (that extended) to the last sea, pouring out great pillars of fire; neither its extent nor its magnitude could I see nor was I able to estimate" (Charlesworth 1983, vol. 1, 24). The Watchers are, presumably, suitably chastened.

This is the story Metatron refers to in his conversation with Mrs. Coulter: "I understood it when the sons of heaven fell in love with the daughters of earth, and I pleaded their cause with the Authority. But his heart was fixed against them, and he made me prophesy their doom" (AS 419–20; HDM 840). Pullman evidently came across it in The Book of Enoch, but changes its focus in order to emphasize Metatron's lustful nature. The apocryphal Enoch says nothing about any sympathy he may have with the Watchers, and certainly does not seem to share their excessive appetite for the flesh; he is depicted as an entirely loyal and pious servant of God throughout the text, which concludes with a lengthy admonition to Methuselah and his other children to live right-eously and avoid the wrath to come (Charlesworth 1983, vol. 1, 73–86). Enoch's empathy for the Watchers is entirely Pullman's invention, as is the suppressed rebelliousness hinted at when Metatron says that the Authority *made* him prophesy the Watchers' doom. The apocryphal Enoch probably had little choice in the matter, but betrays no hint of resentment: in the presence of God, he remains appropriately prostrate and trembling (Charlesworth 1983, vol. 1, 21). Incidentally, as part of his gradual assumption of God's authority, Metatron seems to have borrowed his habit of making himself impervious to human sight; Mrs. Coulter can barely look at him, so brightly does he blaze, and Enoch tells us that God's gown "was shining more brightly than the sun [and] was whiter than any snow. None of the angels was able to come in and see the face of the Excellent and the Glorious One; and no one of the flesh can see him" (Charlesworth 1983, vol. 1, 21).

The Book of Enoch — or its equivalent in Lyra's world, anyway — is, then, one of the "apocryphal scriptures" Lord Asriel refers to in *The Amber Spyglass* (*AS* 393; *HDM* 822). It is also of some interest that William Blake, one of the major influences on Pullman's trilogy, read The Book of Enoch and made some memorable sketches inspired by it (see Brown 1940, 80–85). The book's first English translation appeared in 1821, and it is likely that Blake read it some time between then and his death in 1827, since the five pencil sketches that survive are plainly inspired by Enoch's visions. John Beer (1994, 159–178), however, suggests that Blake had read extracts from the book of Enoch which had been published in translation from the early 1800s onwards and draws attention to Blake's lithograph *Enoch* of 1806–1807. G.E. Bentley (2003, 428–429) suggests that Blake was particularly interested in the sexual relationship between the watchers and human women that seemed to have echoed some of Blake's own thoughts about this complex subject. The most striking in the light of *The Amber Spyglass* is one of Blake's visionary drawings, "Two Angels Descending" (c.1822), in which two angels loom menacingly over a beautiful, naked "daughter of man"; they blaze like stars, while their writhing, snake-like phalli make their sexuality inescapably apparent.[3] Here, perhaps, are figures that inspired Pullman's awesome, lustful Metatron. In another strikingly sex-ualized drawing, "An Angel Whispering" (c. 1822), a descending angel whispers sinful secrets into a woman's ear while in the background loom two of the gigantic offspring of this unholy coupling.[4]

Two other apocryphal texts are attributed to Enoch, and are usually referred to as *2 Enoch* and *3 Enoch*. *2 Enoch*, also known as *The Secrets of Enoch*, survives only in Slavonic and is of uncertain date and authorship; in it, Enoch describes his ascent into heaven and the sights he sees there, before returning to earth for a brief period to warn his children of the necessity to preserve

God's law. He is subsequently "translated" again — this time for good (Charlesworth 1983, vol. 1, 91–221). Of considerably more interest to the Pullman student is *3 Enoch*, a Hebrew text dating from the fifth or sixth centuries CE. It claims to be the work of Ishmael ben Elisha, often known as Rabbi Ishmael, a well-known sage who lived around 90–135 CE, whose views are recorded in the Mishnah, the first major redaction into written form of Jewish oral traditions, the "Oral law" (Charlesworth 1983, vol. 1, 223–315).

The book is Ishmael's account of an ascent into heaven and the various awe-inspiring sights he beholds there; in this respect, the book is not unlike the other apocryphal Enoch texts, with Ishmael playing Enoch's role. Particularly striking, however, is Ishmael's guide during this tour — "the angel Metatron, Prince of the Divine Presence" (Charlesworth 1983, vol. 1, 256). Pullman evidently found the angelic name adopted by his transformed Enoch in this obscure text and suggests extensive scholasticism on his part. This mighty figure fills Ishmael with awe, but he is puzzled to find other angels addressing him as "Youth": he asks Metatron why, and the angel replies that he is

> Enoch, the son of Jared. When the generation of the flood sinned and turned to evil deeds, and said to God, "Go away! We do not choose to learn your ways," the Holy One, blessed be he, took me from their midst to be a witness against them in the heavenly height to all who should come into the world [Charlesworth 1983, vol. 1, 258].

Enoch, then, is elevated here as a sort of living rebuke to God's recalcitrant creation — "a witness against them to future generations" (Charlesworth 1983, vol. 1, 258). This sounds rather more like Pullman's vindictive Authority than the loving God of Christianity (logically enough, since *3 Enoch* is a specifically Jewish text). Metatron goes on to tell Ishmael that the other angels originally objected to his presence, but were forced to accept it by God; nevertheless, they continue to call him Youth "because I am young in their company and a mere youth among them in days and months and years" (Charlesworth 1983, vol. 1, 259). We are thus reminded of Metatron's essential humanity — the humanity that, in Pullman's book, will eventually destroy him. Metatron goes on to describe the process of his transformation into an angel in some detail, and we are given some idea of the brilliance that made Mrs. Coulter unable to look at him directly:

> I was enlarged and increased in size till I matched the world in length and breadth. He made to grow on me 72 wings, 36 on one side and 36 on the other, and each single wings covered the entire world. He fixed in me 365,000 eyes and each eye was like the Great Light. There was no sort of splendour, brilliance, brightness, or beauty in the luminaries of the world that he failed to fix in me [Charlesworth 1983, vol. 1, 263].

He is even granted a throne, and it is announced that "any angel and any prince" who wishes to gain God's presence must first go through him; here, we see the beginnings of the Martin Bormann–like power Pullman's Metatron will eventually come to wield over the Authority (Charlesworth 1983, vol. 1,

264). God also grants Metatron the power to gaze into the human soul which he will come to use against Mrs. Coulter: "before a man thinks in secret, I see his thought; before he acts, I see his act. There is nothing in heaven above or deep within the earth concealed from me" (Charlesworth 1983, vol. 1, 264).[5] Metatron is crowned with a blazing crown, and, seated on his throne, receives the homage of the other angels, who fall prostrate before him; even his body is turned into fire (Charlesworth 1983, vol. 1, 266–7).

So far, the transformed Enoch has remained a loyal servant of his creator, for all his glory. However, there is a hint in *3 Enoch* of the arrogance that leads Pullman's Metatron to attempt to supplant his creator:

> At first I sat upon a great throne at the door of the seventh palace, and I judged all the denizens of the heights on the authority of the Holy One, blessed be he. I assigned greatness, royalty, rank, sovereignty, glory, praise, diadem, crown, and honour to all the princes of kingdoms, when I sat in the heavenly court. The princes of kingdoms stood beside me, to my right and to my left, by authority of the Holy One, blessed be he [Charlesworth 1983, vol. 1, 268].

This Godlike posturing cannot last; the angel Aher, awestruck by Metatron's majesty, bursts out that "there are indeed two powers in heaven!" (Charlesworth 1983, vol. 1, 268). Unsurprisingly, this is a step too far for God, who dispatches an angel to lash the arrogant Metatron with "sixty lashes of fire" and drive him to his feet (Charlesworth 1983, vol. 1, 268). Metatron is humbled and never again betrays any hint of envy of his creator; nevertheless, this brief episode probably suggested the megalomania that so dominates Pullman's Metatron. There is certainly no hint of it in the Bible or the two other relevant apocryphal texts.

The rest of *3 Enoch* is dominated by Metatron's detailed description of heaven and its workings to the presumably suitably awestruck Ishmael (Charlesworth 1983, vol. 1, 269–302). The angels are named and their roles described, and the fates of the souls of both the righteous and sinners revealed. There is no further suggestion that Metatron is anything but the most loyal servant of God.

Conclusion

It is not entirely accurate, then, to claim that Pullman's Metatron is a biblical figure. As we have seen, his origins are far more complex, and testimony both to Pullman's considerable breadth of research and to his imagination. The humanity that lies hidden within Metatron's angelic glory is vital to Pullman, both in terms of his plot — it allows Mrs. Coulter to lure him to his destruction — and, more profoundly, in terms of his attack on organized religion. For all his megalomaniacal posturing at divinity, Metatron is, ultimately, a flawed and all too human being whose desires are shared, to some degree, by all humanity. We are led to believe that the Authority himself once had similar desires — why, otherwise, lie to his fellow angels that he was their creator? — and a more positive depiction of the human within the apparently divine is given to us via Baruch's tragic love for Balthamos. Read in its entirety, Pullman's trilogy powerfully argues that to see any authority as beyond question — particularly any authority that claims to be superhuman, such as that of religion, or God — is a recipe for ignorance, oppression and slaughter; if the human race is to survive, it must reject this sort of immaturity and learn to think for itself. It is a mark of Pullman's considerable skill as a polemicist that he manages to create a character summing up all the menace of authoritarian religion whose origins lie in texts as soaked in irrational reverence as the Bible and the apocryphal scriptures. He is, as it were, pulling down the temple from within.

NOTES

1. In the case of the Christian Bible, the Hebrew Bible (or Old Testament) is based on a Greek translation, and includes the Septuagint, and the miscellaneous collection of lives of Christ, letters of Paul, and other documents that make up the New Testament.

2. There is evidence to suggest that the Bible in Lyra's world is different as it features references to daemons, for a start, though the language certainly sounds very similar.

3. This drawing is available online, see Schuchard (2000). No Blake title exists for this drawing and it has been catalogued under different names by commentators.

4. This drawing is available online, see Schuchard (2000). No Blake title exists for this drawing and it has been catalogued under different names by commentators.

5. This type of ability has been claimed by despotic rulers see for example the dictator Saddam Hussein who is said to have claimed similar powers.

WORKS CITED

Beer, John. 1994. "Blake's Changing View of History: The Impact of the Book of Enoch." In *Historicizing Blake*. Eds. Steve Clark and David Worrall, 159–178. Basingstoke: Macmillan.

Bentley Jr., G. E. 2003. *The Stranger from Paradise: A Biography of William Blake*. New Haven: Yale University Press.

Brown, Allen R. 1940. "Blake's Drawings for *The Book of Enoch*." *The Burlington Magazine for Connoisseurs*. September 1940, vol. 77, no. 450.

Charlesworth, James H., ed. 1983. *The Old Testament Pseudepigraphia* [2 vols.]. London: Darton, Longman and Todd.

Schuchard, Marsha Keith. 2000. "Why Mrs. Blake Cried: Blake, Swedenborg and the Sexual Basis of Spiritual Vision." *Esoterica*, vol II: 45–93. Accessed May 6, 2009. http://www.esoteric.msu.edu/VolumeII/BlakeFull.html.

10

The Republic of Heaven: East, West and Eclecticism in Pullman's Religious Vision

J'ANNINE JOBLING

Introduction

Philip Pullman is notoriously unsympathetic toward organized religion: "This is the religion I hate, and I'm happy to be known as its enemy" (Pullman, n.d.). However, he also acknowledges the centrality and significance of the religious impulse in human life and experience: "It is part of being human, and I value it. I'd be a damn fool not to" (Pullman, n.d.). While *His Dark Materials* offers a stinging critique of the institutional Church, it is also replete with themes associated with spirituality and the religious — such as the metaphysics of being, sin, evil, love, death, salvation, free will, moral choice and moral responsibility. It offers a nontheistic recapitulation of Milton's *Paradise Lost* and explores fundamental themes of the Christian Fall narrative, including the passage from innocence to experience. It culminates, however, in the rejection of the Kingdom of Heaven in favor of the so-called "Republic of Heaven" (*AS* 548; *HDM* 929). Although Pullman (2002) states that he is telling a story — not writing a philosophy, sermon or treatise — the trilogy is infused with philosophical and religious ideas. Much focus has been on Pullman as promulgator of anti-religious mythology and atheism;[1] this chapter seeks to show how Pullman's magisterial moral and metaphysical vision is steeped in the spiritual. In so doing, there is a particular exploration of resonances with certain traditions of Eastern origin, in particular Buddhism. It is nevertheless acknowledged that Pullman's metaphysical categories and concepts locate his universe within the Western context of a post–Christian humanism. He himself says:

> I was brought up in the Church of England, and whereas I'm an atheist, I'm certainly a Church of England atheist, and for the matter of that a 1662 Book of Common Prayer atheist. The Church of England is so deeply embedded in my personality and my way of thinking that to remove it would take a surgical operation so radical that I would probably not survive it [Pullman 2001a, n.p.].

It does not seem problematic, then, to call Pullman post–Christian. More contentious is ascribing to him a spiritual philosophy. He asserts that he never uses the words "spirit," "spirituality," or "spiritual" because he "can see nothing real that seems to correspond with them" (Pullman 2007, n.p.). All the overtones are for him entirely negative, even repulsive: portraits of saints and martyrs as "grubby old men with rotten teeth," or "martyrs having their flesh ripped from their bones as they gaze upwards with an expression of fanatical fervour" (Pullman 2007, n.p.). Yet, spirituality can be seen to exist both inside and outside of the contexts of specific religious traditions; it implies a reference to the frameworks of value, purpose and meaning according to which people orient their lives. Understood in this way, spirituality may or may not entail reference to the divine. Therefore, I will continue to use the language of spirituality for the purposes of analysis, with the understanding that this does not necessarily entail reference to the divine or specific religious traditions.

Pullman's vision is informed by many and various sources. He acknowledges a particular debt to three: William Blake, John Milton and Heinrich von Kleist, but this far from exhausts the materials and mythologies that Pullman has made use of. The eclecticism and enormous scope of influences implicitly and explicitly discernible within *His Dark Materials* are widely recognized. In the acknowledgements to *The Amber Spyglass*, he states himself that he has stolen from every book he has ever read, and that his daemon would appropriately be either a magpie or jackdaw: "One of these birds that pick up bright shining things and doesn't distinguish in terms of shininess between the diamond ring and the KitKat wrapper" (Pullman 2002b, n.p.). Lines from writers such as Samuel Taylor Coleridge, Emily Dickinson, John Keats and Rainer Maria Rilke provide the epigraphs; textual allusions can be found to the Bible, Gnosticism, paganism, Norse mythology, Hermeticism, Kabbalism, alchemy, the story of Odysseus, Doré, Dante and Wagner — amongst many others. While the religious belief systems introduced to us are narratologically dominated by the Church and Magisterium, there are also references to Shamanism, Zoroastrianism, the tiger gods of the Tartars and to the deities of the witches. Pullman's intertextuality sits, then, on a deeply eclectic base. In the analysis below I add the less obvious dialogue partner of Buddhism.

Why Buddhism?

Pullman makes little reference to this worldview,[2] and it is unlikely it acted as an overt influence. Pullman's Republic of Heaven also differs from traditional forms of Buddhism in significant respects. Furthermore, Christopher Hartney (2005) argues that Pullman has failed to incorporate Eastern thinking and that this represents a lost opportunity; emanating from a pervasive Western imperialism, nationalism and conservatism in *His Dark Materials*. As Hartney notes:

> The East remains exotic; rather than a viable alternative consciousness within with problems posed by monoliths such as his Church simply fall away. If Pullman was less Oxonian in his outlook he may have realised that Eastern thinking permits a way to speak of atheism that avoids being trapped in Christian, Western and nationalist discourse [Hartney 2005, 258].

It is undeniable that the structures of the trilogy are heavily dependent on Western philosophies and specifically Christian concepts — as indicated, notably the Christian Fall narrative and symbology, which are then inverted; it is a "fortunate Fall" towards love and self-knowledge. Nevertheless, I would argue that in so doing, Pullman narrativizes a philosophy which does have certain resonances with Eastern themes and modes of conceptualization, specifically in respect to aspects of Buddhism. Buddhism is besides an interesting comparator, given that Pullman with his Republic of Heaven wants to establish a nontheisic mode of conceiving meaning, purpose and morality. Buddhism is the world's primary example of a religion (or according to some, "philosophy of life") which typically does not involve belief in God.[3] It is also worthwhile to consider how Buddhism might inform the construction of a nontheistic ethic. As Douglas Powers argues, Buddhism brings a valuable voice to this debate, as "the appeal of Buddhist ethics is existential — virtue is reasserted not as absolute or transcendent truth but as a pragmatic ground from which to regulate human interaction" (Powers 2001, 73).

David Loy and Linda Goodhew, indeed, identify an explicit Buddhist allusion in Pullman's account of God as fraud. Balthamos reveals to Lyra and Will the truth about the Authority (*AS* 33; *HDM* 569–570). He was never, in fact, the creator, but just another angel, the first, certainly, and the most powerful, but also a being condensed out of Dust. He told the others who came after that he was their creator, but this was not true. In the Brahmajala Sutra of the Pali canon, the Buddha tells the following story (itself a parody of certain Hindu myths). Beings reborn in the Abhassara Brahma world dwell there "mind-made, feeding on delight, self-luminous, moving through the air, glorious" (Loy and Goodhrew 2004, 110). One being falls from the Abhassara world into an empty Brahma palace, where he is eventually joined by others. This causes the first being to believe that he had created the others through wishing for their existence. Those beings who came after then accepted this version of events. There are, then, some parallels between the two stories in the account of a first being who convinced subsequent ones of their status as a Creator God.

Further to this, it is has also been suggested that William Blake's thinking is reminiscent of Eastern philosophies, and it is well established that Pullman's thinking is indebted to Blake. According to Mark Ferrara:

> The similarities between William Blake's philosophical system and that of Buddhism (particularly the Ch'an(a) or Zen School) are no less than astonishing. One is struck by a fundamental similitude underlying the teaching of the Ch'an school and that of Blake's radical epistemology [Ferrara 1997, 59].[4]

This is not a new observation. Northrop Frye notes that Blake's vision of the ultimate identity of all things corresponds with the ultimate identification of nirvana and samsara in Mahayana Buddhism; it is a rejection of the antithesis between being and non-being, between substance and nothingness (Frye 1947, 431–432). Thomas Altizer also asserts that "the true analogue to [Blake's] vision lies in the world of Oriental mysticism," while believing that "Blake himself could not possibly have had any knowledge of Buddhist philosophy" (Altizer 2000, 164). It must also be noted that it was only after the middle of the nineteenth century that Buddhism was constructed in Britain; previously, encounters with Buddhism "remained in British consciousness merely as disparate accounts of the encounter of the West with indistinct aspects of the Orient — but not of the *Buddhist* orient" (Almond 1988, 14).[5]

As a prolegomenon to this analysis, such caveats remind us that Western reception and construction of Buddhist ideas may offer us a blurred and homogenized amalgamation of Eastern modes of conceptualization. Nor should we forget that transcultural exchanges through mission activity, for example, also had effects on indigenous Buddhisms. The distinction between West and East is itself a construct which risks reifying differences and obscuring interchanges. Buddhism is itself far from monolithic, with historical, devotional, philosophical and cultural-geographic differentiations. The broad distinction into Mahayana, Theravada and Vajrayana traditions itself covers healthy growths of sub-varieties. Therefore, it is important to bear in mind that the subsequent allusions to Buddhist thinking are selective and intended to identify moments of affinity — morphic resonance, let us say — or of illuminative divergence: not to offer a comprehensive and systematic account.

In what follows I shall delineate some of the key contours and concepts in Pullman's narrative of the Republic of Heaven, and relate this where appropriate to Buddhist ideas. Before this, however, let us consider what the Republic of Heaven is a reaction *against*: the traditional religion of the Church and the Authority.

The death of God

Pullman has stated that the *His Dark Materials* chronicle is about "killing God" (Pullman in Meacham 2003); this is the horizon and end-time of the trilogy. The denouement of the final novel is the collapse of the Church's Magisterium and the death of the Authority. The defunct and corrupt Kingdom of Heaven is exchanged for the new age of the Republic of Heaven. The battle is rich in traditional apocalyptic tropes: two dualistically opposing forces in a cosmic drama involving God, rebel angels and humans. This battle, indeed, is situated within the threat of an even greater apocalypse: the multi-verse itself is at risk, with the mysterious substance Dust leaking away, thereby endangering life, meaning and consciousness in every world. And both of these apocalypses are actually devices of Pullman's to confront a somewhat different kind of apocalypse — in philosophical terms, the death of God.

The death of God has haunted modernity, stalking philosophy ever since the enthronement of the human subject as the centre of the thinking world. The prospect of the loss of the credibility of God has gone hand-in-hand with anxieties about the disintegration of truth, meaning and purpose. Søren Kierkegaard asked what would life be but despair, if underlying everything was only a "bottomless, insatiable emptiness," or if all was produced by a "wild fermenting force" writhing in dark passions (in Evans and Walsh 2006, 12). It was Friedrich Nietzsche, of course, who gave the death of God its classical formulation on the lips of his madman in *Thus Spake Zarathustra*:

> "Where has God gone?" he cried. "I shall tell you. We have killed him — you and I. We are all his murderers. But how have we done this? How were we able to drink up the sea? Who gave us the sponge to wipe away the entire horizon? [Nietzsche 1961, 14].

Nietzsche, like Pullman, not only announces but also embraces this death of God. For Pullman, the demise of traditional Christianity figures not a threat but an opportunity. Such a view plays into trends which are suspicious of transcendence: as implying a devaluation of the body, immanence and the material world. Nevertheless, Pullman asserts that "not believing in God is not quite like believing in the tooth fairy": there are bigger consequences (Pullman 2001a). He acknowledges that the death of God can fund a sense of meaningless and alienation. So, what is needed is a new myth:

> We need a story, a myth that does what the traditional religious stories did: it must *explain*. It must satisfy our hunger for a *why*. Why does the world exist? Why are we here? ... There's the [why] that asks *What brought us here?* and the other that asks *What are we here for?* One looks back, and the other looks forward, perhaps [Pullman 2001a, n.p.].

Hence for Pullman, having stripped the world of divine sacrality, it is necessary to remythologize: to find new stories, new ways of seeing, which endow life with meaning, purpose, value and a sense that things are right and good. To this end, he ambitiously constructs his Republic of Heaven.

Building a Republic of Heaven out of the Dust

Pullman's claims that he is not writing a treatise or philosophy notwithstanding, he is very clear in his own commentaries and interviews about what values and worldviews are comprehended in the Republic of Heaven. Fundamentally, it is oriented towards the here and now, and a belief in the "preciousness" of the here and now (Pullman 1996). There is no "elsewhere"; humanity is a physical constituent of a physical universe. However, this also entails a feeling of believing, being part of a "real and important story," connected both to our fellow humans (living and dead) and to the universe itself (Pullman 2002a). It stands for a sense that humanity and the universe have a common meaning, destiny and purpose and are profoundly interconnected. It signifies joy, and a democracy of free and equal citizens which it is our duty to preserve and promote (see Pullman 2001b). This is the ethical imperative of the Republic of Heaven: to exercise responsibility and use the qualities we have to make the world a better place (Pullman 2002a)—one open-minded, tolerant and in which nobody "has" the truth (Pullman, 2002d).

So that is what Pullman is seeking to articulate. I will now expand on some of the metaphysical and ethical underpinnings to the Republic of Heaven and where pertinent relate it to Buddhist ideas. The first area for examination is Pullman's conception of Dust, which he uses as a metaphor for the metaphysics underpinning the Republic of Heaven. This mysterious elementary particle clusters around humanity, especially on attainment of puberty and adulthood. This leads the Church to associate Dust with original sin and the advent of sexuality; thus the concept of intercision arises as a means of protecting the individual from sin. There is, in fact, an interesting analogue here in Jainism: in this religion, karma is understood as a physical substance, very commonly referred to metaphorically as "dust"; it is accretion of this karmic dust that locks the soul into the cycle of rebirth; liberation is only achieved through purifying the soul of this karmic matter.[6] Passions, indeed, foster the adhesion of this karma, by creating a stickiness. There are, then, some interesting parallels with the negative view of the accretion of Dust held by the General Oblation Board in Pullman's narrative.

As the mysteries of Dust are unraveled, these negative valuations are shown to be shockingly misguided. It is Mary Malone, in our world, who discovers the connection between Dust (or Shadows), consciousness, and anything associated with human thought or workmanship. Putting this together with the historical arrival of Shadows some thirty or forty thousand years previously leads her to the conclusion that Shadows are actually "particles of consciousness" (*SK* 92; *HDM* 364).

Dust in Pullman's narrative has been likened to the atomism of Leibniz's monadology, which has in turn been likened to certain Buddhist understandings in which the constituent basis of the phenomenal world are dharmas (not to be confused with Dharma: the teachings of the Buddha). C. D. Sebastian explains this with reference to the Abhidharma system of taxonomy: "The conception of dharmas ... discloses itself as a metaphysical theory developed out of one fundamental principle of existence, which is an interplay of a plurality of subtle, ultimate, not further analyzable elements of matter, mind and forces." (Sebastian, n.d.).

Furthermore, Dust for Pullman is not simply a neutral, physical fact; it is intimately connected with purpose and value. Pullman states that Dust is his metaphor for "human wisdom, science and art, all the accumulated and transmissible achievements of the human mind" (Pullman 2007, n.p.). Angels are condensations of Dust, who interfered in human evolution for revenge against the Authority, inciting matter to desire to know itself. Dust represents also raw potentiality — this is evident in its designation as dark materials, which in Milton's *Paradise Lost* (II, 11.915–6) represent the primal matter ordained by the almighty to create more worlds. It is also associated with contemporary physicists' understanding of dark matter, a physical constituent of the mass of the universe.[7]

As in Buddhism, the universe of Dust has no external creator. It is self-organizing, immanent, contingent, and relational; process rather than substance. It has been argued that doctrines of creation, understood as either a unitary moment or as transcendent imposition of order on chaotic or passive matter, support philosophies which marginalize chance and naturalize identities. To the contrary, theories of material self-ordering open up possibilities for multiplicities attributed to changes in the arrangement of and relations between immanent elements (see for example Protevi 2001, 8). Thus a materialist economy can be asserted which disavows transcendent origins and ordering, and in so doing causes us to rethink matter as simply inert, passive or chaotic.

Dust bridges the disjunction between matter and spirit. As the Shadows tell Mary in a conversation about the nature of Shadow particles, spirit and matter are one: in what they are, spirit; in what they do, matter (*SK* 260; *HDM* 480). Dust is matter that has begun to understand itself, and to love itself. It is this tendency towards love and knowledge that leads Dust to cluster in increasing quantities around humans at puberty, as they embark on the journey of loving and knowing themselves as bodies, as matter. Similarly, it is Dust, in the oil of the seedpod, that enables the *mulefa* to know themselves as such and not simply be grazers.

Pullman's concept of Dust, then, visualizes a unity between matter and spirit. It has been suggested by Lois Gresh that Pullman's philosophies might most appropriately be described as "monist idealist," with reality united in a universal, cosmic consciousness (Gresh 2007). This is in contradistinction to "monist materialism," which asserts the epiphenomenal dependence of consciousness upon matter. The designation of Pullman as an idealist is problematic since he himself is on record as a committed materialist. However, Pullman's materialism is a form of panpsychism, for it *includes* consciousness, like mass, "as a normal and universal property of matter ... so that human beings, dogs, carrots, stones, and atoms are all conscious, though in different degrees" (Pullman 2007, n.p.).

This effort to delineate a philosophy which overcomes the matter/spirit dichotomy brings us to a significant point in a comparison and contrast with Buddhism. Gresh also specifically identifies Buddhism, like Pullman's thought, as an example of monist idealism (see Gresh 2007, 36–37); however, the application of materialist/idealist categories to Buddhism is fraught with difficulties. It has been likened to asking where the horns of a rabbit came from.[8] Nevertheless, it can be argued that Western interest in Buddhism corresponded with the rise of modern science, a split between faith and reason, and was specifically to meet a need for an "'alternative altar,' a bridge that could reunite the estranged worlds of matter and spirit" (Verhoeven 2001, 77).[9] So, like Pullman's quest for a post–Christian, humanistic, materialist Republic of Heaven, it can be argued that Buddhism's popularity in the West over the last century has been sparked by a perceived crisis in the capacity of traditional Christianity adequately to inhabit modern and postmodern scientific paradigms. This has exacerbated disjunctions between facts and values, spirit and matter, mind and body. As John Dewey put it: "The problem of restoring integration and cooperation between man's beliefs about the world in which he lives and his beliefs about the values and purposes that should direct his conduct is the deepest problem of modern life (Dewey 1929, 255).

In Buddhism, knowing is not simply a matter of exercising scientific method, but also of morality, self-cultivation and wisdom:

> What all people desire to know is that [i.e., the external world],
> But their means of knowing is this [i.e., oneself];
> How can we know that?
> Only by the perfection of this [citing the *Kuan Tzu*, in Verhoeven 2001, 95].

If we can only know "that" (the world) by knowing "this" (ourselves), traditional distinctions between matter and consciousness are indeed confounded. This plays into another theme within Pullman's narrative: the interconnected nature of all being, which likewise undercuts distinctions between subject and object, knower and known. This has epistemological implications evident in the way Lyra discerns truth in the alethiometer. There are clear parallels between

Lyra's account of how she reads the alethiometer and meditative insight; it is described as a cessation of mental striving after the truth. This centrality of truth — non-deluded and awakened awareness — is itself a point of contact with Buddhist philosophies. When Lyra loses her ability to read the alethiometer through simple grace and is told that she can regain the ability through work the importance of awakened awareness is again visible; she is told that this will lead to a deeper and fuller grace, and better reading, because it would come from conscious understanding (*AS* 520; *HDM* 909).

Truth, death, and rebirth in the trilogy

As Santiago Colás suggests, "truth meter" does not really capture the nature of the alethiometer (see Colás 2005, 41); the divination of the truth through use of this device is more akin to a dialogic and creative process than accession of truth as product. Furthermore, this mode of knowing truth abolishes the division between subject and object inherent in, for example, correspondence theories of truth: the knower is, instead, inseparably part of an immanent and relational process of truth discernment. Therefore, the mode of knowing is more akin to Martin Heidegger's "poetic reason," or John Keats' "negative capability": which, as Mary Malone quotes, involves "uncertainties, mysteries, doubts, without any irritable reaching after fact and reason" (Keats qtd. Pullman *SK* 92; *HDM* 364 and see also Colás 2005, 42–3). Our own enmeshment in reality makes knowledge contingent, open and participatory.

In Buddhism, this fundamental interconnection is primarily expressed in the doctrine of dependent origination. Basically, everything arises in dependence upon conditions; nothing exists in independence; and everything is in a continuous state of flux and dynamic interaction. Everything is impermanent and dynamic, nothing is fixed. This includes the self, which is neither unchanging nor eternal. The human person is comprised of five aspects — bodily forms, feelings, perceptions, dispositions and consciousness — all of which are in a state of constant change. This does not negate the self as such, but renders the notion of fixed identity delusional.

The question of human identity moves us on to Pullman's account of the soul. A preoccupation with and fear of death is often held to be rooted in the Western psyche, leading people to cling to concepts of an afterlife and an eternal soul. Here also Pullman's concern to integrate the spiritual and the material can be seen. He rejects accounts of the soul or fundamental self which see it as separable from the human body, as found in dominant forms of Christianity, Cartesian philosophies and Vedic traditions. This is interesting, since a key innovation in *His Dark Materials* is the idea of the daemon; this seems to posit a clear dualism at the heart of his presentation of the self. However, as Anne-Marie Bird demonstrates to great effect (2001), actually this apparent dualism points at a deeper level to a primary interrelatedness. As Lyra expostulates: "Your daemon en't *separate* from you. It's you" (*SK* 26; *HDM* 318). The externalized daemon, then, models a differentiation which is nevertheless not dualistic; the two cannot be monistically reduced to one, but nor can they be split apart without violent harm, as seen in the procedure of intercision.

What happens to this dynamic and relational self upon death? Pullman's account of Lyra and Will's visit to the world of the dead is central both to the storyline in *His Dark Materials*, and to his construction of an alternative worldview. Pullman's rendition is clearly indebted to a number of religious mythologies, from *Sheol* and Hades to the Christian Harrowing of Hell. According to the latter story, Christ descended into hell after his death, broke down the doors and rescued the souls of all those who had died under the conditions of the Fall. The broad shape of the story, therefore, seems clearly to have its roots in a Christian myth. Given Pullman's eclecticism, however, it is hardly surprising that a range of sources can be discerned, nor that the rescue performed by Lyra and Will leads the souls of the dead to an end very different from the traditional Christian understanding of heaven.

Pullman's version of the world of the dead is bleak indeed. Ghosts, child and adult alike, wander listlessly and mournfully through a landscape bleached of all color. There is no joy, no meaning, just endless apathy. The ghosts are, prison-camp style, guarded by harpies. Lyra and Will effect the escape of the dead through using the subtle knife to cut a window into the outside world; they persuade the harpies to allow the dead to exit by offering them stories as coin for passage.

For the purpose of this analysis, there are two points of particular interest here. The first is the manner through which Lyra and Will carry out this rescue: by telling stories. However, it is highly significant that these are not just any old stories; they are *true* stories. Similarly, upon emerging from the world of the dead, an old woman ghost tells Mary Malone: "Tell them stories. They need the truth. You must tell them true stories, and everything will be well. Just tell them stories" (*AS* 455; *HDM* 864). As is noted earlier in discussing the significance of the alethiometer, truth — awakened awareness — lies at the very heart of Buddhist philosophy. Furthermore, this shows us the personal development of Lyra herself and her own awakening to a deeper understanding. Lyra's actions are rooted in a wholesome intentionality, guided by insight and compassion, and can be compared to Buddhist conceptions of skilful means.[10]

The second significant point relates to the kind of redemption Pullman describes. He is, as has been seen, thoroughly committed to this-worldly spirituality, and argues that "we have to find a way of accepting our own mortality and death" (Pullman, 2001a). So, released from the prison of the world of the dead, the ghosts are finally free to embrace a true death, becoming part of the earth, the night breeze, the trees, and all living things, as their particles loosen and float apart (*AS* 455–456; *HDM* 864–865). This is the "death of death"[11] through reintegration into the cycle of life of which death is part. As Lyra encourages the ghosts, they will never vanish, but be part of everything alive again. In the words of the woman who died as a religious martyr, they will be "glittering in the dew under the stars and the moon out there in the physical world, which is our true home and always was" (*AS* 336; *HDM* 783).

A significant resonance with Buddhism is the importance of letting go; that is why enlightenment is sometimes called the "great death," (Loy and Goodhew, 2004, 115) for it is about the liberation of the ego-self from its fears and attachments, including fear of death and a grasping attachment to this particular life. This demonstrates a graceful acceptance of impermanence, rather than reification of the transient and contingent. Once more, a resonance with William Blake's work can be discerned:

> He who binds to himself a joy
> Does the winged life destroy;
> But he who kisses the joy as it flies
> Live in eternity's sunrise [Blake, 1982, 470].

How does Pullman's account of death accord with Buddhist thinking? This is not an easy issue. Precisely what does happen after death is one of those questions the Buddha chose not to answer. It would appear, however, that here a significant divergence between Pullman's philosophy of existence and Buddhist thought might be identified. In Buddhism, rebirth into another existence marked by suffering (dukkha) is traditionally understood to follow death until liberation is achieved through the realization of nirvana — an awakening that involves "neither annihilation nor some kind of eternal life after death" (Loy and Goodhew 2004, 104). This does not appear to accord well with Pullman's recommendations both to immerse oneself affirmatively in the material world, and to accept the dissolution of self at death.

Pullman lays much emphasis on the significance and value of the sensuous, a this-worldly and material affirmation. Even his angels are envious of human capacity to enjoy the material world — for them to have our flesh and our senses, says Will in *The Amber Spyglass*, would be a kind of ecstasy. This would seem to be in sharp contradistinction to Buddhism, which is often understood to teach asceticism, world-renunciation and the desirability of escaping from the cycle of life, death and rebirth. According to Loy and Goodhew, however, there is a genuine ambivalence regarding this in the Buddhist traditions; they ask whether nirvana amounts to the realization of another reality at the expense of our physicality, or whether it is rather the realization of the true reality of this world, including in bodily and sensuate terms (Loy and Goodhew 2004, 113). The Buddha's teachings support the Middle Way, navigating a path through asceticism on the one hand and self-indulgence on the other; it is also worth noting that while asceticism forms one strand in Buddhist history and practices, other strands such as the tantric traditions, celebrate the sensuality of bodily awakening. So-called engaged Buddhism emphasizes the significance of material conditions and the need for active social compassion. Nevertheless, it should not be overlooked that there are traditions of Buddhism which it would be difficult to reconcile with Pullman's embrace of material, phenomenal immanence.

The concept of rebirth in Buddhism is also subject to debate, with different schools and philosophies expressing varying views. Since Buddhism disavows the idea of an eternal self (*atman*), it is no simple matter to determine just what is, in fact, reborn.[12] The Pali text *The Questions of King Milinda* has King Milinda questioning a Buddhist monk, Nagasena. When asked whether a person who is reborn is the same as or different from the person who died, the monk responded that he is neither; just as curds, butter and ghee are not the same as the pot of milk from which they originated, nor are they something other than it. Hence, the second thing arises in dependence upon the first; there is continuity and a conditioned relationship between them, but there is not a shared, fixed or stable essence that is passed along. In such understandings of Buddhism, a fundamental essence, consciousness or soul neither outlasts death nor is annihilated at death; once more Buddhism steers a middle way, this time between the poles of idealism and materialism.

Interpreting this, the Western Buddhist Nagapriya suggests it is possible to think of rebirth in this manner:

> At death it is possible that we will just flow out into a great karmic ocean, our identity lost forever.... After all, this is what happens to our bodies: they are reabsorbed into the elements. Why should our minds carry on in a discrete form? [Nagapriya, 2004, 128].

There are striking similarities here with Pullman's account in *His Dark Materials*. Depending upon the particular interpretation, then, Buddhist understandings may not always be so far away from his as one might suppose. The mode of liberation from the prison-camp of an artificial afterlife also bears a resonance: it is an awakening, an enlightenment, through the hearing and telling of truth. For Pullman this is not simply an abstract and conceptual mode of truth-telling, but based in the narrativization of experience. Likewise, knowledge, and experience *as* knowledge are important to Pullman. His representation of the myth of the Fall recasts it, in Gnostic fashion, as a move from ignorance to knowledge, from immaturity to maturity: from innocence to experience. This inversion of the traditional Christian understanding leads to a positive valuation of the eating of the forbidden fruit. Pullman identifies this as a primary theme of the books, and comments that, traditionally:

> [The Fall has] been presented as being a very bad thing and Eve was very wicked and we all got covered in sorrow and sin and misery from then on as a result of this ... well, I just reversed that. I thought wasn't it a good thing that Eve did, isn't curiosity

a valuable quality? Shouldn't she be praised for risking this? It wasn't, after all, that she was after money or gold or anything, she was after knowledge. What could possibly be wrong with that? [Pullman 2002c, n.p.].

The centralization of truth and awakened awareness do have resonance with Buddhism; Pullman's enlightenment — as modeled by Will and Lyra at the conclusion of the trilogy — is not directly equivalent, but it does represent a transformation of mind and heart, and is accompanied by heightened insight.

Buddhism: Environmentalism and ethics

Thus far we have seen points of resonance between Pullman's philosophies and aspects of Buddhism in his metaphysics of Dust, his account of the self, his view of afterlife, and his centralization of awakened awareness. Another point of contact between Pullman's philosophy and Buddhism could be located in his environmentalism. This is a persistent theme within *His Dark Materials*, reflecting Pullman's own concerns; in his New Year Message of 2006, he asks "that everybody would just stop destroying the world so that I can stop fretting about it and get on with my proper work" (Pullman 2006a, n.p.). Humanity's lack of respect for the integrity of the universe is seen to have caused severe disruption in all the worlds portrayed. Lord Asriel's actions epitomize this; his violent unleashing of the energy created by separating Roger and his daemon in order to create a bridge between worlds causes climactic upheaval in Lyra's world. Thaws, floods, alterations in migratory patterns testify to an overturning of nature leaving Serafina Pekkala "heartsick" (*AS* 39; *HDM* 574). The world of the *mulefa* is held up as an example of ecological balance gone awry; the years of living "in perpetual joy" (*AS* 139; *HDM* 646) with their trees is under serious threat from the leaking of Dust caused by three centuries of cutting windows between worlds. Pullman's emphasis on environmentalism is consistent with his affirmation of this-world; "where we are is always the most important place" (*AS* 548; *HDM* 929).

Buddhism, in the popular imagination, is also associated with a holistic and environmentally egalitarian worldview. Donald Swearer (2005) cautions that the picture is rather more complex than this, and that five (sometimes overlapping) categories can be identified. These range from holding that environmental ethics are a natural extension of Buddhist worldviews, to actual incompatibility between the two (Swearer 2005, 3). However, the notion that Buddhism promotes a relational, environmentally aware mode of mindful living amounting to a cosmic ecology is also promulgated. This is rooted in the recognition of interdependence and the disavowal of autonomous, stable and separable identities; all are part of a dynamic, changing set of energies with no dualism between life and environment (Badiner 1990, xiv–xv).

The lineage through Blake's influence on Pullman is, again, also worth mentioning. Derek Wall argues that an examination of Green philosophy takes us back, among other influences, to the inspiration of William Blake as poet and holistic philosopher drawing partly from traditions of Western holism and partly from Eastern philosophies: "[t]he influence of William Blake in synthesising and transmitting such ancient knowledge cannot be understated" (Wall 1993, 90). Green philosophy's hallmark is a holism that emphasizes the connection between things, with all life interwoven in transformation and interaction. Wall identifies the importance of the dynamic interplay of opposites and of non-reductive modes of perception in Blake's "The Marriage of Heaven and Hell" as especially inspirational.

This final area I shall touch upon is the nature of ethical action. I suggest here that Buddhist emphasis on action, will and the significance of intentional conduct aligns with Pullman's humanistic views. Pullman has stated that he has an action-based view of identity: "What we are is not in our control, but what we do is ... simultaneously, what we do depends on what we are (on what we have to do it with), and what we are can be modified by what we do" (Pullman 2005, n.p.). This can once more be related to Buddhism, specifically in the understanding of karma. Nagapriya cites the Buddha as reported to have responded to a student: "Student, beings are owners of their actions [*karmas*], heirs of their actions; they originate from their actions, are bound to their actions, have their actions as their refuge. It is action that distinguishes beings as inferior and superior"(Nagapriya 2004, 12).

This rooting of karma in action can, then, be compared to Pullman's conceptualization of action-based identity. Sometimes, karma is understood on a deterministic reward and retribution model. There are a number of philosophical problems with this, including encouraging a passive acceptance of pain and suffering for both oneself and others as just desserts; such an understanding could also be seen to run counter to the centrality of compassion as guiding principle for action. The principle of karma might be more fully understood on a model of action and consequence, rather than reward and retribution. Even here it is important to note that action also arises in dependence on conditions, and intentionality or volition is central to this.

As in Buddhism, so in Pullman — right intention and right action are crucial to morality. Duty is an important part of Pullman's ethics in *His Dark Materials*, as is explicit in the angel Xaphania's strictures to Will and Lyra and the hard choice ultimately made by them in the trilogy's conclusion. Citizens of the Republic of Heaven are free and equal but have responsibilities — "to work hard to make this place as good as we possibly can" (Pullman 2002a, n.p.). Again, we see here analogies with Buddhism, which Powers describes as individualistic, yes, but an individualism of "responsibility, not desire" (Powers 2001, 69). While Buddhism has an emphasis on individual action and karmic liberation, such actions are never divorced from the larger web of existence. To that extent all action is interaction — "a vast net of interreflecting jewels" (Powers 2001, 70).[13] In Buddhism, freedom is not expressed in acting on one's desires or in attaining instant gratifications: which are conceptions common in the consumeristic modern society. The Buddha taught that acting on desire is actually a form of bondage — to those very desires, and patterns of habit conditioning desires.

Conclusion

The philosophy of *His Dark Materials* can, on a broad understanding of the term, be considered a spirituality. It postulates a universe vibrant with love, spirit, meaning and purpose even at the level of the elementary particle. It is a material spirituality, or a spiritual materialism: the divide between matter and spirit is not merely bridged but collapsed. It promulgates an ethic of care and responsibility, where the communal good is favored over individual gratification. It can therefore be argued that Pullman's narrative world in *His Dark Material* is steeped in spirituality. I have in this chapter identified areas where resonances between the spiritual vision of *His Dark Materials* and aspects of Buddhism can be discerned. This is in no way to suggest that Pullman is some sort of anonymous Buddhist; nor is it to deny that similar ideas to those expressed by Pullman can also be found in philosophies of Western provenance (including particular varieties of Christianity). It is, however, to highlight where Pullman's broad structure of an inverted Christian myth is expanded and enriched by alternative ways of thinking about spirit, matter and being. Resonances between Pullman's post–Christian remythologization and Buddhist ideas should not perhaps be surprising. Analysis of the spread and reception of Buddhism in contexts such as Britain and America highlights that it is the very differences from Christianity which render Buddhism appealing, including that it is non-theistic, non-dogmatic and emphasizes spiritual autonomy rather than faith in an external savior figure (*c.f.* Kay 2004, 5). It is possible to identify elements of similarity with a non-theistic humanism which is nevertheless spiritually rich. Therefore, it is argued here that *His Dark Materials* has points of resonance not only with Christian traditions which it overtly rejects, but with Buddhist traditions to which makes no explicit reference and are typically classed amongst the organized religions that Pullman purports to despise.

Notes

1. An earlier version of this essay appeared in J'annine Jobling's *Fantastic Spiritualities: Monsters, Heroes, and the Contemporary Religious Imagination* (London: T. and T. Clark, 2010) and is published with the kind permission from the author and publishers.

2. See Donna Freitas (2007) for an argument that the trilogy is both deeply theological and more specifically, deeply Christian.

3. There is reference in the *The Amber Spyglass* to a Himalayan monastery Cho-Lung-Se with its healer Pagdzin Tulku.

4. Jainism also has no concept of a supreme and ontologically distinct God; every soul is potentially divine.

5. Ferrara also here argues that Blake was known to be familiar with Eastern philosophies through the first English edition of the Hindu Bhagavad-Gita (translated by Charles Wilkins in 1785); that direct influence can be seen in Blake's catalogue entry for piece named "The Brahmins–A Drawing" (*A Descriptive Catalogue of Pictures*, 1809); and cites Blake's opinion that "The philosophy of the east taught the first principles of human perception" (in Erdman 1988, 2). However, even if a case can be made for some Vedic familiarity, it does not thereby demonstrate knowledge of Buddhism.

6. Interest in Buddhism is, however, evident in the writings of German philosophers Leibniz (1646–1716) and Schopenhauer (1788–1860).

7. It is also, perhaps, worthy of note that the process of inflow of karmic dust is known as "asrav." This is intriguingly reminiscent of the *mulefa* word for Dust: "sraf."

8. For an extended discussion of Pullman's Dust and its cultural attributes see Katharine Cox's chapter in this volume.

9. Cited in James Bisset Pratt (1996: 403). It is inherently risky to consider one thought-system in terms developed by another. While there have been numerous attempts to analyze and classify Buddhist thought according to the schools of Western philosophy, it is debatable whether these categories are appropriate.

10. Concerns of this kind, in fact, prompted people like Paul Carus to foster Western interaction with Buddhist thinking. Carus garnered support for Buddhist missionaries to go to the United States in the late 1800s and early 1900s as a response to the perceived spiritual crisis.

11. The principle of "skilful means" is rooted in the Buddha's compassionate aim to assist people to attain enlightenment; it is "the way in which the goal, the intentions, or the meaning of Buddhism is correlated with the unenlightened condition of human beings" (Pye 2008, 1).

12. There is an allusion here to 1 Corinthians 15:26 and Revelations 21:5; typically, Pullman is ironically playing on the Christian idea of the destruction of death, and giving it a vastly different interpretation.

13. For this reason, there is a technical difference between the concepts of rebirth and reincarnation; the latter belief is rooted in the concept of a particular self which reincarnates.

14. This is the model of "Indra's net," described in the Mahayana sutras.

Works Cited

Almond, Phillip C. 1988. *The British Discovery of Buddhism*. Cambridge: Cambridge University Press.

Altizer, Thomas J. J. 2000. *The New Apocalypse: The Radical Christian Vision of William Blake* [1967]. Aurora, CO: Davies Group.

Badiner, Alan Hunt, ed. 1990. *Dharma Gaia*. Berkeley, CA: Parallax.

Bird, Anne-Marie 2001. "'Without Contraries Is No Progression': Dust as an All-Inclusive, Multifunctional Metaphor in Philip Pullman's *His Dark Materials*.' In *Children's Education in Literature* 32.2, 111–123.

Blake, William. 1982. "Eternity." In *The Complete Poetry and Prose of William Blake*. Ed. David V. Erdman. Berkeley: University of California Press.

_____. 1988. *The Complete Poetry and Prose of William Blake*. Ed. David. V. Erdman. New York: Doubleday.

Colás, Santiago. 2005. "Telling True Stories, or the Immanent Ethics of Material Spirit (and Spiritual Matter) in Philip Pullman's *His Dark Materials*." *Discourse* 27.1, 34–66.

Dallmayr, Fred Reinhard. 1996. *Beyond Orientalism: Essays on Cross-Cultural Encounter*. Albany: State University of New York Press.

Dewey, John. 1929. *The Quest for Certainty*. New York: Minton, Balch.

Erdman, David V., ed. 1982. *The Complete Poetry and Prose of William Blake*. Berkeley: University of California Press.

Ferrara, Mark S. 1997. "Ch'an Buddhism and the Prophetic Poems of William Blake." *Journal of Chinese Philosophy* 24, 59–73.

Freitas, Donna. 2007. *Killing the Imposter God: Philip Pullman's Spiritual Imagination in His Dark Materials.* San Francisco: Jossey Bass.

Frye, Northrop. 1947. *Fearful Symmetry: A Study of William Blake.* Princeton: Princeton University Press.

Gooderham, David. 2003. "Fantasizing It as It Is: Religious Language in Philip Pullman's Trilogy, *His Dark Materials.*" *Children's Literature* 31, 155–175.

Gresh, Lois H. 2007. *Exploring Philip Pullman's His Dark Materials: An Unauthorized Adventure Through The Golden Compass, The Subtle Knife, and The Amber Spyglass.* London: Macmillan.

Hartney, Christopher. 2005. "Imperial and Epic: Philip Pullman's Dead God." In *The Buddha of Suburbia : Proceedings of the Eighth Australian and International Religion, Literature and the Arts Conference 2004.* Eds. Carole M. Cusack, Frances Di Lauro and Christopher Hartney. Sydney: RLA, 246–280.

Kay, David N. 2004. *Tibetan and Zen Buddhism in Britain.* London: Routledge.

Kierkegaard, Søren. 2006. *Fear and Trembling* [1843]. Eds. C. Stephen Evans and Sylvia Walsh. Trans. by Sylvia Walsh. Cambridge: Cambridge University Press.

Loy, David R., and Goodhew, Linda. 2004. *The Dharma of Dragons and Daemons: Buddhist Themes in Modern Fantasy.* Somerville, MA: Wisdom.

Mahathera, Nyanatiloka, comp. and trans. 1984. "Extracts from the Samyutta-Nikaya: Dealing with Egolessness." *The Wheel Publication* 202/203/204. *http://www.accesstoinsight.org/lib/authors/various/wheel202.html.*

Meacham, Steve. 2003. "The Shed Where God Died." *The Sydney Morning Herald,* December 13, 2003. *http://www.smh.com.au/articles/2003/12/12/1071125644900.html.*

Nagapriya. 2004. *Exploring Karma and Rebirth.* Birmingham: Windhorse.

Nietzsche, Friedrich. 1961. *Thus Spake Zarathustra* [1885]. Trans. R. J. Hollingdale. Harmondsworth: Penguin.

Powers, Douglas. 2001. "Buddhism and Modernity." *Religion East and West* 1: 67–76.

Pratt, James Bisset. 1996. *The Pilgrimage of Buddhism and a Buddhist Pilgrimage* [1928]. New Delhi: Asian Educational Services.

Protevi, John. 2001. *Political Physics: Deleuze, Derrida, and the Body Politic.* London and New York: Athlone.

Pullman, Philip. n.d. "Comment on Religion." *Philip Pullman website. http://www.philip-pullman.com/pages/content/index.asp?PageID=12.*

_____. 2001a. "The Republic of Heaven." *The Horn Book Magazine,* November/December. *http://www.hbook.com/magazine/articles/2001/nov01_pullman.asp.*

_____. 2001b. "Interview with Joan Bakewell." *Belief* series, BBC Radio 3. *http://darkadamant.betterversion.org/BBC_Belief_Philip_Pullman.txt.*

_____. 2002a. "A Dark Agenda: Interview with Susan Roberts." November. *http://www.surefish.co.uk/culture/features/pullman_interview.htm.*

_____. 2002b. "I am of the Devil's Party." Interview with Helen Bertodano, *Telegraph.co.uk,* January 29 *http://www.telegraph.co.uk/arts/main.jhtml?xml=/arts/2002/01/29/bopull27.xml&page=1.*

_____. 2002c. "Faith and Fantasy." Interview on *Encounter* series, ABC Radio National, March 24. *http://www.abc.net.au/rn/relig/enc/stories/s510312.html.*

_____. 2002d. "Are you There, God? It's me." *Book,* November/December *http://web.archive.org/web/20050211151440/http://www.bookmagazine.com/issue25/inthemargins.shtml.*

_____. 2005. "Identity Crisis." *Trinidad and Tobago Humanist Association,* November. *http://www.humanist.org.tt/forum/article/guest/identity_crisis.html.*

_____. 2006a. "New Year Message 2006." *Philip Pullman Website,* January. *http://www.philip-pullman.com/pages/content/index.asp?PageID=120.*

_____. 2006b. "Carnegie Medal Acceptance Speech." *http://www.randomhouse.com/features/pullman/author/carnegie.html.*

_____. 2007. "FilmChat: Philip Pullman: The Extended E-Mail Interview (with Peter T. Chattaway)." November 28. *http://filmchatblog.blogspot.com/2007/11/philip-pullman-extended-e-mail.html*

Pye, Michael. 2008. *Skilful Means.* London: Routledge.

Sebastian, C.D. n.d. "Theory of Psyche in Buddhism: An Appraisal of Buddhist and Scientific

Psychology." *Omega: Indian Journal of Science and Religion* 6. 1, 39–51. *http://www.lfseminary.org/htm/articlesonline2.html.*

Singh, Nagendra Kr., ed. 2001. *Encyclopedia of Jainism.* New Delhi: Anmol.

Swearer, Donald K. 2005. "An Assessment of Buddhist Eco-Philosophy." December 10. *http://www.hds.harvard.edu/cswr/resources/print/dongguk/swearer.pdf.*

Verhoeven, Martin J. 2001. "Buddhism and Science: Probing the Boundaries of Faith and Reason." *Religion East and West* 1, 77–97.

Wall, Derek, ed. 1993. *Green History: A Reader in Environmental Literature, Philosophy and Ethics.* London: Routledge.

11

"Walking into Mortal Sin": Lyra, the Fall, and Sexuality

TOMMY HALSDORF

Introduction

Part of Philip Pullman's ambition in creating *His Dark Materials* was to rewrite John Milton's *Paradise Lost*. However, by adhering to the satanist interpretation championed by Pullman's inspiration William Blake, and thus reversing standard Christian morality, the novels have stirred up controversy. One aspect of this is that Eve subversively functions as a female savior figure. The original Fall of man was an unjust punishment for daring to acquire knowledge, which in Pullman's story is seen as a positive act. The heroine Lyra Belacqua is, unbeknown to her, the subject of a prophecy casting her as Eve reborn, and her second Fall acts as a means of redemption not damnation of mankind. Her "fault" becomes fortunate, and it will be argued that it represents a reestablishment of the male-female balance upset by the events related in the Book of Genesis.

I shall discuss how *His Dark Materials* reworks the Fall, and its prelude, the temptation, in the light of the previous renderings of the Bible, Milton, and Blake. Importantly, the essay will not only trace the intertextuality back, but it will also examine the theatre adaptations of the books, thus offering a perspective on both the stage productions and the novels simultaneously.

The focus of this essay will lie with the temptation and Fall scenes and the subject of sexuality, bodily awareness and sexual awakening, with which it is heavily linked. This represents a transgression of a traditional boundary in children's literature. Pullman's writing breaches this taboo, which forms another highly contentious issue among critics of his work. The death of God aside, the physical relationship between Lyra and Will is undoubtedly the most polemical part of the story. I will analyze what happens when the sexuality which Pullman can be said to merely suggest, must be dealt with visually on stage — arguably an even more controversial proposition.

I shall be concentrating on the original version of the stage production[1] in Britain which ran from December 2003 to April 2004, referring to the revised and slightly shorter version of Christmas 2004 to April 2005 (with a different cast, but the stage version was likewise adapted by Nicholas Wright and directed by Nicholas Hytner) only when there are major differences concerning the scenes important to the analysis, as most revisions do not significantly affect the plot.[2]

The essay will furthermore look at some of the other changes that the stage version makes to Pullman's original episode of the temptation and Fall.[3] This concerns for example the female temptress figure playing the role of Satan in the Garden of Eden, and includes the means the theatre employs to compensate for the descriptive, reflective and emotional passages that it must necessarily omit in its rendering of the climax of the story.

Sexuality and the Fall

Taking the Bible as a starting point, we can establish that the actual information provided by the Book of Genesis is sparse. The scene of temptation, and the actual moment of the consumption of the fruit and the Fall, covered in Genesis 3:1 to 3:6, is brief, and there is no direct reference to Adam and Eve having sexual intercourse; it is only after their Fall and expulsion from Eden that it is explicitly stated that "Adam lay with his wife Eve" (Genesis 4:1). Sex cannot then be said to have caused the Fall, it is rather a shameful consequence of it.

This is a long way from the detailed description of Adam and Eve's life in *Paradise Lost*. Here, Adam and Eve also have sex as soon as they are banned from Eden, which, assuming they were virgins before this, points to sexuality as a Fallen value. The Bible does not say otherwise; however Milton's poem can be read in a completely different way. According to *Paradise Lost*, lovemaking has nothing to do with the Fall, as Adam and Eve already had sexual intercourse earlier. Freshly married, they retreat "into their inmost bower" (Milton 2004, IV.l 738.), and

> Straight side by side were laid, nor turned I ween
> Adam from his fair spouse, nor Eve the rites
> Mysterious of connubial love refused [Milton 2004, IV.l 741–43].

Milton justifies their sexual union by referring to God's command to multiply: "Our Maker bids increase, who bids abstain / But our destroyer" (Milton 2004,

IV.1 748–749). Pullman's story inverts this; it is the Authority who condemns sexuality and the serpent's role to promote it.

If we take prelapsarian sex as a given, it cannot be shameful as such (after all angels do it too), so the only argument can be that the act itself has somehow changed. John Beer suggests that Milton is affirming that the nature of sexual congress was transformed with the Fall. Carnal desire, a negative value, arose as a consequence, whereas previously lovemaking represented a pure corporeal and spiritual bonding, nearer to the order of angelic love (Beer 1968, 31). Easthope argues to the contrary, seeing Adam's desire for Eve as heightened by the Fall: "For never did thy beauty [...] so inflame my sense / With ardour to enjoy thee" (Milton 2004, IX. l 1029; ll 1031–2), so their lovemaking has grown from the childish act in the prelapsarian Garden to adult maturity (Easthope 1999, 139). Similarly, as we shall see, Lyra and Will pass the threshold from childhood to adulthood through their sexual awakening.

In *Paradise Lost* the Fall is not a direct consequence of sexual relations, although sex is affected by it. In *His Dark Materials* it is triggered by physical contact and love between Lyra and Will. The difference is that in the former sex is not necessarily a negative deed, and certainly not a decisive one, whereas in the latter it becomes the crucial positive act.

Eve's conversation with the serpent initiates the Fall and the ensuing loss of paradise, sealed through this gesture: "Forth reaching to the fruit, she plucked, she ate" (Milton 2004. IX. l 781). The serpent willfully seduces Eve with his crafty rhetoric: "can it be sin to know" (Milton 2004, IV. 517), and she is convinced. Gnostics have interpreted the serpent's action as promethean rather than evil, as argued for example by Elaine Pagels (1989, 69) giving man experience which is identified with knowledge, instead of innocence, equated with ignorance. There is no mention of the temptation being of a sexual nature, neither in *Paradise Lost*, nor in the Bible. However Christian apocryphal writers such as Tatian have interpreted the gained knowledge as sexual awareness (see Pagels 1989, 27), and the consumption of the fruit itself can be seen as a metaphor for sexuality. From this point of view Adam and Eve's discovery of their sexuality then nonetheless becomes the Fall, resulting in bodily shame.

Blake too maintains that if sex provides pleasure it must also have existed before the Fall, being as the Fall could not produce any pleasure that had not already been present in the Garden of Eden (Beer 1968, 32). Though Blake does not pick up on the story of Adam and Eve directly, the theme of sexuality is prominent in his work as an integral and joyous part of life, a source of physical fulfillment and bliss. He speaks of desire in almost spiritual, religious terms and deplores Christianity's vilification of it, as his poetry repeatedly testifies.

"A Little Girl Lost," in the Experience section of his *Songs of Innocence and of Experience*, combines the religious and the sexual, foregrounding the latter with the girl's Fall into experience. Interestingly, Ona's Fall is not due to her first sexual encounter, with the youth, but rather because of her father's subsequent sarcastic "loving look" as he deems love "a crime" and is bitterly disappointed by his daughter (Blake 1977, 131, l 27; l 4). The girl realizes this and thus a sense of guilt is instilled within her that will forever be connected to sexual matters, a guilt that she will invariably transmit to the youth. Blake is appalled by this situation, and hopes that his appeal to future children will be heard, as he assumes that then love will be accepted and the story of his poem only a bad memory to show that once things were different. This Fall story is timeless, symbolized by Blake's tense-mixing, alternating between present, past and future. Ona and the youth represent Adam and Eve; they are Everyman figures (Gillham 1973, 54–5). Blake is keen to visualize the Fall as taking place throughout our lives, a culmination of our shortcomings, and always applying to us, not just in one specific moment.

Like Milton's couple, Blake's is innocent but by no means ignorant because of it. Before the Fall they know what work is (tending the garden), and they know sexuality. Afterwards of course the work becomes hard labor, without pleasure, and sexuality becomes shameful, tinged with the father's gaze — comparable to the gaze of God on Adam and Eve. Mere awareness ("they knew that they *were* naked" [Genesis 3:7]) is enough to shatter their innocence. Thus the activities themselves do not change fundamentally, but their perceptions of them do.

The pair of poems "The Little Girl Lost" and "The Little Girl Found" are similarly about a girl's entrance into the world of experience, however with the positive outcome found in *His Dark Materials*. Not only does the name of the protagonist Lyca resemble Lyra, but there are obvious parallels in their respective stories. Lyca grows to independence from her parents. She discovers sexual passion in the process, which is symbolized by wild beasts of prey. These lions and tigers are however portrayed as benign creatures in the text. Whereas Lyca's passions themselves are of an innocent nature and she enters them naturally, she is distraught by her parents' reaction to this new stage of her life. They are deeply concerned about her new behavior, and fear the beasts. Lyra too awakens to sexuality innocently, and has her mother fearing for her to the point of kidnapping her to keep her safe. Like Lyca's parents, Mrs. Coulter finally comes to realize that her daughter must be left to grow up freely, of which sexuality is an integral part, and have "their fears allay[ed]" (Blake 1977, 122, l.30).

Pullman's Eve reincarnation, whose coming the Church dreads as "the fount of original sin" (Wright 2003, 133) and whose renewed Fall they want to prevent at all cost because it will end their control over mankind, is revealed to be Lyra: "she will be life — mother — she will disobey [...] Eve, again! Mother Eve!" (*SK* 328; *HDM* 527).

Mary Harris Russell (2005, 214) argues for several different characters that could be interpreted as having an Eve function, namely Mary Malone, Mrs. Coulter and of course Lyra. What these three women have in common with Eve is a fervent thirst for knowledge. Likewise, the figure of Satan is split into multiple roles. In this Pullman follows Blake's Zoas as well as pre–Christian ideas. Lord Asriel is Satan, the adversary of God. Lyra, his daughter, is sin, though sin equated with sexuality is actually good in line with Pullman's inversion of convention. The tempter role falls to a different character in Mary Malone, a former nun turned scientist. Sexuality is a central theme of the story. Every human in Lyra's world has a daemon, a physical manifestation of the soul in animal form, of fixed nature with adults but changeable with children. The abominable intercision, the Church's severing of the human-daemon bond serves to prevent "all sorts of troublesome thoughts and feelings" (*NL* 285; *HDM* 209–210) connected with puberty and sexuality, and thus avoid Falling. For Pullman, clearly, the Fall is of a sexual nature.

Lyra's temptation in *His Dark Materials* is separate from her actual Fall. It occurs when Mary Malone, who "must play the serpent" (*SK* 261; *HDM* 480), tells Lyra of her own experiences of romance. Her story of how she rediscovered her sensual side stimulates Lyra and Will's sexual awakening. A taste of marzipan at a science conference brought back forgotten memories of her first kiss, her first love, when she was twelve and this boy gently fed her a piece of marzipan before kissing her. She also talks about the bliss of her relationship with a man she met at the conference. Lyra's reaction to this story is forceful and intense, a bodily epiphany, as she starts to discover a hitherto unknown side of her:

> Lyra felt something strange happen to her body. She felt a stirring at the roots of her hair: she found herself breathing faster. [T]he sensations in her breast [...] were exciting and frightening at the same time, and she had not the slightest idea why. The sensation continued, and deepened, and changed, as more parts of her body found themselves affected too. She felt as if she had been handed the key to a great house she hadn't known was there, a house that was somehow inside her, and as she turned the key, deep in the darkness of the building she felt other doors opening too, and lights coming on. She sat trembling, hugging her knees, hardly daring to breathe [*AS* 467–468; *HDM* 873–874].

Pullman's serpent really did eat from the forbidden fruit as well: Lyra is tempted by the enchanting words of Mary the serpent, but Mary is not trying to deceive but simply relating honest feelings of a true experience, and little does she know what she is triggering in the girl. She knows from the rebel angels who contacted her that it is her mission to be the catalyst of the Fall, but arguably she does not consciously aim to achieve what she does. Lyra later reproduces the temptation gesture of Mary's story when she "tempts" Will. The new Eve is offering the fruit to the new Adam:

> Then Lyra took one of those little red fruits. With a fast-beating heart, she turned to him and said, "Will...." And she lifted the fruit gently to his mouth. She could see

from his eyes that he knew at once what she meant, and that he was too joyful to speak. Her fingers were still at his lips, and he felt them tremble, and he put his own hand up to hold hers there, and then neither of them could look; they were confused; they were brimming with happiness. Like two moths bumping clumsily together, with no more weight than that, their lips touched [*AS* 492; *HDM* 890].

Just before the kissing scene, Lyra and Will are already reminiscent of Adam and Eve walking together in paradise, surrounded by untouched, lush nature as far as the eye can see; "They might have been the only people in the world" (*AS* 483; *HDM* 884), and then they progress into a "little wood of silver-barked trees [into] a little clearing [...] floored with soft grass and moss-covered rocks [where] the branches laced across overhead" (*AS* 489, 491; *HDM* 888, 889). Protected from view, in idyllic surroundings, like Adam and Eve in their "nuptial bow'r" (Milton 2004, VIII. 1 510), they speak out their reciprocal love.

"I love you, Will, I love you—"
The word *love* set his nerves ablaze. All his body thrilled with it, and he answered her in the same words, kissing her hot face over and over again, drinking in with adoration the scent of her body and her warm honey-fragrant hair and her sweet moist mouth that tasted of the little red fruit [*AS* 492; *HDM* 890].

Love is here a deeply fulfilling experience, both spiritual and intensely sensual. The reaction of the body is emphasized, nerves, body, touch, smell and taste, upon hearing the word. Like in Milton's Eden the physical manifestation of love follows the declaration. The unspecified little "sweet, thirst-quenching red fruits" (*AS* 481; *HDM* 883) that spark their moment of sensual, pure passion, evoke the commonly accepted red apple[4] of Eden in their color. It is a fitting metaphor because like love itself the fruit is sweet to the senses, intoxicates them and develops sexual arousal. It provokes a feeling of divinity growing inside, they become as gods, having eaten from the tree of knowledge, and makes love advance from the platonic to the sexual (Blamires 1971, 228, 236).

When they start kissing passionately and declare their deep mutual love, an immediate calm and peace surrounds them, a virtually religious respect: "Around them was nothing but silence, as if all the world were holding its breath" (*AS* 492; *HDM* 890). Lyra and Will's love is integrated with the landscape around them, which seems to react to them in a manner reminiscent of the pathetic fallacy. Nature itself silently worships the couple, instinctively knowing the implications and consequences of this act. This physical contact and the simultaneous declaration of love is the moment of salvation, the instant where the flow of the all-nourishing Dust, the mysterious cosmic life-force of all conscious life, turns back away from the fateful abyss it is draining into.

The Dust pouring down from the stars had found a living home again, and these children-no-longer-children, saturated with love, were the cause of it all [*AS* 497; *HDM* 893].

Let us compare this to the moment of Eve's Fall in *Paradise Lost*:

> ...her rash hand in evil hour
> Forth reaching to the fruit, she plucked, she ate.
> Earth felt the wound, and nature from her seat
> Sighing through all her works gave signs of woe,
> That all was lost [Milton 2004, IX. ll 780–84].

Nature's reaction is here somewhat different to that in *His Dark Materials*; indeed the opposite is happening. Whereas Lyra is saving Dust and nature rejoices, here in *Paradise Lost* it is lamenting the destruction of the paradisal state.

The controversial scene which has caused so much uproar occurs later. It is where the two lovers touch each others' daemons. They have already Fallen at this point and saved the parallel universes. As Mary Harris Russell observes, they know what they are doing at this stage; knowledge has happened (Harris Russell 2005, 220). "*Knowing* exactly what he was doing [Will] stroked the red-gold fur of her daemon. Lyra gasped [...] and as her fingers tightened in the fur, she *knew* that Will was feeling exactly what she was" (*AS* 527–528; *HDM* 915; my emphasis).

Since this incident is not essential to the denouement of the story, it is not entirely certain why Pullman added it. Granted, it could be to emphasize the settling of the daemons into their final forms, which happens here, and so complete the children's Fall and their transition to adulthood. However this could easily have occurred with the kiss, as the text already claims they are "no-longer-children" (*AS* 497; *HDM* 893) twenty pages earlier. Looking at the strongly suggestive, erotically charged language, this scene is arguably a metaphor for Lyra and Will having sex. Nothing is however stated explicitly, and it is possible that nothing beyond what is literally explained happens; it is open to the reader's interpretation and imagination. As Stanley Fish wrote about satanic readings of *Paradise Lost*, the Fallen reader interprets differently, so we[5] are bound to see a sexual act in our Fallen state (Fish 1971, 1).

The debate is not resolved, as it is not entirely clear either whether Adam and Eve had sex in paradise. Purists such as Pierre Bayle vehemently deny this, but just as many voices affirm it, Milton included (Turner 1993, 11–12). In the Bible of Lyra's world, Adam and Eve change, and their daemons settle when they partake of the fruit. Sex is not mentioned, so either it is omitted from the story, plays no part, or is suggested by the fruit metaphor. In *His Dark Materials* the eating and the lovemaking scene are linked but distinct, as they are in *Paradise Lost*.

Staging Will and Lyra's Fall

Let us now look at the stage production, which necessarily has different emphases to the novel. Cuts, textual and scenic rearrangements and manipulations are unavoidable to resolve the space and time constraints nonexistent for the books. To illustrate, the unabridged BBC audio book version read by Pullman takes approximately thirty-five hours, which is compressed into six hours stage time (Butler 2003, 28). Complex ideas and feelings need to be shown and explained visually and rhetorically to the audience, although the expression of thought through the characters' conversations with their daemons is a convenient device to avoid some of these problems. The narrative must be strong and effectively coupled with the visual performance to compensate for the lack of description; every word and gesture counts. The setting and the props must speak too, and a vital role falls to the lighting and the music to establish moods or mark highlights. The production admirably surmounts most of the difficulties, keeping the life force of the books and forming a valid interpretation in its own right rather than simply being a pale replica of the novels.

Robert Butler sees the plays, like the novels, as situated "firmly in the alternative tradition that believes Eve did the right thing [...] a heresy that runs through English literature and drama from Marlowe to Milton to Blake" (Butler 2003, 116). The ambiguities in Milton's retelling became controversial when picked up by the Romantics to support their revolutionary ideas. Indeed, Pullman talks about Milton's influence on Blake and Wordsworth's poetry, as if these poets were "taking hold of a torch passed to [them] by Milton" (Pullman 2005, 9). Pullman himself is the latest recipient of this torch, whose flame burns all the fiercer now, fed by centuries of dissidence and Romantic and Gnostic ideas. I shall scrutinize in how far the stage production follows the story, and above all the morality, of the books, concentrating on the controversial temptation and Fall. Whereas *The Amber Spyglass* contains two love scenes, the red fruit episode and the daemon caress, the play fuses them into a single event — and the daemon-touching does not happen, they simply turn up after the love scene in their settled forms.[6]

Serafina Pekkala assumes the role of Lyra's protector and tempter. The witch Queen's role is magnified as she merges the roles of the missing characters Mary Malone and the leader of the rebel angels Xaphania, perhaps in this condensation of characters she is standing for the Gnostic figure of wisdom, Sophia. Indeed, for the purpose of the temptation, her love story with Farder Coram, which is given more prominence than in *Northern Lights*, and modified to include a fruit-feeding scene, works effectively as a substitute for Mary's marzipan tale. Both Hytner and Pullman seemed to have agreed on this plot solution to the cutting of the characters of Mary Malone and Xaphania thereby arguably combining pragmatism which helps reduce the play's plot and running time with a symbolic aggregation based on the function of subversive female figures in the story (Haill 2004, 82). Furthermore, Serafina fits the role of the satanic tempter because the Church sees witches as "daughters of evil, determined to seduce" (*AS* 105; *HDM* 622), and they are sensual superhuman beings who take human lovers, like the Fallen angels did according to the Book of Enoch (Forsyth 1987, 163).

Serafina tells Lyra her story, overheard by the allegedly sleeping Will. It is all much more explicit than in the books; with Lyra being told what her destiny is and that she and Will are "bound together" (Wright 2003, 143). In addition these events happen much earlier than in the novels, only a half hour into play II (scene 5 of 24), with nearly half of the story yet to unfold. In my view, this foreknowledge for the spectator results in the climax of the story being weakened in the play, as the temptation and Fall are too far apart to form one coherent whole. In the stage version, Serafina brings the children the fruit into paradise, and in doing so she is almost commanding them to act — one has the impression that in the books they have more of a choice rather than being guided or nudged, which goes against the idea that Lyra's destiny should be fulfilled in ignorance. Fate is being given a helpful hand by the witch queen rather than coming about organically. Compared to the books, in the play we lose out on the rich, powerful emotions the story unleashes in Lyra.

The Fall is preceded by Serafina's comment, waiting for them[7] in the new world they visit: "Lyra. Will. I've brought you blackberries" (Wright 2003, 228). The strange choice of fruit aside, although blackberries are of course juicy and fruits of the summer, this seems an overly broad hint to the children after her story, even given the constraints of the play's running time, of the need for brevity and a more direct action. In *The Amber Spyglass*, Mary packs them a picnic including some red fruits (which are not mentioned in her tale although the Biblical hint may be clear to some readers), but it is not this obvious in terms of the symbolism of the fruit. A more subtle solution would perhaps have heightened the romantic atmosphere provided by the picnic.

The scene is presented as follows: Lyra enters the stage holding the basket of fruit given to them by Serafina, followed by Will, into the unknown Edenic world they have just cut through to with the magical knife. Both are giggling, Will tries to grab the basket from Lyra, and failing, flops down center stage. Lyra then kneels down facing him. They are in a clearing, surrounded by flowers. The mood is quiet, pastoral, and there is romantic, and nervous, tension emphasized by a clear though soft blue light playing on the circle of greenery surrounding the children, whereas the rest of the stage is dark. Lyra takes a blackberry from the basket,[8] they declare their mutual affection, before Lyra slowly raises the berry to Will's lips and presses it against his lips, while he clasps her wrist. Lyra speaks: "I love you, Will" (Wright 2003, 230). They kiss, Will cupping Lyra's face with his hands and Lyra touching his arm. They then slowly lie down together. The attention shifts to a raised platform and Serafina Pekkala looking through the amber spyglass and then commenting on the scene and its repercussions, a stream of golden Dust pouring over her, behind her. Lyra and Will lie entwined throughout Serafina's speech until the blackout. The following scene has the two lovers wakening in the presence of their daemons who have returned to them and who are now settled. The event is reinforced by the music, which provides a suggestion of the magical: the scene is initially accompanied by peaceful, but clear flute music representing childhood. After the kiss it changes into soft classical orchestra tones, creating a more complex, mature atmosphere in line with the transformation the children have undergone, the richer sounds of adulthood.

There is however one serious difference between the two National stage versions: The original reads "two children are making love in an unknown world" (Wright 2003, 230), whereas the re-run has them "lying in each others' arms in an unknown world" (Wright 2004, 224). A watered-down version of this crucial sentence might be more suggestive and open to interpretation, but if we want to follow the books' highly provocative celebration of love and sexuality, with scantly dressed witches, gay angels, the passion of Mrs. Coulter and Lord Asriel, Serafina's relationship with the Gyptian Farder Coram, and Ruta Skadi's one night stand with Asriel added to Mary's story and Lyra and Will's love, it seems slightly weak. However, as noted above, the novels are not entirely clear about what happens, whether the children lose their virginity or not, so the revelatory statement of the first version of the play by Nicholas Wright is maybe too explicit and leaves no room for alternative interpretation. Other comments in the first version of the play suggest Will and Lyra's love-making too. The original Fall is explained by the fact that "a young woman fell, in the physical sense" (Wright 2003, 176). Serafina and Coram had sexual intercourse for sure (though the episode is not staged) because she says that "nine months later I bore his child" (Wright 2003, 143). Mary's story in *The Amber Spyglass* mentions nothing similar.

Suddenly the trilogy does not seem as extreme when positioned side by side with the first play, which seems to radicalize the whole possibility of a feminist reading of the value of sexuality. The second play however leaves it more open by its more modest version of that crucial sentence. Like in the novels, there is erotically allusive language, but any explicit action beyond kissing is kept behind closed doors. The daemon-touching scene comes very close to crossing this boundary though, especially with the additional information that daemons settle only "having felt a lover's hands" (*AS* 528; *HDM* 915).

I assume that Lyra and Will have some kind of physical sexual contact which completes their move from innocence to experience, though whether they actually lose their virginity is not revealed for certain in the trilogy. Pullman, confronted with this very question, does not feel it appropriate to comment on this scene. He says he does not know if they made love, although he does not exclude the possibility:

> I don't know what they did. I wrote about the kiss — that's what I knew happened. I don't know what else they did. Maybe they did, maybe they didn't. I think they were

rather young to, but still.... [...] My imagination withdrew at that point. If you want to follow them under the tree and watch what happens, you must bear the responsibility for what you see. Personally, I think privacy is a fine and gracious thing. I describe a kiss: and there are some turning-points in life for which a kiss is quite enough [Pullman quoted in Watkins 2004, 201].

We could be treading dangerous waters here: if we see more than him we're in danger of being accused of anything from voyeurism to pedophilia, however this is precisely what the initial stage production affirms — though the theatre-goer is not shown more than words (though stage images of characters making love are seldom as realistic as their counterparts in film and television). Pullman refuses all responsibility, laying the interpretation of his own words firmly in the lap of the reader. He can be accused of opting for the easy way out, though to be fair, to argue that human beings and readers should take responsibility for democratic government and interpretation is what *His Dark Materials* advocates as a condition of the utopian new regime after the end of Church rule, in the Republic of Heaven. Still, the story bears dangerous undercurrents of not only teenage, but legally underage sexuality, as the main protagonists are only adolescents. Granted, Adam and Eve have sex in *Paradise Lost*, but the difference is that they are married adults and not teenagers.

The actors playing the children at the National, Lyra (Anna Maxwell Martin) and Will (Dominic Cooper) in the original play, were all in their twenties.[9] A different problem presents itself when you have child actors,[10] which is why any motion picture will probably have to cut this scene; on stage actors do not have to be as true to the age of the characters, on film which is a more realist medium this is much harder — and the main protagonist of *The Golden Compass* (2007), Dakota Blue Richards, was born in April 1994. With a young lead character, the film is aimed much exclusively at a child audience unlike other productions, and we can expect a declaration of love, and maybe a chaste kiss, but nothing else — the film will surely steer well clear of this controversy (obviously also for legal reasons). To be true to the original, though, Lyra must be aware of her emerging sexuality, and Pullman's positive embrace of love in both its emotional and physical expression is as such commendable, age issues aside.

Writing pleasure: Lyra and *Jouissance*

Lyra's first experience of love can be considered in the light of the (psychoanalytic and literary) concept of *jouissance*. It signifies an extreme or deep pleasure, which, although it may also mean innocent enjoyment, coterminous with sexual pleasure and the orgasm. It was employed by Jacques Lacan in 1972 to mean the "sexual, spiritual, physical, conceptual at one and the same time" (Hawthorne 1997, 119). *Jouissance* is not necessarily a purely pleasurable phenomenon, but "arises through augmenting sensation to a point of discomfort" (Clark, 2004). More negative connotations include self-disruption and loss of the self. In *His Dark Materials*, Lyra's experience is a much more positive version of the term *jouissance*. Lacan also sees *jouissance* as signifying the condition of merging with the other, and a "desire to abolish the condition of lack *(la manque)* to which we are condemned by our acceptance of the signs of the symbolic order in place of the Real." (Clark, 2004). We can take Lyra's world as a metaphor for this: Lyra desires to abolish her condition of lack of love through her relationship with Will. Condemnation of love and the symbolic order here is the Church, whose doctrine is not real but enforced through repression and ideology, and accepted by, the masses, who are blinded to the reality of things. She however succeeds, and consequently shatters the old order, and breaks through to the reality of Dust, the Real.

The two lovers' experience has been profound on all levels, true to the Lacanian definition of *jouissance* and their spiritual bliss is matched by physical ecstasy. Will is, upon Lyra's gesture with the fruit, "too joyful to speak," her hand trembles, and "they were confused; they were brimming with happiness" (*AS* 492; *HDM* 890) the situation is too strong, too intense for their own minds to cope with rationally; they lose themselves in this previously unknown, and hardly describable delight. It then takes over their bodies: "The word *love* set his nerves ablaze. All his body thrilled with it, and he answered her in the same words, kissing her hot face." (AS 492; *HDM* 890). Then their surroundings are caught up, the world holds its breath, as the energy released by their feelings sets alight the universe and acts upon the Dust. Their love goes beyond consciousness and relates to the bigger picture, to the overall idea of Dust in a special and unique manner, as the children influence and save the essence of being. To illustrate their newly discovered passion, Pullman uses a repetition of words like joy, love, delight, bliss, dazed or confused, describing their state of mind, a "trance of happiness," (*AS* 509; *HDM* 902) but he also insists upon the physical, sensual and sexual side of their expression of love, the touch, as the vocabulary demonstrates: "kissing," "tasted," "drinking in" (*AS* 492; *HDM* 890). This sublime mixture of feelings, or this higher feeling composed of so many different emotions and sensations recurs when they touch each others' daemons.

> Lyra gasped. But her surprise was mixed with a pleasure so like the joy that flooded through her when she had put the fruit to his lips that she couldn't protest, because she was breathless [*AS* 528; *HDM* 915].

This is a virtually orgasmic reaction to Will's touch. *Jouissance* produces a state of bliss enabling a person to transcend his normal state of being or subjectivity, and this can be triggered by sexual activity, satisfaction at a major or defining achievement in life, and also art. Lyra and Will indeed merge with each other, and their minds and bodies can in that moment no longer be distinguished in what they sense. It is a higher experience, a contact with Dust.

After the brief time of pure love and happiness, in the play Serafina reappears the next morning to explain: "you were tempted and fell" (Wright 2003, 231), so the Fall is indeed sexual. In the novels she tells the children's daemons, they must now leave their Edenic world of love to build the Republic of Heaven in their own respective worlds. The difference to Genesis is that Paradise is lost not as a punishment but rather out of altruistic self-sacrifice.

The result of their love and physical union is that Lyra, as an alternative 'everyman' symbol, has lost her childhood innocence and grace, but this grace can be regained by hard work, after which it will return consciously rather than intuitively, and as such be deeper and wiser. The Fall is about shame and the body, this is what happens to all adolescents. Lyra moves from innocence and childhood to experience (sin) and adulthood, maturing mentally and physically. If she were to stay as a Peter Pan eternal youth she would be seen to be missing out on a full life. The progression to experience is not only natural; it is to be embraced as a phase of development not decline. The example of Lyra's guiltless and shameless joy of love and sexuality ruins the Church's imposition of fear and guilt, redeems womankind from original sin and sets up the potential for a happier and freer society. Lyra's Fall turns out to be a *felix culpa*, a paradoxically fortunate Fall not a tragic lapse, thus reversing standard Christian doctrine.[11]

His Dark Materials is not the first modern feminist rewriting of Eve's role that is keen to alter the traditional negative perception of women — Angela Carter's *The Passion of New Eve* (1977) being one example. Pat Pinsent underlines the female roles in *His Dark Materials*, saying that the story comes to many of the same conclusions as feminist interpretations of theology, with the Gnostic figure Sophia and original sin as enlightenment (Pinsent 2005, 203). But Pullman's is not a feminist text as such. He refuses an oppressive masculine deity and creates a number of strong female characters to redress the male-female balance rather than tipping the scales the other way. The male figures are already there in our patriarchal subconscious.

Conclusion

Influenced by Romantic and Gnostic ideas, sexuality is often associated with experience and knowledge. In the trilogy, these are positive values. Sexuality is absolutely crucial to the outcome of Lyra's Fall. It redeems mankind and in doing this, it is cleansed of all the negative baggage it has had to carry. Sexuality is after all normal and natural, nature's method of survival and growth. Pullman eliminates what he perceives as harmful and unnatural stigma of sin and shame associated with it. It becomes the joyous and natural act that it was always meant to be, the one that Adam and Eve experienced in Paradise before the original Fall (according to Milton), the act that Blake as we have seen defended. *His Dark Materials* follows the belief that sexuality is a metaphor for the Fall itself. If Lyra and Will are indeed "walking into mortal sin," (*AS* 489; *HDM* 888) then we should rejoice at the fact.

NOTES

1. It actually consists of two plays, as a single session would have been too long, and the trilogy form of the books would have meant theatregoers would have had to attend too often.

2. There have been other major stage productions of *His Dark Materials* in Britain. In April 2006 at the Dream Factory, Warwick, the Playbox Theatre Company used a more "abstract, almost futuristic stage installation" and divided the stage into different levels to compensate for the lack of a revolving drum as at the National's Olivier theatre (Pullman 2006). Subsequent versions were realized in 2007 by the Scottish Youth theatre at the Scottish Summer Festival, and by the Belvedere College Dramatic Society at Dublin's O'Reilly theatre, using the National's music and some of the original costumes. In April 2008 the Young People's theatre of Bath performed it at the Bath Theatre Royal, creating their own puppets. All these productions however used Wright's script. See Karian Schuitema's interviews in this present volume for further accounts of some of these productions.

3. For the National Theatre's production see the archival website containing video clips and interviews ("Stagework" 2003/4).

4. The Bible incidentally also gives it no other name than fruit. The almost universally established tradition, the conventional image of it being a red apple that Eve ate stems from a confusion of words: Eve ate the fruit of the tree of the knowledge of good and evil, not an apple tree, but the Latin word for apple, *malum*, is also the word for evil (Wieland 1997, 40).

5. We are experienced adult readers as opposed to an innocent child reading.

6. In the play, Lyra's daemon Pantalaimon settles as a cat, not a pine marten as in the novels, presumably to be more compatible with Will's cat-daemon Kirjava.

7. How she guessed the right world to wait in, or even got there so quickly, remains a mystery.

8. In the first play, Will takes and eats one first; this stage direction is not important and is omitted from the second play.

9. As Karian Schuitema's interviews in this volume suggest, there are other ways of staging this by using child actors.

10. The Warwick production interestingly had underage actors, in fifteen-year-olds Olivia Meguer (Lyra) and Calum Finlay (Will), as did the Irish production (Hannah Osbourne and Paul O'Connor). The Scottish and the Bath versions both used different actresses for Lyra as she grows up, ranging from ages thirteen to eighteen.

11. It was A.O. Lovejoy who first suggested that the Fall represented in Milton's *Paradise Lost* could be understood as fortunate because without it Christ could not have been able to redeem the world (see Lovejoy 1937).

WORKS CITED

Beer, John. 1968. *Blake's Humanism*. Manchester: Manchester University Press.

Blake, William. "Songs of Innocence and of Experience." In *The Complete Works*. Ed. Alicia Ostriker. London: Penguin, 273–475.

Blamires, Harry. 1971. *Milton's Creation: A Guide through Paradise Lost*. London: Methuen.

Butler, Robert. 2003. *The Art of Darkness: Staging the Philip Pullman Trilogy*. London: NT/ Oberon.

Clark, Robert. 2004. "Jouissance." *The Literary Encyclopedia*. January 1. *The Literary Dictionary Company*, University of East Anglia. Accessed April 22, 2006. *http://www.litencyc.com/php/ stopics.php?rec=true&UID=602.*

Easthope, Anthony. 1999. "Paradise Lost: Ideology, Phantasy and Contradiction." In *New Casebooks — Paradise Lost*. Ed. William Zunder. Basingstoke and London: Macmillan, 136–44.

Fish, Stanley E. 1971. *Surprised by Sin: The Reader in Paradise Lost*. Berkeley: University of California Press.

Forsyth, Neil. 1987. *The Old Enemy: Satan and the Combat Myth*. Princeton, NJ: Princeton University Press.

Frost, Laurie. 2006. *The Elements of His Dark Materials: A Guide to Philip Pullman's Trilogy*. Buffalo Grove, IL: Fell.

Gillham, D.G. 1973. *William Blake*. Cambridge: Cambridge University Press.

Haill, Lyn, ed. 2004. *Darkness Illuminated*. London: NT/Oberon.

Harris Russell, Mary. 2005. "'Eve, Again! Mother Eve!': Pullman's Eve Variations." In *His Dark Materials Illuminated*. Eds. Carole Scott and Millicent Lenz. Detroit: Wayne State University Press, 212–222.

Hawthorn, Jeremy. 1997. *A Concise Glossary of Contemporary Literary Theory*. London: Arnold.

Lovejoy, A.O. 1937. "Milton and the Paradox of the Fortunate Fall." *English Literary History* vol. 4, no. 3, 161–179.

"His Dark Materials: Scottish Youth Theatre to Stage a Piece of Scottish Theatre History." 2007. January 19. Accessed April 29, 2008. *http://www.scottishyouththeatre.org/?node_id=1.6.1&id=122*.

"His Dark Materials." 2008a. Accessed April 9, 2008. *http://www.wiltshiretimes.co.uk/display.var.2185182.0.0.php*.

"His Dark Materials." 2008b. Accessed April 29, 2008. *http://www.belvederecollege.ie/College%20Productions%20Detail.html*.

The Holy Bible: New International Version. 1990. London: Hodder and Stoughton.

Milton, John. 2005. *Paradise Lost*. Eds. Stephen Orgel and Jonathan Goldberg. Oxford: Oxford University Press.

Pagels, Elaine. 1989. *Adam, Eve and the Serpent*. New York: Vintage.

Pinsent, Pat. 2005. "Unexpected Allies: Pullman and the Feminist Theologians." In *His Dark Materials Illuminated*. Eds. Carole Scott and Millicent Lenz. Detroit: Wayne State University Press, 199–211.

Pullman, Philip. 2005. "Introduction." In *Paradise Lost*. John Milton. Oxford: Oxford University Press, 1–10.

_____. 2006. "A New Production of His Dark Materials," Accessed April 6, 2008. *www.philip-pullman.com/pages/content/index.asp?PageID=124*.

"Stagework." 2003/4. Accessed April 29, 2008. *http://www.stagework.org.uk/webdav/harmonise@Page%252F@id=6004&Section%252F@id=35.html*.

Turner, James Grantham. 1993. *One Flesh: Paradisal Marriage and Sexual Relations in the Age of Milton*. Oxford: Clarendon.

Watkins, Tony. 2004. *Dark Matter: A Thinking Fan's Guide to Philip Pullman*. Southampton: Damaris.

Wieland, Carl. 1997. "Did Eve Eat an Apple?" *Creation* 20 (1):40 (December 1997): 40. Accessed April 7, 2008. *http://www.answersingenesis.org/creation/v20/i1/apple.asp*.

Wright, Nicholas. 2003. "Notes on *His Dark Materials*." London: Royal National Theatre Archive.

Wright, Nicholas, and Philip Pullman. 2003. *His Dark Materials*. London: Nick Hern.

_____. 2004. *His Dark Materials,* 2d ed., revised. London: Nick Hern.

12

Becoming Human: Desire and the Gendered Subject

Sarah Gamble

Introduction

However wide-ranging and imaginative, children's literature retains a tendency to leave both their subjects and their readers in a state of innocence. While attraction between individuals may be acknowledged, and desire hinted at, the majority of children's authors fall short of writing their characters into a fully-fledged sexual identity. Philip Pullman, however, is unusual in what Claire Squires terms his "espousal of adolescent sexual activity" (Squires 2004, 64); the consequence of which is to suggest, as Kristine Moruzi also quite rightly observes, "that ascent into adulthood through sexual experience is the desired goal for children" (Moruzi 2005, 55).

In *His Dark Materials*, this sexual awakening is foregrounded by being an integral part of the plot. When, at the end of the final novel, *The Amber Spyglass*, Will and Lyra finally achieve the fulfillment of their desire for each other, it is not only a moment of private satisfaction, it saves the world — in fact, it saves a potentially infinite number of interlinked worlds. Dust, the material that empowers human consciousness, is pouring out of the universe, leaving a wasteland behind. Were it to disappear completely, "[t]hought, imagination, feeling, would all wither and blow away, leaving nothing but a brutish automatism; and that brief period when life was conscious of itself would flicker out like a candle in every one of the billions of worlds where it had burned brightly" (*AS* 476; *HDM* 879). The union of Will and Lyra reverses the Dust flow. In them, Dust finds its "living home ... [and] these children-no-longer-children, saturated with love, were the cause of it all" (*AS* 497; *HDM* 893). In Pullman's anti-biblical schema, Will and Lyra achieve a second Fall, rejecting a moral system bound to the dictates of an authoritarian theology in order to become "the true image of what human beings always could be, once they had come into their inheritance" (*AS* 497; *HDM* 893).

Because the assumption of an active sexuality is presented as the key to autonomy and knowledge, it is towards this moment of the loss of innocence that the entire trilogy has been driving. So what interests me most in relation to these books is the evolution of Lyra and Will into desiring subjects, a process which can be profitably read in relation to Judith Butler's theoretical analyses of sex and gender, and the "radical critique of the categories of identity" (Butler 1990, ix) that ensues from such an enquiry. Butler laid the foundations of her most widely-known arguments in *Gender Trouble*, published in 1990, in which she famously claimed that "gender reality is created though sustained social performances" (Butler 1990, 141). Once one recognizes that gender identity is not innate, but is instead "an identity tenuously constituted in time, instituted in an exterior space through a *stylized repetition of acts*" (Butler 1990, 140: Butler's italics), one gains an awareness of "the performative possibilities for proliferating gender configurations outside the restricting frames of masculinist domination and compulsory heterosexuality" (Butler 1990, 141).

Butler does not intend to suggest, however, that the subject is free to choose their gender. As Sara Salih says, "Butler does *not* mean that a 'free agent' or 'person' stands outside its gender and simply selects it. This would be impossible, since one is *already* one's gender and one's choice of 'gender style' is always limited from the start" (Salih 2002, 46; Salih's italics). In her later work, Butler has explored constraints surrounding the acquisition of gender identity in more detail; a project that has led her into a wider ethical consideration of what it means to be human. In *Undoing Gender*, a collection of essays published in 2004, Butler reiterates her earlier paradoxical conception of gender as a site of both potentiality and curtailment:

> If gender is a kind of doing, an incessant activity performed, in part, without one's knowing and without one's willing, it is not for that reason automatic or mechanical. On the contrary, it is a practice of improvisation within a scene of constraint. Moreover, one does not "do" one's gender alone. One is always "doing" with or for another, even if the other is only imaginary [Butler 2004, 1].

Insofar as gender produces desire, it becomes inextricably bound up with the necessity of *recognition*; a conclusion that leads Butler to "the question of power and ... the problem of who qualifies as the recognizably human and who does not" (Butler 2004, 2). The extent to which the subject is recognized within its wider social context depends upon its intelligibility according to the norms by which that context is structured: not to be recognized is to be undone as a person, to be placed outside the category of the human. At that point, the subject no longer experiences what Butler terms a "liveable life" (Butler 2004, 8).

Nonetheless, the tension generated by nonconformity can also be productive: "As a result, the 'I' that I am finds itself at once constituted by norms and dependent on them but also endeavors to live in ways that maintain a critical and transformative relation to them" (Butler 2004, 3).

Butler and Pullman

These arguments would seem to be to be very pertinent to Philip Pullman's trilogy, which can be read as a chronicle of the journey towards an adult subjectivity which seeks to negotiate a path between dependence on and critique of the norms that render it intelligible. Both Lyra and Will undergo a process of maturity that will make of them gendered and desiring subjects situated within a wider social order, and redefine the meaning of "human-ness" itself. However, the novels' stress upon rebellion also brings to the fore the risk inherent in resistance to the norm, which may entail becoming unintelligible, unrecognizable and therefore less than human.

In the first essay of *Undoing Gender*, "Beside Oneself: On the Limits of Sexual Autonomy," Butler speaks for the value of fantasy as a practice capable of subverting the truth claims upon which the real is founded, and of transforming social norms in order to stake an identity claim. As she says:

> I think that when the unreal lays claim to reality, or enters into its domain, something other than a simple assimilation into prevailing norms can and does take place. The norms themselves can become rattled, display their instability, and become open to resignification [Butler 2004, 27–8].

However, Philip Pullman's dismissal of the fantasy tag in connection with his trilogy, which he describes as "a work of stark realism" (Parsons and Nicholson qtd. in Squires 2004, 17), creates a point of tension in any attempt to align the *His Dark Materials* trilogy with Butler's views regarding the function of fantasy. Claire Squires, who outlines this debate in her reader's guide to the trilogy, points out that when Pullman terms his work realistic, he is referring to psychological, not generic, realism, and argues that it is his "way of promoting his own skill in developing character motivation: although the worlds of *His Dark Materials* may be unknown to us, the psychological manner in which the characters traverse them is instantly recognizable" (Squires 2004, 17). So, insofar as, for Pullman, fantasy is not a *way out* of reality, but a method of *engaging with* the real more fully, his work can be seen to correspond with what Butler in "Beside Oneself" terms "part of the articulation of the possible" (Butler 2004, 28) that fantasy represents.

But while there may be agreement between Pullman and Butler on this point, it is far from total, for I would argue that Pullman's espousal of the concept of psychological realism in relation to this trilogy suggests that he may be setting his characters on a trajectory towards the very social norms that, as far as Butler is concerned, should be interrogated and subverted:

> Fantasy is not the opposite of reality; it is what reality forecloses, and, as a result, it defines the limits of reality, constituting it as its constitutative outside. The critical promise of fantasy, when and where it exists, is to challenge the contingent limits of what will and will not be called reality. Fantasy is what allows us to imagine ourselves and others otherwise; it establishes the possible in excess of the real; it points elsewhere, and when it is embodied, it brings the elsewhere home [Butler 2004, 29].

Thus, the question that is central to this essay is whether Pullman's adolescent characters smoothly move towards convergence with normative understandings of personhood, or, alternatively, are fixed on a collision course which will fragment such norms, leaving new configurations of subjectivity to be constructed from the wreckage. In answer, I want to examine what, for Pullman, constitutes a liveable life in Butlerian terms, concentrating particularly on the models of relationality between (gendered) bodies and between bodies and societies.

Reading Pullman's trilogy

The first volume of the trilogy, *Northern Lights*, centers upon Lyra, charting her adventures until just before the moment she meets Will, an encounter that takes place at the beginning of *The Subtle Knife*. A girl who believes herself to be an orphan, bereft of family apart from her formidable uncle Asriel, Lyra has been raised in the male-dominated environment of Jordan College in Oxford. This alternative world is one in which feminism has not happened: women's access to positions of power is limited, and few women have access to education. Those who do are segregated in all-female enclaves far from the center of university power. Not yet having reached puberty, however, Lyra lives outside the strict segregation of gender roles to which adults in her society are subject. Instead, she is "a barbarian," whose preferred pursuit is "clambering over the College roofs with Roger, the kitchen boy who was her particular friend" (*NL* 35; *HDM* 26). She is presented as physically daring from the novel's opening episode, in which she trespasses into the Scholars' Retiring Room, a place from which mere females (*NL* 4; *HDM* 3) are strictly forbidden.

Although Lyra's inherently transgressive nature is established from the outset, it is transgression of a qualified sort. Brought up in a society that is rigorously divided along gender lines, Lyra displays no wish to subvert a system which is inherently discriminatory towards her gender: in fact, she is its staunchest advocate. Possessing a firm allegiance to the male bastion of Jordan College, Lyra "regard[s] female Scholars with a proper Jordan distain: there *were* such people but, poor things, they could never be taken more seriously than animals dressed up and acting a play" (*NL* 67; *HDM* 50). She may be rebellious, but Lyra rebels with no consciousness of her gender, for the models of power and authority to which she aspires are virtually all male — Lord Asriel (who is later revealed to be not her uncle, but her father); the Master of Jordan College; and, later on in *Northern Lights*, the Gyptian leaders John Faa and Farder Coram.

Yet the scorn Lyra pours upon female Scholars, her belief that they are "animals dressed up and acting a play" is a conviction that is in many ways borne out in the novel's presentation of the female gender. While masculinity is also presented in animalistic terms, it is far more elemental and hence admirable: a force to be in awe of rather than a laughable spectacle. When it is presented in these terms it is therefore not surprising that Lyra idolizes an idealized assertive masculinity based upon the unquestioning appropriation of power and authority:

> Lord Asriel was a tall man with powerful shoulders, a fierce dark face, and eyes that seemed to flash and glitter with savage laughter. It was a face to be dominated by, or to fight: never a face to patronise or pity. All his movements were large and perfectly balanced, like those of a wild animal, and when he appeared in a room like this, he seemed a wild animal held in a cage too small for it [*NL* 13; *HDM* 10].

Embodied in the figure of her uncle, masculinity is presented here as the ultimate state of nature, confined within the walls of a society that strives to contain it. This places masculinity, though, in exact counterpoint to femininity, which is strongly identified in Pullman's text with what Butler would term "performativity." If Lord Asriel represents a world of self-motivated agency and intellectual enquiry founded upon an innate and naturalized masculinity, the feminine sphere is one of acute self-consciousness and assiduous self-fashioning.

The prime representative of the performative characteristics of femininity in the trilogy is its main adult female character, Mrs. Coulter, Lord Asriel's erstwhile lover and Lyra's mother. The world of difference that she represents is literalized in Pullman's description of her flat, which exists in aesthetic opposition to the starkness of the innately masculine world of Jordan College:

> In Jordan College, much was magnificent, but nothing was pretty. In Mrs. Coulter's flat, everything was pretty. It was full of light ... and the walls were covered in a delicate gold-and-white striped wallpaper. Charming pictures in gilt frames, an antique looking-glass, fanciful sconces bearing anabaric lamps with frilled shades; and frills on the cushions too, and flowery valances over the curtain-rail, and a soft green leaf-pattern carpet underfoot [*NL* 76; *HDM* 56–57].

Mrs. Coulter systematically proceeds to induct Lyra into such an environment, initiating her into a world of "feminine mysteries" (*NL* 78; *HDM* 58) such as shopping, fashion and grooming, and taking her to ladies' tea parties, where she meets women who appear to her "almost to be a new sex altogether, one with dangerous powers and qualities such as elegance, charm, and grace" (*NL* 82; *HDM* 61).

Contrary to appearances, all this is actually empty display, for Mrs. Coulter's frilly furnishings and pretty clothes conceal the fact that like her daughter she is wholly male-identified — even though she is far more devious in her tactics, calculatedly deploying a sexuality that Lyra has yet to develop. She no more sees herself as a representative for her sex as does Lyra: working for a conservative wing of the Church, the Oblation Board, she schemes only to further her personal ambitions. So, while she may be the epitome of femininity, Mrs. Coulter lacks the attributes conventionally associated with female attributes socially conceived of as natural — most notably, maternal instincts. She does not take Lyra in because she wants to mother her, but because Lyra is vital to her schemes, which also involve the abduction of children for experimental purposes.

In fact, Mrs. Coulter enacts the kind of masquerade defined by Joan Riviere in her 1929 essay "Womanliness as a Masquerade," in which she argues that "women who wish for masculinity may put on a mask of womanliness to avert anxiety and the retribution feared from men" (Riviere 1929, 130). In this way, femininity is presented as a masquerade from the outset: a performance, indeed, which contains many of the elements of the double-cross, because it is inherently duplicitous. Masculinity, on the other hand, is naturalized; for while aspiring to power makes the female subject something less than a woman, it only confirms the inherent manliness of the masculine subject. This is the paradox with which Lyra has to contend: how to evolve a conception of female subjectivity that does not depend upon identification with the male as the only legitimate source of agency. While she is pre-pubescent, not yet fully contained within a dualistic gender system, Lyra is free to play as if she were a boy; but an adult female in her world does not have such an option. One either becomes a despised anomaly, such as a scholar, or one becomes properly feminine.

Family, community and the individual

The dislocated family structure with which Lyra is presented in *Northern Lights* thus suspends her between an elemental masculinity and a femininity manufactured to disguise "unwomanly" ambitions. Gender may, as Butler asserts in her introduction to *Undoing Gender*, "figure ... as a precondition for the production and maintenance of legible humanity" (Butler 2004, 11), but that does not mean that gender itself is the natural ground upon which all configurations of the human depends. What *His Dark Materials* appears to endorse, though, is a traditional binary that naturalizes masculinity as the norm, while femininity is only recognizable to the extent that it operates as the opposing principle within a dialectic that ultimately endorses the superiority of the male.

Her decision to run away from Mrs. Coulter sets Lyra on a picaresque course in which she is presented with other models of femaleness, all of which reflect other ways of being a woman without espousing Mrs. Coulter's extreme version of the masquerade. Taken in by the Gyptians, travelers on the barges that trade up and down the canal network, she is reunited with a figure she has known intermittently throughout her childhood: the "boat-mother" (*NL* 130; *HDM* 96) Ma Costa, formidable matriarch of the Costa family. If Mrs. Coulter is pure artificial femininity without a heart, Ma Costa is the incarnation of fiercely protective maternity. Described as "stout and powerful" with "hands like bludgeons" (*NL* 105; *HDM* 79), she is tender and nurturing, "fold[ing] her great arms around Lyra and press[ing] her to her breast" (*NL* 106; *HDM* 79). Nevertheless, Ma Costa is only a temporary staging post for Lyra, who must travel further afield in order to discover women unconfined within the sphere of the domestic. The Gyptians remain a society led by men and, redoubtable though she is, the domain of Ma Costa's authority is limited to her family and the running of their boat.

It is only when Lyra has travelled with a group of Gyptians to Lapland on a quest to rescue the kidnapped children that she encounters women who exists wholly outside the gender dualisms so clearly enforced within her own culture. The witches of Lapland possess extraordinary abilities — they have extended lifespans, can fly on branches of cloud-pine, and are skilled archers. Living in matriarchal clans, their relationships with men are tenuous, as the witch Queen Serafina Pekkala describes to Lyra:

> There are men who serve us ... and there are men we take for lovers or husbands. You are so young, Lyra, too young to understand this, but I shall tell you anyway and you'll understand it later: men pass in front of our eyes like butterflies, creatures of a brief season. We love them; they are brave, proud, beautiful, clever; and they die almost at once. They die so soon that our hearts are continually racked with pain. We bear their children, who are witches if they are female, human if not; and then in the blink of an eye they are gone, felled, slain, lost [*NL* 314; *HDM* 232].

The witches' social structure appears to offer Lyra (and, beyond her, the adolescent female reader) a model of a social system centered around women, rather than offering them only limited options as second-class citizens. Not all is as it seems, however, for Serafina Pekkala's speech here is not a paean to female independence so much as a description of a world of women in mourning for the heterosexual relationships they cannot preserve. There is a price to pay for being a witch, and that is to live in a permanent state of loss — a conclusion which is later reinforced by the love-suicide of another witch at the end of *The Subtle Knife*.

This suggests that Pullman's world is one firmly bound to dualistic conceptions of gender identity: no matter how independent, the female subject is always bound to the imperatives of desire. The result is that any move to destabilize heterosexual dualisms is baffled in these texts. Butler's proposal that neither gender nor sex are intrinsic to the subject, but are the products of "historically specific organization[s] of power, discourse, bodies and affectivity" (Butler 1990, 92), is ultimately not endorsed by the trilogy. The primary means by which Pullman naturalizes sex, gender and desire is through his most striking invention: the figure of the dæmon, an aspect of the self externalized in animal form. Everybody in Lyra's world has their dæmon, who is their most intimate companion from birth, and both will die if separated by more than a few feet. Before puberty, dæmons are able to change forms at will, but at the onset of puberty, they adopt a fixed form, the reasons for which are explained to Lyra by a seaman on the voyage to Lapland:

> "Why do dæmons have to settle?" Lyra said. "I want Pantalaimon to be able to change for ever. So does he."
> "Ah, they always have settled, and they always will. That's part of growing up. There'll come a time when you'll be tired of his changing about, and you'll want a settled form for him."
> "I never will!"
> "Oh, you will. You'll want to grow up like all the other girls" [NL 167; HDM 124].

This conversation hints at the role dæmons play as indicators of the existence of sexual desire. They are hedged around with taboos — for example, it is unthinkable to touch another person's dæmon, and to do so is conceived of as an assault of the most intimate kind. When Lyra and her dæmon Pantalaimon are captured at the research station at Bolvangar, where the kidnapped children are being held, his abduction is described in terms akin to rape: she feels "faint, dizzy, sick, disgusted, limp with shock," "as if an alien hand had reached right inside where no hand had a right to be, and wrenched at something deep and precious" (NL 276; HDM 203).

But, fluid as the *bodies* of children's dæmons might be, their *gender identities* are irrevocably fixed at birth, for they cannot experiment with changing sex. And because the dæmon takes on the opposite sex to its human, this fixes both human and dæmon within a binary gender system in which no configuration other than male/female is possible. Pullman does admittedly allow for the odd exception to this rule, such as Bernie Johansen, the pastry-cook at Jordan College, who is "a kindly, solitary man, one of those rare people whose dæmon was the same sex as himself" (NL 125; HDM 93). However, Bernie Johansen is a peripheral figure in the text; mentioned in passing, but never appearing directly, which means that the implications of having a dæmon the same sex as oneself is never explored. He is a "queer subject," to be sure, but his anomalous position means that he is situated on the edge of what Butler terms "our grids of intelligibility" (Butler 2004, 35). In order to be articulated at all, the difference he embodies must be occluded — he is reduced and simplified through the rather vague designation of a "kindly, solitary man."

The reason for this silence surrounding same-sex dæmons stems from the central role all dæmons play in the enactment of desire — which, in this trilogy, is almost always heterosexual. And although Pullman, given the fact that he is writing a children's book, is understandably slightly coy about this, his use of dæmons in this way does allow him to be quite explicit in his delineation of sexual passion. At the end of *Northern Lights*, for example, Lyra sees her parents Mrs. Coulter and Lord Asriel together in a scene in which their dæmons — a golden monkey and a snow leopard — dramatize the intense sadomasochistic bond that drives their otherwise disconnected relationship:

> His hands, still clasping her head, tensed suddenly and drew her towards him in a passionate kiss. Lyra thought it seemed more like cruelty than love, and looked at their dæmons, to see a strange sight: the snow leopard tense, crouching with her claws just pressing in the golden monkey's flesh, and the monkey relaxed, blissful, swooning on the snow [NL 395; *HDM* 290].

A very similar scene occurs towards the end of *The Subtle Knife*, when Mrs. Coulter, never reticent about using her sexual wiles to get what she wants, seduces Sir Charles Latrom in order to discover the secret of the subtle knife. The fact that Sir Charles's dæmon (with peculiarly Freudian appropriateness) is a snake only acts to intensify the sexual suggestiveness of the episode, in which "the golden monkey slowly ran his hands along the emerald serpent again and again, squeezing just a little, lifting, stroking, as Sir Charles sighed with pleasure" (*SK* 326; *HDM* 525).

Scenes such as this, in which the dæmon takes on an overtly metaphorical function, can certainly be read a dramatic enactment of the kind of decentered subjectivity endorsed by Butler. Butler argues that it is simply not possible to make a genuinely autonomous identity claim, particularly where gender is concerned, since: "One only determines 'one's own' sense of gender to the extent that social norms exist that support and enable that act of claiming gender for oneself. One is dependent on this 'outside'" to lay claim to what is one's own [Butler 2004, 7].

The dæmon is an aspect of the self that exists in correspondence with, and yet outside, the self, and in this sense renders the self intelligible and classifiable. In Lyra's world, a living person without a dæmon is an abomination, "like someone without a face, or with their ribs laid open and their heart torn out: something unnatural and uncanny that belonged to the world of night-ghasts, not the waking world of sense" (*NL* 215; *HDM* 159). When Lyra comes across a little boy whose dæmon has been amputated in the course of Mrs. Coulter's experimental program (further confirmation of her monstrous and unnatural femininity), he is described in terms that render him sub-human — he is a "severed child" (*NL* 214; *HDM* 159), a "half-boy" (*NL* 215; *HDM* 160) and a "hideously mutilated creature" (*NL* 217; *HDM* 160). The loss of a dæmon has, in other words, caused him to drop out of the category of the recognizably human: his unutterable isolation does not just relate to the loss of his life-long companion, but also his right to participate within a community. The fact that he dies soon after Lyra's discovery of him is a mercy, since neither dæmon nor community is recoverable.

Models of masculinity

In the book that follows *Northern Lights*, *The Subtle Knife*, such a definition of the human is challenged in only a limited way by the introduction of Will Parry, a boy from a world that is recognizably the readers' own, and hence lacking a dæmon. It is a glaring absence that Lyra reconciles in her own mind by imagining the dæmon as present but hidden:

> "You *have* got a dæmon," she said decisively. "Inside you."
> He didn't know what to say.
> "You have," she went on. "You wouldn't be human else. You'd be ... half-dead.... Even if you don't know you've got a dæmon, you have. We was scared at first when we saw you. Like you was a night-ghast or something. But then we saw you weren't like that at all."
> "We?"
> "Me and Pantalaimon. Us. Your dæmon en't *separate* from you. It's you. A apart of you. You're part of each other" [*SK* 26; *HDM* 318].

Because to be human means to say "we," and never solely "I," to be always a self-in-community, identifiable both sexually and socially, Lyra is unable to accept that Will does not have a dæmon, only that she cannot see it. To come to any other conclusion would mean that Will would become unintelligible to her.

In fact, later events prove her to be right, because in *The Amber Spyglass* it is established that Will does indeed possess a dæmon. She becomes externalized following Will and Lyra's sojourn in the land of the dead, where no dæmons can go, "born," she says, at the moment "I was torn away from his heart" (*AS* 500; *HDM* 896). The advent of Kirjava is a significant moment in Will's own evolution as a gendered subject, which is analogous to Lyra's: in order to reach their destination at the end of the road to sexual maturity, both children have to evolve a coherent gender identity within the boundaries of the heterosexual matrix, a process in which dæmons play an integral part.

Just as Lyra begins the trilogy in a state of male identification from which she must move away in order to evolve a feminine sense of self, Will has to work hard in order to sever a dyadic attachment to the mother. Following the mysterious disappearance of his father Will's mother declines into mental illness, and Will becomes her carer, "fear[ing] more than anything ... that the authorities would find out about her, and take her away, and put him in a home among strangers." The result is to bind mother and son together into a tight-knit unit, in which Will "could think of no better companion, and wanted nothing more than to live with her alone for ever" (*SK* 11; *HDM* 308). But in the course of his travels within alternate worlds, in during which he (albeit briefly) rediscovers his father, Will begins to evolve a more appropriately masculine sense of self.

This is achieved primarily through his acquisition of a relic known as the subtle knife. It bears an obvious similarity to the artifact carried by Lyra, the alethiometer, a device that conveys knowledge through the manipulation of symbols. The symbols must be read intuitively, for each conveys many different levels of meaning, and many possible interpretations. Likewise, the subtle knife, which cuts the membranes that keep alternative worlds apart, requires sensitivity and instinct in order to be used effectively, for "[i]t's not only the knife that has to cut, it's your own mind. You have to think it" (*SK* 191; *HDM* 431). But where the two artifacts differ is that the knife is also a deadly and effective weapon traditionally possessed by men, while Lyra's alethiometer remains the traditional fantasy object that allows knowledge suitable for a female child but doesn't allow her to practice violence, as proven by the fact that Will wins the knife from its previous bearer in a fight to the death.

From then on, he becomes increasingly firmly established as the fitting heir to his father, John Parry, "a handsome man, a brave and clever officer in the Royal Marines, who had left the army to become an explorer and lead expeditions to remote parts of the world" (*SK* 10; *HDM* 307), and the journey he makes is, quite literally, one that takes him away from his mother and towards the elusive paternal figure. This meeting takes place at the end of *The Subtle Knife*, when he finally encounters John Parry, who is not dead, only trapped in Lyra's world, where he has become known as the shaman Stanislaus Grumman. The reunion of father and son, however, is only partial and fleeting, the moment of mutual recognition cut short by the intervention of the witch Juta Kamainen, who kills John Parry in revenge for his rejection of her love for him. At the very moment when "there came just the first flicker of something else to both of them," "as the lantern light flared over John Parry's face, something shot down from the turbid sky and he fell back before he could say a word, an arrow in his failing heart" (*SK* 336; *HDM* 533). It is his father's death, though, that triggers Will's affirmation that he will obey his father's injunction to use the subtle knife in the service of Lord Asriel: "[W]hatever you wanted me to do, I promise, I'll swear I'll do it. I'll fight. I'll be a warrior, I will" (*SK* 338; *HDM* 534). Will's adoption of an actively masculine role in accordance with his father's wishes triggers a corresponding diminution in Lyra's function as active tomboy heroine. Kidnapped by Mrs. Coulter at the end of *The Subtle Knife*, *The Amber Spyglass* opens with her lying in a drugged sleep, passively awaiting Will's rescue.

Brief though it is, the father's intervention within Will's journey acts a catalyst that maneuvers both children into their appropriate places within the heterosexual matrix in preparation for their transition into adolescence. It is, however, left to Lyra's mother Mrs. Coulter to complete the process that Will's father has begun. Following his father's death, Will is still alienated from the world of adult desire, unable to understand what emotions might have motivated Juta Kamainen's (self)destructive act born of unrequited sexual passion:

> Will felt no horror, only desolation and bafflement.
> He stood up slowly and looked down at the dead witch, at her rich black hair, her flushed cheeks, her smooth pale limbs wet with rain, her lips parted like a lover's. "I don't understand," he said aloud. "It's too strange" [SK 338; HDM 534].

Pullman deliberately eroticizes Juta Kamainen's body in his description precisely in order to emphasize Will's estrangement from an autonomous sexual self— he regards her only with bafflement, not desire, which remains nascent until aroused by Mrs. Coulter. She justifies her treatment of her daughter on the grounds of maternal duty, arousing in Will memories of his own mother: yet she also looks "uncannily like her daughter" (AS 149; HDM 653). This initiates a powerful erotic confusion within Will, who is caught between his first love-object — his mother — and the possibility of an attachment to a new erotic ideal: "He had been captivated by Mrs. Coulter. All his thoughts referred to her: when he thought of Lyra, it was to wonder how like her mother she'd be when she grew up; [...] and if he thought of his own mother..." (AS 151; HDM 654). Will's disturbance culminates in the breaking of the subtle knife in the course of his rescue attempt. He begins to cut a window between one world and another through which he and Lyra can escape, but when Mrs. Coulter wakes up and looks at Will

> the glare from the sky, reflected off the damp cave wall, lit her face, and for a moment it wasn't her face at all; it was his own mother's face, reproaching him, and his heart quailed from sorrow; and then as he thrust with the knife, his mind left the point, and with a wrench and crack, the knife fell in pieces to the ground [AS 162; HDM 662].

It is the conflict aroused in Will's psyche between prohibition and desire that shatters the knife, symbol of masculine mastery. Yet its fragility demonstrates that the subtle knife has always symbolized the precariousness of masculine identity as much as its authority to control: the assumption of Will's role as knife bearer is signaled by another symbolic castration, when he loses two fingers in course of the fight which wins him the subtle knife. The bearer, as Will's predecessor observes, "should not be a child" (SK 197; HDM 435), and his use of it is inhibited by his ongoing struggle to evolve a sexual subjectivity.

It is therefore the knife, which on one level can be interpreted as the ultimate masculine signifier in this novel, which also opens up an opportunity to read against the apparent grain of the text. On the surface, as I have argued throughout this essay, Pullman appears to be endorsing an extremely conventional conception of gender as dualistic and oppositional. While Lyra and Will both begin their quests exhibiting a primary attachment to the opposing gender — Lyra actively masculine and Will passively feminine — the whole point of their adventures seems to be to re-orientate them in relation to their "proper" gender identity. Lyra begins the trilogy as a feisty tomboy while she ends as a dutiful young woman; Will starts as a feminized carer of his mother and ends as a masculine warrior. Hence, Will comes to identify himself with his father rather than his mother and learns to turn his desire outwards towards a separate, non-maternal, love-object. In turn, Lyra develops a more submissive, intuitive character more in keeping with conventional conceptions of the feminine. Like Will, she learns to direct her desire outwards towards the opposite other, and stops striving to incarnate it within her self. It is only having gone through this process that the two can adopt their ordained symbolic roles as the new Adam and Eve, orchestrators of a truly fortunate Fall.

The result is to ensure that theirs is an utterly conventional heterosexual union. While it is true that other sexual identities have been hinted at in the trilogy — most notably the love between the two male angels Balthamos and Baruch — it is quite literally rendered spectral; almost as invisible as the intangible and ghostly bodies of the angels themselves. It is the heterosexual principle that dominates this novel, externalized in the dæmons that confer and confirm humanity, as seemingly non-negotiable as the process by which their bodies are rendered fixed and immutable in adolescence.

Pullman's trilogy is, however, perhaps more subtle in its intentions than this surface interpretation allows. Although the subtle knife is mended, it is marred, "shorter, and much less elegant.... It looked ugly now; it looked like what it was, wounded" (*AS* 205; *HDM* 691). It has, in actuality, only been temporarily patched up before its second, and more devastating, breaking. For the trilogy does not finish with Lyra and Will's sexual initiation, but goes on beyond the conclusion of a traditional romance. In order to stop the leakage of Dust from the worlds, the gaps between them cut by the subtle knife must be closed, and the knife destroyed for good. Moreover, Lyra and Will must each remain alone within the world within which they were born, for it is impossible for anyone live for long in a world which is not their own. However, their separation ensures Lyra and Will a future in which they can become something more than the complement of the other.

Will breaks the knife for a second time, using his grief for the loss of Lyra as the means to do so, and returns to his mother. The loss of the knife thus signals his loss of an assertive martial masculinity; but not necessarily of his independence, for his reunion with the mother-figure does not entail his re-assumption of the role of lonely champion. This time, he has the assistance of the Oxford scientist Mary Malone, who offers Will both a home and help in finding his mother "some proper treatment" (*AS* 540; *HDM* 923–924). Through her intervention, Will is able to discard the crushing sense of obligation to care for his mother that he has labored under since he was seven years old and "first realized his mother was different from other people, and that he had to look after her" (*SK* 8; *HDM* 306). Nor is it any coincidence that he is simultaneously also freed from the duty to be the bearer of the subtle knife; a decision which, as the previous bearer confirms, is never made by choice. Re-emerging with Mary into their old world, Will finds that both it and his gender identity have been made anew: masculinity is no longer something that has been conferred upon him as a sword is given to a warrior, but something that he has to develop in the midst of continually evolving social relations.

Simultaneously Lyra, who has lost the ability to read the alethiometer intuitively, ends the novel staking a claim within the world of female academia she so despised at the trilogy's outset. Although still "too young to become an undergraduate," she is offered a place at a girl's boarding school run by "a clever young woman, energetic, imaginative, kindly" and an opportunity to gain "the friendship of other girls of your age" (*SK* 545; *HDM* 926–927). This will pave the way not only for a lifetime of study, reading the books that will teach her to interpret the alethiometer again, but also for new possibilities for female fellowship and identification which extend beyond the shallow performativity offered by Mrs. Coulter.

Conclusion

One of Judith Butler's final questions in "Beside Oneself" is this:

[H]ow might we encounter the difference that calls our grids of intelligibility into question without trying to foreclose the challenge that the difference delivers? What might it mean to learn to live in the anxiety of that challenge, to feel the surety of one's epistemological and ontological anchor go, but to be willing, in the name of the human, to allow the human to become something other than what it is traditionally assumed to be? [Butler 2004, 35].

There is indeed some correlation between Butler's interrogation of closed categories of the human, and Pullman's portrayal of rebellion, for both lay a similar stress upon the necessity for actively pursuing new conceptions of being. Transformations, be they of the self or society, do not just happen, but must be labored over: furthermore, as Butler implies in the passage quoted above, the *process* of becoming — the willingness to embrace change without necessarily knowing what the end product will be — is as important as the final destination itself.

It is this endorsement, not just of change, but of the process of change, that, for me, pulls the *His Dark Materials* trilogy back from an uncritical reification of conventional gender binaries. *The Amber Spyglass* concludes with Lyra poised on the edge of adult life, realizing that the overthrow of the Authority opens up new possibilities of living and thinking. And this realization includes the acknowledgement that there are ways of being beyond the limits of the heterosexual couple:

> "We shouldn't live as if it mattered more than life in this world, because where we are is always the most important place."
> "He said we had to build something...."
> "That's why we needed our full life, Pan. We would have gone with Will and Kirjava, wouldn't we?"
> "Yes. Of course! And they would have come with us. But–"
> "But then we wouldn't have been able to build it. No one could, if they put themselves first. We have to be all those difficult things like cheerful and kind and curious and brave and patient, and we've got to study and think, and work hard, all of us, in all our different worlds, and then we'll build" [AS 548; HDM 929].

This is certainly a moment when Pullman's didactic intentions for his text are most clearly evident, but this vision of a liveable life also contains, surely, an acknowledgement of diversity and difference that provides a tentative opportunity for the re-imagining of gender. Will and Lyra may have been inducted into the heterosexual norm in the course of the trilogy, but as the breaking of the subtle knife indicates, such identities may not be as secure as they at first appear. Both characters have, by the end of the final novel, surrendered the artifact that has confirmed them as elect and, along with it, they begin to develop their own chosen, evolving and worked-upon gender identities which exist in perpetual relationship with the Other — whatever that might be.

WORKS CITED

Butler, Judith. 1990. *Gender Trouble*. New York and London: Routledge.
_____. 2004. *Undoing Gender*. New York and London: Routledge.
Moruzi, Kristine. March 2005. "Missed Opportunities: The Subordination of Children in Philip Pullman's *His Dark Materials*." *Children's Literature in Education*, vol. 36, no. 1, 55–68.
Riviere, Joan. 1929. "Womanliness as a Masquerade." In Anna Tripp. 2000. *Gender*. Basingstoke: Palgrave, 130–138.
Salih, Sara. 2003. *Routledge Critical Thinkers: Judith Butler*. London: Wiley Blackwell.
Squires, Claire. 2004. *Philip Pullman's His Dark Materials Trilogy: A Reader's Guide*. New York and London: Continuum.

13

After the Fall: Queer Heterotopias

SALLY R. MUNT

Introduction[1]

The modern bounded self has to manage intelligibility of itself through time, and it achieves this through *narrative*, through becoming the hero of its own story. This self is very durable: techniques of the self such as writing (confession, diary, autobiography) render the self visible and plausible to itself, and to others.[2] The folding of the outside into the inside creates intelligible interiority, over time, this gathering accrues the force of a plot, it is retrospectively submitted to a sense of ordering, it is made to mean, it contains narrative devices such as cause and effect, heroes and villains, major themes, disruptions, and the emplotment of random events. These elements cohere into the thing we call a life. This is not to say, incidentally, that the self being produced here is a fiction, in the pejorative sense of the word, nor is it simply a sum of habits. This is, I think, what Mary Malone is musing upon towards the end of *His Dark Materials*:

> This was the very thing she'd told Will about when he asked if she missed God: it was the sense that the whole universe was alive, and that everything was connected to everything else by threads of meaning. When she'd been a Christian, she had felt connected too; but when she left the Church, she felt loose and free and light, in a universe without purpose [*AS* 473; *HDM* 878].

She has a profound confidence in connection and proliferation, rather than the more conventional separation and individuation inflicted by God, through the concept of sin, shame and the Fall.

202

Daemonic Heterotopias

Philip Pullman's trilogy *His Dark Materials* is a substantial investigation of the Christian, Western self. He is, like Michel Foucault, convinced that the self is produced as fundamentally sexual, and like feminist critic Adriana Cavarero, dependent upon narrative, a story that is a gift from another. In Philip Pullman's novels selfhood is profoundly sexual, spatial and textual, illustrated in his distinctive proposition of a self that is not an "I," so much as a rather Irigarayan "we."[3] The first novel takes place in a single parallel world, a heterotopia based on an extrapolation of our own.[4] It is an uncanny fantasy, in which one twelve-year-old girl, Lyra Belacqua, goes on a quest to rescue her friend Roger from the Gobblers (in Pullman's post–Christian theology: the General Oblation Board). Pullman establishes the strangeness of this world by granting each person a daemon, which can be variously interpreted as the individual soul, spirit, emotional expression, unconscious, child, companion, or perhaps the irreducible "it-ness" of a particularized life. Daemons take the shape of an animal, and cannot be far removed from their person's body. Until puberty, daemons self-determine their shape, their animal form changes in relation to external events and the emotional state of their human; they are highly mutable. When the human reaches sexual maturity (around the age of twelve/thirteen), the daemon fixes constantly as one specific animal, its typography then permanently alluding to the "who-ness" of the person it emulates, usually a bird, reptile or mammal; for example a poodle, a snake, or an eagle (fish obviously present practical difficulties, and are rare). The vividness of the self/daemon relationship is impossible to convey here: daemons can talk, usually conversing with their human out loud, although thoughts can also be shared, and communication is instinctive.[5] They sleep and die simultaneously, their life is lived as one breath, a shared consciousness that is dialogic. Lyra's daemon is Pantalaimon, who is effervescently playful, he also protects, advises, and at times, sulks. Most human/daemon selves are heterosexually paired, although same-sex combinations do appear occasionally.

The intricacy of the human/daemon union is developed throughout the trilogy, in the second book, *The Subtle Knife*, two new worlds are introduced with a third fleetingly glimpsed. Firstly, Pullman presents Will Parry (also aged twelve), the second hero of the trilogy, who comes from our reality, a kind of palimpsest Oxford, whose daemon, Kirjava, Lyra claims to recognize as being inside of him.[6] Secondly he designs a third world, entered through the city of Cittàgazze, which is haunted by soul-eating vampiric Spectres who kill *sexually mature* adults, their victims are made into pallid zombies by having their consciousness "eaten."

In *The Subtle Knife* the author hones his post–Christian theological precept of Dust, preparing the reader for the republican war in Heaven that becomes more fully delineated in *The Amber Spyglass*. But it is in the second volume that we begin to understand empathetically the human/daemon relationship, through a secondary character Lee Scoresby and his daemon Hester. Lee is introduced in the first book as a Texan aeronaut and explorer. He is the archetypal lone adventurer whose role in the novelistic structure is of helper and good father. His plot function is twofold: to protect Lyra, and to find Will's father, although the latter results in the death of both fathers, symbolic and real. Lee is cast as an alternative, loving, heterosexual male, complemented in his relationship with Hester, his daemon hare who is "as thin and tough-looking as he was" (*NL* 192; *HDM* 142). When Lee is traveling, he keeps his daemon Hester close sometimes tucked into his clothing (see for example *SK* 302; *HDM* 509), but she is far from infantilized even when being carried, as it is often Hester who warns or curtails Lee. She is dry, wise, and alert, and in this unusual marriage they share an intimate ambience: "He was used to her silence, and she to his. They spoke when they needed to" (*SK* 217; *HDM* 449).[7] In the depiction of Lee/Hester the author has rendered a most ideal intimacy, in which profound knowledge and acceptance occurs between elements of the "us," making visible "the necessary 'inside' of the subject." In the terms of the feminist philosopher Adriana Cavarero (2000),[8] Hester is that Lover/Other that is part of the self:

> Lee looked for Hester in alarm, and found her sleeping, which never happened, for when he was awake, so was she; so when he found her asleep, his laconic, whip-tongued daemon looking so gentle and vulnerable, he was moved by the strangeness of it, and he lay down uneasily beside her [*SK* 304; *HDM* 510–511].

When Lee and Hester are faced with their personal Alamo, a gunfight with the soldiers of the Magisterium Guard who are chasing them in order to capture to Lyra, Lee becomes mortally wounded:

> Another crack, and this time the bullet went deep somewhere inside, seeking out the centre of his life. He thought: it won't find it there. Hester's my centre [...]. Then she was pressing her little proud broken self against his face, as close as she could get, and then they died [*SK* 318–19; *HDM* 520–521].

The death of Lee and Hester is detailed in the chapter "Alamo Gulch" and is incredibly moving, depicting an idiosyncratic love relationship between a man and a hare. Principally it is because in the daemon/human structure Pullman has invented, there is displayed something profound regarding our internal spatiality. This is a kind of compound-gendered private collectivity, dependent upon love, sometimes non-human love. It is this difference in perspective, choosing to creatively emphasize an inter- and intra-subjectivity, which echoes the optimism of Cavarero, it also forms the premise of much of Luce Irigaray's philosophy too, "[t]o love together with her, porous to a multiple familiarity" (2000, 114). Rather than the gloomy aggrandizing self/other preponderant in contemporary critical approaches, then, it challenges us to radically reconfigure the split subject of shame.

There is a queer attachment, a physical space of containment for this self; the daemon cannot be separated too far from the human without extreme physical pain. In an early scene reminiscent of Freud's *fort-da* game, Lyra and Pantalaimon try to rescue the bear-king Iorek Byrnison, and in doing so Pantalaimon alters shape, becoming a badger to pull away from her causing them both much anguish: "It was such a strange tormenting feeling when your daemon was pulling at the link between you; part physical pain deep in the chest, part intense sadness and love" (*NL* 194; *HDM* 143–144).

This passage offers a stirring visualization of the compelling vagaries of emotional attachment. Throughout the trilogy appears another haunting notion of disattachment, "intercision," a torture that separates daemon from person, either by the internal evisceration of the daemon by the Spectres, or in the mechanistically sadistic guillotining deployed by the General Oblation Board, a wing of the Church. This forced division, or metaphorical castration, is tested upon pubescent children in a Northern prison camp in Lyra's world, in a place that resembles Siberia. The first book, *Northern Lights* has its plot driven by this horror of intercision, while some of the advantages of this practice are advanced by Coulter in the second volume (see for example *SK* 209; *HDM* 444), when she details the behavior of the soldiers who, like automatons, will fight on until destruction as they have no fear or any free will left. More often, the daemon-less just wither and die as this disconnection is spiritual and permanent. The *His Dark Materials* trilogy is immersed thematically with the various perils of separation, isolation, and seclusion, the daemon-less are detached from the collective good and existentially lost, in loops of shame, unable to reconnect.

At sexual emergence intercision becomes no longer possible because at the point where the daemon defines its shape, the self becomes settled. In this Pullman could be criticized for sentimentalizing actual childhood for its endless potential, which is something nostalgically deluded adults tend to do. Pullman has described the Blakean movement in the novels as from innocence to experience,[9] it is through experience the self becomes integrated as a moral, accountable entity, chiming with Foucault's late injunction for building an ethical self. The human/daemon self is a social structure, but it is demonstrably a symbolic psychic split, split in a Kleinian sense of projection (1975).[10] However, unlike in classical psychoanalysis, this splitting is not pathologized: Pullman makes materially visible a modern, multiple self underpinned by association, negotiation and cooperation, rather than rejection, fragmentation and alienation. In that sense, Pullman creates a synergy between the Enlightenment Man of Reason, linked inexorably to the rise of the Church, a self formed through the exercise of will, choice, and accountability, and the postmodern decentered self that is founded upon doubt, diversity, and narrative. The taboo against touching someone else's daemon unless the humans are lovers clearly indicates the erotic intimacy of this self-daemon bond. Each real-world sexual self, of course, is multiply intersected by social discourses. Beverley Skeggs has argued that the construction of selfhood is inevitably classed, and linked to cultural property (Skeggs 2003). That the self is produced through status, that only some persons are created with interiority, dimensionality, and that the ability to propertize oneself depends on one's value as proscribed by others, are all conditions of the emergence of the bourgeois subject. Experience (of the right kind) accrued through the methodical operation of history and memory, is interpreted critically to form a concept of personal depth and interiority, of reflexive selfhood. This selfhood, which is intrinsically spatial and accrues through sexual experience, is then possessed by the individual as a form of authorization. This model of middle class selfhood is also carved out via appropriation, and accumulation, defined against the working class as the limit-site; they form the constitutive outside that is sexually excessive, abject and immoral. Selfhood can thus be perceived as a kind of appetite.

In order to be hegemonically acceptable, discursively readable, working class narratives of selfhood are frequently rendered through the rhetoric of redemption, of moral correction and aspiration. Skeggs has argued that "[t]he self then becomes an ethical imperative: it has to be displayed as a sign of one's social responsibility, one's morality" (Skeggs 2003, 33). Fantasy fiction for children and young adults is heavily strewn with these social and moral signifiers, think, for example, of the remarkably classed signifiers of the *Harry Potter* series, or the overbearingly repressive class politics of J.R.R. Tolkein's *Hobbit* and *The Lord of the Rings*. Elements of typecasting all too familiar to this genre are also present in Pullman: Lyra is a resoundingly upper-class child who sets out to find herself in a tale teeming with moral messages. As Nicola Allen explores in this volume, certain working class stereotypes are plentiful within the epic, where servants have rather plain daemons that are usually dogs, as Lyra explains when she makes the link explicit between servants and their dog daemon hinting at their subservient nature (*AS* 483; *HDM* 884). These types always seem to be grammatically challenged in the novel's dialogue; there is a Traveler group or pseudo–Gypsy tribe called Gyptians who are jolly folk who perform the function of rosy-cheeked helpers who have lots of cheerfully ungovernable children. If Lyra (towards the end of the trilogy) claims that servants' "real nature" is to be dogs, then we are seeing here the hoary animalization of the lower classes. Fantasy as a genre is replete with strictly hierarchical societies, it is often the most intransigent of representations in otherwise quite radical novels. This seems to be a political slip by Pullman, who is otherwise very careful to challenge received notions. The middle/upper class characters in *His Dark Materials* seem to be either more mendacious, or more honorable, or just more individuated, in that classic economy of accumulative interest. Even Will, despite his single-parent-family status, has a missing heroically masculine father who is a famous explorer and ex-marine (officer class, we presume). *But* even though the novels do deploy some clichéd class representations, there is also some visible effort directed into challenging them.

Angelic sodomites

Principally Pullman's remaking of the Christian self is pictured through the pairing of characters, with the self/daemon as described, but this coupling structure is present elsewhere and powerfully communicated in *The Amber Spyglass* with the story of two male angels, Balthamos and Baruch.[11] The witch Ruta Skadi's first meeting with a group of angels stresses their delicacy, size and immense intelligence (*SK* 147; *HDM* 402), but they shown themselves at times to be envious of human bodies and experience. Balthamos and Baruch are two aged homosexuals, and in spite of these creatures' fearsome intelligence they are also knowingly familiar: the Muscle Mary (Baruch) and the Biting Queen (Balthamos). Pullman has some fun with these gay stereotypes: we recall that they would be very familiar images to teenagers, whose chat is peppered with anti-gay cliché. Balthamos, already charming the reader with his trenchant sarcasm, his sour sulking, his disdain and physical ineptitude, is every angelic inch a reluctant, rescuing hero. Pullman takes these worn out typologies and resignifies the homosexual in a creative rewriting of Foucault's imperative to remake ourselves. Balthamos and Baruch become the archetypes of love, a love that is transcendental and eternal, but not at all sentimental. What is striking in this pairing in *His Dark Materials* is that Baruch and Balthamos are the perfect, passionate lovers (bound like Lee and Hester as a self manifestation of one whole, thinking and feeling as though one) (see for example *AS* 24; *HDM* 563), and when Baruch dies, the representation of Balthamos' grief is profound. These two aged sodomites love without shame, they are "advanced democratic beings" who love with a passion and who benefit from an ancient wisdom, as the angel Balthamos comments on the origins of the Authority who is "formed of Dust as we are, and Dust is only a name for what happens when matter begins to understand itself" (*AS* 33; *HDM* 569). Attaining self-consciousness is perhaps a more prosaic, universal formulation of Foucault's injunction to galvanize an "aesthetics of the self" (1985, 1986). Baruch and Balthamos are rogue angels not obedient to the Authority, they are unbound militants who have escaped the shame-ties of convention and their function in the novel is to aid the revolution in Heaven. These two angels are in fact a perfect visualization of the sodomitical sublime. In producing an anti-religious polemic, what purposeful irony to make one of the most aspirational love relationships of the text revolutionary, anti-authoritarian, and heroically homosexual — and all this for teenagers.

Of "other spaces"

To return to Cavarero's literary model of the self, explained as "a flesh and blood existent whose unique identity is revealed *ex post facto* through the words of his or her life story" (Kottman 2000, xiii). Pullman's fiction exemplifies this, for example in this scene in *The Amber Spyglass* where Lyra descends to the land of the dead, a purgatorial wasteland of abandoned souls. Chapter 23 is entitled "No Way Out," however, its epigram is taken from the Gospel of St. John "And ye shall know the truth, and the truth shall make you free" (see *AS* 321; *HDM* 773). The *truth* of the self is contained in the life-story, embodied by Lyra as she journeys down through the spatial/spiritual land of the dead in order to liberate Death, to end the rule of the Authority. When Lyra tells her story to the harpy called No-Name,[12] it becomes clear that the appointed role of No-Name has been to torment the souls that were sent there, to fill them with fear, remorse, and self-hatred by reminding them of their life's worst and wicked deeds, for eternity. They are the damned, castigated by perpetual guilt and condemned to eternal shame. However the harpies have a kind of warped sincerity, in that they can detect truth from fiction, so when Lyra spins a tale in order to deflect them, they attack her. Lyra redeems the harpies by giving them the task of hearing the true tales or life-stories of the recent dead, in exchange they promise to lead them out from death; as these ghostly souls emerge into a new pastoral world in which their atoms disperse, they become one with nature, transformed into life again. When this new treaty for the dead is reached, Lyra kisses No-Name, and in an act of love she gives the harpy a name: Gracious Wings, and hence, a self. The whole scene evokes a Foucauldian aim to distinguish truth, but also woven through are Western Christian principles of oral confession and absolution.

Critic Millicent Lenz has drawn attention to how Pullman deploys storytelling in *The Amber Spyglass* to enable children to come to terms with the idea of death, by appropriating Platonic and also Romantic sources from Keats and Percy Bysshe Shelley, "providing a kind of armor for the psyche" (Lenz 2003, 48). Lenz claims that "Escape from the Land of the Dead can be won only by those who have lived aesthetically and soulfully, who have enjoyed the gift of life through their intellects and senses. Only then, it is implied, will they have stories to tell" (Lenz 2003, 52). Plato expressed the hope that stories could provide a way of salvation, through their power to transform, to imagine a way out from suffering. It is this act of storytelling, demanded by the harpies, that releases the dead, but it is also effortless to read this as a metaphor for release from despair and shame. Stories nourish the soul, but only if the storyteller has an active listener who is able to receive the gift. This quality of mutual listening is an extended sensibility of openness, the role of the "You," in Cavarero's terms, the one who gives the subject her story.

In Pullman's trilogy everyone has their own personified death, a spirit-world character similar to a shadow, an unseen companion who ensures that life and death have their proper resolution. Pausing on the outskirts of the land of the dead, Lyra and Will encounter an old woman's Death says this: "You must call up your own deaths. [...]But they're not far off. Whenever you turn your head, your deaths dodge behind you. Wherever you look, they hide" (*AS* 278; *HDM* 742).

Death is an internal entity that must be negotiated with, kindly. The model is integrative, it is anti-psychoanalytic in the sense of Freud, offering instead a philosophical construct located historically with the nineteenth century Romantic's concept of a sympathetic imagination, Lenz relates it to empathy, another critic Naomi Wood calls it "a Coleridgean distinction between fancy and imagination" (Wood 2001, 253). In Pullman's trilogy this quality of listening and telling depends not a superficial, fanciful whimsy, it is a redemptive extrapolation sourced from a kind of deep consciousness, from the emotional integrity of self-acceptance. It is an authorization of self-narrative, with a reflective understanding of dependency as connectivity, rather than subjectivity. Lenz quotes Mary Watkins as saying that what this active imagination offers is a capacity for visualizing "what the Romantic poets called 'a heterocosm — a world other than this one — which, once alive imaginally, can inspire action'" (Watkins 1987 in Lenz 2003, 53). This seems very akin to Foucault's heterotopic imagination, his idea of the enabling other space.

The title of *His Dark Materials* is taken from Milton's *Paradise Lost*, Book II, line 915, from the passage on chaos. Satan is just getting his ticket out of hell from Sin in order to go off and make trouble for mankind. The reference to dark materials is to two kinds of controversy: firstly the *ex nihilo* problem, which wonders what there was before God made the world, whether He made the world out of something, or out of nothing. But what would nothing be, and how can any thing come from it? The second controversy is the other worlds problem: might God have made a multiplicity of worlds, or could He make new ones if this one goes wrong? Would the Fall take place in all of these worlds, would Christ be incarnated in all of them, would He be the same in each?[13] Both of these branched theological questions had a long history in Milton's day. Pullman is investigating the potential for the creation of a self that is complicated by the indeterminable freedoms of human will, and that lives beyond/after shame. Seeking the domicile of the Authority, Mrs. Coulter makes this observation when pondering an example of heresy in *The Amber Spyglass*:

> He had suggested that there were more spatial dimensions than the three familiar ones [...]. He had even constructed a model to show how they might work, and Mrs. Coulter has seen the object before it was exorcised and burnt. Folds within folds, corners and edges both containing and being contained: its inside was everywhere and its outside was everywhere else [*AS* 415; *HDM* 836–837].

In this heresy there is no longer an interiority that is a site of injury formed through shame, and in shame. Instead there is a less rigid, more playful sense of the layerings of potentially joyous intersubjectivities. This idea of space as dynamic possibility emerges out from under Newtonian physics, following Da Vinci, with Kant's island universes, it consolidated in the twentieth century with the theory of the expanding universe popularized by Hubble's telescope, and is epitomized in Einstein's theory of relativity, and more recently, in quantum physics. Thus — in what Pullman so wittily describes as experimental theology — we can envisage a dynamic cosmic architecture with its own organic history: a Big Bang that produced curved, expanding space. This space seethes and ripples and produces any number of space-time dimensions, most famously in the form of strings. Cyber-idealism is one contemporary casualty of this free-floating, Gnostic, disorienting swarm. Dizzying as these possibilities are for human potential, Pullman insistently grounds his figures in a self-space that is clearly collective and accountable, presenting his characters with moral choices that are old-fashioned and fleshly. He retains an idea of shame that is closer to guilt, less of an ontological separation and more so an internalized ethic that is reached through the Foucauldian exercise of self, something profoundly optimistic. In his models of other- and same-sex couplings, whether human-daemon, human-human, or angelic, the dark materials of self-making are irrepressibly and dynamically anti-heteronormative and queer.

After the Fall

The trilogy is centrally concerned with a Blakean rewriting of the story of the Fall of Adam and Eve, from innocence to experience. Pullman describes Milton as being one of the two other sources for *His Dark Materials*, the third being an essay written in 1812 by Heinrich von Kleist called "On the Marionette Theatre" that offers three metaphors for the Fall. In an interview when asked how important this central conceit is Pullman calls it "Completely essential. It's the best thing, the most important thing that ever happened to us, and if we had our heads straight on this issue, we would have churches dedicated to Eve instead of the Virgin Mary. That's basically it" (Parsons and Nicholson 1999, 118).

In *Northern Lights/The Golden Compass* the Genesis story is reworked, the serpent tells Eve that if she eats the fruit knowledge shall be hers and Adam's and their daemons will adopt their true forms (*NL* 372; *HDM* 273). The end of shame brings knowledge, once their eyes are opened Adam and Eve can fully see themselves and each other, their selves are formed through recognition and accountability. Pullman declares they have the capacity to become gods, in non-theological terms they are able to claim full agency only through this act of radical disobedience. Rejecting authority/repression brings the responsibilities of free will ("Will" Parry[14]), and consequently the gifts of discernment and ethical discretion. As Wood has claimed "Pullman argues that storymaking should not be an escape from the world but a way to reinvent it," she continues, "Mary Malone's role [in *The Amber Spyglass*] as 'serpent' in this new Garden of Eden is to tell her own true story of her "deconversion" from celibacy to joyful sexuality" (Wood 2001, 255). Anne-Marie Bird analyses Pullman's reworking of the myth of the Fall and points out that the original creation story is charged with naming, making distinctions, classification, and articulating opposites; she helpfully observes that the Judeo-Christian creation story opens with the concept of division and separation: God dividing the light from the darkness, the heaven from the earth, the day from the night. Bird points out that by appropriating William Blake's concept of the "Contraries": "Pullman attempts to synthesize the opposing principles that lie at the core of the myth while leaving the innocence-experience dichotomy firmly in place" (Bird 2001, 112). Because Adam and Eve opt for knowledge rather than paradise, Satan can be said to have liberated Man "from a place of temporal and moral stasis with no opportunities for growth or development.... Adam and Eve were trapped in a preconscious state" (Bird 2001, 121). Adam and Eve are not trapped in immovable shame, shame impels them away from God toward an allegorical journey we call the human condition. The appearance of shame is thus imbricated with the revelation of sex and death, it is synonymous with becoming fully human, with *becoming*. This is what Deirdre F. Baker calls Pullman's metaphysical map (Baker 2006, 243), as Will says, repeating words from his father: "We have to build the Republic of Heaven where we are" (*AS* 516; *HDM* 907). *His Dark Materials* is an extended dissertation on human limitations and moral accountability.

Bird asserts that Pullman is reworking a story of disobedience and punishment into a narrative of self-development, based on his theory of interconnectedness and the necessary interplay of opposites. Dust is the matter that unites all that is known and unknown. Pullman's worlds and the subjects within them are predicated on this mutual, affective energy. Dust links sexuality to the life-force, to the reproduction of selves, and in this association of Dust with Original Sin, as the General Oblation Board claims, Pullman tries to reinvigorate an argument of sex-as-biological drive that Queer Studies has often tried to refute. However, it is not too different from the more Deleuze and Guattarian preconceptions of sex as proliferating desires, Dust as the precondition for desire, a "desiring-machine" (1977). The conflation of sex with possibility, sex with life, depicted in its magnificent complexity, is something that stories can explore with imaginative impunity. Pullman tries to remake sex as a foundational principle of life, as something to positively embrace as mystery.

We recall that the original Fall also inaugurated the creation of sexual differentiation. In an early scene from *Northern Lights*, when Lyra is first installed in the home of her mother in London, Mrs. Coulter tries to, like a good mother, install femininity in Lyra. The dense and overwhelming excessiveness of Coulter's flat is seen by Lyra, indeed: "In Mrs. Coulter's flat, everything was pretty [...] and every surface was covered, it seemed to Lyra's *innocent* eye, with pretty little china boxes and shepherdesses and harlequins of porcelain" (*NL* 76; *HDM* 56–57, my emphasis). Pullman goes on to associate seductive femininity with the horrors of the upwardly mobile suburban boudoir. The vision of Lyra, which is blurred and unrecognizable in the flat's reflective surfaces is an identity constructed through shame:

> Pantalaimon watched with powerful curiosity until Mrs. Coulter looked at him, and he knew what she meant and turned away, averting his eyes modestly from these feminine mysteries as the golden monkey was doing. He had never had to look away from Lyra before [*NL* 78; *HDM* 58].

This chapter, "The Alethiometer," is densely significant: on the one hand Lyra, as the "new Eve" is being auto-seduced by femininity, something to which she retains ambivalence toward in the later books. Secondly, Lyra is surprised by a sensuality that is rather perversely tendered by her mother. Then thirdly, and principally, the chapter epitomizes how essentially the spatial self is a sexual self, illustrated here through the mechanism of shame. Shame instigates a state of uncomfortable self-knowledge that becomes an internal consciousness of differentiation, and this is Pullman's rendering of Francis Broucek's "keystone effect" (Broucek 1989, 369), which can substantiate a recursive moment of recognition of our place in the social world. Shame is based upon separation and loss, in this instance, it presages the excision of self/other that constitutes Lyra's loss of her daemon in the final volume. Yet, it is this separation from Pantalaimon that ensures the radical success of Lyra's redemptive narrative. In this depiction Pullman is suggesting that even in selfhood, desire for the other internal self must be spatially negotiated.

His Dark Materials is a secular humanist attack on institutionalized religion, and its role in war. The Roman Catholic Church has perceived the trilogy as an attack on itself, Pullman's archaic and apocalyptic version has certainly annoyed conventional Christians. But Pullman's aim is wider than that, for example he has also roundly attacked fundamentalist Protestantism in public debate, and he notoriously castigates the Narnia books of C.S. Lewis. *His Dark Materials* focuses upon the Old Testament Judeo-Christian origins in Genesis because that is what Pullman sees as the core falsehood. In his project of critiquing and remaking the model of the shamed Christian self, Lyra is a central conceit. Her destiny as the new Eve (or "Eve again" as the witches call her) is explicit, and it is her function in the fable to eat from the tree of knowledge and thus gain true consciousness through sexual experience. In *His Dark Materials*

Eve's tragic disobedience in eating the forbidden fruit makes her a hero, not a villain, it inaugurates a new era of sexual love without guilt forcing religion to relinquish its power. The symbolic re-enactment of the Fall is written from the perspective of what if the serpent was right, it is a heresy that has fascinated literature from Marlowe to Milton to Blake. The dark matter of Dust — the creative erotic force of the Universe — brings consciousness, and through it the agency to resist the religious tyranny of the Church. Pullman is adamantly opposed to religious fundamentalism, as his public comments attest.[15] Rewriting *Paradise Lost* for teenagers allows the author to radically dissent from the ideologies of the Christian Right in their popular mobilization of teenage celibacy in such campaigns as True Love Waits. It is fair to say though that the Calvinistic, Talibanesque Church of *His Dark Materials* is a parody, an ironic intensification, albeit one constructed out of the ecclesiastical scaffolding of our own Roman Catholic Church. The trilogy structure depends systematically upon the grand narrative forms and logic of Christianity, not just the Fall but also the pilgrim's journey, temptation and redemption, the descent into Hell, the resurrection after death. The author has repeated the convention and turned away from it, only to be reconnected in a new way.

The queer spatiality of *His Dark Materials*

I have described aspects of sexual subjectivities in the trilogy that can be interpreted as non-normative or queer. Experimentation with gender includes for example Will's father turning out to be a chaste shaman, a healer and spiritual figure who integrates the feminine and masculine, and Lyra is the consummate tomboy who likes to climb over College roofs spitting plum stones on passing scholars and hooting like an owl. Nevertheless, the narrative imperative of the series might still be read as heteronormative, in that the plot is resolved by the emerging sexual knowledge and experience of its two main heterosexual protagonists. The climax of the trilogy comes at the end of book three, *The Amber Spyglass*, when Will and Lyra re-enact the Fall. They become Adam and Eve in the Garden of Eden, reunited with their daemons, and make love. In the stage adaptation, Lyra is seen kissing Will as a stream of gold pours over them, and the witch Serafina declares "two children are making love in an unknown world." Pullman has taken the classic narrative convention of Western culture but given it a characteristic twist. Firstly, we recall that Lyra and Will, the archetypal heterosexual couple that anchor the novel, are with their daemons, who also cavort with each other sexually, they are *more than* a pair, their sex is explicitly not private in a traditional sense, they are "to be two" (Irigaray 2000). Secondly, the couple do not end up together in romantic wedlock at the conclusion of the books, they remain apart in separate yet parallel worlds to become more fully themselves (Russell 2003). Thirdly, at this point in their lives, Lyra and Will are still *children*; it's hard to imagine a more radical gesture in the current climate of paranoia about child sexuality and pedophilia than to suggest under-age sex, in a teenage novel and a play at the National Theatre (UK). Fourthly, Lyra is a firmly feminist action hero, and it is Will who out of the two of them is the most introspective, troubled and sensitive. Their re-enactment of the Fall is all the more powerful for its insistence upon the full agency of the two/four sexually charged participants, and its outcome is their joy, spiritual knowledge and accountability, not their shame. Original sin becomes transformed in *His Dark Materials*.

Pullman's trilogy is a queer heterotopia in that it insists upon a self-fashioning, or self-work that is achieved through being responsive to the collective good, and by holding fast to ethical truths, achieved dialectically in many forms. By presenting this narratable self as an ethical and accountable self, Pullman gives a moral map to agency by dispensing with the sovereign, split, subject forged through shame. He optimistically reworks the Fall of Man into the rise of the posthuman, an ascent to adulthood via sexual experience. *His Dark Materials* is a very Foucauldian project, by looking to spatial and textual realms of the imagination Pullman attempts to redefine what is to love as a human. His writing fulfils the Foucauldian injunction to actively queer aesthetics; he asserts that techniques of the self are intrinsically narrational ["tell them stories"], and therefore intertextual. He is gnomic, Foucaldian even, when he comments upon his aims, contending that his trilogy "is not fantasy. It's a work of stark realism. I don't read fantasy" (Parsons and Nicholson 1999, 131). These self-stories are an effort to form different truths: Pullman gives us a moral accountable self, accrued by means of a diversity of sexual experience and pleasure, and the rejection of shame. Pullman's self is one stirred toward connectivity, of fundamental openness and vulnerability, aligned with Cavarero's faith in the non-shaming You, and the Irigarayan "to be two."

Michel Foucault saw his last work, the three-volume *History of Sexuality*, as a project that returned to the precepts of the Enlightenment that he had spent his previous career refuting. His modern ethics of the self is infused with emancipatory potential, it is opposed to the idea of split, alienated subjectivities that are trapped in cycles of shame and rejection, and it eschews large-scale belief systems that demean and restrict the ordinary person. Pullman's fiction is engaged with a similarly trenchant criticism of religious orthodoxy, and an extended refutation of the biblical theology of sexual shame. Instead, he offers us in creative story-writing what Foucault couldn't: the reimagination of queer heterosexuality, of prelapsarian opposite-sex love that is outside of the phallic economy. Foucault rebuked Christianity for its heteronormativity, for its contrived values, and its subordination of individuals, posing instead a locally emergent ethic, what he called the "autonomous aesthetics of the self," a Kantian attitude of critical self-awareness, the person as a "work of art." It is in fantasy fiction then, that we can find clues to Foucault's project of the constructive reworking of Enlightenment self-fashioning. This genre opens up more fluid spaces where alternative truths of the imagination — thinking and being in the world — can be invented:

> ...the critical ontology of ourselves ... has to be conceived as an attitude, and ethos, a philosophical life in which the critique of what we are is at one and the same time an historical analysis of the limits that are imposed on us and an experiment with the possibility of going beyond them [Foucault in Rabinow 1994, 49–50].

This torque of possibility is reminiscent of the elastic tendon binding self and daemon, and of the twisting and turning dynamics of shame.

NOTES

1. This essay is a revised version of the longer "After the Fall: Queer Heterotopias in Philip Pullman's His Dark Materials Trilogy" in Sally R. Munt, *Queer Attachments: The Cultural Politics of Shame* (Aldershot: Ashgate, 2007).

2. These techniques are resources not equally accessible to all. See further Bridget Byrne (2003) on how some women do not narrate.

3. This idea is at the core of the work, illustrated when the stage version performed at the National Theatre in two separate three-hour plays in January 2004. The first play opened with a scene that immediately addressed this conjunction by deliberately foregrounding the main characters' interdependence:

"The first person to speak a line of the new play was Anna [playing Lyra]. 'Will?' she said.... The second person to speak was Dominic [playing Will]. 'Lyra?.' Dominic playing Will, told Anna playing Lyra, that he missed her, and he missed Pantalaimon too. In fact, he missed Pantalaimon as much as he missed Lyra, 'because he *is* you'" (Butler 2003, 9).

Foucault famously saw heterotopias as: "something like counter-sites, a kind of effectively enacted utopia in which the real sites, all the other real sites that can be found within the culture, are simultaneously represented, contested, and inverted" (Foucault 1986, 24). Heterotopias are kinds of mirrors to utopias, a counterpoint of the real to the unreal, in which the utopic glance returns to reconstruct the real, in a new way of seeing. See further his essay "Of Other Spaces."

4. In the film *Northern Lights*, released in 2007, the ability to use computer generated imagery to illustrate the human/daemon relationship gave us new but limited possibilities for imagining its meaning. The dramatic production at the National Theatre in 2004 used translucent puppets with little lights inside controlled by the hand of the actor. See Butler (2003) for more detail.

5. "You *have* got a daemon," she said decisively. Inside you" (*SK* 26; *HDM* 318).

6. This relationship recalls Hester's name, as Greek Goddess of the Hearth she is the physical representation of home (eds.).

7. Italian feminist philosopher Adriana Cavarero in her book *Relating Narratives: Storytelling and Selfhood* returns us to look back at the idea of a self, and through it an appreciation of what she prosaically calls the "you." Cavarero revives the writerly tradition of Roland Barthes, and echoing his emphasis on eros, love and desire. Drawing also from Hannah Arendt, Cavarero is keen to revivify notions of individual "who"ness, in recalling the uniqueness of each human story. Cavarero doesn't reproduce the Cartesian remoteness so preponderant in modern versions of the self. Her self is distinctive, but entirely dependent upon the love, recognition, and *narration* of the other, the person she calls "you."

8. Pullman is evoking Romantic poet, artist and philosopher William Blake, whose epigrams open nine of the 38 chapters in *The Amber Spyglass* (this is the only volume of the trilogy to use such quotations).

9. For a fascinating psychoanalytic interpretation of the trilogy see the three consecutive journal articles by authors Margaret and Michael Rustin (2003).

10. Pullman clearly sexes his angels rather than detailing hermaphrodite angels; see for example *SK* 146; *HDM* 401 (eds.).

11. The harpy No-Name and this descent passage into the underworld of the dead are reworkings of Homer's *The Odyssey* (when Odysseus gives his name as No-body/No-man) and the descent into Hades by Aeneas in Virgil's *Aeneid*. See Falconer (2004) for a discussion of the descent into Hell in contemporary literature (eds.).

12. This explanation was given to me by Brian Cummings, University of Sussex.

13. Will is of course also short for William, and there must be an allusion here to William Blake.

14. Pullman has given many interviews at which he has been explicit about his political aims in writing *His Dark Materials*. Useful sources include: De Bertodano, Helena (2002); Parsons, Wendy and Nicholson, Catriona (1999); Sharkey, Alex (1998); Tucker, Nicholas (2000). For an enjoyable twist on this see Minette Marrin's comments in the week following the Archbishop of Canterbury's suggestion to a group of theologians at 10, Downing Street [the home of the British Prime Minister] that the trilogy be taught in Religious Education classes in schools (Marrin 2004).

Works Cited

Baker, Deirdre F. 2006. "What We Found on Our Journey Through Fantasy Land." *Children's Literature in Education* 37, 237–251.

Bird, Anne-Marie. 2001. "'Without Contraries Is No Progression'": Dust as an All-Inclusive, Multifunctional Metaphor in Philip Pullman's His Dark Materials." *Children's Literature in Education*, 3:2, 111–123.

Broucek, Francis. 1991. *Shame and the Self*. New York and London: Guilford.

Butler, Robert. 2003. *The Art of Darkness: Staging the Philip Pullman Trilogy*. London: National Theatre/Oberon.

Byrne, Bridget. 2003. "Reciting the Self— Narrative Representations of the Self in Qualitative Interviews." *Feminist Theory* 4:1 (April), 29–49.

Cavavero, Adriana. 2000. *Relating Narratives: Storytelling and Selfhood*. Trans. Paul A. Kottman. London and New York: Routledge.

De Bertodano, Helena. 2002. "I am of the Devil's Party." *Sunday Telegraph*, January 27.

Derrida, Jacques. 2005. *On Touching, Jean-Luc Nancy*. Stanford, CA: Stanford University Press.

Elden, Stuart. 2001. *Mapping the Present: Heidegger, Foucault and the Project of a Spatial History*. London and New York: Continuum.

Falconer, Rachel. 2004. *Hell in Contemporary Literature: Western Descent Narratives Since 1945*. Edinburgh: Edinburgh University Press.

Foucault, Michel. 1979. *A History of Sexuality: An Introduction, Volume One*. Trans. Robert Hurley. Harmondsworth: Penguin.

_____. 1982. "On the Genealogy of Ethics: An Overview of Work in Progress." In *Michel Foucault: Beyond Structuralism and Hermeneutics*. H. Dreyfus and P. Rabinow. Chicago: Chicago University Press.

_____. 1984. "What Is Enlightenment?" In *The Foucault Reader*. Ed. P. Rabinow. Cambridge: Polity.

_____. 1986a. "Of Other Spaces." In *Diacritics* (Spring), 22–7.

_____. 1986b. *Care of the Self: The History of Sexuality, Volume 3*. Trans. Robert Hurley. Harmondsworth: Penguin.

_____. 1991. "Politics and the Study of Discourse." In *The Foucault Effect: Studies in Governmentality*. Eds. Graham Burchell, et al. Chicago: University of Chicago Press.

_____. 1993. "About the Beginning of the Hermeneutics of the Self." Trans. Thomas Keenan and Mark Blasius. In *Political Theory* 21.2, 198–227.

Foucault, Michel, and Catherine Baker. 1984. "Interview with Michel Foucault." In *Actes* 45–46 (June).

Gooderham, David. N.d. "Fantasising It As It Is: Religious Language in Philip Pullman's Trilogy, *His Dark Materials.*" *Project Muse.* Accessed May 10, 2010. *http://muse.jhu.edu.*

Grosz, Elizabeth. 1994. *Volatile Bodies: Towards A Corporeal Feminism.* Bloomington: Indiana University Press.

_____. 2004. *The Nick of Time.* Durham: Duke University Press.

_____. 2005. *Time Travels.* Durham: Duke University Press.

Irigaray, Luce. 2000. *To Be Two.* London: Athlone.

Kottman, Paul A. 2000. "Translator's Introduction." *Relating Narratives: Storytelling and Selfhood.* Ed. Adriana Cavarero. Trans. Paul A. Kottman. London and New York: Routledge.

Lenz, Millicent. 2003. "Story as a Bridge to Transformation: The Way Beyond Death in Philip Pullman's *The Amber Spyglass.*" *Children's Literature in Education* 34:1 (March), 47–55.

Russell, Mary Harris. 2003. "Ethical Plots, Ethical Endings in Philip Pullman's *His Dark Materials.*" *Foundation: The International Review of Science Fiction* 32:88 (Summer), 68–74.

Rustin, Margaret, and Michael Rustin. 2003a. "Learning to Say Goodbye. An Essay on Philip Pullman's *The Amber Spyglass.*" *Journal of Child Psychotherapy* 29:3 (December), 415–25.

_____. 2003b. "Where is Home? An Essay on Philip Pullman's *Northern Lights [The Golden Compass].*" *Journal of Child Psychotherapy* 29:1 (April), 93–105.

_____. 2003c. "A New Kind of Friendship — An Essay on Philip Pullman's *The Subtle Knife.*" *Journal of Child Psychotherapy* 29:2 (August), 227–34.

Sharkey, Alex. 1998. "Heaven, Hell, and the Hut at the Bottom of the Garden." *Independent on Sunday,* December 6.

Skeggs, Beverley. 2004. *Class, Self, Culture.* London: Routledge.

Slouka, Mark. 1995. *War of the Worlds: The Assault on Reality.* London: Abacus.

Squires, Claire. 2003. *Philip Pullman's His Dark Materials Trilogy: A Reader's Guide.* London and New York: Continuum Contemporaries Series.

Tucker, Nicholas. 2000. "Paradise Lost and Freedom Won." *Independent* October 28.

_____. 2003. *Darkness Visible: Inside the World of Philip Pullman.* Cambridge: Wizard, 87–186.

Watkins, Mary. 1987. "In Dreams Become Responsibilities: Moral Imagination and Peace Action." In *Facing Apocalypse.* Eds. Valerie Andrews, Robert Bosnak, and Karen Walter Goodwin. Dallas: Spring, 70–95.

Wood, Naomi. 2001. "Paradise Lost and Found: Obedience, Disobedience, and Storytelling in C.S. Lewis and Philip Pullman." *Children's Literature in Education* 32: 4 (December), 237–259.

14

Staging the Impossible: Severance and Separation in the National Theatre's Adaptation

PATRICK DUGGAN

Introduction

Nicholas Hytner, director of England's National Theatre's adaptation[1] of Philip Pullman's *His Dark Materials*, said that when he was contemplating a production of the books the idea "felt crazy, it felt unstageable" (qtd. in Butler 2003, 8).[2] Others disagree. In his review of the production, John Nathan makes the claim that "no vision is beyond the reach of the stage" (Nathan, 2004, 15), a claim which Pullman himself upholds when he suggests the nothing is impossible in the theater (*c.f.* qtd. in Butler 2003, 36).

Indeed, the books' theatrical connections are made explicit in the first book of the trilogy, *Northern Lights/ The Golden Compass*, when the Armored Bear, Iorek Byrnison is tested by Lyra to see if he can be tricked by her feints and lunges in a deliberate echo of Kleist's famous essay "Über das Marionettentheater" [On the Marionette Theater] in which a young adolescent tries to attack a fighting bear: "thrusts and feints followed thick and fast, the sweat poured off me, but in vain. It wasn't merely that he parried my thrusts like the finest fencer in the world; when I feinted to deceive him he made no move at all. No human fencer could equal his perception in this respect" (Kleist trans. Parry 2008).[3] This use of Kleist is acknowledged at the end of *The Amber Spyglass* in the acknowledgements and here is what Pullman writes:

> "You cannot trick a bear. You want proof? Take a stick and fence with me."
> Eager to try, she [Lyra] snapped off a stick of snow-laden bush, trimmed all the side-shoots off, and swished it from side to side like a rapier. Iorek Byrnison sat back

on his haunches and waited [...]. Finally she decided to thrust at him directly....
Instantly his paw reached forward and flicked the stick aside [*NL* 225; *HDM* 167].

This evocative and very theatrical scene in the first novel perhaps shows how
far Pullman's novels depend upon showing through the interaction of characters
in dramatic scenes, rather than telling in terms of third person narration, as
regards the novels' mode of narration. This fact among others may help to
explain why Hytner and Nicholas Wright recognized the potential offered by
the trilogy for successful drama. In addition, the scene in the novel shows Iorek
Byrnison cannot be tricked by a human because of his non-human bear nature
which allows him to see in a way humans have forgotten, to see what is true
and what is dishonest (which he compares to Lyra's own similarly uncanny
ability with the alethiometer). The scene therefore sets up by means of narrative
irony and a framework of thematic resonance a strong connection to Lyra's
great success later in *Northern Lights/The Golden Compass*, where she successfully
tricks King Iofur Raknison of the *Panserbjørn* of Svalbard. Raknison has deserted
his bear nature to try to become human, baptized a Christian and to obtain a
daemon (*NL* 334; *HDM* 246). It is for this reason that she will earn the name
Lyra Silvertongue from an impressed Iorek (*NL* 348; *HDM* 257). This example
shows the detailed working through of themes at the level of the plot which is
common throughout *His Dark Materials* and may also explain a further reason
why the novels seemed to such potent dramatic potential.

Despite the novels' theatrical elements and Pullman's own endorsement
of the stage's powers, it might appear upon first glance that adapting three
novels, totaling over thirteen hundred pages with an estimated reading time
of over thirty five hours (*c.f.* Berninger 2008, 160), into only *circa* seven hours
of theatrical endeavor may indeed be an impossible task, even for a stage as
versatile as the Oliver.[4]

Even before the rehearsal process began Hytner cautioned that the production "could easily not work. He could be wrong about the whole thing" (qtd.
in Butler 2003, 3). The financial, critical and popular success of the National's
production(s) would, however, suggest that it did work. In his lucid and valuable
critical analysis of the production, Mark Berninger concludes that the production
was a *Gesamtkunstwerk* which "was a highly popular show [... that] tuned in
with the zeitgeist at the beginning of the 21st century" (Berninger 2008, 164).[5]

The notional impossibility discussed here is in regard to the "insanely
ambitious" (*c.f.* Butler 2003, 100) task of adaptation which faced the creative
team at the time, an impossibility which was overcome by a production team
of countless busy and talented minds, technical support most musical productions would have been jealous of, a budget to match, and a director whose
single minded drive pushed the process forward relentlessly.[6] But, while the
production's various successes and failures (in the eyes of some critics) are useful
for contextualization they are not the central focus of this essay, rather I hope

to suggest that through the specific staging strategy of the National's production, employing the full technical might of the Olivier stage, it was able to achieve another impossible task: staging a phenomenologically/viscerally experienced representation of trauma through a series of repetitious and violent separations.

The turn to the traumatic

Throughout the 1990s there was a discernable turn towards the traumatic, the violent, and the visceral in theatrical productions and in representational media more generally. Roger Luckhurst suggests that during the 1990s there was a notable rise in interest in what we might call the "traumatological"; trauma, he argues, became a discernable presence throughout popular, academic, artistic, medical, and political discourses (*c.f.* Luckhurst 2003, 28–33).

With the first production of *His Dark Materials* coming so quickly on the heels of the millennium and the critical furor surrounding much theater of the previous decade, it is worth momentarily pausing on that historical moment as it presents a socio-historical framework which is not only pertinent to my concerns here, but also more widely helps explain the centrality of trauma in both adult and children's literature of the time, and society more generally. This turn towards examinations of trauma is evidenced in the emphasis on the effects of trauma as a noticeable factor in both children's literature written in the period as well as in adult literature and something that critics have increasingly considered. To choose just one example, in this case one of the best-selling children's books of all time, J. K. Rowling's *Harry Potter* series is centered on a child, Harry, who discovers that his parents were brutally tortured and murdered by Voldemort and his own life consists, in the main, of learning to deal with this trauma (and experiencing new ones).[7]

The traumatological turn is similarly noticeable in the theater of the 1990s; writers such as Sarah Kane, Martin Crimp, Mark Ravenhill and Anthony Neilson, to name but a few, wrote plays which presented and repeated images which ranged across multifarious notions of traumatic suffering. From the abusive relationship of Cate and Ian in *Blasted*, to represented sodomy with a screwdriver in *Shopping and Fucking*, to the frenzied violence of *Normal* and what Dan Rebellato (2008) has shown is a persistent trope of self-harm in many plays, there was a general trend in much new theatrical endeavor to represent the un-representable; images and acts which were previously the domain of film and, to a lesser extent, television were now finding a home on the 1990s stage. This trend established new dramaturgies which were engaged in attempting to present irreconcilable traumas. Much like the reality of performance art, these writers employed compositional and dramaturgical styles which intentionally tried to present a constant sense of traumatic presence, a traumatic reality through theatricality. It is a lineage to which *His Dark Materials* is doubly indebted, if not in such explicit content being staged dramatically, then most certainly in its attempt to deliberately and viscerally stage unstageable acts of trauma in the form of Wright's adaptation.

It is the convergence then of several elements that provide the framework for understanding and which contextualizes the importance of trauma in Wright's adaptation of *His Dark Materials*: British theater's 1990's obsessions in trauma and its unrepresentability; the correspondent emphasis on trauma in children and young adult's literature; the traumatological turn in 1990's British culture; the growing interest in crossover literature (literature for young adults read by adults) that is discussed in Rachel Falconer's account of *His Dark Materials* as a contemporary cross-over novel (2008). I would further argue that these aspects when taken together suggest there was a ready and prepared audience interest in the adaptation of *His Dark Materials* as text about trauma; an argument perhaps given more substantiation by several productions that followed *His Dark Materials* at the National of texts for young adults, which continue this focus on the representation of trauma. In one way or another while ostensibly aimed at young audiences, these adaptations have been just as popular with adults and they would include: Helen Edmundson's adaptation of *Coram Boy* (2005–2006); Nick Stafford's adaptation of *War Horse* (2007–2009); and Mark Ravenhill's adaptation of *Nation* (2009–2010).[8]

From physical violence to psychological abuse *His Dark Materials* is littered with representations and accounts of traumatic experience. The National's production staged much of this trauma, so much indeed that it could be identified as a central performance trope of the production. The signal for these representations comes, of course, from Pullman's trilogy of novels, themselves variously peppered with traumatic encounters, losses and actions. But it is on the specific recurring trauma of separation, dislocation and severance that I wish to focus on here.

A very present absence

Timothy Dalton, playing Lord Asriel, strides confidently across the stage, leather trench-coat billowing behind him.[9] Dalton is variously slapped on the back, shaken hands with, smiled at, and otherwise variously applauded and welcomed to the fictional Oxford of Lyra's parallel Earth, which the characters inhabit. All the while a small, excited figure, slightly upstage left of the main hubbub of action, and tries desperately to catch his attention:

> *LYRA tries hard to attract Fhis [Asriel's] attention*
> LORD ASRIEL (to a SCHOLAR): Professor Tonkin, I hear your book's been a great success.
> LYRA: Hello!

LORD ASRIEL ignores her, and the MASTER bustles her aside.
MASTER: Out of the way!
LORD ASRIEL (to another): Congratulations on your professorship, Richard.
LYRA is back.
MASTER: Now then, Lyra!
She is shunted out of the way [Wright 2004, 13].[10]

Anna Maxwell Martin, playing Lyra, looks forlorn as Dalton is led out by the assembled crowd of actors, her body language is, momentarily, dejected, almost as if the character is broken by this failed encounter. Lyra thinks at this stage, as we do that, she is an orphan who has never known her parents and that Lord Asriel is her uncle and only known relative, and it is in this context that his rejection of her occurs. Moments later the external scene has been transformed into an interior as the Retiring Room rises from the stage floor carried by the behemoth which is the Olivier's drum revolve. And only moments after this Dalton has violently grabbed Martin's arm, twisting it into what appears to be an agonizingly unnatural, painful position, and although the lines aren't uttered on stage the presence of Lord Asriel's words from the novels are powerfully evoked, "what the hell are you doing [in here]? ... I'll break your arm" (*NL* 14; *HDM* 10).

For many people the relationships we forge throughout life, from the first moment to the last, define who we are and how we move in the world around us. From our first attachment with our mothers, the human animal needs contact with other humans in order to develop and to move productively through life. As we grow older we become increasingly able to negotiate the complexities of these relationships, layering and categorizing the different types of bond which we live with. Most of the relationships of greatest importance are those which involve deep emotional investment such as with family members, lovers, and friends — it is these relationships, as the attachments theorists discuss, that help form, develop and sustain our notion of self.[11] Psychoanalyst and attachment theorist John Bowlby has argued that "a liability to experience separation anxiety and grief are ineluctable results of a love relationship, of caring for someone" (Bowlby ctd. in Holmes 2008, 86). It stands to reason then that when these attachments are disturbed, ruptured and severed that they impact upon that constructed self.

PANTALAIMON: There's nothing here.
LYRA: Look
A small figure can be seen a distance away from them.
Roger? Rodge, is it you?
The figure becomes clearer as it turns towards them. It's BILLY COSTA. He looks white, drained and half-alive, and speaks in a feeble whisper.
BILLY: You seen my Ratter?
LYRA: That ain't Rodge. It's Billy Costa. Billy, what's wrong?
BILLY: Ratter?
PANTALAIMON, very alarmed, approaches BILLY and searches all around him.

PANTALAIMON: He's got no daemon!
BILLY: I lost my Ratter.
LYRA: Oh Billy! Billy, what happened?
BILLY: Ratter? Ratter?
He collapses [Wright 2004, 62].

In *His Dark Materials* one of the closest and most important attachment bonds is that between a person and their daemon. Very near the beginning of the National's adaptation the Oxford scholar called Hopcraft asks, "Why, if a man ran away from his daemon, would he experience, first discomfort ... then pain ... then a grinding sense of loss, and finally death?" (Wright 2003, 10). The question makes it textually clear to the audience from the outset of the piece that this relationship is at the very core of human existence. But the importance of the daemon bond is signified and highlighted through a number of different theatrical/dramaturgical layers, both textual and extra-textual; sound, lighting, set and, of course, an embodied/acted layer, all interact to both semiotically and phenomenologically iterate and reiterate this central element of the story to the audience.

As with all theatrical criticism it is important to recognize that while semiotics and phenomenology may be very different ways of approaching the live experience they are essentially the inescapable flip-sides of each other; Stanton B. Garner suggests, they are "complimentary ways of seeing that disclose the object two ways at once" (Garner 1994, 15).[12] Garner's assertion is built from Bert O. States' call for a "binocular vision" (States 1985, 8) when approaching performance criticism, a call to recognize the value in approaching criticism through both critical approaches. It is a call which has been supported and reiterated by many others,[13] Mick Wallis has usefully postulated that by acknowledging the semiotic and the phenomenological we are able to read and map the "play of signifiers below the level of signification" in order that we might more fully become aware of "a multifarious flow of possibilities" and so navigate the "multivocality" and "slippery signification" of the stage image (Wallis 2005, 70).

Wallis further suggests, in his analysis of *The Fate of Sparta* (*c*.1788), that it might be possible to identify levels of textual meaning (textual in this case being applied to the whole of a production as a text) which are both natural to the shape of the play (the harrow-like machine of Bolvangar, described below) and a ritualized layer of coincidence, what I refer to as an uncanny echo of sorts, which creates an unexplainable presence (the slicing in and out of worlds through the use of the drum revolve, echoing the action of the subtle knife).

His central contention is that this layering operates as a system of production of phenomena, and that such coincidental repetitions operate as "a mode of productivity not only of meanings but also of phenomena" (Wallis

2005, 74), the idea being that there is "interplay between signification and constructed [phenomenological] presence" (Wallis 2005, 70). The daemon bond is one such presence, a presence which is established not only through the progression of the narrative fiction, but coincidentally through the staging structures of the piece. It is a constructed phenomena, an unexplainable, uncanny presence which the audience experience fully but which is inherently absent; it cannot be pointed at, seen or heard but is constantly there nonetheless.

In his account of the making of the play Robert Butler points out the daemon bond is a bond which "could not be closer" and one which Hytner went to great lengths to illustrate as "unbreakable" (Butler 2003, 108). This creature, which takes on an animal form that can change shape until such time as its human reaches the age of puberty, is part of the human. There is no separation or distinction between the daemon self and the human self, they are part of the same entity. Although Pullman distances himself from such claims (*c.f.* Butler 2003, 24), the relationship has been described as similar to what we might think of as our relationship or interaction with our soul or perhaps conscience. Whether this is accurate or not is not my concern, but what is patently clear throughout the stage adaptation is that the relationship is a deeply embedded one. Daemon and human form one being, one self; it is a relationship which cannot be separated without terrible and lasting consequences.

In the scene cited above, the audience witness a staggering Jamie Harding, playing Billy Costa, appear on stage and it becomes apparent he has been severed from his daemon, Ratter. In the novel this doesn't happen to Billy Costa, but instead to Tony Marakios. Samuel Barnett, the actor/puppeteer who voices and animates/embodies Pantalaimon, makes the puppet daemon twitch and writhe in discomfort, similarly vocalizing the emotions. Anna Maxwell Martin, playing Lyra, also reacts with fear and revulsion, though she necessarily overcomes this in order to be able to interact with Billy Costa.[14] The embodied reactions of the characters to the event of encountering a daemon-less human quite clearly signifies that something is terribly amiss; Billy is now somehow made "other" through the act of severance from Ratter. The scene dramaturgically establishes the daemon bond's centrality to human existence within Lyra's world, and while the act of separation is not represented its aftermath is apparent in the fearful, agitated and shocked reactions of the characters around Billy.

Throughout the books and the seven or so hours of performance, a theme of separation and split is repeated time and again, and whether it is imposed upon one character by another or self inflicted the action is always violent, a tear, a disruption, a trauma. So deeply painful are these separations for the characters within the diegetic world(s) of *His Dark Materials* that they can be seen to mimetically echo the central edict of trauma theory, namely that trauma is an event outside the realm of human experience the impact of which cannot be felt until after the event itself has ended, and that this impact manifests itself in a disruption of the survivor-sufferer's understanding of self.[15] Trauma theorist Judith Herman describes it thus:

> traumatic events call into question basic human relationships. They breach the attachments of family, friendship, love, and community. They shatter the construction of self that is formed and sustained in relation to others. They undermine the belief systems that give meaning to human experience. They violate the victim's faith in a natural or divine order and cast the victim into a state of existential crisis [Herman 2001, 51].

An untouchable phenomena

As noted trauma has become an increasingly important point of reference in today's society but through this the term has become overused, so much so that it has almost lost all sense of meaning in its everyday uses. It is a term which pervades all levels of our interactions in the world, from the most personal and private traumas which we experience throughout life, to its most banal use in television insurance adverts which claim that taking out a policy with such-and-such a broker will prevent traumas. We live in a society which is bound to its traumatic experiences, a society in which trauma has become, as Christina Wald has recently argued, a "cultural trope" (Wald 2007, 3). Wald goes on to suggest that the rise of this cultural trope has pushed the notion of trauma to "the point of meaninglessness" on one hand, but that the relatively recent rise in trauma theory as a focus of academic interest has galvanized trauma as a frame through which to examine cultural issues "of experience, memory, the body, and representation" (Wald 2007, 3).

Western academic, artistic, journalistic, psychiatric, psychoanalytic and cultural discourses, in particular, have become increasingly engaged in analysis of traumata and people's experience of them. Contemporary British society has been described by Luckhurst as a "traumaculture," a term he suggests is born out of the "notable academic turn to questions of memory, trauma and identity during the past ten years" and which is responding both to Mark Seltzer's notion of "wound culture" and to "a pervasive sense of the organising power of the notion of trauma in the 1990s" (Luckhurst 2003, 28).

The rise in academic interest in trauma theory has been most easily seen in the fields of history, literature, cultural studies, and fine art. But trauma theory suggests a performative bent in traumatic suffering. This is not to be flippant or insensitive to the memories of trauma sufferers, a concern elucidated in much commentary on trauma, but to suggest that the increasing take up of trauma theory as a means of exploring theater and performance is long since due. [16] Dominic LaCapra, a prominent historian and trauma theorist, inadvertently draws attention to this performative element in *Writing History, Writing Trauma* when he suggests that trauma sufferers have a tendency to "relive the past, to be haunted by ghosts or even to exist in the present as if one were still in the past, with no distance from it" (LaCapra 2001, 142–143).

There is in this statement a sense in which trauma performs itself within a collapsing of time, a sense in which the inability to exist in the present is a traumatic performative disruption/disturbance of time. Performance critic Adrian Heathfield has suggested that the linear narrative of life is what enables us to live productively in the world. He argues that we constantly "evaluate and, listening to what the past tells, draw lessons for life in the present" and he goes on to say that through this process of evaluative learning, "you might come to believe that you have survived the thing that has ended, you might create a bar between you and it, and so consign it to the past" (Heathfield, 2000 105). Sally R. Munt, in her chapter in this volume, suggests, through Foucault, that "the self negotiates both the spatial and the temporal in order to have a sense of individuation" and goes on to say that we construct a narrative of our lives in which we become "the 'hero' of our own story."

The self, then, is constructed through and around relationships and our personal histories or narratives. But traumata collapse this linear succession of things through the constant performative irruptions of the trauma symptom or memory. LaCapra further compounds the notion of trauma as a performative suffering, suggesting that survivor-sufferers act out compulsive repetition of actions, words, and situations from traumatic occurrences (LaCapra 2001, 142–143).[17] Trauma, then, can be seen to rehearse, repeat, and re-present itself in performed ghosts that haunt the sufferer.

Despite the relatively recent critical attention on trauma in the non-literary representational arts (film, fine art, photography, theater), trauma remains elusive and slippery to them. Like Lacan's Real, trauma is seemingly ungraspable, impossible. In her musings on loss and (its) survival in the introduction to *Mourning Sex*, Peggy Phelan touches on trauma as already existent within human kind from the moment of birth, her language evoking a sense of evisceration at birth as we are "severed from the placenta and cast from the womb" only to enter the world as "amputated" bodies defined by our own mortality (Phelan 1997, 5); and interestingly, she goes on to position the self as constructed through and in relation to trauma suggesting that "maybe bodies come to be 'ours' when we recognise them as traumatic" (Phelan 1997, 18).

It would seem, in light of Phelan's arguments, that trauma is a fundamental part of the creation of human existence. During these opening pages she taps into the widely shared argument that "trauma is untouchable [...] it cannot be represented. The symbolic cannot carry it: trauma makes a tear in the symbolic network itself" (Phelan 1997, 5). Trauma, in other words, is beyond representation. Yet despite the tear that trauma makes in representational orders, despite its evisceration of language and the impossibility of capturing and/or repeating the impact of traumata adequately, it seems to me that the theater is one representational form in which an attempt at articulation of, or bearing of witness to, trauma might be possible.[18] Karen Malpede concurs, commenting that "[b]ecause theatre takes place in public and involves the movement of bodies across a stage, theatre seems uniquely suited to portray the complex interpersonal [and intrapersonal] realities of trauma" (Malpede 1996, 168).

Indeed Hans-Thies Lehmann, in his examination of postdramatic theater, uncannily traces the trauma theorists (such as Herman, cited above) when he claims that "performance has the power to question and destabilise the spectator's construction of identity" (Lehmann 2006, 5). Not only can trauma-symptoms be considered as performative disturbances of self, time and psyche but it would further appear, under Lehmann's assertion, that theater/performance shares this destabilizing power. Thus theater/performance, more than any other art form, is perfectly placed to attempt a dialogue with trauma, and potentially, working against Phelan's assertions, even a representation of it.

The parting is agonizing

A large building, displaying the letters *G. O. B* on its roof, dominates the stage. It is an austere looking structure, cold and institutional, penal even. A sliding door which covers almost half the length of the building is open, revealing cage after cage of quivering and agitated animal-like figures. A girl, holding a similar creature in her arms, stands beside the opening; she is completely dwarfed by the structure's size and dominance of the space. The girl's shrinking stature is further compounded by two extra diegetic elements — the enveloping size of the Olivier auditorium and an underscore which plays "danger" music. Two men appear and see the girl standing beside the open sliding door; they lurch forward to roughly grab the girl and close the door to the cage room in a flurry of panicked action:

> DR. CADE: We can't let her go back to the other children. She'll blurt it all out, and we'll have total panic all around.
> DR. WEST: There's only one thing we can do, it seems to me.
> DR. CADE: What, now?
> DR. WEST: Why not?
> DR. CADE: But Mrs. Coulter hasn't arrived. I thought she had to be there for each experiment.
> DR. WEST: That's what she says ... but there's no scientific justification for it. She simply enjoys watching [Wright 2004, 63].

And with that we move to the interior of the Bolvangar camp. The girl is violently struggling against her captors, but she is no match for their strength. Again the scenography is the overwhelmingly dominant part of the stage image; a huge scientific laboratory slices into the space on the drum revolve, the central component of which is a Kafkaesque machine comprising of a chair reminiscent of the electric chairs of countless films, connected by a long, covered, rectangular trough to a raised cage.

The connection is bisected by a third item, a large "guillotine-blade" (Wright 2004, 63), and just as the prisoner in Kafka's *In the Penal Settlement* is confused and frightened by the macabre Harrow (Kafka 1949, 195), so too does the girl embody a sense of fear and confusion as she sees the blade and the rest of the torturous device. She is manhandled into the chair and bound down as the creature she holds to her chest is torn away from her by one of the men. The instant the creature is touched the music screeches and the lighting changes; we know something terrible has happened. Girl and creature scream in agony, and as the distance between them increases the discomfort for both seems to increase; the creature writhes and wriggles, desperate to return to the comfort of girl's bosom, and she in turn struggles against her bonds, taught muscles digging deep for extra strength with which to break free.

Their screams fill the auditorium despite their small size, the dominance of the scenography only adding the audience's sense of fear for the two characters now bound by cage or chair. The girl screams out repeatedly, "You can't touch him! You can't touch him!" (Wright 2004, 63), as a lighting effect makes visible the bond between her and the creature, her daemon, a bond which we are sure is about to be violently severed. Jeremy Holmes has suggested that this type of behavior is typical of those experiencing a split in an attachment relationship suggesting that if one:

> Tr[ies] to prise a limpet away from its rock [...] it will cling all the harder. The best test of the presence of an attachment bond is to observe the response to separation [...]. Crying, screaming, shouting, biting, kicking — this "bad" behaviour is the normal response to the threat to an attachment bond [Holmes 2008, 72].

The reaction to this scene and to the Bolvangar scene is primarily a phenomenological one, each audience member will embody what is happening and so experience it in a slightly different way. Yet what is particularly interesting is the way in which there is a dual layer meaning making process in operation between the scenography and the actor. At times the scenographic elements of the production might be seen to naturalistically augment the embodied and textual actions. This is to say that the design elements of the production are passively adding to what is already on stage.[19] However, there is a second layer in which the meaning is uncannily echoed through the scenographic elements, rather than a coincidental meaning making process. The juxtaposition between the enormity of the machines, the stage and auditorium spaces, and the cacophony of the sound effects against the actor's screaming and struggling sets the audience on the track of traumatic witnessing. [20]

The scream is at once dwarfed by the staging and openness of the Olivier space, and in the same instant piercingly real, creating an experience which is viscerally embodied, a reaction against the attempt to cut the self, the result of which we witnessed only a few scenes ago. The daemon bond is again illustrated and made palpably present through the reaction of both Pantalaimon and Lyra to the threat of its severance, and also by Mrs. Coulter's breathless and aggressive dismissal of the doctors, her evident relief (though not necessarily for the right reasons) in uttering "I was beside myself. I've never been so upset" (Wright 2004, 64), and her shifting, squirming (vocal and physical) awkwardness as Lyra asks "Why do you do it? How can you be so cruel?" (Wright 2004, 64).

Despite its obvious theatricality, the scene I have just described is hard to witness; the screams of Lyra and Pantalaimon resonate in the audience's ears and rattle through their bodies, reaching, as Garner has suggested representations of pain can, "across the boundary [...] between stage and spectator" (Garner 1994, 180), to touch and impact upon the bodies of the spectators. A moment of rhetorical performative *punctum* which, just as Barthes suggests of the photographic *punctum*, "rises[es] from the scene, shoots out of it like an arrow, and pierces me," it reaches out and across the space to prick the audience, to bruise them (*c.f.* Barthes 1982, 26–27).[21]

Furthermore, we layer this performative prick with the numerous other recognizable significations present in the representation; child abuse, Nazi concentration camps, and Dr. Mengele's experimentation with twins are just a few which, to my mind at least, sit closely and deliberately to the surface of the scene. Jill Bennett has observed that "[t]he fact that we live in a post–Holocaust world is understood to compel us to deal with Holocaust memory, and to account for the ways in which the Holocaust has touched us directly or indirectly" (Bennett 2005, 6). It is a socio-cultural trauma memory which we continually attempt to bear witness to in various ways; the signification of the Nazi concentration camps, and of other right wing regimes, in the National's production of *His Dark Materials* is by no means accidental.

Robert Butler notes that in both the books and the plays there are "hints of Communist Russia and Nazi Germany" (Butler 2003, 6), but these hints are designed into the stage adaptation and repeated with frequency that, for an adult audience at least, it difficult to categorize them as merely hints, instead they seem to take centre stage, so to speak. In the Bolvangar scene I have outline above it is hard not to implant the specter of Dr. Mengele onto the stage as the calculating and calm voice of the on stage Dr. Sargent turns to Lyra saying, "keep still for a moment for me. That's perfect" (Wright 2004, 64). After all, the violence is an "experiment," "for scientific progress [... and] the child's own good," as Mrs. Coulter puts it moments later (Wright 2004, 65). Pullman's novels make this move too, but the connection is made explicit by National's scenographic design. The austerity of the staging, the institutional quality and intimidating grandeur of the stage buildings, coupled with the

Olivier's own austere concrete interior, speak explicitly to the numerous images of the camps that pervade film and literature, which, according to Dominic LaCapra, can be seen as part of the problem of "canoniz[ing] the Holocaust" (LaCapra 1996, 1; 19–41). The images are common currency and so the link from the stage images to the concentration camps and experiments of Mengele is not a particularly difficult one.

"Feel the pain of separation"

I would like to turn now to the Boatman scene in the underworld (c.f. Wright 2004, 198–200). It is the scene in which Lyra and Will cross over into the Land of the Dead, and in order to do so Lyra must part ways with Pantalaimon, an act which we know to be both painful and dangerous, against the natural order of Lyra's world.[22] The massive Olivier stage is, for the first and only time in this production, completely bare save the three actors, one of whom is wearing a black body suit as he embodies the daemon Pantalaimon, standing stage right, slightly toward the down stage edge. High above them a rowing boat appears, as if it is floating in the darkness. The Boatman inside pulls gently on the illuminated oars, his aged face highlighted by the lighting inside the boat and framed by a sharp dark suit and bowler hat. The boat descends toward Lyra, Pantalaimon and Will all of whom stare on in what might be fear or just as likely awe and anticipation. A haunting brass/wind instrument accompanies the Boatman's journey to the children.[23]

> *A rowing boat is heard*
> WILL: It's the boat.
> LYRA: Will? You ready?
> *Pantalaimon howls.*
> Ssh, Pan.
> *The boat appears and comes to a rest, rowed by a very old BOATMAN.*
> WILL: I'll go first.
> PANTALAIMON: No!
> BOATMAN: Not him.
> LYRA: Not who?
> *The Boatman indicates Pantalaimon.*
> I can't leave Pantalaimon behind. I'll Die!
> Boatman: Isn't that what you want?
> *Pantalaimon howls and whimpers* [Wright, 2004,198–199].

Dominic Cooper, playing Will, has moved away from Lyra and Pantalaimon's fierce embrace and tearful goodbyes to climb onboard the boat. Lyra begins to move away from Pantalaimon, the small puppet is agitated and flicks frantically around Anna Maxwell Martin's ankles as Samuel Barnett, voicing Pantalaimon, repeatedly pleads with her, "No! No!" Martin climbs in to the boat, her character's determination to rescue her companion Roger dictates that she must tear herself away from her daemon. The Boatman was very clear, "Not him."

> *Lyra embraces Pantalaimon.*
> LYRA: Pan, I love you. If I have to spend the rest of my life finding you again, I will. But I can't go back. I can't. I'm going to push you away now. I'm sorry.
> *She pushes Pantalaimon away and steps on to the boat.... Pantalaimon crouches, forlorn and desolate. The Boatman pushes off and the boat moves away from the shore. Lyra and Pantalaimon feel the pain of separation. Lyra cries in agony.*
> Oh Pan! [Wright 2004, 200].

As boat begins to move away it is enveloped by the darkness of the empty space, highlighting both the physical distance between Pantalaimon and Lyra and the growing tear in their unseen but palpably felt bond. This element of the sceno-graphic design is another uncanny echo of the textual story, without the empty space the phenomenological sense of emptiness, isolation and violent rupture which is made present in this scene would have been lost. This scene is one in which the "interplay between signification and constructed presence" (Wallis 2005, 70) is at its most effective, heightening the emotional resonance of what Butler describes as "one of the most heart-rending events in the story" (Butler 2003, 108).

As the boat moves further into the darkness, Samuel Barnett's voice quivers through the space in a remarkable moment of emotionally charged vocal work as he simply cries out "Lyra" in a prolonged and agonizing vocalization of the pain of this separation. The sound is tortured and imbibed with a palpable sense of the emotion the characters must be experiencing. It is hard to ade-quately describe Barnett's cry but his slightly West Country accent seems to elongate Lyra into what might be written as "Lyyyyyrraaaaaa" (or something equally inadequate). This emanation created an awareness of both the character of Pantalaimon and his puppeteer, the presence of whom is made manifest in a why which I do not believe happens at any other point in the play — it is this tripartite presence, Lyra-Pantalaimon-Puppeteer, which helps to explain the deeply embodied and emotionally resonant experience of the scene. Theater academic and phenomenologist Bruce Wilshire suggests that we go to the the-ater in order to "see ourselves" (Wilshire 1982, 5), and that through the mimesis we are able to position ourselves on the stage with and/or in the place of the actor because of our identification with them. He claims that an "actor cannot stand on-stage without standing in for a type of humanity" (Wilshire 1982, 6) and so phenomenologically we relate our experiences to that of the actor, or more specifically to the character they are playing: "The actor playing a character stands in for all persons of this sort, and we in the audience, iden-tifying with him and his characterization, stand in through his standing in. We try out another life for size" (Wilshire 1982, xiii).

The voice work and the embodied manipulation of the puppet collide and circulate with the echoic darkness of the stage space (and indeed auditorium) to create and underpin a phenomenological experience of this traumatic split. This scene (like the one described earlier) is not experienced within a semiotic field in the first instance, but rather it seems to rupture the symbolic divide between audience and performance spaces; the scene seems to reach across and touch us both emotionally and physically. James Elkins usefully postulates that the image one has of oneself is mingled with the way we respond to depicted bodies and that "the act of beholding a body affects [ones] ability to form propositions and to use language, blurring the capacity to judge and finally erasing it when [one is] in the presence of excessive pain" (Elkins 1999, vii).

The Boatman scene is, again, a moment of performative *punctum* which captivates the audience; it is pertinent to them but is also viscerally/emotionally painful to them. It is emotional, "slightly overwhelming," as a colleague put it to me and very strongly felt in the pit of the stomach and tightening of the throat.[24] Butler reiterates this point noting that "[o]n stage an actor was saying goodbye to a puppet and in the auditorium there were members of the audience in tears" (Butler 2003, 108). There is a sense when watching this scene that it is a deeply private and overwhelming real pain that is being put before is. So uncomfortable is this scene that through a series of embodied and phenomenologically experienced spatial and body-to-body (spectator to actor) relations this moment in *His Dark Materials* creates what Jonas Barish, might call a moment of "ontologically queasiness" (Barish 1981, 3) in which the spectator is set into a position, as Nicholas Ridout suggests, of not knowing if they "want to 'be' there or not" (Ridout 2006, 3). To be at the event of the Boatman scene is to experience the effect of presence in traumatic severance, so to speak.

"Flies cue 61. Go."

At the beginning of both parts of the National's adaptation the audience enter the space to find a large tree, with a bench circling it, positioned down stage center. This represents the botanic gardens, a recurrent venue in which the story can unfold and the relationship of Will and Lyra can develop. It is a cyclical setting too, the play begins and ends here.

At the end of the play Lyra and Will fall in love, and make love, but even in the union of desire and finding of self in the act of copulation (which is not actually staged) the split, traumatized self is again reared as the two lovers are informed that they must part ways — news with is scenographically doubled as the deputy stage manager calls for "flies cue 61" and "the sliders pull back and the tree divide[s] in two" (Butler 2003, 117). Despite being reunited with Pantalaimon moments earlier, Lyra is left devoid of the object of her desire and the person who helps define her (proto-adult) sense of self, Will, who is himself now given a daemon, but one which cannot stand in for his love for Lyra. The divided, split, severed self, the traumatized self, is the self that ultimately survives at the end of the play. Even though the lovers can become complete again once a year as they meet "only inches apart on stage; ... [but in] parallel universes [in the fiction]" (Butler 2003, 116–117), but they must repeat this traumatic split again as they part ways at dawn. The repetition of traumatic severance and disrupted selfhood is perpetual.[25]

The acts of severance are a repetitive and cyclical bearing witness to trauma. It is through the stage dynamic and its uncanny echo of the embodied and textual elements of the theater event that *His Dark Materials* is able to make present both the daemon bond and the subsequent phenomenological experience of its split. It is the layering of stage imagery with Pullman's original story which is so evocative for an audience; by embodying the physical and emotional traumata the reader is able to phenomenologically engage with and bear witness to the traumata in a much more adequate, which is to say engaged or personal, way. Signification through the stage imagery is layered upon the dialogue and action to reinforce the repetition of traumatic separation. The daemon bond is built through the dramaturgical and semiotic strategies of the production, creating a sense of the bond's presence in the theater space despite its ontological absence. This semiotically constructed bond is then violently severed, in an experience which is deeply embodied by the audience. To write of the experience in this way is potentially however, as Wallis cautions, to attempt to write about the ungraspable (*c.f.* Wallis 2005, 71); but that is of course the point, for to write or think about traumata and performance events is precisely to engage in attempting to write, grasp, re/present the un-writable, un-graspable, un-re/presentable.[26]

It is entirely appropriate, then, to talk of what we might term a phenomenological "presence-in-trauma effect," which is caused by the staging of separation in *His Dark Materials*. Indeed, while Phelan claimed that to represent trauma is impossible this production makes if not a representation of trauma then at least an embodied articulation of it which makes that impossible phenomenon present to the assembled audience. To read and write about the experience of traumatic separation in relation to *His Dark Materials* is to become entangled in a web of presence effects; the invocation of the presence of the daemon bond through stage effects and strategies, and through this the effect of being *in* traumatic separation.

Wallis states that "phenomenology illuminates theatre, but theatre is also a privileged apparatus for revealing some existential truths" (Wallis 2005, 72), so, linking back to Herman's assertion that trauma casts the victim into existential crisis, theater is again illustrated as a space in which the exploration of traumata might not only be appropriate but possible. While the novels of *His*

Dark Materials contain a litany of representations of trauma the stage adaptation embodies those representations in much more viscerally embodied and so, potentially, meaningful ways. This is not to deny the emotional resonance of the books but to suggest that through the utilization of the Olivier's enormity and mechanical sublimity in juxtaposition to the human body, the trauma of severance and separation is played out and borne witness to with a resonance which is impossible in other media. Both due to the lack of bodily proximities and also because the uncanny echoes of cutting and severance made by the staging strategy of the production would be absent. Berninger suggests that the National Theatre, and the Olivier stage in particular, is the only venue in the world that could have produced this spectacular production (*c.f.* Berninger 159–160). [27]

The same could be said for the creation of the phenomenological experience of trauma and severance which is palpably made present by this production, and in particular the Boatman scene. The ability of the drum revolve to so seamlessly slice through the scenes of the play and the worlds of the fiction, like the National's very own Subtle Knife, is central to the embodied experience of the audience. The importance of the space-body relationship cannot be underestimated in creating a presence-in-trauma effect. Gay McAuley has convincingly argued that the

> Experience of theatregoing teaches us to look at the stage, but the spectator in the theatre is always involved first and foremost in the phenomenological experience of being there, of the space in relation to oneself, of one's self *in* the place, of the "height in the air," of the "feeling" (what ever that is) of being in a theatre [McAuley 2000, 256].

One might add to this description the relation of one's body to the bodies of the actors, to their voices and movement, and to the other spectators' bodies. The experience of the theater is a phenomenally active one, which is first and foremost experienced in and through the body rather than cognitively, though the two are of course inescapably braided. By opening up the stage space in the moment of Lyra's separation from Pantalaimon, and through the continued dramaturgical and scenographic strategies, both natural to the story and coincidental, the audience are opened to a phenomenological experience of traumatic separation which is created by both the experiential and referential elements of the production.

Notes

1. We use the English word "theatre" when referring to the (English) National Theatre, located on the South Bank in London, UK (eds.), elsewhere the American spelling "theater" is used.

2. I would like to thank the National Theatre archive, Gavin Clarke and Zoë Wilcox in particular, for their generous help while researching this essay.

3. Berninger also highlights this point in discussing the notion of falling from grace which is present in both Pullman's novels and Kleist's piece.

4. The Olivier stage is named after the famous British actor Lawrence Olivier (1907–1989).

5. For further discussion of the plays as *Gesamtkunstwerk* see MacDonald (2007).

6. Berninger gives an excellent account of the productions scale, cost and the number of people involved in relation to other theatrical types and to film (*c.f.* Berninger 2008, 155–156; 160–161; footnote 8). Butler's description of the technical rehearsals gives a good gloss of Hytner's determination and drive (see Butler 2003, 93–101).

7. For further discussion of trauma and children's literature as a specific connection that has become very important recently see: Bosmajian (2002); Kidd (2005); Homans (2006).

8. Helen Edmundson's adaptation is based on Jamila Gavin's novel *Coram Boy* (2000), Nick Stafford's adaptation is based on Michael Morpurgo's novel *War Horse* (1982), and Mark Ravenhill's adaptation is based on Terry Pratchett's novel *Nation* (2008).

9. The references I make to the production refer to the first run from the previews in December 2003 until March 2004, staging of *His Dark Materials*. For a full cast list refer to Butler (2003). The second run of the play was from 20 November 2004 to 2 April 2005.

10. Unless otherwise stated, all following citation of the play will be taken from the 2004 Revised Edition of the play script that was used for the second run of the production.

11. On the importance of the figure of the orphan in the novels, see Laura Peters' essay in the present volume.

12. The "at once" here is important, for while is has been suggested that the phenomenological experience happens first and the cognitive/semiotic second, it is reductive to try and delineate the readings in this way as in actual fact we may need to decode what is happening before it is able to phenomenologically impact upon us. To think of the experiential and the referential as mutually beneficial readings which we always already hold open and active is thus much more productive.

13. See, for example, Wilshire (1982), Garner (1994), and Wallis (2005).

14. Although there is still an emotional resonance to this scene, the play puts much less emphasis on this scene than the novel does (see *NL* 215–216; *HDM* 159–160).

15. See Caruth (1995 and 1996), LaCapra (1996), and Herman (2001) for further discussion.

16. See, especially, the Dominic LaCapra (1994 and 1996) and Ruth Leys (2000).

17. "Acting out" is, of course, a widely accepted and used psycho-medical term which is employed in much writing on and in psychotherapeutic practices.

18. In terms of adequately bearing witness to the survivor-sufferers' memories of the event.

19. The opening Oxford scenes and the scenes in the Master's study are good examples of this (*c.f.* Butler 2003, 44–47; also see "The Production" (2003/4a), section "Lyra Meets Mrs. Coulter on Stage," and "The Production," Stagework (2003/4b), section "The Alethiometer: Performance."

20. The Olivier auditorium can seat over 1000 audience members, thus its scale comes to be part of the theater experience in a very direct way. For an excellent account of space and performance see McAuley (2000).

21. It is worth noting that Barthes somewhat fetishizes the *punctum*, it is a positive element of the photograph which captures his interest and draws him further into the image. By employing the term here my intention is both to utilize the sense of violence which Barthes' writing conjures, but also to stay true to the term's meaning, i.e., the performative *punctum* has a violently felt impact but it is one which, while uncomfortable, draws the audiences interest, captivates them, is poignant to them (See Barthes 1982, 26–28).

22. For a short, edited video clip of this scene visit see "The Performance" (2003/4d), "Boatman on Stage."

23. Robert Butler clarifies that the sound is that of a trombone, and also provides further description of the scene (Butler 2003, 107).

24. An early draft version of this chapter was presented at a research seminar at the University of Leeds, School of Performance and Cultural Industries, April 2008, at which I received much valuable feedback. I am particularly grateful to Dr. Kara McKechnie and Professor Mick Wallis for their insightful comments and critical engagement.

25. For a short, edited video clip of this scene see "The Production" (2003/4c), "The Botanic Gardens On Stage."

26. See Heathfield (2006, 179) for further elucidation on writing "the event" of performance.

27. It is, however, worth noting that Wright's adaptation has been frequently and successfully staged, in a number of vastly different ways, using quite different staging and performance strategies, at other theatres in Britain and elsewhere. See, for example, Karian Schuitema's essay and interview in the present volume.

Works Cited

Barish, J. 1981. *The Anti-Theatrical Prejudice*. Berkley: University of California Press.

Barthes, R. 1982. *Camera Lucida: Reflections on Photography*. Trans. Richard Howard. London: Jonathan Cape.

Bennett, J. 2005. *Empathic Vision: Affect, Trauma, and Contemporary Art*. Stanford, CA: Stanford University Press.

Berninger, M. 2008. "A Fantasy Epic as a Theatrical Event —*His Dark Materials* at the National Theatre." *Contemporary Drama in English: Non-Standard Forms of Contemporary Drama and Theatre*. Eds. E. Redling and P.P. Schnierer. Trier: WVT Wissenschaftlicher Verlag Trier, 153–169.

Bosmajian, H. 2002. *Sparing the Child: Grief and the Unspeakable in Youth Literature about Nazism and the Holocaust*. New York: Routledge.

Butler, R. 2003. *The Art of Darkness: Staging the Philip Pullman Trilogy*. London: Oberon.

Di Benedetto, Stephen. 2003. "Sensing Bodies: A Phenomenological Approach to the Performance Senssorium." *Performance Research* 8:2, 101–108.

Edmundson, Helen. 2000. *Coram Boy* [based on the novel by Jamila Gavin]. London: Nick Hern.

Elkins, J. 1999. *Pictures of the Body: Pain and Metamorphosis*. Stanford, CA: Stanford University Press.

Falconer, Rachel. 2008. "Coming of Age in a Fantasy World: Philip Pullman's *His Dark Materials*." *The Crossover Novel*. London: Routledge, 73–94.

Garner, S. B. 1994. *Bodied Spaces: Phenomenology and Performance in Contemporary Drama*. Ithaca: Cornell University Press.

Heathfield, A. 2000. "End Time Now." In *Small Acts: Performance, the Millennium, and the Marking of Time*. Ed. A. Heathfield. London: Black Dog.

_____. 2006. "Writing the Event." In *A Performance Cosmology: Testimony from the Future, Evidence from the Past*. Eds. J. Christie, R. Gough, and D. Watt. London and New York: Routledge.

Herman, J. L. 2001. *Trauma and Recovery: From Domestic Abuse to Political Terror*. Rivers: Oram.

Homans, M. 2006. "Adoption Narratives, Trauma, and Origins." *Narrative* 14:1, 4–26.

Kafka, Franz. 2001. *In the Penal Settlement*. Trans. E. Muir and W. Muir. London: Secker and Warburg.

Kidd, K. B. 2005. "'A' is for Auschwitz: Psychoanalysis, Trauma Theory, and the Children's Literature of Atrocity." *Children's Literature* 33, 120–149.

Kleist, H. 2008. *On the Marionette Theatre*. Trans. I. Parry. Accessed May 20, 2008. *http://www.southerncrossreview.org/9/kleist.htm*.

Luckhurst, Roger. 2003. "Traumaculture." *New Formations* 50, 28–47.

MacDonald, L. 2007. "Imagining *His Dark Materials* as a Gesamtkunstwerk." *Studies in Musical Theatre* 1, 2: 199–211.

Malpede, K. 1996. "Teaching Witnessing: A Class Wakes to Genocide." *Theatre Topics* 6, 2: 167–179.

McAuley, G. 2000. *Space in Performance: Making Meaning in the Theatre*. Ann Arbor: University of Michigan Press.

Nathan, J. 2004. "Review of *His Dark Materials*." *Jewish Chronicle*, *Theatre Record* 1–28 (January), 18.

Phelan, P. 1997. *Mourning Sex: Performing Public Memories*. London: Routledge.

"The Production: *His Dark Materials*: Lyra Meets Mrs. Coulter on Stage." 2003/4a. *Stagework*. The Royal National Theatre. Accessed October 30, 2007. *http://www.stagework.org.uk*.

The Production: *His Dark Materials*: The Alethiometer: Performance." 2003/4b. *Stagework*. The Royal National Theatre. Accessed October 30, 2007. *http://www.stagework.org.uk*.

"The Production: *His Dark Materials*: The Botanic Gardens On Stage." 2003/4c. *Stagework*. The Royal National Theatre. Accessed October 30, 2007. *http://www.stagework.org.uk*.

"The Production: *His Dark Materials*: Boatman on Stage." 2003/4d. *Stagework*. The Royal National Theatre. Accessed October 30, 2007. *http://www.stagework.org.uk*.

Ravenhill, Mark. 2009. *Nation: The Play* [based on the novel by Terry Pratchett]. London: Corgi.

Rebellato, Dan. 2008. "'Because It Feels Fucking Amazing': Recent British Drama and Bodily Mutilation." In *Cool Britannia? British Political Drama in the 1990s*. Eds. Rebecca D'Monté and Graham Saunders. Basingstoke: Palgrave Macmillan, 192–207.

Ridout, N. 2006. *Stage Fright, Animals, and Other Theatrical Problems*. Cambridge: Cambridge University Press.

Stafford, Nick. 2007. *War Horse* [based on the novel by Michael Morpurgo]. London: Faber and Faber.

States, B.O. 1985. *Great Reckoning in Little Rooms: On the Phenomenology of Theatre*. Berkley: University of California Press.

Wallis, M. 2005. "Translating Bodies: Siddons, Cowley and the Stage Sublime." *Performance Research* 10:1, *On Theatre*, 68–80.

Wilshire, B. 1982. *Role Playing and Identity: The Limits of Theatre as Metaphor*, Bloomington: Indiana University Press.

Wright, N. 2003. *His Dark Materials* [based on the novels by Philip Pullman]. London: Nick Hern.

_____. 2004. *His Dark Materials*, rev. ed. [based on the novels by Philip Pullman]. London: Nick Hern.

15

Staging and Performing *His Dark Materials*: From the National Theatre Productions to Subsequent Productions

KARIAN SCHUITEMA

Introduction: Restaging the National Theatre's production of *His Dark Materials*

Creating theatrical adaptations from literary works will always prove to be a healthy challenge. When taking much loved classics and popular novels and bringing them to the stage, the production team are in the dangerous business of taking numerous ideas from a particular story and rendering these into one single interpretation, a product of the producer, adapter, director, designer and actors. Inevitable criticisms will follow such as "the actor was nothing like the character" or "the play was nothing like the book." Besides the acknowledgment that using a well-loved story as a foundation of a play has obvious advantages, especially in terms of commercial interests, the final performance perhaps still needs to critically justify how well it succeeds in adapting the original story. For example, the argument that the stage version by Nicholas Wright was a success has been made forcefully by Robert Butler (2003).

It could be argued that with the adaptation of children's literature, the added difficulty lies within specific features; for example, the talking animals, magic and fantasy that so often makes books of young adult fantasy so popular with their readers. When transferring these elements to stage and creating a quality performance, with only small to moderate budgets, what is needed is much ingenuity and creativity, as well as a real commitment to both audience and story. The particular focus in this chapter is therefore to explore stage productions of *His Dark Materials* which, while based on the National Theatre (UK) version adapted by Nicholas Wright, did not have the large budgets and available resources which the National Theatre originally brought to the process of this adaptation. These versions have used Nicholas Wright's adaptation of the text of *His Dark Materials*, despite their varying budgets and resources, which allows us to ask questions and make interesting comparisons about different theatrical solutions to the staging and performance of the play.

Given the commercial and critical success of *His Dark Materials* trilogy by Philip Pullman, the question was not *if* these highly acclaimed pieces of literature would be adapted for the cinema, but rather *whether* this would be done also for the stage. While there is a tradition of adapting children's literature for the stage it has typically been classic children's literature that has been adapted for large scale theater work, such as the English National Theatre's version of *A Wind in the Willows* in 1990 (Olivier stage, directed Nicholas Hytner). More importantly was the question of *who* would do it, *where* this would be done and especially *how* the three books could be transferred onto stage. Indeed, the story takes up to 35 hours on audiotape, is set in at least four different universes and not only features talking and fighting ice bears and the daemons, but also creatures like *mulefa* who are part of a different evolutionary pathway from bipedal and quadrapedal animals.

The following interview and critical analyses attempt to answer the above questions and particularly focuses on those who chose to attempt to re-imagine by restaging the National Theatre's successful production. Interviewing the director Stewart McGill from Playbox Theatre Company (UK) based in Warwickshire explores his approach and motivation for staging the text, while at the same time the interview highlights the difficulties and complexities of the story when it is moved to the stage. In order to contextualize the interviews, therefore, it would be useful to first look at the National Theatre's productions and related publications.

The National Theatre (UK) productions

The National Theatre was the first theater with the resources and the vision to stage *His Dark Materials* in Britain. The National's staging process, from the original books to the actual production and its aftermath, is recorded in two books written by Robert Butler and published by the National Theatre in association with Oberon Books. With various interviews, observations and post-show discussions, Butler outlines the grandness of a project that rather unsurprisingly had an equally grand budget of £850,000 (Butler 2004, 28). Nicholas Hytner, director of the National's production of *His Dark Materials*, made arguably the first influential decision, in terms of future productions elsewhere, when he argued that the production should condense the books into two, three hour-long plays. The logic of this decision being that it would be too much to ask from an audience to come to three separate plays or to sit through three plays that mirror the three books all in one day (Butler 2004, 18). Interestingly, in the *Art of Darkness: Staging the Philip Pullman Trilogy*, Pullman himself mentions his relief of not having to rework his original books for the stage (Butler 2003, 36), a challenge that was instead accepted by the playwright Nicholas Wright after Nicholas Hytner's invitation.

On seeing the play staged at the National Theatre (UK), the results of the decision to put all three books and 35 hours of material into two three-hour plays becomes apparent. The performance is visually an amazing spectacle, which is underlined by the use the drum-revolve (on the Olivier Stage). It spirals out of the stage creating lavish sets that expertly incorporate the actors, before continuing its relentless tempo, and revolving to the next scene with technical proficiency. Moreover, the crafted trees in the Botanic Gardens under which Will and Lyra meet at the beginning and end of the two plays, as well as the vast and incredibly detailed set of Lyra's Oxford, both suggest that the production has spared no expense in creating a visually stunning piece. However, it is possible that the technical wizardry and the speed of the performance enabled by the drum-revolve may overwhelm certain subtleties of the story. Moving through many different and often integral scenes, with at the same time numerous and complicated set changes, perhaps creates the feeling in the audience that the play may be sacrificing story development for performance tempo and to fit within the allotted time. The development of the complex plot, the rich growth of the three-dimensional characters and the continual use of the drum-revolve may become slightly vertiginous and excessive in the short time span.

At other moments the National's production feels more rewarding while ironically using less high-tech stage methods. One such moment occurs when Lyra and Will go to the land of the dead where they encounter the harpy named No-Name and find Lyra's friend Roger with the other ghost-children. The scene feels absolutely haunting with the ghosts entering the stage via the auditorium, before walking slowly through the audience with their dark clothes and pale faces. Significantly it was the scene that was singled out for most praise by theater reviewers such as Michael Billington (2004) and Charles Spencer (2004) as genuinely harrowing and moving in its intimacy. On stage Lyra beautifully contrasts the dead with her bright, colorful clothes. A mirror, raised from the ceiling and reflecting those characters on stage, was a clever way to create an almost claustrophobic feeling of a cave with death everywhere you look. More atmospheric still are the shrieks of the harpy, so effective that you can almost feel the character's pain as a member of the audience. This scene (perhaps unusually for this event crammed and fast-paced production) takes ample time to present and explore the emotion of the characters on the stage and succeeds in creating a very moving moment where the ghost children reminisce about their daemons. This is an example where simplicity and low technology as well as unrushed narrative combined to poignant effect.

This raises the question as to whether the entire production at the National Theatre could have benefited from an approach more focused on dialogue and narrative rather than the slick visual stage imagery, elaborated through the power of complex stage scenery. During the play's rehearsal process it was already known that Tom Stoppard was also working on a film script and it would be interesting to know whether the proposed film would have affected Nick Hytner's choices in terms of visualizing Lyra's story on the stage. A film can not only show the journey of Lyra and the different worlds she encounters in greater realist and realistic detail than the theater can, but with the use of post-production technology all the obvious (theater) problems like the magical daemons and talking polar bears are more easily resolved. In this case the need to highlight the theatrical potential of the story becomes even more important. Significantly, the national's production highlights Hytner's choice of theatrical solution such as the use of the beautiful puppets, designed by Michael Curry, to represent the daemons, polar bears, angels and Gallivespians. This shows how the theater requires, and finds, different solutions, thus enhancing the performance and making it belong inherently to the stage. Hytner's theater production therefore played up to the imaginations of the audience to make sense of the theatrical and stylized puppets whereas the film version offered fully realized and realistic portrayals of the fantasy creatures which essentially left no room for an audience's imagination.

Assuming that the technical difficulties of staging the three books in the space of two plays are acceptable, a second problem can be highlighted in terms of the motive and justification for this decision to condense the three books into two plays. As mentioned earlier, director Hytner felt that it would be too much to expect an audience to come to the theater to see three plays, one after the other. Theater makers, especially those involved in theater for young people, typically argue an audience cannot be completely trusted to show the same commitment as they would when reading books or seeing films. While sitting in the theater for nine continuous hours in one day is probably as much as you can ask from a younger audience, the plays could arguably have worked as independent pieces, with audiences waiting a week, a month or even a year for the next part, as they would for a new installment of the book or a film.

Taking the commitment of the audience to one side, it is perhaps understandable that a larger theater like the National will have a problem with committing to such a large project, as multiple productions of the same play would presumably get in the way of other projects. This leaves one other solution: to only stage certain elements of Lyra's story and strip the books to their narrative bare bones. Wright does achieve this to some extent, as for example the story of Mary Malone and the *mulefa* is cut out which in effect erases much of the scientific dimension of Pullman's story. Furthermore, Mary Malone's absence, together with the lack of information on Will's background and his struggle to keep his mother safe, means that what can be called "dimension earth" is almost completely left out in the theater adaptation, thus collapsing the broad sweep of the Pullman multi-verse. So the text when staged becomes more of a fantasy without reference to its realist elements that are set in our world. On the other hand, however, it can be argued that Wright has not been ruthless enough. Robert Hanks, for example, writes in his review of the play for the *Independent*, that it suffers from something he calls the "Harry Potter syndrome" meaning that "the effort to satisfy the fans by keeping in characters and incidents has led to an overcrowded, at times barely coherent, drama" (Hanks 2004).

Billington, writing in the *Guardian*, draws a similar conclusion reviewing the National's creative team as "ultimately overcome by the vastness of the enterprise" (2004). Billington feels that by adapting Pullman's "quintessentially literary work" to the stage, the intertextuality of the novels is party lost, which is, for many, the origin of reading pleasure and the work's particular strength. Drawing such a clear distinction between stage and page, or the literary and the theatrical in this way is interesting because, taking Shakespeare as a prominent example, the English theater tradition is normally recognized for its textual strength and literary quality. However it could be inferred that Hytner has chosen to move away from this tradition, instead prioritizing the visual and performative aspects of the production over literary quality and textual content, which is perhaps a more contemporary way of approaching the question of adaptation. For British theater audiences this has become a familiar experience, because of the work of physical theater companies such as Shared Experience who have adapted many classic literary novels such as George Eliot's *The Mill on the Floss* or Tolstoy's *War and Peace* in vivid, exciting and audacious ways that emphasize performance more than they do the text (see the Shared Experience website, in bibliography below). For example, the National production has a chorus of striking, black-garbed witches standing apart from the main action who used choreographed movement to music to create the illusion of flying and it is noticeable that several of these actors (such as Samantha Lawson) came from physical theater traditions. Another example would be the equally strongly choreographed fight between the two actors who played bears, which again depended on evocative music and stylized action. At times then, it appears that the dialogue for *His Dark Materials* have been written to enable and bring to life the vast scene designs and stage imagery of the National's production, rather than the other way around. As the adaptor Nicholas Wright writes: "There were certainly times when I'd have to write a scene in a particular way to fit this technical marvel beneath our feet, which is making the whole thing work-the Olivier drum-revolve" (Butler 2004, 76).

Small theater companies in Cornwall and Bath

Small theater companies, however, following the National in the staging of *His Dark Materials* could potentially struggle with the script which as I have argued is effectively written for the Olivier's drum-revolve and extensive resources. Working with contracts that simply do not allow major alterations to Nicholas Wright's text or its structure, directors have an even bigger job in trying to make scene changes appear smooth. For example, director Ann Garner from Next Stage Theatre Company, a non-professional theater company based in Bath, spoke to me about the staging *His Dark Materials*. Next Stage is a company with over a hundred adult members, which stages regular performances. With a slot at the atmospheric Minack open-air theater in Cornwall in the summer of 2007, the choice for staging Pullman's work was made with the intention primarily to appeal to a family audience. At the same time, the play would also be a good opportunity to interest both the young and the older actors of the company and this is important for a non-professional production. Even though the play turned out to be a great success with the actors and was generally well received by the press, Garner did express some misgivings about their working with the text. The intentions of the National when making the initial adaptation essentially bound the text to the original venue of the Oliver stage which perhaps suggest that it was never meant (or was thought, would) to be performed anywhere else.

To be able to stage the play at the Minack, Garner decided to work with no sets whatsoever and trust her actors to be able to provide settings for the story and to show travel through different dimensions and worlds using their theatrical skills alone.[1] Even the props to indicate settings were reduced to the bare, but metonymically evocative essentials: a cage, a rowing boat and a set of gates for when the story moves to Bolvanger and then, of course, the masks and puppets used to portray the various daemons. Although one should say that the spectacular setting of the Minack theater, built into a cliff at Porthcurno, Cornwall and overlooking a dramatic costal vista tends to dominate any production that is undertaken there, so extensive props and stage sets are arguably less necessary. The stage additions consisted of a high platform over the Minack's back arches, used for the flying witches and the moments the characters jump into a different dimension, and a back walkway with steps down to create multiple exits and entrances, vital to a story with so many scenes changes. Other production essentials were the lights and the music accompanying the story. Garner worked with a composer to create a completely new score with reoccurring themes for key moments or characters. The costs, however, were steep, with the highest expenditure being new masks and puppets created completely from scratch. In spite of this, it seems probable that the company will return to the production in the future especially considering it is such an excellent play to be performed with larger casts, as it provides so many different parts for the company's members, as well being popular with the audience.

In comparison, Lee Lyford has created an opportunity for the participating young people to enjoy the excitement of Lyra's story in a production in the main house of Theatre Royal Bath. Following not only the National and the Playbox version, the 2008 production in Bath also came after the film version of the first novel, and looking back at his production, which provides the possibility to create something different and new from what had preceded but also reflects on the issue of religion, which had been fore grounded by the release of *The Golden Compass.*

Theatre Royal Bath Young People's Theatre offers young people the chance to experience and participate in multiple aspects of the process of making theater, by organizing classes and projects running from acting and dancing to working backstage or even as a theater reviewer. With regular performances in the Young People's Egg Theatre, as well as the Ustinov Studio and Theatre Royal Bath Main House Theatre, the company has build up a reputation of creating productions of professional quality. Lee Lyford works as artistic director within the Acting Group, which staged *His Dark Materials* from 13 April 2008. This production was staged at the Main House Theatre and had a run of one week, playing both parts in one day. It was the result of many months of rehearsing and overall it involved about 160 young people aged between 9 and 19, performing on stage as working well as backstage. The spectacle also included puppetry which was directed by Lizzy Philps and designed by Karen Mckeown (who was also responsible for the design of numerous costumes for the production). Hayley Grindle designed the elaborate set in which some of young actors even had an opportunity to experience some stage flying. Overall the production was a great success and was lauded not only by the viewing public, but also praised by the press.

Both the Next Stage production at the Minack theater in Cornwall and the production at the Theatre Royal Bath, Young People's Theatre, highlight the importance of the elements of puppetry and music to enable the staging of Lyra's story. This theme is also elaborated upon by Laura MacDonald in her essay titled "Imagining *His Dark Materials* as a *Gesamtkunstwerk*," where she deals with the interdisciplinary nature of Hytner's creation as a complete and total work of art drawing on the theories of those such as Richard Wagner the composer who was one of the first to use the term *Gesamtkunstwerk*. She argues that an interdisciplinary theatrical approach is essential to staging Pullman's epic, but more importantly this has to be realized through the transparency of this interdisciplinary collaboration. She states: "Nicholas Hytner and his team invited the audience to enter the worlds of the play as participants in the collaborative work, free to mould their own experience of the heroes' adventures and complete the adaptation with their own imagination" (MacDonald 2007, 199).

For MacDonald the use of the drum-revolve and other technicalities in combination with live musicians and the daemon puppeteers reveals the process of theatricality to the audience, something which she recognizes as both courageous and directly engaging (MacDonald 2007, 209). Although these techniques, along with interdisciplinary approaches, have been used in both adult theater and theater for the child, it is mainly the latter, especially where puppetry has made a regular appearance throughout its history, that such an approach has been more often utilized. Unsurprisingly therefore, many young people's theater companies use interdisciplinary aspects in their productions, and the Oily Cart theater company provides a good example of this. Established in 1881, they make extensive use of puppetry, live music and techniques such as lights and video projection (more often than not used all at once), to create multi-sensory productions especially aimed at early years or young people with disabilities. However even if the interdisciplinary approach is not a necessarily new phenomenon, the question still remains as to whether *His Dark Materials* can also be successfully performed without these collaborative elements in play. At the same time it is interesting to see if the interdisciplinary approach is as viable on a limited budget in comparison to the £850,000 the National had to make their production work.

Audiences and performers

As well as the interdisciplinary collaboration MacDonald also highlights the importance of the audience in this process, and its composition is of particular interest. Pullman's novels were originally categorized as children's literature, something which Pullman himself recognized as a great help when he explains: "If they'd been published by an adult publisher, they would have been called fantasy and would have gone on fantasy shelves with all the mock-Tolkiens and what-have-you, and the majority of adults who have read them would never have seen them" (Butler 2004, 59). However when transferred to the stage the story was more aimed at a teenage and adult audience. Indeed, Hytner explained his decision to employ Nicholas Wright, who had no previous experience in writing for young audiences, because he felt that the books were essentially written for adults, thus explaining the popularity amongst teenage audiences. In some respects Hytner's view could be taken as slightly negative, in that young people's playwrights are somehow incapable of writing a supposed mature play. Audiences, it seems do not like to be treated like kids and be spoken down to (Butler 2004, 18).

His Dark Materials as a play written for a young audience is in itself an interesting choice in terms of its religious or rather anti-religious themes; as such themes tend to be avoided. It is easy to find issues such as drug use, sex and teenage pregnancies, racism and bulling and other matters that are associated with teenagers, however not many plays deal with, or are adapted from stories that deal with, religious questions and openly criticize aspects of organized religion. It is interesting to note that Spencer, reviewing the play in the *Daily Telegraph* (2004) was concerned that the play might not really be suitable for children because it challenged Christianity so strongly and was therefore more suitable for adults. However, it should be said against this view that throughout the two runs at the National Theatre, a very considerable section of the audience was spell-bound children, albeit accompanied by adults. A possible explanation could be found in the inclusion of diversity and equality policies adopted by theaters or companies staging for young people. In effect it means that productions and workshops should be created to be accessible for all young people from every background. Yet although a novel can be chosen, bought and read by young individuals, theater for young people often attracts groups such as classrooms and consequently individual choice may be lost. While encouraging group and school attendance is a good way of making theater accessible for all and introduces those who would otherwise have not come to the theater, a particular theme could nevertheless prove to be offensive to some in the audience and this could have disastrous results commercially.

When *The Golden Compass* opened in cinemas in 2007 the religious aspects came to the fore, as the U.S. based Catholic League launched a boycott campaign against the film (Joyce 2007). At the same time Pullman was criticized by others for supposedly allowing the producers to dilute the so-called anti-religious connotations embedded in his books. Comparing the play with the movie, however, it would be fair to say that criticism of the clerical institution is much more apparent in the stage version, especially through the portrayal of the members of the consistorial court who are all stereotyped evil men with a range of reptilian daemons, openly showing disgust at any mention of sex and sexuality. Billington feels this is a real weakness of the play version of *His Dark Materials* as he writes: "in his didactic anti-clericalism, Pullman demonises religion to the point of absurdity" (2004). With this in mind it is very interesting if not surprising to observe that the companies staging Pullman's work in Britain are most often youth theaters and not as one might expect adult theaters. Among these are Playbox and the Young People's Theatre of Theatre Royal Bath, but there are many more, such as York's Stagecoach Youth Theatre (April 2006) and the Scottish Youth Theatre (July 2007). Various school productions have also been staged, such as the Lancaster Royal Grammar School and Lancaster Girls' Grammar School who performed *His Dark Materials* in The Grand Theatre in Lancaster (May 2006) and Crestwood College at The Point theatre in Hampshire (March 2008).

This popularity of the stage adaptation with young performers is also rather remarkable because of the intensity and duration of the two three hour plays. Hytner states that it never once occurred to him to cast younger actors, as a twelve year old actor would simply not be able to carry a play in the National or anywhere else (Butler 2004, 21–22). According to Hytner the reasons for this can be located in elements such as stamina, vocal resource, concentration and imagination, a rationalization that allowed him to opt for actors in their twenties. He states: "I think it's a straightforward and conventional acting challenge for a 25-year-old to come on stage and say, 'I'm twelve.' If the actor is convincing enough you believe the actor's twelve. But for a twelve-year-old actor to come onto the stage and say, 'Believe every single thing I'm going through.' It is much harder" (Butler 2004, 22). His statement highlights a substantial difference between theater work and the more commercial musicals, where young actors are not only expected to act for around three hours, but to also sing and dance, think for example, of young actors in West End musicals such as *Billy Elliot* or *The Lion King*. Hytner's view may also be consistent with his judgment as already detailed above, that the text is aimed at an adult audience rather than a young adult audience.

The following interview highlights and continues the issues discussed above. The detailed accounts of Stewart McGill's direction offers a unique insight into the difficulties, but also excitement, of staging Pullman's epic. Those involved in the original production, Hytner, Wright and Pullman (Butler 2004, 28, 59, 78), believe it is possible to stage the play away from the National with its drum-revolve and resources that come from an epic budget. McGill provides examples of how to carry out this process of restaging in smaller venue successfully. McGill shows how his company feels passionately about returning the story to those who own it, and how the young actors of his company showed total commitment to Pullman's creation. His view that this is a young adult play for young adult audiences contrasts very significantly with that of Hytner.

Interview with Stewart McGill, artistic director Playbox, Theatre (Warwick, UK)

Stewart McGill joined Playbox Theatre as artistic director in 1989. Having studied at Dartington College of Arts and developed the performing arts faculty at Chelmsley Wood's Simon Digby Campus, he wanted to put all his theories of child-centered artistic education into practice without the restrictions of a curriculum. At that point, according to vision of founding director Mary King, the company had been successfully making theater with children for three years. Playbox has a very strong philosophy about the involvement of children and young people in the arts, and has a strong child-centered approach. The respect the young performers receive is obvious through the productions delivered, which are high in quality, complex and challenging. At Playbox children and young people are not seen as imitators of art, those that need to learn and develop to become like the "real thing," the adult. Instead of being external to the creative process, the child and young person is at the center, creating art instead of imitating. It is therefore not surprising that it was this company that took on the challenge to be the first to perform *His Dark Materials*, after the National Theatre. Involving up to 150 young people in this performance, the rehearsal process was under direction of three directors: Emily Jane Quash, Mary King, as well as Stewart McGill. The production was performed from 5 to 23 April in 2006, alternating part one and two during weekdays. However in the weekends both parts were played back to back, lasting for up to seven hours in a departure from the pattern established at the National.

Confirming the principles of Playbox, the spectacle was received with great admiration not only for the actors, but also for the way in which their production was innovative and dared to move away from some of the National Theatre production's artistic choices and decisions. It was an audacious attempt to re-imagine how the play could be staged.

Q: To start, I would like to ask you what was the initial motivation for Playbox to stage the story of *His Dark Materials*?

A: I had been hearing a lot about the books when they first came out. However, I am the sort of person who is often put off by long commitments. Reading one book is fine but when you have to make a journey through three books, for example something like the *Lord of the Rings*, I start to wonder if I can commit to that. It was my daughter who said: "You've got to read it, you will love it." So, I picked it up expecting to read a few chapters to put it down again, thinking that I had made a token gesture. However from the moment I started *Northern Lights*, the moment I started wandering through the Oxford corridors, it just struck a real cord of resonance. I loved the story; I loved the characters, and most of all I loved the questioning of religion, the power of religion and the possibilities within that.

When I finished the books the National Theatre made the announcement that they were actually going to stage them. I thought that was wonderful! Absolutely wonderful! I think it was also at the same time that New Line commissioned Tom Stoppard to create a screenplay. Around that time there was a lot of excitement about the books, however I had never thought about it for Playbox until it occurred to me that it would be wonderful to bring that work to the people who feel they own it.

At the moment there is a lot of crossover literature, children's literature that adults take under their wing, and eventually start thinking they own it. The

Harry Potter books are a good example. There is a kind of saying that goes like "well, they are books for everyone not just for children." However with *His Dark Materials* I feel that the issues of growing up, friendship, reaching adolescence, are all young people's issues, and in a way the crossing over of literature is taking them away from young people. I therefore thought that *His Dark Materials* would be a wonderful piece to explore with Playbox, although we knew we could not do at the time because the National had it, and would consequently form two, possibly three years, of commitment from the National Theatre. As it happened it was only two, but it could have possibly been three, so we put the idea on the back burner.

I got incredibly exited seeing *His Dark Materials* staged at the National, especially because of Michael Curry's puppetry, whose work I find brilliant. With the excitement of a fan I went to see it, and I really enjoyed it. Nevertheless I enjoyed it like a fan, as I enjoyed Indiana Jones, almost like a comic book piece of story telling. What the show did not have, wonderful as it was, was that I did not get the humanity of Pullman's original story, because it was swept away with the big theatrics. I subsequently spent a lot time on the phone to various people connected with National's production agents saying: "Look once the National has finished use of it, I really want to do it, I desperately want to do this show." However, I kept being told: "Wait and see, wait and see." Nevertheless at that point we set up a think-tank in the studio and we took the script and used it as a starting point for improvising and discussion, just to see how things might go if the production was ever given the go-ahead. After a while and I remember this very clearly, I was in Cornwall in a café having a coffee when the phone rang. It was Nicolas Wright's agent and he said you can have it, the National do not want it for a third year and now you can do it. I was so thrilled.

It is a long ended way to answer the original question, but in effect it was from the love of reading the book, to being excited by what young people were saying and their reaction, and the possibility to offer the story to young people through their own company instead of taking it away. The only people who act on stage here are young people; we are a theater devoted to young people.

Q: Would you agree that it is this sense of ownership, which makes *His Dark Materials* fit in with Playbox's existing work?

A: At the moment we have been asked to go out to schools to do a workshop on *Blue Remembered Hills*. It is a play about wartime and children who are evacuees, and the whole point of the play is that the adults play the children. I was talking to a girl running the workshop and she has told me that it simply does not work as well when adults play children because you tend to loose their vulnerability. You might miss out on the technical expertise that an adult may bring to the role; however, nothing is missed in terms of vulnerability.

Olivia Meguer as Lyra and Mike Hood as Pantalaimon consult the Alethiometer in the Playbox (UK) production of *His Dark Materials* (photograph by Andy Brining).

This is also the key to Lyra and Will. Our company worked on the plays by taking the young people's ownership as the core of our work. There are three directors who all have ideas, but not at the expense of the young actors, as it is essentially their production. At Playbox we motivate the young people to be at the centre of the creative process by telling them: "It is going to be your work which you are going to bring to us, your age, your enthusiasm and your beliefs and it is our job to make that into the show." I hope very much they felt a sense of ownership, even though we went in with designs and very strong ideas. In this way it ended up as very much a company show.

Q: It would be useful to get a brief idea of the way it was staged. In the press release you are quoted as taking a different route to Pullman's work with the creation of an abstract, almost futuristic, stage installation. Could you explain this further?

Commedia featuring Mairin O'Hagan as Seraphina Pekkala, left, Theo Lamb as Lee Scoresby, center, and Izzie James as his Daemon, Hester, right, in the Playbox (UK) production of *His Dark Materials* (photograph by Andy Brining).

A: Did I say that? What a pompous thing to say. What I think I was trying to say was the National Theatre was beautifully picturesque. They had the whole panorama of Oxford but we simply cannot do that here. What we try to do is to find a series of metaphors, visual metaphors in story telling. At Playbox it is about the story and the characters within that story, and the rest of what is seen on stage in terms of sets and props supports but never dominates. For this show we wanted to get away from the whole idea of an adventure yarn, and make it much more a piece of story telling. Essentially, the play was rooted in one environment, consisting of an open space with a raised platform and a huge central tower that went from the floor of the stage to gallery level. When Asriel, for example, crossed over into a different dimension he used the top of this tower as an exit point. Throughout the play, this tower, with cascading dry ice coming over the top, functioned as a metaphor for crossing universes.

At the same time I wanted to make our production very filmic, because I had a problem with the rhythm at the National. I mean the rhythm of moving from one location to another, and even though the drum-revolve did wonders, it still takes a couple of minutes to get from one scene to another. While the audience is watching that great drum move, while listening to the musical cues going over, the story telling still tends to get slowed down. What I wanted with our team was to have a kind of cinematic approach where you cross fade. In this manner one scene is coming in while another is still playing, and by switching and turning the focus swiftly the play becomes like a series of fast film cuts. The influence comes from the way film is edited.

When I said our production was going to be futuristic, I did not mean futuristic in the sense that we were saying that the story was set in twenty or thirty years down the road. I think we were saying that the story could be set now, in the past, but also in the future. The story is what is important, not the geography or the time line. Our idea was to refer a little bit to the past, a little bit to the now, but the audience needed to put it together in their own head. I think that is the thing our company wants to achieve: *we* want to give people suggestions, but *your* job is to finish it off in your head. If it had been a film there is nothing to finish, it is presented to you in complete form.

Q: You also mention in a press release that the Playbox version is aiming to create a total theater event. Why is this important to the company, and do you think the production has achieved this?

A: It is a question concerning the nature of theater. I love theater but when I go, I always find myself nodding off. I know young people have problems with going to the theater and with becoming engaged with the material. It could be that theater is often perceived as boring because it is too long and too heavy on the dialogue, whereas with film, television and music this is not the case. Take for example contemporary music which is so exciting and so immediate; when young people have been to a gig they are so adrenaline fuelled. This is something that I want to achieve with theater, to offer a similar experience and to create excitement. I do not want to do it through cheap tricks, you can sell theater as being like a gig but at the end of the day, theater is theater. However I think there are ways in which actors and audience can come together, and this interactive quality is unique to theater.

With *His Dark Materials*, we wanted the audience to feel very much a part of this work. We wanted them to think: "All right we are sitting down, we are in our seats but we are very close to the actors. We are close enough to touch them, we are close enough to really see the emotions very clearly, and for the moments of spectacle we are close enough to wonder at the world they are in." This is what we tried to achieve, we wanted to share this experience and enjoy the story telling together. Most of the work we do here is influenced by this idea. We try to vary the space, sometimes the seats will be out and the audience will stand, so we have promenade work. We also have thrust work, work in the round, and have a lot of work in the air (we have a very good circus director). We use all the spaces to make every performance exciting, so when an audience member comes in they do not know what they are going to get. At the same time it must serve the story. For example, if we would be doing *Romeo and Juliet*, and we had actors on trapeze, it would only be because we felt that it was the most important thing to do, we would not simply do it just for the sake of it. Audiences are so important to us; we feel that theater is the whole adventure of actor, space, and audience. This is what made *His Dark Materials* such a wonderful opportunity for Playbox, because the book is about a journey from location to location, from earth to beyond, and it just gave us the opportunity to really explode the space and have a lot of adventure.

Q: What were the major differences between your production and that of the National?

A: I do not think we set out to consciously say: "Well the National did it that way, we will do it this way." There was never anything like that. From the start we knew the way we wanted to approach the play. [...] There was a lot of pressure because many expressed their amazement and asked: "How on earth can a young people's theater, in a fairly small auditorium, stage *His Dark Materials*?" The idea that people thought we had to be mad to undertake such a project did not change our minds, instead it set a great challenge. There was pressure, but we knew from the start that the way we had cast the show, with such a wonderful line up, audiences would fall in love with the actors from the start, and our show would be built around that.

There were fan sites for *His Dark Materials*, containing lots of gossipy bits and pieces that occasionally we would be told about. We would have a look and people would say, "I do not think she is like Lyra at all, she's not what I expect Lyra to be." However I think that such comments, interest and speculation surrounding a show can work to be very positive.

[In terms of what we did differently to the National's production,] I think the biggest change has to be the daemons, as we did not want to use puppets to portray them. In workshops we tried using different forms of manipulation and different types of puppets. I did think Michael Curry's puppets were wonderful. In fact I did have a meeting at the National because their puppet makers (they set up a puppet workshop with a head of puppetry) got in touch with us and said they felt a bit frustrated now the show was finished because there where things they had wanted to do with the puppets which they felt had never gone completely right, as the time was too short. They said that they would have loved to have another go, and asked me if they could work on our production and develop the puppetry. This offer was so tempting but in the end we did turn it down. We told them we were going to do it without, because we wanted to explore the characters of the daemons as perceived by young actors. As an alternative we spent a lot of time looking at movement. Together with the young actors we explored how the daemons would move, how they would change, and how an audience would be able to create them in their heads through the suggestion of the actor's movements. That became a huge challenge and a major difference, and I think something quite unique, because a lot of people said you ought to be using puppets. However puppetry is such a fine art and it is not enough to have the puppet and say: "Look here is the daemon." The manipulator and the puppet need to be as one, similar to using masks. I just felt that was a totally different dimension of performance and we did not want to go down that road. In contrast we wanted to explore movement and the way the daemons were characterized.

Another big difference was the design and the emblematic set that we used in our production. I guess you could say our production was less spectacular, in the way that it focused much more on the way the story was told. I believe it is right that when you are the National Theatre and you are doing *His Dark Materials* you should spend a huge amount of money and I do think they spent it well. Here at Playbox, we can still stage Pullman's work because we can still tell the story, and we can still reach the heart of an audience, but we had to do it in a very different way. The director who has greatly influenced my work is the theater director Robert Lepage from Quebec, and our production of *His Dark Materials* is influenced by his way of using acting, multimedia, and acrobatics to tell a story.

Q: Returning to the example of the daemons and considering your decision not to use puppets, could you please expand on the way the actors were able to portray the daemons in Pullman's story?

A: The performances were very physical. Even though they had specially designed make-up, it was still essential that the actors worked with their bodies to make the daemons recognizable. For example the Golden Monkey was completely gold, however the actor was chosen for the role because of his superb styles of movement. For the daemons of the younger characters we had very neutral costumes, to enable them to change. This meant that the daemon changes could be found in their body, their shape and movement not in their costume. The audience had to make the changes in their heads, as the actors would do. Pan remains in the same costume throughout, but changes physically.

This was incredibly challenging, but because we were not worried about costume or puppetry, we could focus and worry about the huge emotional power of Pan and Lyra, and the moment of separation. When those two actors were working together, the pain of that scene could really be felt. It is such a relief that you could just focus on these moments rather than thinking: "Well it is great that you are playing it so well but what about the puppet here, and what about the costume." We did not have to worry about that, we were going for the jugular with the emotion and the result was pretty powerful.

Q: The age difference between the lead actors is an obvious point of departure between your production and that of the National.

A: I think that young actors, young people, are *very* underestimated in the arts, especially in theater. This is a prominent debate for our company. If you are a young musician between 15 and 25 years old, and you are in a band, you are listened to. Your opinions and thoughts, either political or emotional, matter. Audiences will listen to what you have to say because you are in a band. However if you are in the theater the perception of young actors is that youth theater is not very good, it is amateur and it is emulating adult theater. That perception is wrong, and it is a perception through ignorance! I think where Nick Hytner is right [in his decision to cast older actors], is because of the scale in terms of the size and the enormity of that theater. At the same time you could not have a company of young people out of school, September through to March to do it.

Our space is much smaller and therefore it is very possible to get young people to the level where they can convince an audience of the role they are playing. Now it is hard when you are Asriel and it is hard when you are Mrs. Coulter, but we were not giving ten or eleven years old the part of Asriel. I think this particular actor was about eighteen or nineteen, the actor playing Mrs. Coulter was nineteen and has gone off to drama school. In other words we did have an age range, and would cast accordingly. I think young actors when treated professionally and treated with respect as well as listened to, will deliver. They will not deliver when you treat them like a bunch of kids and when you do not respect what they bring to a project. A young persons' theater should be fully committed. Playbox works as a full time operation for young people, which is ultimately the reason it exists. It does not work as a part time or youth wing of another theater, which means that the work with the young people becomes the core reason for existence.

For us young people can deliver. They can deliver classical work (Shakespeare), as well as medieval and contemporary drama. However, never attempt to make young people cardboard copies of adults, because you will fail. Do not try to stage *King Lear* with a fifteen-year-old actor because that actor will not have the experience to play King Lear. However a fifteen-year-old girl playing Lyra will know what it is like. She will have gone through, or will be going through, some of the experiences Lyra is going through: that first love and awareness for example. The question is how the actress is going to tackle those areas with her own idea's and knowledge. That is what makes working with young people so exiting and that is why I think a lot of us staff enjoy the work we do. We are continuously confronted with surprises.

Because these actors have no history of the theater tradition, they bring to it a kind of recklessness and immediacy, which is great. If you are working on Shakespeare with an actor at the RSC they will know the history of Richard

III, they will refer to the production in 1972, and study how it was done back then. This however does not matter to young people, they will just respond to it directly in the here and now. They will say: "Look, this is what I think, can I try it this way." My reaction is always: "Yes, let's try it, let's see what happens." As a result it becomes very immediate, without being flashy or trying to be trendy. I would not stage this play with young people on stage at the National, the Royal Shakespeare Company, or anywhere else like that, as I think they cannot vocally sustain it. However here, in a theater that is designed and build for young people, and where everything is done to provide the appropriate support for young people, it worked well.

If you are not used to working with young people there is a fear. There is a real fear that they are not going to take it seriously, that they are not going to be able to do it. If you work with young people you know how serious and passionate they are.

Young people do have stamina. They have more stamina than many adult actors. You will see that a lot of adult actors in the rehearsal room will be sitting in the corner with their coffee and a copy of The *Guardian*, and wait until they are called. Instead of this, our actors are around the building trying to improve what they were doing when they are not in the rehearsal room with us. If you would come in on a regular rehearsal day you will find daemon movement going on everywhere and young people trying different things, you have to pull them all back together. It brings us back to the point I made earlier. You do not say to a rock band: "My goodness what a lot of stamina," you take it for granted because they are young, they hold that audience and play two and half hour sets, the stamina is just there. It is the same with young actors, they are brilliant, and they have more stamina than us.

Q: It would be an understatement to say that Pullman's work is a challenge to stage and to make the Playbox version possible, three directors were in place. Could you expand on the directorial process and the working method that was employed?

A: I basically did not want to do the whole thing on my own. I thought it would be boring for the actors to have one voice all the time. It was therefore great that I could co-direct with both Emily Jane Quash and Mary King. Emily was also a passionate lover of the book and Mary King is a very exciting director. We all work in slightly different ways. I was more interested in the religious other-worldliness content of the plays; the witches, Asriel and Lyra's journey with Asriel, and therefore I worked on all these points. Emily was passionate about Lyra and Will, and Lyra's world, so Emily took all the Lyra scenes. Mary took the Oxford world and directed everything around these moments in the story.

Mairin O'Hagan, foreground, as Seraphina and her witch clan in the Playbox (UK) production of *His Dark Materials* (photograph by Andy Brining).

Q: I can imagine that a cast of 50 people requires detailed planning and organized logistics, how was this achieved?

A: As our young actors come from quite a wide region, I had to liaise with all the different authorities, which in turn have different rules and regulations for young people on stage. Once this process was completed and we had all the relevant licenses in place, we had to liaise with the actor's parents and schools. We have to make sure we are not abusing any moments in their lives in terms of hours, so we have to finish rehearsing at a certain time and we cannot start the next day until a certain time. Because Playbox is a large organization, it is considered a kind of model of good practice. At the same time we are inspected on a very frequent basis and we have the authorities breathing down our necks to make sure that everything is as it should be. It is a huge logistical job especially when there are fifty in the cast which, I have to say, is one of Playbox's largest casts, as we normally have about twenty or thirty at most and sometimes as small as ten or fifteen. With a show like this the planning was enormous and it all adds up: the process of liaison with local authorities and obviously the support for the families, for example the parents were constantly driving the young actors back and forth to rehearsals. This means that a production like this becomes such an enormous logistical operation. However, the company is used to it because we have been going for a long time. I do not think that if we had just opened up, we would have said: "Let's stage *His Dark Materials* ... that would be good." Over the years we have been building those relationships and building those trusts, which enable us to be able to do it.

Q: And on the day of the performance was there a very organized back stage area?

A: Absolutely. We have to have a team of chaperones who are officially called matrons. To work as a matron you have to be CRB (Criminal Record Bureau) checked to enhanced status, which is quite a detailed police check to make sure you are fit to be back stage. For every performance there is a team of matrons who supervise the wellbeing of the young people. Their duty is to make sure that the working conditions are good for the actors that they are fed properly and everything is fine. These matrons *will* tell you if there is anything not up to standard. Also during the rehearsal process the matrons continually inform us about the actors, for example one of the young persons has been working too hard or somebody is not feeling well. It does feel that they are breathing down your neck and this can really get on your nerves at times, but at the same time, you know that they are there for the child's interest, which is paramount. Being a young person's organization that is what we have to do.

Q: The National Theatre made use of their drum-revolve and some advanced technology throughout where, for example, Will used his knife to make an opening in between two worlds. How did Playbox find equivalents or alternatives for such technology?

A: Simplicity, for example when Will cuts with his knife to reach a different dimension, we used a light and just synchronized to the actor's movement, a very simple solution. We had some special effects up our sleeves, for example we have a big trap in the stage through which Asriel and Mrs. Coulter used to exit the stage surrounded by a lot of smoke. We also had the big tower that could be useful for other effects. In the scene where the witches were flying, they would be actually up on the tower, but we only put the lights on the actors making them appear in motion. Throughout the entire production we used a great amount of lighting, as well as many sound effects and sound tracks. Nevertheless it was all based on the simplicity of story telling. It is as if we would say to the audience: "Look, if you suspend your disbelief for a bit, we will provide you with some images and if you put them altogether in your mind, then together we will have made something special." It is not that we do not like effects, because we definitely do. We do like having spectacle in our show and when, for example, Asriel crossed to another dimension at the end of play one, we had marvelous effects such as cascades of dry ice, projections and sound effects. For a moment it is great and really spectacular. I think ultimately the answer is that you use what you can. You use the resources that are available and attainable.

I think you could do *His Dark Materials* with no set and no costumes, in an empty room with a group of people. The reason that you could succeed when you strip away everything else is ultimately because the narrative around Lyra and Will is strong enough to carry the entire story, as they are such wonderful characters. I was really excited about the film; I thought it was going to be the kind of ultimate visual trip. However, on the contrary, I really did not like it and was very disappointed, because visually it was too much. It was too much a film about effects. For example, the bear was wonderful CGI but at the same time there was too much emphasis on these elements. The book is not about a bear, he is a part of the journey, whereas the posters, and everything about the film, simply say: "Come and see this giant bear in combat." I do believe that simplicity can sometimes reach the heart, whereas the over the top CGI is impressive, but just misses the point. It will be interesting to see if they do the other two books. I tend to feel they may not, as I do not feel it has been a great success. I went to a talk by Phillip Pullman in Oxford about six weeks ago, and you kind of feel he was not overly passionate about the film as he was about the stage production at the National.

Q: Playbox used the adaptation of Nicholas Wright for their production. Was it an instant choice to use this play text and did you use the first or second publication? Also, did Playbox make any alterations?

A: We did not make any alterations to the text. I think we might have done if this would have been allowed. We used the second revised text but there is a little clause in the contract that says you cannot change anything, so we did not do this. A great amount of the original story has been left out in this adaptation. I think if the National had not taken the initiative to create an adaptation and if there had not been a movie, I think we may have talked to Phillip Pullman about trying to develop an adaptation with a different writer, because we felt very passionate about the three books. However Nicholas Wright's version was available and it tells the story well. At the same time it is very workable, especially for a production with young people as the text is not overly complicated, so we stuck to Wright's version. We made our own visual decisions, but we did not change the text.

Q: Again returning to the press release it is written that at the heart of the story is Lyra's journey to find love and awareness. I wonder how Will's story finds a place in this, and how his character is developed in comparison to Lyra's character?

A: With Will it was a less complex journey. We did not have as much questions about his character and journey. The actress who played Lyra brought so many questions and perspectives to the character, whereas with Will it was a more linear journey. I was not as committed to Will's story in terms of how his character was developed. Not in the way I was committed to Lyra's story and journey. My co-director Emily tended to handle more of the Will scenes.

There is a major part of Will's story line missing [from Wright's adaptation]. In the adaptation you come to Will really as a foil for Lyra, rather than a character in his own right. It is also a long time before he comes into the story, which means that you have really created an understanding about Lyra's character and you are following her specifically on that journey. I remember the most important moments for Will were the parting scenes of him and Lyra. The agony portrayed by both actors playing that scene is fantastic; I really think that that is when Will's scenes become deeply moving.

Q: Having seen the National Theatre's version, the speed in which the scenes followed each other stood out the most. Therefore, how does the Playbox version deal with the length of the play? And could a high tempo, especially with the more dramatic scenes, create a problem for the young audience to become emotionally involved with the story?

A: I think it could present a problem, but because we tended to move quite quickly and very cinematically, we cut time off the National's version. I think the National's running time was three hours per show, however we brought it down to about two hours and ten minutes. We achieved this through the speed of the changeovers, as there was no drum-revolve and no changing of props. We did not have many props at all. We did not have any furniture coming on or going off, unlike the National, which had big tables and chairs for the committees. At the same time, when the members of the consistorial court made an entrance it is quite a slow, processional kind of arrival. However I think our audiences could have stayed there longer, they absolutely lapped it up. It was a real crossover audience, as you had young people who had read the books, fans of *His Dark Materials* who had traveled across the country, and you had the Playbox's regular audience who wanted to experience what the excitement was about without having any prior knowledge about the books. Hopefully they all went away with something, but certainly we did not feel it was too long for audiences.

Q: Is there a danger that the transition between scenes cuts them short, inhibiting or breaking any emotional connection the audience may have, or may have had, with a particular scene?

A: I do not like it when high impact moments are broken. I remember when we first got into this building. I was rehearsing *Henry IV* and I could not get into the theater for some reason. Instead I had to use the studio for pre-school children, to rehearse the death of Henry IV. At first I really did not want to work in the space, but then the two young actors brought most of those attending the rehearsal to tears with the way they captured the father and son relationship, which was so magnificent. I remembered this moment when we were working on *His Dark Materials*, and decided that we did not want to lose those moments. We did not want to say: "Right, get out, let's go for the next scene." The aim was to exploit these moments as much as we could so, for example, we used musical underscoring to highlight these emotional scenes. One of the things I love about film is the way they blend the score, the way they heighten the emotion for an audience, and so we tried to use these effects on stage. We aimed to stage an emotional type of story rather than a comic book type. I did love the National's production and I went to see it both years. However each time I came out of the theater, I still felt that its style took away the story's emotion. You get adventure as it is told in a really good comic book, something like Indiana Jones. Even though I like this style, it does not move me, and I wanted to feel moved. With our own version of the story, I was moved. I remember sitting up-stairs in the gallery with the guy operating the lighting who said: "We seem to have got a choky moment here," and that was a really great moment for me.

Q: How did your company deal with the religious aspects of the play?

A: We did talk a lot about extremism in religion, about the threat of religion, and about the diversity of religions. I think you make a big statement if would reduce the religious element of the story, something which the movie did, because I feel that you cannot take out the fundamental reason of the book. This is why we did not shun the religious aspect of the story. However, I think we played religion as a central metaphor for what this society has at its heart. We did not say that this is what Christian religion or Muslim religion is like, rather we just said that this religion is whatever is at the center of these people's lives. However we did not sweep the issues under the carpet. We did not try to push our audience through images or through symbolism to a definite conclusion, we left that open. We did have a huge shaft of light for the casket of the Authority to imply there was some supernatural presence there.

I felt the play was very topical because of the war of Iraq, and I think that since 9/11 everything we do has to engage in discussions about our world. Young people have to grow up in this world and I think in their lifetime living with religious extremism will remain a prominent issue. Therefore it has become very pertinent to look at these issues without taking sides. We focused on how the young people felt about religion and whether it was a dominant aspect of their lives.

We did not have many post-show discussions on this show. This was

The company as the world ends featuring Ed Miller as Lord Asriel, standing left, James Lewis as Brother Jasper, center, and Sophie Danks as Mrs. Coulter, right, in the Playbox (UK) production of *His Dark Materials* (photograph by Andy Brining).

because we were doing the show quite intensely over a short period of time, with sometimes two shows on one day. We felt that it would be best to let the plays speak for themselves. I think we probably had one post-show discussion, but I do not think these really focused on the religious elements. Instead it was more a standard kind of discussion and an opportunity to ask the actors how they felt playing Lyra and Will.

Theater is a battleground for arguments and for diversity. Theater should be challenging every perception in a diverse, multi-ethnic, multi-cultural and multi-disciplinary way.

Q: Did the performance of *His Dark Materials* change your regular viewing audience and attract a different kind of audience? Did you do any research examining audience composition?

A: You tend to know your audience quite well. Playbox has been going since 1986 and before we settled in this building, we did a lot shows at Warwick Arts Centre as well as touring our productions. In this way, we had already built an audience that would trust the work that we were doing and say: "Let's see the Playbox take on whatever it might be." This could be Shakespeare, or rather a cut down version of Shakespeare, which usually comes in just under two hours, or any other play for that matter. Our audiences are very loyal and they like to see the kind of things that we do. They are less enthusiastic about things they do not know, which is the reason why staging new work or a new commission is quite hard. *His Dark Materials* did bring a new audience. It brought a lot of people who would normally come, but it also brought some really extreme *His Dark Materials* fans into the building. These fans argued a lot which was great and interesting to hear.

In the interval of a show, I tend to go and sit out in the entrance area and listen to what people say. I am always quite interested in the reception of our work. With *His Dark Materials* there was diversity in the response. Some people thought Olivia, who played Lyra, should have also been in the film version because they thought she was wonderful. Others disagreed, which is great because when you read a book, you have your own perception and your own interpretations. It was fascinating to listen to their responses, fascinating to pick up on the little things that they had liked, such as the piece of music we had used for introducing the show and the fact that we brought it back at the end of the six or seven hours.

We said to the cast when we started that we were dealing with very precious property, because *His Dark Materials* is owned by its readership. For the young actors this would mean that from the moment they would walk on stage and say: "I am Lyra," the audience may say: "No you're not! I know who Lyra is, and that's not you." The production introduced a lot of new people to Playbox's theater and hopefully some of them will come back for other things.

Q: Looking back on your production, are there any changes you would make in hindsight, and are you tempted to revive the production at a future date?

A: Tempted to revise it, yes, it would be wonderful. Logistically it would be very hard because a lot of the people who were involved have moved on. Lyra would now be too old and at the time she was perfect. It is always a temptation to revive any show. I think it was technically the most challenging piece we have ever done, and I would like to go back and try to rework some of the technical side of it. We always felt that we nearly got there with the projections, but it was never quite right. The lighting was brilliant, but we knew there were areas where we could do even more. So I think if we did revive it we would try to really improve the technical side, which was good but we could move that on. I also think it would have been nice to have a bigger budget, I cannot remember what the budget was in total, but they are never very large here. With a slightly bigger budget you can take it a little bit further. However the only reason we would revive if there was a need for doing so, in other words if the young people of Playbox said to us: "We have rediscovered these books so let's do it again," or we felt there was an audience out there who did not know the work very well and through the show we could reintroduce the book.

I think if the films continue then we probably would see no reason, and meanwhile there are many other things that we want to do. So, I think we will just treasure this as a really wonderful moment.

Concluding remarks

Inevitably any discussion of productions of *His Dark Materials* must start with the strengths, virtues and possible weaknesses of Nicholas Wright's play text adaptation of the trilogy. His play condenses the span of three large volumes into a two-part play which, as has been suggested here, leaves out certain key elements such as Mary Malone and the *mulefa*, which could be considered to make the action of the plays more fantastic and less connected to the world in which we live. Secondly, it has been suggested here that Wright's text was very much written with the resources (both financial and technical) of the National Theatre in mind. This is not to say that the play text of *His Dark Materials* does not offer significant virtues, but it is surely not the only way the trilogy could be adapted and this should be perhaps be remembered.

In the National Theatre script the visual perspective and stage imagery, in terms of what technology could achieve, was emphasized perhaps to the detriment of the narrative and the centrality of language and storytelling. By comparison the regional theater groups I've spoken to placed a greater emphasis on the importance of the story and this was perhaps exacerbated by their small budgets and limited resources, in relation to the National's production. Speed, in terms of the length of the production, and what can be done with the pace of the play, seems to have been an interesting issue for all of these productions. This aspect would seem to be linked to questions about the attention span and capabilities of children and young adults as audience and actors, but also determined by technological resources in terms of the stage and the importance or not accorded to visual imagery over straightforward storytelling. The Minack theater production in particular was as bare bones as it is possible to imagine and even the puppets were no more than sketches for the imagination. Put simply, these productions encouraged the audience's imagination to engage with the story presented, while the audience of the National Theatre was treated to a full display of the capabilities of one of Britain's leading theater company on the world-famous Olivier stage.

While it seems that the three theater companies interviewed in this chapter were able to build their own distinctive interpretations of Wright's play into very individualized productions, this re-imagining required a strong and original directorial perspective. One of the most interesting elements of these productions by Playbox Theatre, Next Stage Theatre Company and Theatre Royal Bath, Young People's Theatre was the way in which they found such different theatrical solutions to staging key elements of the plays, these involved: how characters were presented on stage, whether to use adult or child actors, whether to use puppets or actors to represent the daemons, how to adapt their production to the theater space in which they working. One noticeable difference between the National's production and that of these smaller theater companies is that at least two of them (Playbox Theatre and Theatre Royal Bath, Young People's Theatre) were determined to see the plays and books as written for children/young adults and to use children/young adults as actors, whereas the National only used adults in its production. Arguably, these smaller young adult theater companies returned ownership to the audience for which the books were originally written.

Notes

1. Images from the production are available on the Minack's web site and details are supplied in the bibliography below as "His Dark Materials (Part 1) presented by the Next Stage Theatre Company, August 20 to 24" and "His Dark Materials (Part 2) presented by the Next Stage Theatre Company, August 20 to 24."

Works Cited

Billington, Michael. 2004. "*His Dark Materials*." *The Guardian*, January 5, 2004. Accessed September, 1 2009. *http://www.guardian.co.uk/stage/2004/jan/05/theatre.fiction*.

Butler, Robert. 2003. *The Art of Darkness: Staging the Philip Pullman Trilogy*. London: Oberon.

_____. 2004. *Darkness Illuminated*. London: National Theatre and Oberon.

Hanks, Robert. 2004. "His Dark Materials, National Theatre London." *The Independent*. December 14, 2004. Accessed September 1, 2009. *http://www.independent.co.uk/arts-en tertainment/theatre–dance/reviews/his-dark-materials-national-theatre–london-686118.html*.

"His Dark Materials." N.d. Accessed November 10, 2008. *http://arts-archive.com*.

"His Dark Materials (Part 1) presented by the Next Stage Theatre Company, August 20 to 24." N.d. *Minack Theatre*. Accessed June 15, 2008. *http://www.minack.com/theatregoers/hisdark-materials.htm*.

"His Dark Materials (Part 2) presented by the Next Stage Theatre Company August 20 to 24." N.d. *Minack Theatre*. Accessed June 15, 2008. *http://www.minack.com/theatregoers/his-darkmaterials2.htm*.

Joyce, Julian. 2007. "Golden Compass Author Hits Back." *BBC News Channel*. November 29, 2007. Accessed January 10, 2009. *http://news.bbc.co.uk/1/hi/uk/7115300.stm*.

MacDonald, Laura. 2007. "Imagining *His Dark Materials* as a *Gesamtkunstwerk*." *Studies in Musical Theatre* 1: 2.

"Minack Theatre." N.d. Accessed January 10, 2009. *http://www.minack.com/*.

Next Stage Theatre Company. N.d. Accessed June 15, 2008. *http://www.next-stage.co.uk/*.

"Playbox Theatre." N.d. Accessed January 10, 2009. *www.playboxtheatre.com*.

"Playbox Theatre: Regional Premiere of Philip Pullman's Award-Winning *His Dark Materials* at Warwick Next Month." March 2006. Accessed January 10, 2009. *www.bridge tothestars.net/index.php?d=stage&p=playbox_release*.

Shared Experience. N.d. Accessed June 15, 2008. *http://www.sharedexperience.org.uk/company.html*.

Spencer, Charles. 2004. "Working with the Wrong Material." *The Daily Telegraph*, January 5, 2004. Accessed January 10, 2009. *http://www.telegraph.co.uk/culture/theatre/drama/36 09641/Working-with-the-wrong-material.html*.

"Theatre Royal Bath: *His Dark Materials* Press Release." March 2008. Accessed June 15, 2008. *www.theatreroyal.org.uk/page_attachments/0000/1477/HIS_DARK_MATERIALS_-_Press _Release.doc*.

"Theatre Royal Bath: Young People's Theatre." N.d. Accessed January 10, 2009. *www.the-atreroyal.org.uk/young-peoples-theatre*.

Wright, Nicholas. 2005. *His Dark Materials*. Oxford: Heinemann Educational.

Bibliography

Selected works by Phillip Pullman

PLAYS

1990. *Frankenstein: The Play*. Oxford: Oxford University Press.
1992. *Sherlock Holmes and the Limehouse Horror*. N.p.: Nelson Thornes

BOOKS

1979. *Galatea*. New York: E.P. Dutton. (Adult science fiction/magical realist fiction.)
1990. *The Broken Bridge*. London: Macmillan.
2001. *The Butterfly Tattoo* [originally published in 1990 as *The White Mercedes*]. London: Macmillan.
2010. *The Good Man Jesus and the Scoundrel Christ*. London: Canongate.

The Sally Lockhart Quartet

1985. *The Ruby in the Smoke*. Oxford: Oxford University Press.
1999. *The Shadow in the North*. London: Scholastic.
1999. *The Tiger in the Well*. London: Scholastic.
2000. *The Tin Princess*. London: Scholastic.

His Dark Materials

1995. *His Dark Materials: Northern Lights*. London: Scholastic.
1997. *His Dark Materials: The Subtle Knife*. London: Scholastic.
2000. *His Dark Materials: The Amber Spyglass*. London: Scholastic.
2003. *Lyra's Oxford*. N.p.: David Fickling. (A short story set after the action of *His Dark Materials*. The adventure sees Lyra confront her assumptions about witches.)
2008. *Once Upon a Time in the North*. N.p.: David Fickling. (Set some thirty-five years before *His Dark Materials*, this prequel tells the story of how aeronaut Lee Scoresby met the bear Iorek Byrnison. The book is richly prodcued with engravings and a board game.)

The New Cut Gang (the stories of a gang of Lambeth urchins)

1996. *Thunderbolt's Waxwork*. Harmondsworth: Puffin.
1998. *The Gasfitter's Ball*. Harmondsworth: Puffin.

FAIRYTALES

1999. *I Was a Rat!* N.p.: Doubleday.
1995. *The Fire-Maker's Daughter.* N.p.: Doubleday.
1996. *Clockwork or All Wound Up.* N.p.: Doubleday.
2005. *The Scarecrow and His Servant.* N.p.: Yearling.

FOREWORDS

2005. Introduction to *Paradise Lost* by John Milton. Oxford: Oxford University Press, 1–10.
2008. Foreword to *Doctor Who: The Writer's Tale.* Davies, Russell T., and Benjamin Cook. London: BBC.

JOURNALISM (ADVERSARIES AND INFLUENCES)

1998. "The Darkside of Narnia." *The Guardian,* October 1. Accessed September 24,2007. http://reports.guardian.co.uk/articles/1998/10/1/p-24747.html.
2002. "What! No Soap?" *Notes from the Royal Society of Literature* 20.
2005. "Prize Winning Lecture at the Swedish Royal Library by Philip Pullman at Swedish House of Parliament — on Receipt of Astrid Lindgren Memorial Award." May 23. Accessed December 1, 2007. http://www.alma.se/templates/KR_Page.aspx?id=3131&eps language=EN.
2002. "The 2002 May Hill Arbuthnot Lecture, 'So She Went into the Garden.'" *Journal of Youth Services in Libraries* (JOYS), 15.4, 35–41.
2006. "A New Production of His Dark Materials." Accessed April 6, 2008. www.philip-pullman.com/pages/content/index.asp?PageID=124.
2005. "Boatyard Statement." *Philip Pullman's Website.* March 8. Accessed June 1, 2005. http://www.philip-pullman.com/pages/content/index.asp?PageID=112.
n.d. "Philip Pullman Interview Transcript." Scholastic Books. Accessed March 1, 2009. http://web.archive.org/web/20000816094721/http:/teacher.scholastic.com/authorsand books/authors/pullman/tscript.htm

JOURNALISM (TRADITIONS AND LEGACIES)

2000. "Revisiting Suvin's Poetics of Science Fiction." In *Learning from Other Worlds: Estrange ment, Cognition, and the Politics of Science Fiction and Utopia.* Patrick Parrinder, ed. Liver pool: Liverpool University Press, 36–51.
2002. "I am of the Devil's Party." Interview by Helena de Bertodano. *Daily Telegraph,* Janu ary 2002. Accessed March 1, 2009. http://www.telegraph.co.uk/culture/donotmigrate/357 2490/I-am-of-the-Devils-party.html.
2002. "Faith and Fantasy." *Radio National Encounter Interview,* March 24. Accessed Octo ber 29, 2010. http://www.abc.net.au/rn/relig/enc/stories/s510312.htm.
2002. "Writing Fantasy Realistically." *Sea of Faith Network.* Accessed October 28, 2010. http://www.sofn.org.uk/conferences/pullman2002.html.
2004. "The Science of Fiction." *The Guardian,* August 26. Accessed June 1 2005.
2005. "Miss Goddard's Grave." Lecture Given at the University of East Anglia. Accessed October 28, 2010. www.philip-pullman.com/assets_cm/files/.../miss_goddards_grave.pdf.
2008. "The Elementary Particles of Narrative." *The Lion and the Unicorn.* Vol. 32, 2 (April), 127–147.
2009. "'I Must Create a System…': William Blake Society Lecture 2005." Accessed March 1, 2009. http://www.philip-pullman.com/pages/content/index.asp?PageID=110.
n.d. "Philip Pullman Interview Transcript." Scholastic Books. Accessed March 1, 2009.

http://web.archive.org/web/20000816094721/http:/teacher.scholastic.com/authorsand
books/authors/pullman/tscript.htm.

JOURNALISM (RELIGION, SEXUALITY AND GENDER)

2001. "Interview with Joan Bakewell." *Belief* series, BBC Radio 3. http://darkadamant.better
version.org/BBC_Belief_Philip_Pullman.txt.

2001. "The Republic of Heaven." *The Horn Book Magazine*, November/December. http://
www.hbook.com/magazine/articles/2001/nov01_pullman.asp.

2002. "I am of the Devil's Party." Interview with Helen Bertodano, *Telegraph.co.uk*, January 29. http://www.telegraph.co.uk/arts/main.jhtml?xml=/arts/2002/01/29/bopull27.xml
&page=1.

2002. "Faith and Fantasy." Interview on *Encounter* series, ABC Radio National, March 24.
http://www.abc.net.au/rn/relig/enc/stories/s510312.html.

2002. "A Dark Agenda: Interview with Susan Roberts." November. http://www.surefish.
co.uk/culture/features/pullman_interview.htm.

2002. "Are You There, God? It's Me." *Book*, November/December. http://web.archive.org/
web/20050211151440/http://www.bookmagazine.com/issue25/inthemargins.shtml.

2004. "Archbishop Wants Pullman in Class." March 10, 2004. Accessed October 29, 2010.
http://news.bbc.co.uk/1/hi/education/3497702.stm.

2005. "Identity Crisis." *Trinidad and Tobago Humanist Association*, November. http://www.
humanist.org.tt/forum/article/guest/identity_crisis.html.

n.d. "Comment on Religion." *Philip Pullman website*. http://www.philip-pullman.com/pages
/content/index.asp?PageID=12.

JOURNALISM (DRAMATIZING *HIS DARK MATERIALS*)

2007. "FilmChat: Philip Pullman: The Extended E-Mail Interview (with Peter T. Chattaway)." November 28, 2007. http://filmchatblog.blogspot.com/2007/11/philip-pullman-
extended-e-mail.html.

Critical editions on *His Dark Materials*

Freitas, Donna, and Jason E. King. 2007. *Killing the Imposter God: Philip Pullman's Spiritual
Imagination in His Dark Materials*. San Francisco: Jossey Bass.

Gray, William. 2008. *Fantasy, Myth and the Measure of Truth: Tales of Pullman, Lewis,
Tolkien, MacDonald and Hoffman*. London: Palgrave Macmillan.

Rayment-Pickard, Hugh. 2004. *The Devil's Account: Philip Pullman and Christianity*. Darton,
Longman and Todd.

Scott, Carole, and Millicent Lenz, eds. 2005. *Dark Materials Illuminated*. Detroit: Davidson,
H.R.

Wheat, Leonard, F. 2007. *Philip Pullman's His Dark Materials: A Multiple Allegory: Attacking
Religious Superstition in The Lion, The Witch and the Wardrobe and Paradise Lost*. N.p.:
Prometheus.

Readers' guides to *His Dark Materials*

Colbert, David. 2007. *The Magical Worlds of Philip Pullman*. London: Puffin.

Freitas, Donna, and Jason E. King. 2007. *Killing the Imposter God: Philip Pullman's Spiritual
Imagination in His Dark Materials*. San Francisco: Jossey Bass.

Frost, Laurie. 2006. *The Elements of His Dark Materials*. London: Scholastic.

Gifford, Clive. 2006. *So You Think You Know His Dark Materials?* N.p.: Hodder Children's.

Gresh, Lois H. 2007. *Exploring Philip Pullman's His Dark Materials: An Unauthorized Adventure Through The Golden Compass, The Subtle Knife, and The Amber Spyglass*. London: Macmillan.

Gribbin, John, and Gribbin, Mary. 2005. *The Science of Philip Pullman's His Dark Materials*. London: Hodder.

Haill, Lyn, ed. 2004. *Darkness Illuminate*d. London: NT/Oberon.

Houghton, John. 2004. *A Closer Look at His Dark Materials*. Eastbourne: Kingsway.

Parkin, Lance, and Mark Jones. 2007. *Dark Matters: An Unofficial and Unauthorized Guide to Philip Pullman's Internationally Bestselling His Dark Materials Trilogy*. N.p.: Virgin.

Simpson, Paul. 2007. *The Rough Guide to Philip Pullman's His Dark Materials*. N.p.: Rough Guides.

Squires, Claire. 2003. *Philip Pullman's His Dark Materials Trilogy: A Reader's Guide*. London and New York: Continuum Contemporaries Series.

_____. 2006. *Philip Pullman, Master Storyteller: A Guide to the Worlds of His Dark Materials*. London: Continuum.

Tucker, Nicholas. 2003. *Darkness Visible: Inside the World of Philip Pullman*. Cambridge: Wizard.

Vere, Pete, and Sandra Miesel. 2007. *Pied Piper of Atheism: Philip Pullman and Children's Fantasy*. N.p.: Ignatius.

Ware, Jim, and Kurt Bruner. 2007. *Shedding Light on His Dark Materials: Exploring Hidden Spiritual Themes in Philip Pullman's Popular Series*. N.p.: Tyndale House.

Watkins, Tony. 2004. *Dark Matter: A Thinking Fan's Guide to Philip Pullman*. Downer's Grove, IL: Intervarsity.

_____. 2006. *Dark Matter: Shedding Light on Philip Pullman's Trilogy His Dark Materials*. Downer's Grove, IL: Intervarsity.

Yeffeth, Glenn, ed. *Navigating the Golden Compass: Religion, Science and Daemonology in Philip Pullman's His Dark Materials*. Dallas: BenBella.

Suggested further reading (adversaries and influences)

Davies, Caroline. 2005. "Author Attacks School League Tables for Killing Off Curiosity and Joy." *Telegraph*, September 3.

Falconer, Rachel. 2008. "Coming of Age in a Fantasy World: Philip Pullman's *His Dark Materials*." *The Crossover Novel*. London, Routledge.

Joyce, Julian. 2007. "Golden Compass Author Hits Back." *BBC News Channel*. November 29, 2007. Accessed January, 10 2009. http://news.bbc.co.uk/1/hi/uk/7115300.stm.

Oziewicz, Marek, and Daniel Hade. 2010. "The Marriage of Heaven and Hell? Philip Pullman, C.S. Lewis, and the Fantasy Tradition." *Mythlore*, 28:109/110, (Spring), 39–54.

Shohet, Lauren. 2005. "Reading Dark Materials." In *His Dark Materials Illuminated: Critical Essays on Philip Pullman's Trilogy*. Millicent Lenz with Carole Scott, eds. Detroit: Wayne State University Press, 22–36.

Suggested further reading (traditions and legacies)

Butts, Dennis. 2010. "Children's Literature and Social Change: Some Case Studies from Barbara Hofland to Philip Pullman." Cambridge: Lutterworth.

Hines, Maude. 2005. "Second Nature: Daemons and Ideology in *The Golden Compass*." In

His Dark Materials Illuminated: Critical Essays on Philip Pullman's Trilogy. Millicent Lenz with Carole Scott, eds. Detroit: Wayne State University Press, 37–47.

Holderness, Graham. 2007. "'The Undiscovered Country': Philip Pullman and the 'Land of the Dead.'" *Literature and Theology*, 21, 3: 276–292.

Lambert, Angela. 2002. "A Golden Age for the Kids? Is Children's Fiction More Interesting Than That Being Written for Adults? Angela Lambert Talks to Philip Pullman." *Prospect Magazine*, March, 72. Accessed May 1, 2008. http://www.prospect-magazine.co.uk/article_details.php?id=4989.

Markman, Arthur B. 2006. "Science, Technology and the Danger of Daemons." In *Navigating the Golden Compass: Religion, Science and Daemonology in Philip Pullman's His Dark Materials.* Glenn Yeffeth, ed., 61–70. Dallas: BenBella.

Moruzi, Kristine. March 2005. "Missed Opportunities: The Subordination of Children in Philip Pullman's *His Dark Materials.*" *Children's Literature in Education*, Vol. 36, No. 1, 55–68.

Oziewicz, Marek. 2010. "Representations of Eastern Europe in Philip Pullman's *His Dark Materials,* Jonathan Stroud's *The Bartimaeus Trilogy,* and J. K. Rowling's *Harry Potter Series.*" *International Research in Children's Literature,* 3:1 (July), 1–14.

Russell, Mary Harris. 2003. "Ethical Plots, Ethical Endings in Philip Pullman's *His Dark Materials.*" *Foundation: The International Review of Science Fiction* 32:88 (Summer), 68–74.

Rustin, Margaret, and Michael Rustin. 2003. "Where Is Home? An Essay on Philip Pullman's *Northern Lights [The Golden Compass].*" *Journal of Child Psychotherapy* 29:1 (April), 93–105.

_____. 2003. "Learning to Say Goodbye: An Essay on Philip Pullman's *The Amber Spyglass.*" *Journal of Child Psychotherapy* 29:3 (December), 415–25.

_____. 2003. "A New Kind of Friendship — An Essay on Philip Pullman's *The Subtle Knife.*" *Journal of Child Psychotherapy* 29:2 (August), 227–34.

Said, Edward. 1978. *Orientalism.* Harmondsworth: Penguin.

Thomson, Stephen. 2004. "The Child, the Family, the Relationship. Familiar Stories: Family, Storytelling, and Ideology in Philip Pullman's *His Dark Materials.*" *Children's Literature: New Approaches.* Basingstoke and New York: Palgrave Macmillan, 144–167.

Suggested further reading (religion, sexuality and gender)

Billen, Andrew. 2003. "The Andrew Billen Interview: A Senile God? Who Would Adam and Eve It?" *The Times*, January 21, 14–15.

Bird, Anne-Marie. 2001. "'Without Contraries Progression': Dust as an All-Inclusive, Multifunctional Metaphor in Philip Pullman's 'His Dark Materials.'" *Children's Literature in Education*, 3:2, 111–123.

Bird, Ann-Marie. 2005. "Circumventing the Grand Narrative: Dust as Alternative Theological Vision in Pullman's *His Dark Materials.*" In *His Dark Materials Illuminated: Critical Essays on Philip Pullman's Trilogy.* Eds. Millicent Lenz and Carole Scott. Detroit: Wayne State University Press, 188–198.

Bruner, Kurt, and Jim Ware 2007. *Shedding Light on His Dark Materials: Exploring Hidden Spiritual Themes in Philip Pullman's Popular Series.* Carol Stream, IL: Salt River.

Butler, Andrew. 2005. "The Republic of Heaven: The Betrayal of Philip Pullman's *His Dark Materials* Trilogy." *Children's Fantasy Fiction: Debates for the Twenty First Century.* Eds. Nickianne Moody and Clare Horrocks. Liverpool: Liverpool JMU, 285–298.

Chrisafis, Angelique. 2002. "Pullman Lays Down Moral Challenge for Writers." *Guardian*, August 12. Accessed December 30, 2002. http://education.guardian.co.uk/Print/0,3858,4479940,00.html.

Colás, Santiago. 2005. "Telling True Stories, or The Immanent Ethics of Material Spirit (and Spiritual Matter) in Philip Pullman's *His Dark Materials.*" *Discourse,* 27.1, 34–66.

Garrahy, Jessica. 2009. "His Controversial Materials: Philip Pullman and Religious Narrative Identity." *Literature and Aesthetics: The Journal of the Sydney Society of Literature and Aesthetics,* 19:2 (December), 105–122.

Gooderham, David. 2003. "Fantasizing It as It Is: Religious Language in Philip Pullman's Trilogy, *His Dark Materials.*" *Children's Literature,* 31, 155–175.

Graham, Karen. 2010. "Paradise Lost? Adolescent Alienation in Philip Pullman's His Dark Materials." In Spark, Gordon, et al., ed. *Alienation and Resistance: Representation in Text and Image.* Newcastle upon Tyne, England: Cambridge Scholars, 268–286.

Harris Russell, Mary. 2005. "'Eve, Again! Mother Eve!' Pullman's Eve Variations." In *His Dark Materials Illuminated: Critical Essays on Philip Pullman's Trilogy.* Millicent Lenz with Carole Scott, eds. Detroit: Wayne State University Press.

Hartney, Christopher. 2005. "Imperial and Epic: Philip Pullman's Dead God." In *The Buddha of Suburbia: Proceedings of the Eighth Australian and International Religion, Literature and the Arts Conference 2004.* Eds. Carole M. Cusack, Frances Di Lauro and Christopher Hartney. Sydney: RLA, 246–280.

Jacobs, Alan. 2004. "The Republic of Heaven." *Shaming the Devil: Essays in Truthtelling.* N.p.: Wm. B. Eerdmans.

Lenz, Millicent. 2003. "Story as a Bridge to Transformation: The Way Beyond Death in Philip Pullman's *The Amber Spyglass.*" *Children's Literature in Education* 34:1 (March), 47–55.

Nathan, J. 2004. "Review of *His Dark Materials.*" *Jewish Chronicle, Theatre Record,* 1–28 (January), 18.

Voogd, Susanne. 2010. "From the Plains of Childhood to the Peaks of Adolescence in Philip Pullman's *His Dark Materials.*" In Besson, Françoise ed., *Mountains Figured and Disfigured in the English-Speaking World.* Newcastle upon Tyne, England: Cambridge Scholars, 372–378.

Suggested further reading (dramatizing *His Dark Materials*)

Berninger, M. 2008. "A Fantasy Epic as a Theatrical Event—*His Dark Materials* at the National Theatre." *Contemporary Drama in English: Non-Standard Forms of Contemporary Drama and Theatre.* Edited by E. Redling and P.P. Schnierer. Trier: WVT Wissenschaftlicher Verlag Trier, 153–169.

Billington, Michael. 2004. "*His Dark Materials.*" *The Guardian.* January 5. Accessed September 1, 2009. http://www.guardian.co.uk/stage/2004/jan/05/theatre.fiction.

Butler, R. 2003. *The Art of Darkness: Staging the Philip Pullman Trilogy.* London: Oberon.

Butler, Robert. 2004. *Darkness Illuminated.* London: National Theatre and Oberon.

Greenwell, Amanda M. 2010. "'The Language of Pictures': Visual Representation and Spectatorship in Philip Pullman's *His Dark Materials.*" *Studies in the Novel,* 42:1/2, 99–120.

Hanks, Robert. 2004. "His Dark Materials, National Theatre London." *The Independent.*

MacDonald, Laura. 2007. "Imagining *His Dark Materials* as a *Gesamtkunstwerk.*" *Studies in Musical Theatre,* 1: 2.

Wright, Nicholas. 2003. "Notes on *His Dark Materials.*" London: Royal National Theatre Archive.

About the Contributors

Nicola Allen, a lecturer at the University of Northampton, is the author of *Marginality in the Contemporary British Novel*, and co-author of a chapter in *Reading Chuck Palahniuk: Monsters, Mayhem and Metafiction* and an article in *Critical Engagements*. She is co-editing a collection on twentieth century canonical texts.

John Haydn Baker lectures in English literature at the University of Westminster. His study of the relationship between Robert Browning and William Wordsworth, *Browning and Wordsworth*, was published in 2004. He is editing a collection of essays on Nick Cave.

Steven Barfield's major research interests are in the work of Samuel Beckett, contemporary British drama and theatre, fantasy/children's literature, and postcolonial literature. He is a senior lecturer at the University of Westminster. He is working on co-edited collections of essays about contemporary British theatre companies, Beckett and modern theatre and Harry Potter. He is joint editor of *Critical Engagements*.

Phil Cardew is the pro-vice chancellor at London South Bank University. His major research interests are medieval literature and language (especially Icelandic) and computing and the humanities.

Martyn Colebrook is completing a Ph.D. at the University of Hull focusing on Iain Banks. His publications include "The Gothic and Mental Disorder," "Alienation and *The Music of Chance*" and "J.G. Ballard and *The Atrocity Exhibition*."

Katharine Cox is a principal lecturer in English at the University of Wales Institute, Cardiff, and head of the Department of Humanities. Her research concentrates on contemporary authors; in particular, the ecological writings of Philip Pullman, Iain Banks and Jeanette Winterson. She is currently working on a monograph on labyrinths in contemporary detective fiction.

Patrick Duggan is a lecturer in theatre and performance studies at the University of Northampton. Patrick writes on, curates and creates performance and theatre. He completed his Ph.D. at the University of Leeds (2009) and he is writing *Trauma-Tragedy: Symptoms of Contemporary Performance* based on that research.

Elisabeth Eldridge studied English at Exeter College, Oxford, before joining the children's literature M.A. course at the University of Reading. Her dissertation at Reading explored retellings of biblical narratives and ideas of spirituality in children's books. She is working on constructions of contemporary Christianity in books for children.

Rachel Falconer is a professor of modern English literature at the University of Lausanne. Some recent publications include *Hell in Contemporary Literature: Western Descent Narratives since 1945* and *The Crossover Novel: Contemporary Children's Fiction and Its Adult Readership*, and she was co-editor of *Face to Face: Bakhtin Studies in Russia and the West*. She is working on a historical-critical survey of fantasy, as well as a monograph on climate change fiction, and is editing two collections, one on Tolkien, the other on the concept of re-reading.

Sarah Gamble is a reader in English with gender at Swansea University. She is the author of *Angela Carter: Writing from the Front Line* and *Angela Carter: A Literary Life*, and is the editor of *The Fiction of Angela Carter: A Reader's Guide to Essential Criticism*. She is writing a book on Angela Carter and the gothic and doing research for a study of twenty-first century women writers.

Tommy Halsdorf is a secondary school teacher in Luxembourg. His academic work focuses on fantasy and children's literature. He studied and taught English at the University of the West of England, Bristol, and has completed his Ph.D. at the University of the West of England, Bristol, which was entitled "Temptation and the Fall in Philip Pullman's *His Dark Materials* Trilogy."

J'annine Jobling's interests focus on religion and spirituality in literary texts, particularly within the theoretical contexts of feminism and postmodernism. Her most recent publication, *Fantastic Spiritualities*, examines spiritual themes in selected young adult fantasy fiction, including *His Dark Materials* and *Harry Potter*. She is an associate professor at Liverpool Hope University.

Sally R. Munt is director of the Sussex Centre for Cultural Studies, University of Sussex. She is the author of several books including *Queer Spiritualities: Sexuality and Sacred Places* with Andrew Yip and Kath A. Browne, and *Queer Attachments: The Cultural Politics of Shame*. She is also a cognitive behavioral therapist.

Laura Peters, a principal lecturer at the University of Roehampton, researches and teaches nineteenth-century fiction. She maintains an interest in the concept of the orphan and its popularity in post-colonial writing as a vehicle through which identity formation is enacted, and her first book (*Orphan Texts: Victorian Orphans, Culture and Empire*) addressed this in particular. Her research is on race and racial theory in nineteenth- and twentieth-century writing and theory.

Karian Schuitema is working toward a Ph.D. on children's theatre at the University of Westminster. She focuses on aspects of interculturalism, multiculturalism and internationalism in theatrical performances for the child and actively works to promote research into theatre for young audiences.

Index

Aaronovitch, David 25*n*1
Abiah 105
ACHUKA 41, 43–44, 46–47, 51, 52
Acton, Lord 32
Adam 12, 14–15, 18, 22, 25*n*5, 68, 111, 122,
    130, 133, 140, 140*n*3, 140*n*10, 143–147,
    173–178, 182, 185, 199, 210–211, 213
Aidinoff, Elsie V. 25*n*5
alethiometer 23, 35, 36, 61, 84–85, 97, 103,
    106, 121, 162, 197, 200
Altizer, Thomas 157
Amato, Joseph 128, 140*n*6
Amis, Kingsley 58, 63; *The Alteration* 63
angels 8, 15, 20, 22, 25*n*7, 35, 57, 64, 66,
    67–69, 71*n*4, 71*n*10, 72*n*16, 80, 83, 84, 130,
    143, 146–153, 156, 158, 160, 164, 167, 174,
    176, 179, 180, 181, 199, 207, 210, 216*n*10,
    242; *see also* Balthamos; Baruch; Xaphania
Apocrypha 5, 143, 146–153
Armitt, Lucie 70
Asimov, Isaac 59, 64, 71*n*7; *Nightfall* 64
Asriel, Lord 13, 49, 64, 68, 69, 70, 71*n*3,
    72*n*19, 78, 80, 82, 85, 95, 97, 103, 106, 128,
    129, 134–135, 143–144, 146–148, 150, 166,
    176, 181, 190–191, 197, 222–223, 252, 256,
    257, 259, 263
Authority (Pullman's God) 64, 67, 99, 109,
    133, 143, 151, 153, 156–158, 160, 207–209

Babbage, Charles 81, 90*n*13
Baker, Deirdre F. 211
Balthamos 68, 72*n*19, 146, 153, 156, 199, 207
Bardi, Abby 114
Barish, Jonas 233
Barrie, J.M.: "The Little White Bird" 45
Barthes, Roland 40, 215*n*7, 230, 236*n*21;
    "Death of the Author" 40
Baruch 68, 143, 146, 153, 199, 207
Bate, Jonathan 138
"The Battle of Maldon" 32

Baum, L. Frank (*The Wizard of Oz*) 94
bears 19, 20, 21–22, 32, 36, 64, 71*n*2, 71*n*10,
    98, 99, 101, 106, 205, 219–220, 240, 242,
    243, 260; *see also* Byrnison, Iorek
"Bear's Son Folk Tale" 32
Beer, John 150, 174
Bentham, Jeremy 125*n*10
Bentley, G.E. 150
Beowulf/Beowulf 31–32, 34
Bible 5, 29, 53, 127, 130, 140*n*10, 145, 147–
    148, 152–153, 153*n*1, 153*n*2, 155, 172–174,
    178, 185*n*4; Genesis 12, 14, 66, 122, 133,
    145–147, 149, 172–175, 184, 210, 212; Job
    130; *see also* Apocrypha
Bildungsroman 11
Billington, Michael 63, 241, 243, 247
Billy Elliot 248
Bird, Anne-Marie 126–127, 139, 140*n*4,
    141*n*12, 163, 211
Blake, William 5, 12, 14, 16, 21, 25*n*7, 69,
    72*n*18, 90*n*18, 93, 109, 127, 140*n*4, 153*n*3,
    153*n*4, 150, 155, 157, 164, 167, 169*n*5, 172,
    174–176, 179, 185, 205, 210, 211, 213,
    215*n*8, 216*n*13; works 25*n*7, 150; *see also*
    Romanticism
Blake Society 14, 72*n*18
Bloom, Harold 55
Blue Remembered Hills 250
Book of Dust 126
Botting, Fred 59
Bourdieu, Pierre 120
Bowen, Lizzie (*Cared For; Or the Orphan
    Wanderers*) 99
Bowlby, John 223
Boy's Own 101, 109*n*3
Braddon, Mary Elizabeth 4
Brontë, Anne (*The Tenant of Wildfell Hall*)
    95
Brontë, Charlotte (*Jane Eyre*) 95
Brontë, Emily (*Wuthering Heights*) 95

Broucek, Francis 212
Buchan, Peter (*The Orphan Sailor: A Tragic Tale of Love, of Pity, and of Woe*) 100–101
Buddhism 5, 154–157, 160–168, 169*n*5, 169*n*6, 169*n*10, 169*n*11
Bunyan, John 32
Burke, Edmund (*A Philosophical Enquiry into the Origin of Our Ideas of the Sublime and the Beautiful*) 79
Butler, Judith 6, 112, 188–190, 193–194, 200; *Gender Trouble* 188; *Undoing Gender* 6, 188–189, 200
Butler, Marilyn 59
Butler, Robert 179, 215*n*3, 215*n*4, 219, 220, 225, 230, 232–234, 236*n*6, 236*n*9, 236*n*19, 236*n*23, 239–240, 241, 243, 246, 248
Byrnison, Iorek 19, 22, 85, 98, 205, 219–220
Byron, Lord George 87–88

Calvin, John 50, 63, 99, 213
Carroll, Lewis (*Alice's Adventures in Wonderland*) 3, 94
Carter, Angela (*The Passion of New Eve*) 184
Cavarero, Adriana 203–204, 208, 214, 215*n*7
Chase, Carole F. 67
childhood 2–3, 6, 8, 9*n*2, 9*n*3, 11–17, 18, 19, 20, 21, 22–23, 24, 25*n*1, 25*n*5, 30, 33–35, 36, 37*n*1, 40–42, 43, 44–48, 50, 51, 52, 53–55, 59, 61, 63, 67, 69, 77, 79, 82, 84, 85, 89*n*2, 94–109, 109*n*1, 109*n*4, 111–112, 113, 115, 117, 118, 122, 124, 124*n*4, 125*n*7, 130–131, 134, 139, 144, 149, 163, 172, 174, 175–176, 177, 180, 181, 182, 183, 184, 185*n*5, 185*n*9, 187–188, 192–194, 195–198, 203, 205–206, 208, 213–214, 221–222, 228, 230–231, 236*n*7, 239–240, 241, 246–247, 248–249, 251, 259, 262, 265; constructions of 40, 42–43, 45–48, 50, 52, 54, 113; daemons 13, 82, 131, 176, 184, 194, 205; growing up 2–3, 11–15, 21–23, 30, 34, 36, 37*n*1, 42–48, 50–55, 124, 131, 178, 181, 184, 198, 214; literature/reading 3, 6, 9*n*2, 9*n*3, 11–13, 16–17, 18, 19, 23, 24, 25*n*5, 30, 33, 34–35, 36, 40–42, 44–48, 50, 53, 54–55, 67, 89*n*2, 94, 97–99, 101, 105, 107, 111–112, 115, 118, 172, 185*n*5, 187, 195, 206, 221–222, 239–240, 246–247; Romantic figure 22, 98, 106–107, 139
Church 13, 14, 49–50, 54, 63–64, 68, 78, 82–83, 94, 97, 99, 103, 105, 107–109, 119, 124*n*5, 128–131, 136–137, 148, 154–159, 175–176, 179, 182–183, 184, 192, 202, 205, 210, 212–213
Cittàgazze 13, 22, 61, 83–84, 108, 131, 133, 203

Clare, John 139
Clarke, Arthur C. ("Third Law of Prediction") 60
Clockwork 6, 8*n*2
Clute, John 77
Colás, Santiago 162
Coleman, John 11
Coleridge, Samuel Taylor 155; *see also* Romanticism
Collings, Michael 57
Collins, Wilkie 4
Conan Doyle, Sir Arthur 4
Cook, Benjamin 59
Cooper, Dominic 182, 215*n*3
Cooper, Susan 30
Coulter, Mrs. 13, 35, 67–69, 72*n*19, 78–82, 85, 88, 95, 96–97, 100, 103, 105–106, 107, 113–117, 119–122, 129, 135–136, 143–144, 146–147, 149–150, 151–152, 175–176, 181, 191–193, 195, 197–198, 200, 205, 209, 212, 228, 230, 236*n*19, 256, 263
Count Karlstein 8*n*2
Crimp, Martin 221
cross-over literature 12–13, 16–17, 25*n*1, 115, 172, 222, 246, 249
Crossley-Holland, Kevin *see Gatty's Tale*
Curry, Michael 242, 250, 254

daemons 3, 4, 9*n*3, 13, 15, 21, 22, 24, 25*n*13, 36, 69, 78–79, 80, 81–82, 85, 89*n*4, 97, 98, 105–107, 116, 121, 125*n*9, 130, 131, 141*n*21, 155, 162–163, 166, 176, 178, 179, 181, 183–184, 185*n*6, 203–206, 207, 210, 212, 213, 215, 215*n*4, 215*n*5, 220, 224–225, 229–232, 234, 240–242, 244, 246–247, 254–255, 257, 266; intercision/separation 131, 176, 203, 205–206, 212, 224–225, 230–232, 234, 241; sexuality 121, 131, 163, 178, 179, 181, 183–184, 203–206, 213, 215, 229–230, 247; staging 215*n*4, 232–233, 240–242; 244, 246–247, 254–255, 257, 266 *see also* Hester; Pantalaimon
Dalton, Timothy 222
dark matter 8, 25*n*2, 60, 65, 71*n*4, 72*n*22, 83, 126–127, 131–133, 141*n*15, 160, 213; *see also* Dust
Davies, Russell T. 59
de Beauvoir 114–116, 122–123
Dee, Dr. John 87, 147–148
Deleuze, Gilles 211
de Quincey, Thomas 141*n*20
Dewey, John 161
Dickens, Charles 87, 140*n*6
Dickinson, Emily 155
Dickinson, Peter (*Eva*) 25*n*5
Dixon, Bob 112
Doctor Who 59

Dodd, Celia 132
Douglas, Mary 134–135, 141n13
Dracula 77
"The Dream of the Rood" 30, 32
Duchen, Jessica 115
Dust 5, 60, 61, 65, 67, 83, 84, 97, 126–140, 140n4, 141n15, 156, 159–161, 169n7, 177, 178, 180, 183, 184, 187, 199, 203, 207, 211, 213; dark matter 127, 131–132, 141n15, 160; theological responses to 126, 127, 128, 129–131, 133, 136, 137, 139–140, 140n4, 156, 159–161, 183, 213

Edmundson, Helen 222, 236n8
Eliot, George (The Mill on the Floss) 243
Eliot, T.S. 16, 130, 140n11
Elkins, James 233
Empire 8
Enoch 143–154; see also Apocrypha
Eurydice 21
Eve 12, 14–16, 18, 21–22, 25n5, 25n8, 48, 68, 111–113, 122–123, 124n1, 131, 140, 165, 172–179, 182, 184–185, 185n4, 199, 210–213

Falconer, Rachel 222
the Fall 12, 16, 18, 21, 25n5, 48, 52, 64, 66, 68, 71n15, 111, 113, 130–131, 138, 154, 156, 163, 165, 172–181, 184–185, 185n11, 199, 202, 209–214
fantasy 3–4, 9n3, 14, 15, 19–20, 23–24, 29, 36, 40, 57–58, 60–61, 63, 69, 77, 80, 82–83, 90n15, 106, 189–190, 197, 203, 206, 214, 215, 239, 242, 243, 246
feminism 70, 114, 117, 121, 124, 181, 184, 190, 203–204, 214, 215n7
Ferrara, Mark 157, 169n5
The Firework-Maker's Daughter 6, 8n2
Fish, Stanley 18
Foucault, Michel 40, 114, 117, 122–123, 125n10, 203, 205, 207, 209, 214–215, 215n3, 227; History of Sexuality 214; "Of Other Spaces" 215n3; "What Is an Author" 40
The Foundling 105
Frankenstein/Frankenstein 59–60, 90n11
Franklin, Sir John 101
Fredericks, Casey 69
Freitas, Donna 5, 72n16, 168n2
Freud, Sigmund 30; application of theory 37n2
Frye, Northrop 30–31, 33, 157; Anatomy of Criticism 30
Furedi, Frank 25n1

Galatea 60
Gallagher, Catherine 63
Gamble, Sarah 135–136
Garner, Alan 9n3

Garner, Ann 244
Garner, Stanton B. 224
Gatty's Tale 111–113, 118–120, 124n4
gender 5–6, 15, 43, 70, 77, 101, 111–112, 115, 117–121, 124, 133, 135–136, 187–196, 199–201, 204, 213; femininity 4, 49, 111–117, 119–120, 122–123, 136, 191–193, 195, 212; masculinity 70, 101, 122–123, 184, 188, 191–192, 196–200, 206, 213; see also Astriel, Lord; Coulter, Mrs.; daemons; Parry, Will
Genette, Gérard 31
Gibson, William (The Different Engine) 81, 90n13
Gilliam, Terry (Brazil) 7
Going, K.L. (The Garden of Eve) 25n5
The Golden Compass (film) 6–8, 182, 215n4, 242, 245, 247, 260, 262, 264, 265; Pullman's reaction 7–8
Goldthwaite, John (A Natural History of Make Believe) 43–47, 51
The Good Man Jesus and the Scoundrel Christ 5
Goodwin, Linda 156, 164
Goss, Cory 76–77, 90n6
Greene, Mark 50–54
Gresh, Lois 161
Guattari, Félix 211
Gypsies 102–104, 114–115, 206; see also Gyptians
Gyptians 4, 36, 37n5, 82, 84, 96, 99, 102–106, 111, 113–115, 117, 121, 124, 181, 191, 193, 206

Hanks, Robert 243
Harris, Robert (Fatherland) 63
Harris Russell, Mary 124n1, 176, 178
Hartney, Christopher 156
Heaney, Seamus 139
Heathfield, Adrian 227
Heidegger, Martin 162
Hein, Rolland 67
Herman, Judith 226
Hester 204, 207, 215n6
heterosexuality 15, 121, 135, 146, 188, 193–196, 198–199, 201, 203–204, 213
historiographic metafiction 94
Hitchens, Peter 5
Hollinger, Veronica 70
Holmes, Jeremy 229
Holmes, Sherlock 77, 135
Holocaust 230
Homer 19, 155, 216n11
homosexuality 207
Hooke, Robert 128
Hooper, Walter 66
Houghton, John (A Closer Look at His Dark Materials) 50

Hughes, Ted 139
Hutcheon, Linda 94
Hytner, Nicholas 173, 179, 219–220, 225, 236n6, 240–243, 245, 248, 256

I-Ching 71n4
I Was a Rat! 2, 8n2
the Inklings 93
Intertextuality 3–4, 8, 9n3, 11, 14, 28–29, 83, 93, 155, 172, 214, 243
Irigaray, Luce 204, 213–214

Jacobs, Alan 49–50, 52
Jacobson, Howard 25n1
James, Edward 62
Jeykll, Dr. 90n11

Kafka, Franz 228–229
Kane, Sarah 221
Kaveney, Roz 77
Keats, John 22, 140n4, 155, 162, 208; works 162
Kierkegaard, Søren 123, 158
Kimball, Melanie 94
Kincaid, James R. (*Child-Loving: The Erotic Child and Victorian Culture*) 47
King, Jason E. 5, 72n18
King, Mary 248–249, 257
Kingsley, Charles (*The Water Babies*) 3
Klaw, Rick 75
Kleist, Heinrich von 6, 20, 93, 155, 210, 219, 235n3; *On the Marionette Theatre* 93, 210, 219
Kristeva, Julia 21
Kruks, Sonia 114, 122

Lacan, Jacques 182, 227; *jouissance* 182–183
LaCapra, Dominic 226–227, 231
Lambert, Angela 124
Lawrence, D.H. 114
Le Guin, Ursula K. 70
Lehmann, Hans-Theis 228
L'Engle, Madeleine (*A Wrinkle in Time*) 66–68
Lenz, Millicent 208–209, 124n1
Lewis, C.S. 3, 7, 25n9, 28, 30–33, 34–35, 37, 40–45, 46, 47–48, 49–50, 53, 66–68, 71n14, 93, 212; *The Chronicles of Narnia* 7, 35, 40–43, 48, 53–55, 66; construction of the author 40–45, 46, 47–48, 49–50, 53; *The Horse and His Boy* 25n9; *The Lion, the Witch and the Wardrobe* 28–29, 32, 34, 45; *Out of the Silent Planet* 34, 66; *Perelandra* 66; *That Hideous Strength* 34, 66; *The Voyage of the Dawn Treader* 41, 42
Lide, David 128
The Lion King 248

London 20, 77, 86–89, 80n20, 113, 116, 125n9, 135–136
Lovejoy, A.O. 185n11
Loy, David 156, 164
Luckhurst, Roger 71n6, 221, 226
Lucretius 128
Luther, Martin 63
Lyford, Lee 245
Lyra's Oxford 140n2

MacDonald, Laura 245–246
magic 8, 18, 58, 60–61, 71n10, 80, 83–85, 87, 90n16, 128, 148, 180, 181, 239, 242; *see also* Dee, Dr. John; *see also* witches
Malone, Mary 64, 70, 71n3, 71n4, 72n22, 80, 83, 133, 159, 162, 163, 176, 179, 199–200, 202, 211, 243, 265
Malpede, Karen 228
Manlove, Colin 40
Marlowe, Christopher 213
Maxwell Martin, Anna 182, 215n3, 223, 225, 231
McAuley, Gay 235
McCaughrean, Geraldine (*A Little Lower Than the Angels*) 25n5
McGill, Stewart 240, 248
McKenna, Terence 71n4
Metatron 67, 68, 70, 85, 133, 143–144, 146–147, 149–152
Milner, Andrew 86
Milton, John 4, 5, 11–12, 14–22, 24, 25n6, 25n7, 25n10, 30, 57–58, 59, 69, 93, 133, 154, 155, 160, 172–175, 178–179, 185, 185n11, 209, 210, 213; works 4, 11–12, 14–22, 24, 25n10, 57–58, 59, 93, 133, 154, 160, 172–175, 177–179, 185, 185n11, 209
Minack theater 245
Montgomery, Lucy Maud (*Anne of Green Gables*) 94
Moorcock, Michael (*The Warlock of the Air*) 90n12
Mootoo (*The Orphan: A Romance*) 102–103
More, Hannah 96
Moruzi, Kristine 187
Mossycoat 8n2
Moylan, Tom 89
mulefa 58, 64–65, 71n4, 108, 130, 137–138, 140, 160, 166, 169n7, 240, 243, 265
Munt, Sally R. 6, 136, 215n1, 227
Murchison, Dr. Charles 129
music 4, 11, 16–18, 123, 179, 181, 185n2, 220, 228–229, 243, 244–246, 248, 254, 256, 262, 264; Orpheus 4, 16–18
myth 3, 21, 30, 33, 67, 69–70, 77, 82–83, 84, 86, 144, 154–155, 158, 163, 165, 168, 211

National Theatre UK 6, 214, 215n3, 219–221, 223–224, 229, 231, 233, 235, 235n1,

236*n*20, 239–250, 252, 257, 259–262, 265–266
Neilson, Anthony 221
Nevins, Jess 76, 90*n*6, 90*n*7
New Cut Gang series 9*n*6, 89*n*2
New Labour 11
New Line 7
Newitz, Annalee 132
Next Stage (theater company) 244, 266
Nicholls, Peter 86
Nietzsche, Friedrich (*Thus Spake Zarathustra*) 158
Nord, Deborah Epstein 114–115

Oblation Board 14, 98–99, 101, 103, 108, 159, 192, 203, 211
Oily Cart (theater company) 246
Once Upon a Time in the North 140*n*2
Onion, Rebecca 80–81, 90*n*12
orphan 4, 36, 93, 94–105, 108, 109*n*1, 118, 190, 223, 236*n*11; Romanticism 97–98
The Orphan 105
Oxford 16, 23, 87, 89*n*2, 90*n*9, 96, 105, 116, 122, 134–135, 140*n*1, 140*n*2, 199, 222, 224, 249, 252, 257, 260

Pantalaimon 21, 95, 116, 121, 131, 141*n*21, 212, 153*n*2, 185*n*6, 203, 205, 212, 215*n*3, 230–232, 234, 251, 255
Pantheism 5, 71*n*4, 127, 128, 139–140, 140*n*4
Parry, William (Will) 13–15, 19, 22–24, 35, 37, 49, 61, 63, 65, 68, 70–71, 72*n*19, 78, 79, 84–85, 90*n*16, 94–99, 101, 103, 105, 106–108, 109, 121, 131, 134, 135, 137, 143, 156, 163, 164, 166, 167, 173–174, 176–178, 180–183, 185, 185*n*6, 185*n*8, 185*n*10, 187–190, 196–201, 202, 204, 206, 209, 211, 213–214, 215*n*, 216*n*13, 231, 233, 234, 241, 243, 251, 258, 259–261, 263
Pearce, Philippa (*Tom's Midnight Garden*) 25*n*5
Pekkala, Serafina 49, 68, 78, 123–124, 166, 179–181, 184, 193, 213, 258
Phelan, Peggy 227
Philips, Lawrence 86
Playbox (theater company) 6, 240, 245, 247–251, 254–255, 258–261, 264–266
postmodernism 20–21, 24, 76, 89*n*5, 127, 161, 205
Powers, Douglas 156
Propp, Vladimir 31
Puss in Boots 8*n*2

Quash, Emily Jane 249, 257, 261
queer 194, 202, 205, 210–211, 213–214, 215*n*1
The Questions of King Milinda 165

Ratt, Margaret P. 80
Ravenhill, Mark 221–222, 236*n*8
Raymond-Pickard, Hugh 5
realism 3–4, 11, 19–21, 23–24, 189, 214
Rees, Jasper 25*n*1
Richards, Dakota Blue 183
Ridout, Nicholas 233
Rilke, Rainer Maria 155
Ringrose, Christopher 118
Riviere, Jan ("Womanliness as a Masquerade") 192
Roberts, Adam 58, 71*n*6, 72*n*21, 89
Röhrich, Lutz 29
Romanticism 2, 12, 14, 76, 86, 94, 96–99, 106–107, 115, 127–129, 131, 133, 138–139, 179, 184, 208–209, 215*n*8; *see also* Blake, William; Keats, John; Wordsworth, William
Rose, Jacqueline 45–47, 52, 54; *The Case of Peter Pan or the Impossibility of Children's Fiction* 45
Rousseau, Victor (*The Messiah of the Cylinder*) 65
Rowling, J.K. 2, 6, 12, 13, 25*n*11, 30, 94, 111–113, 121, 221; *The Goblet of Fire* 113; *Harry Potter* series 6, 12, 30, 94, 111–112, 121, 124*n*2, 221, 243, 250
Ruby in the Smoke 9*n*4, 9*n*5, 109*n*5
Rushdie, Salman (*Haroun and the Sea of Stories*) 12; *Satanic Verses* 12, 25*n*4
Ruskin, John 129
Russ, Joanna 70

Said, Edward (*Orientalism*) 94
Salih, Sara 188
Sally Lockhart quartet 4, 9*n*6, 87, 89*n*2, 109*n*5
The Scarecrow and His Servant 6
Schwartz, Sanford 66
science fiction 4, 34, 57–62, 64–70, 75–77, 82, 86, 144, 71*n*5, 71*n*6, 72*n*21
Scott, Carole 124*n*1
Scottish Youth Theatre 247
Sebastian, C.D. 160
Seltzer, Mark 226
Serviss, Garrett (*Edison's Conquest of Mars*) 89*n*3
Shadow in the North 9*n*5
Shakespeare, William 16, 25*n*10, 130, 243, 256–257; *Hamlet* 25*n*10, 130, 140*n*11; *Henry IV* 261–262; *King Lear* 256; *Romeo and Juliet* 254
Shared Experience (theater company) 243
Shelley, Percy Byssche 14, 140*n*4, 208
Shippey, Tom 29, 90*n*5
Shohet, Lauren 137
Skadi, Ruta 64, 68, 82, 105, 181, 207
Skeggs, Beverley 206

Smith, Leapidge (*Abiah; Or, The Record of a Foundling*) 105
Snickett, Lemony (*A Series of Unfortunate Events*) 6–7
Spencer, Charles 241, 247
Spring-Heeled Jack 8n2
Squires, Claire 124n1, 137, 187, 189
Stafford, Nick 222, 236n8
Stagecoach (youth theater company) 247
Stapledon, Olaf (*Last and First Men: A Story of the Near and Far Future*) 66
Star Trek 79
Stasheff, Christopher (*The Warlock in Spite of Himself*) 60
States, Bert O. 224
Staume, David 137
steampunk 58, 61, 75–78, 80–87, 89, 90n12, 90n13, 90n17; *see also* Victoriana
Sterling, Bruce (*The Different Engine*) 81, 90n13
Stoker, Bram 140n9
Stoppard, Tom 7, 242, 249; *Rosencrantz and Guildenstern Are Dead* 7; *Shakespeare in Love* 7; *see also* Gilliam, Terry
Suvin, Darko 62, 70, 72n21, 86, 90n21
Swearer, Donald 166

Tambling, Jeremy 87
theater 219, 221–222, 226–228, 232, 234–235, 240–266
Theatre Royal Bath 245, 247, 265–266
Tolkien, J.R.R. 3, 18, 28–33, 34–35, 37, 93, 246; *The Lord of the Rings* 28–29, 35; *The Return of the King* 29, 33
Tolstoy, Leo (*War and Peace*) 243
Toynbee, Polly 45
trauma 221–222, 225–230, 233–235, 236n7
Tucker, Anand (*Shopgirl*) 7
Turtledove, Harry 62–63; *Agent of Byzantium* 63; *How Few Remain* 62
Tyndale, John 128

Unicorn theater company 6
Uselton, Matthew 69

VanderMeer, Ann and Jeff (*Steampunk*) 75
Verne, Jules 76–77
Victoriana 58, 75–77, 80, 83–84, 86–87, 89n2, 90n5; *see also* steampunk
Virgil (*Aeneid*) 216n11

Wald, Christina 226
Wall, Charles (*The Orphan's Isle*) 102
Wallace, Alfred Russell 129
Wallis, Mick 224, 234
Ward, Glenn 125
Watkins, Mary 209
Weitz, Chris 7; *American Pie* and *About a Boy* 7
Wells, H.G. 61–62, 66, 76–77; *The Shape of Things to Come* 66; *The War of the Worlds* 61–62
Whitbread Book of the Year 23
Williams, Dr. Rowan (Archbishop of Canterbury) 5, 55n1
A Wind in the Willows 240
Winston, Lord Robert 132, 141n17
witchcraft *see* magic
witches 8, 20, 21, 22, 30, 35, 36, 49, 64, 68, 70, 71n10, 80, 82, 84, 90n16, 98, 99, 101, 106, 113, 123–124, 130, 155, 179–181, 193, 197–198, 207, 212, 213, 243, 244, 257–259; *see also* Pekkala; Ruta; Serafina; Skadi; *see also* magic

The Wonderful Song of Aladdin and the Enchanted Lamp 8n2
Wood, Naomi 209
Woolf, Virginia 114
Wordsworth, William 97–98, 131, 133, 138–139, 140n4; works 97–98, 133, 138–139
The Workhouse Orphan 100
Wright, Nicholas 173, 175, 180–181, 184, 185n2, 220, 222 223, 224, 228–230, 231, 232, 237n27, 239–241, 242–244, 246, 248, 260–261, 265

Xaphania 68, 70, 72n19, 167, 179